D1395648

COOKING IN SPAIN

Janet Mendel

Cooking in Spain (Second Edition)
Published by Ediciones Santana, S.L.
Apartado 41
29650 Mijas-Pueblo (Málaga)
Spain

Tel.   (0034) 952 48 58 38 Fax. (0034) 952 48 53 67
E-Mail   info@santanabooks.com

First published in 1987 by Lookout Publications, S.A.
Copyright © 2006 Janet Mendel
Photography Copyright © 2006 Jean Dominique Dallet & Jerónimo Alba

Designed by Imigiz S.L. (www.imigiz.com)

Printed in Spain by Gráficas San Pancracio, S.L.
ISBN-13: 978-84-89954-61-8
ISBN-10: 84-89954-61-5
Depósito Legal: Ma-1.467/2006

ACKNOWLEDGEMENTS

Thanks to the many cooks, both professional and housewifely, throughout Spain, who have shared their recipes with me. Thanks to Ken and Arlene Brown who first published Cooking in Spain in 1987 and to its original editor, the late Mark Little.

Thanks to David and Thea Baird for editing the revised edition; to Jean Dominique Dallet and Jerónimo Alba for new photos; to editorial assistant Emma Walkiden; to Phill and Fiona Coe for design; and to Harry and Charlotte Gordon for advice.

ABOUT THE AUTHOR

American-born journalist, Janet Mendel, has been researching and writing about Spain's national and regional cuisine from her home in southern Spain for more than thirty years. Since its first publication in 1987 COOKING IN SPAIN has become a classic in its field. Other publications include Great Dishes From Spain, also published by Santana, the award-winning Traditional Spanish Cooking and the highly praised My Kitchen in Spain. She has also written numerous articles for newspapers and magazines worldwide.

CONTENTS

INTRODUCTION

I learned about Spanish cooking in pueblo kitchens. When I first came to live in an Andalusian village in the late 1960s, I enjoyed tasting the local foods at tapa bars, where a tiny plate of food was served free with every glass of wine.

One day, when I asked what flavoured the chicken dish, the owner sent me back to the kitchen to talk to his wife.

The women in the kitchen were delighted to talk about food. I returned day after day, watching the preparations, tasting, making notes, sometimes helping. One kitchen led to another and an enquiry about new dishes got me sent off to other homes. We would talk about recipes while the women of the house fanned the fire under the *olla,* the great soup pot set on a tripod in the hearth. In those days, very few village homes had butane-fuelled cookers and almost none had refrigerators. Against whitewashed walls hung pots and pans burnished to satin brilliance. Earthy pottery jugs, the family collection of glassware and colourful ceramic bowls lined the tile counters and mantel. Ropes of garlic bulbs and branches of bay-leaves adorned these simple kitchens.

On travels throughout Spain I found that people everywhere love to talk about food and are delighted to share their recipes. In simple bars and restaurants in small villages, I would soon be in the kitchen, absorbing the local culture and customs by way of food. In fine restaurants in the cities, where the cooks were most often men, I found the same generosity. A chef with a few minutes free would come and sit with me and share the secrets of his specialities.

Experimenting with the many new dishes in my own kitchen was also the best possible initiation into the Spanish marketplace. I slowly learned the names of fruits and vegetables, kinds of seafood, cuts of meat, spices, herbs and wines.

In the almost 20 years since *Cooking in Spain* was first published, Spain's culinary scene has changed in several important ways. Instead of a very local market, globalisation, for better or worse, means we can buy a huge variety of foods at local supermarkets—Asian, Middle Eastern, Mexican, as well as Spanish. Inevitably, "fast food" and prepared convenience foods have made inroads on traditional cooking. Nevertheless, in village homes housewives still cook daily fare much like their grandmothers did—fish soups, lentil pots, meat stews, *paella* on Sundays. Treasured recipes for sweets and cakes appear for holiday feasts. Tapa bars still prepare old favourites such as crispy croquettes, potato *tortilla,* sizzling prawns, garlicky grilled pork and meatballs in almond sauce. (Recipes for all these dishes can be found in this book.)

The quality of Spain's food products has grown exponentially. The finest olive oil in the world, extraordinary ham, wonderful fruits and vegetables, an array of artisanal cheeses and superb wines make Spain's cuisine a real delight. These gourmet products are increasingly known, not just in Spain, but on the export market too.

In the 21st century, the art and genius of some wildly creative restaurant chefs working in every region have put Spain on the world culinary map. These super-chefs have turned dining-out in Spain into entertainment of the highest order. While you and I may not want to "deconstruct" a traditional tortilla in our own kitchens, nor prepare smoke ice cream, ham "dust" or strawberry-beet foam, such culinary creations have generated tremendous excitement in the food world.

Cooking in Spain is still about the traditional and authentic dishes of Spain. The new edition keeps all the best of the original—it's a useful guide to the market. It provides an introduction to the regional cuisines of Spain plus it includes more than 300 recipes for all the best-known traditional dishes. But we've given the book a fresh look with new photos and a new, more cook-friendly format.

Cooking in Spain is intended both for residents of Spain who, like myself, shop and cook here, and for those visitors who would like to reproduce some of the flavour of Spain in kitchens back home. More than just a cookbook, it's a cook's guide to good eating throughout Spain, to marketing and to cooking, with lots of recipes for favourite Spanish dishes. This is a book about cooking in Spain and I hope you will enjoy your introduction to the Spanish kitchen as much as I have.

Janet Mendel, 2006

THE FLAVOUR OF SPAIN

Spanish food, as I learned to cook it, was without pretensions, simple fare. It was the subtlety of flavourings, the combinations of ingredients — sometimes truly inspired — and the freshness of the raw materials that made it very special.

Cooking in Spain today is still the traditional fare of the pueblo kitchen, but it has changed. Where once rang the sound of the brass mortar and pestle, now there is the whirr of the electric blender. Fruits and vegetables which once came by donkey from nearby fields now are trucked in from distant regions. In addition to the local fishermen's catch, there is frozen seafood from far-off seas. All this has greatly enriched Spanish cooking and, with prosperity, people today eat much better than they did 50 years ago.

The availability of produce beyond what is raised on local farms plus the talent of a new generation of cooks, both professional and housewifely, have led to *la nueva cocina española,* Spain's new cuisine, with its adaptation of traditional recipes to modern tastes and the imaginative use of old products in new ways and new products in old ways.

Tourism and the influx of foreigners who have settled on Spain's sunny coastlines have also influenced the cooking. Markets and supermarkets catering to new demands import everything from Norwegian smoked salmon and Chinese vegetables to Indian chutneys and English Christmas puddings.

This culinary cross-fertilisation is nothing new in Spain. The Romans may have started it. They had a passion for Spanish olive oil, figs, grapes, wine and fish, which were exported to Rome and points beyond. In turn, the colonisers contributed dishes — such as the original *cocido,* a boiled dinner which could be considered the national dish of Spain.

The Moors, who ruled much of the Iberian peninsula for more than seven centuries, contributing to science, literature, philosophy, art and gastronomy, left their culinary calling card which can still be savoured today. Moorish settlers, who were Arabs and Berbers, with complex systems of irrigation and water-wheels, turned vast barren regions into rich agricultural lands. They introduced into Spain the cultivation of rice, sugar cane and many fruits and vegetables previously unknown. The cooking was vastly influenced by both the Moors and the Sephardim Jews who cohabited peacefully much of the time. Dishes from this era included exotic spices such as saffron, the use of fruits and almonds with savoury dishes, honeyed sweets and pastries. It is this Moorish flavour that makes Spanish cooking so distinctive from that of the rest of Europe.

Then came the discovery of the Americas. Though gold was of foremost interest to the *conquistadores,* the discovery of tomatoes, potatoes, peppers, beans, squash, avocados, corn and chocolate, which were introduced to Europe from Spain, were of longer-lasting importance. The famous gazpacho, of Moorish origin, didn't develop into the dish so well known today until tomatoes came from the New World.

A COOK'S TOUR OF SPAIN

Many of us who live in Spain frequently travel throughout the country, discovering a wealth of art, history and culture as well as exciting foods, cheeses, wines and sweets, some very local indeed. For the traveller, this survey of regional specialities can provide suggestions of what to eat in Bilbao, Barcelona or Badajoz and, for the enthusiastic and adventurous cook, a culinary tour of this most fascinating country.

A few dishes have no culinary frontiers, such as: the *cocido,* a one-pot feast of meats, sausages and vegetables; the *tortilla* or Spanish omelette, made with eggs and potatoes; and *sopa de ajo,* garlic soup. Though each varies from region to region, incorporating local produce and flavours, they are all truly "national" dishes. Additionally, all three are simple to prepare, wonderful introductions for the novice into the complexities of Spanish food.

Regional variations are best characterised by the Spanish saying, referring to both climatic conditions and to cooking techniques: "In the north you stew; in the central region you roast; in the east you simmer and in the south you fry."

We'll start in the north.

ASTURIAS
Green meadows and mists, thick forests of oak and chestnut, fat cattle and fast-running trout streams...can this really be Spain? The Principality of Asturias can seem like a corner of Brittany, Normandy or Ireland, which is not so extraordinary considering all these regions were settled by Celts.

Tucked away at the top of this sub-continent on the Bay of Biscay and behind the rugged slopes of the Picos de Europa, Asturias may actually be the most Spanish of all Spain's regions. It was here the Visigothic kings fortified themselves and, through all those centuries, was the only region never conquered by the Moors. It was from Asturias that the Christian reconquest of Spain began.

Asturias has another claim to fame: the *fabada,* beans and sausages at their most elegant. To know the landscape of Asturias is to understand the *fabada.* Bitterly cold in the winter, all life centres around the warm hearth where the beans gently bubble on the fire. There is no winter growing season and summer harvests must feed the family until spring. Maize, grain, beans, vegetables are hung in sheds to dry. Pigs are slaughtered, salted and cured to provide meat for winter eating. No wonder that Asturias is famous for its cured meats: *morcilla,* black pudding; *longaniza,* smoked sausage; *chorizo,* paprika-flavoured red sausage; and hams, salt pork and bacon.

The rivers of Asturias provide wild salmon and trout and the Bay of Biscay a plentiful array of seafood. Also famous: 250 varieties of apples; a blue cheese called Cabrales, one of the best in Spain; lentils, chestnuts and cider. Little wine is produced in Asturias. Instead there is the "wine of the apple", *sidra* (cider), which seems to contain the essence of the crisp and green countryside. Dispensed in the *chigres* or taverns, cider is good with seafood on a summer's day.

Besides *fabada,* excellent dishes are *caldereta de pescado,* a seafood stew, *sardinas trechadas,* boned and stuffed sardines, and trout fried with ham.

BASQUE COUNTRY

"*Apalaurreaudiak*", "*txitxardiñak*", "*kokotxas*" and "*txangurro*". It looks like a typewriter gone berserk, but those are actual words for culinary specialities in that crazy language, Basque. No one knows how the language originated. Though it has borrowed from both French and Spanish, the native tongue of the Basques bears no relation to either. Or to anything else, though some theorists have suggested the Basques can understand the fish in the seas, which doesn't seem too far-fetched considering their ability to catch and prepare them.

One tale, acknowledging both the impossibility of the language and the sternness of the women, says the devil decided one day he wanted to learn Basque. So he hid himself behind the door in a Basque kitchen to listen. At the end of a whole year he had learned two words in Basque: "Yes ma'm."

Language aside, the devil or anyone else can learn fabulous things in a Basque kitchen, for the Basques are reputedly Spain's best cooks. Not stingy with their expertise, these people have spread their talents throughout Spain. There are probably more Basque restaurants in other provinces of Spain than any other one kind. They're also prolific cookbook writers, both in Basque and the more readable Spanish.

Two factors condition life in the Basque country — sea and mountain. It is located in the corner of the Bay of Biscay, where Spain curves around to meet France, and straddles the Pyrenees. This enclave ignores national borders for Basques claim there are seven Basque provinces, four in Spain (Vizcaya, Guipúzcoa, Álava and Navarra) and three in France (Laburdi, Zuberoa and Benabar). Culinary boundaries are even less distinct. Álava, not on the sea, seems more akin to the Rioja region, and Navarre, gastronomically, is closer to Aragón.

The Basques take their cooking and eating seriously. A *tripasais* is one who looks after his belly, a gourmand and a gourmet. They are members of cooking societies, open only to men, where kitchen facilities and a well-stocked pantry invite fine cooking. This gourmet tradition may explain why many Basque chefs are in the forefront of Spain's innovative cuisine.

Apalaurreaudiak is lunch, and it might include those famous dishes *txangurro*, a crab casserole, or *kokotxas*, a morsel of flesh from the jawbone of the hake, sautéed with onion and garlic, or *txitxardiñak*, baby eels sizzled with garlic. Other great seafood dishes are: *marmitako*, a casserole of fresh tuna and potatoes; *bacalao al pil pil*, salt cod cooked with garlic; *merluza a la vasca*, hake in a green sauce; *chipirones en su tinta*, cuttlefish in its own ink sauce; and *besugo a la donostiarra*, bream grilled on a charcoal fire by street vendors on fiesta days. Also clams, mussels, oysters, lobster and even *percebes*, an edible and much-appreciated sea barnacle.

Back in the mountains, meat is excellent and the *chuletas de buey*, beef chops, are famous, each weighing more than half a kilo! There are good lamb and good game. Quail wrapped in grape leaves is a speciality. *Setas a la kashera* are sautéed wild mushrooms. There are many good egg dishes, including *piparrada*, an omelette with tomatoes and peppers. The Basque *cocido* is cooked in three pots — in one goes beef and chicken, in the second red beans, ham bone and salt pork, and in the third cabbage, *chorizo* and sausages. There are good cheeses in this region, especially the smoky *Idiazábal*. The local wine, *txacolí*, is a light, tangy white wine. The flavour is attributed to vineyards seasoned by sea breezes and, indeed, the wine pairs perfectly with seafood dishes.

RIOJA

Hardly a touristic region, it's been off the beaten path since the days of medieval pilgrimages. Yet the names of its towns — Haro, Logroño, Cenicero, Fuenmayor — are hauntingly familiar, as well known as the names of Spain's resort towns. The connoisseur and the inveterate reader of labels know immediately what's so special about the Rioja. It is *the* best-known wine-producing region of Spain, where some of the country's finest table wines are made.

Looking at the map, one wouldn't think the Rioja (named for the river Oja) had any claim to exist as a separate region. Tucked in between the Basque country, Navarre and Castile, the Rioja is a swath carved out of other lands by the river Ebro.

Like most good wine-producing areas, the Rioja is famed for its food. It is not delicate food, any more than the wines are delicate wines. "Full-bodied" is probably the best adjective for both.

The Rioja is famous for beans: red beans, white beans, green beans…they have them all. And they do marvellous things with them. Also good are: potatoes *a la riojana*, with paprika, garlic and slices of pork loin; sweet peppers, both red and green, and hot peppers, *guindillas*, used with discretion for flavouring; good hams and sausages; garlic soup; snails; *pisto*, a vegetable medley that appears in other regions, but here served with lamb or partridge; and several excellent chicken dishes.

NAVARRE

This historical and varied land is closely associated with the Basque provinces, though its culinary tradition is closest to neighbouring Aragón. It ranges from the deep forests, torrential rivers and green mountain meadows of the Pyrenees — a land of cattle and sheep — to the wide valleys of intensive cultivation to the south and low flatlands crossed by the Ebro and its tributaries. As ever with Spanish food, the culinary customs are determined by the products of the land.

The Navarrese are known for their gigantic appetites and digestive powers. Famous are the *chorizos* of Pamplona, the quality of the lamb, wild dove, partridge and quail, legumes and vegetables, trout, and the cheeses of the high mountain villages, particularly one called Roncal. Lamb chops *a la navarra* and *cochifrito*, fried lamb, are two excellent dishes. *Garbure*, a dish of pork, ham and sausages, is hardly different from a dish of the same name served in nearby Béarn (France). Other dishes worth trying are partridge in a sauce enriched with chocolate; *huevos al Roncal*, eggs fried with sausages; *trucha a la navarra*, trout wrapped in ham and fried; and *chilindrón*, a lamb dish also a speciality of Aragón.

ARAGÓN

The ancient kingdom of Aragón, comprising the provinces of Huesca, Teruel and Zaragoza, conjures up romantic images of Roman legions, kings and queens, Moors and Christians, convents and castles. More than once it has been a decisive battleground in Spanish history — in the Roman conquest, the Christian reconquest and, more recently, during the Spanish Civil War. It stretches from the French border and the high mountains in the north almost as far south as Valencia.

The region has strong reminders of its past. An often desolate landscape hardly changed since Caesar Augustus (corrupted to "Zaragoza") added Spain to the Roman empire. Shepherds in the fields. Medieval towns hung on cliffs. Narrow, winding streets and surprising towers that recall the Moorish domination. Wolves, bears and wild chamois in the wilderness areas of Ordesa, now a national park.

The food, grave and simple, like the land seems ancient. Lamb, roasted on a wood fire; shepherds' stews whose recipes are biblical; ham and sausages cured as they have been for centuries; fresh trout from fast-flowing mountain streams. No adornments, no refinements, just quality products, particularly fruits and vegetables, lamb and game.

The most famous dish of Aragón is *chilindrón*, lamb or chicken braised with tomatoes and strips of sweet red pepper. It's a holiday dish and no *alifara* or country outing is complete without *chilindrón*. *Ternasco* is baby lamb roasted on a wood fire with little more than salt, garlic and bacon fat. *Criadillas* are a speciality, lamb's testicles, blanched, soaked, cooked, sliced, batter-dipped and fried. And lamb's head, split and stuffed with pork and roasted. Another Aragón lamb dish is *espárragos montañés* (mountain "asparagus"), which are really lambs' tails braised in tomato.

Where winters can be bitter, good soups are important. Aragonese garlic soup is made with almonds and eggs. Another is flavoured with tomato, pepper and *chorizo,* to which quantities of bread are added, making a thick porridge which is browned in the oven. Another is *presa de predicador* (preacher's game) containing beef, mutton, pork, chicken and sausages.

Aragón is well watered by rivers, most notably the Ebro and new-born streams plunging down from the Pyrenees. Besides trout, there are crayfish and eels. *Bacalao,* salt cod, is prepared in several ways, *a la baturra* (with potatoes and garlic mayonnaise) and *al ajo arriero,* mule-driver's style.

Charcuterie is excellent in Aragón, which is known for its *morcilla,* black pudding, here confected with rice and pine-nuts. The ham from Teruel is famous, prepared batter-dipped and fried or bathed in a tomato sauce. Hearty, winter dishes include hare and partridge and bean potages with sausages, such as the well-flavoured *recao de Binéfar.*

Sweets are, as in Andalusia, well-spiced with the Moorish flavour. Marzipan and candied fruits are festive offerings. The region also produces fine apples, cherries and peaches.

The Aragonese wines of Cariñena are among Spain's classics. Almost black in colour, the red wines go nicely with the region's hearty, simple foods. Newer in style are the wines of Somontano, Calatayud and Campo de Borja.

CANTABRIA

Verdant meadows, rolling hills, pastures where cows graze and an extensive coastline make this region — also called La Montaña — not unlike its neighbours, Asturias and the Basque lands. The food is not as sophisticated as the Basque, more subtle than the Asturian, and much more complex than the austere cuisine of Castile.

Inland, deep valleys, rivers and mountains where deer and bears are not uncommon, separate one village from another. A rich and varied agriculture, plus the riches of the sea, make this a land of wonderful eating.

Seafood is exalted. This is real *merluza* country. This fish, the hake, mild of flavour and flaky of texture, is one of the best loved all over Spain. Here it is featured in many ways. There's also an exquisite variety of other salt-water fish, plus trout and salmon, dairy products, chicken, game and pork. An extraordinarily varied cuisine.

Rabas are breaded bits of squid, crisply fried; *sorroputún* is a tuna casserole; *cabracho al ajillo,* scorpion fish or rascasse cooked with garlic; *almejas a la marinera,* clams sailor style; *pollo a la campurriana,* chicken with rice and white wine; *habas a la montañesa,* broad beans flavoured with thyme; and *arroz santanderino,* rice with salmon. Best known of several cheeses is Pasiego, from the valley of Pas, a milder version of Cabrales-type blue cheese.

GALICIA

Tucked away in the topmost corner of Spain, the four provinces of Galicia — Lugo, La Coruña, Orense and Pontevedra — seem hardly related to the rest of the country at all, at least not to the picture-postcard image most foreigners have of Spain. Once called Finisterre, the end of the world, beyond which roared the winds of the unknown, Galicia is a region hardly touched by the Moorish influence which flavours much of the peninsula and its cooking.

This is a region of lush, green pastures and greystone towns, of fat livestock, cold trout rivers, pine-clad hills, witchcraft, bagpipes and lashing Atlantic storms. Deep estuaries, or *rías,* provide sheltered inlets for fishing fleets and small populations. Provincial boundaries are only an administrative convenience; because of the irregular terrain, Galicia actually divides itself into small districts, many very isolated.

The cooking of Galicia, too, is different from that of the rest of Spain. This is not a Mediterranean country. The sombreness of its people and the baroque splendour of some of the dishes as well as the architecture reflect another world. Galicia is, of course, Spain's very first "tourist" centre. Way back in the Middle Ages Santiago de Compostela, the shrine of St. James, was a pilgrimage destination almost as important as Rome and Jerusalem. The *vieira,* or sea scallop — to this day a much appreciated dish in Galicia — is also called the *concha peregrina,* or pilgrim's shell. Considered a symbol of St. James, the shells were collected by pilgrims.

Well-watered pastures mean excellent meat and dairy produce. In Galicia, butter and lard are used much more extensively than oil in cooking. Rye flour, maize flour and whole-wheat breads were widely used in Galicia, though modern agriculture and milling has finally begun to make inroads on what was once a very local cuisine. Cool-season vegetables (Galician summers are pleasantly cool) such as carrots, turnips and cabbages appear in many dishes. Game is superb: partridge, pheasant, quail, duck, game hen, hare, rabbit, roe deer, boar. Specialities are partridge pie, partridge and cabbage, duck with chestnuts, marinated boar steaks.

Seafood of all kinds, and shellfish in particular, come from Galician coasts and fjords. The oysters of Arcade, dipped in corn meal and crisply fried, and the scallops of Vigo are famous. Sardines are grilled on iron spikes over grape-vine prunings and served with *cachelos,* jacket potatoes. *Caldeirada* is a fish stew and *sopa de ostras* is oyster soup.

The famous Galician threesome from the land are *lacón con grelos, pote gallego* and *caldo gallego*. *Lacón* is cured pork hand or shoulder; *grelos* are bitter turnip greens, said to counteract nicely the fattiness of the pork. To concoct the dish one also needs a pig's ear, potatoes and Galician *chorizo*. The *pote* contains white beans, beef or pork bone, *chorizo, morcilla,* potatoes and greens. The *caldo*, a thick soup, is similar.

Picnics, fiesta days and hunting expeditions in Galicia call for another speciality, the *empanada,* a pastry which is a cross between a sandwich, a pizza and a pot pie. The pastry is a yeast dough and the filling can be sliced pork loin, chicken or fish in a thick tomato sauce. Cut into wedges, the *empanada* can be eaten out of the hand.

Spain's finest white wine, made from the Albariño grape, comes from the Rías Baixas district of Galicia. Other wine denominations are Monterrei, Ribeira Sacra, Ribeiro and Valdeorras.

OLD CASTILE AND LEÓN

The ancient kingdoms of Old Castile and León, now the autonomous region of Castilla y León, have many claims to fame, historically and touristically. This is truly the land of castles in Spain, the birthplace of kings and saints and great warriors, the home of *castellano*, the Spanish language. The provinces of the region — Ávila, Segovia, Valladolid, Palencia, Burgos, Soria, León, Zamora and Salamanca — share a treasure-trove of Spanish monuments, landmarks and art.

For the casual tourist with limited time, the memory of St. Teresa's birthplace in Ávila, El Cid's birthplace in Burgos, the fabulous gardens of La Granja or the wondrous stained-glass windows of the León cathedral may blur with time. But no one on this cook's tour is likely to forget the experience of eating roast suckling pig, fragrant and crackling from the big ovens, in the shadow of the great Roman aqueduct, at one of the famous *mesones* of Segovia.

Most of the region is a high plain where, contrary to the lines of the song, the rain in Spain doesn't fall. It can be an austere and bleak land, with a severe climate that makes for robust foods. This is also called *tierra de pan,* Spain's bread-basket, for the vast stretches of wheat fields which produce much of the country's grains.

Ávila, the "roof of Castile", is the highest provincial capital in Spain. A huntsman's paradise, all kinds of game are found here, including the ibex or wild mountain goat. It is a land of severe winters and an almost medieval cuisine that suits its great walled city. Burgos provides a contrast between fertile valleys and high plateaux. *Chacinería,* the curing of meats, is important here as in other cold climates.

Palencia, dotted with monasteries on the old pilgrim route, is also known for pork products as well as trout and freshwater crayfish. Soria, where the River Duero is born, is more pastoral. Valladolid, where Columbus died and where Cervantes' home is preserved as a museum, is a land of excellent wines, game and trout. Segovia represents the classic Castilian cuisine with the emphasis on roast meats. León, once capital of Christian Spain, presents strong contrasts in landscape, from intensely cultivated fields to mining country to pastureland to wheat fields to trout streams to craggy peaks where wild ibex roam. Salamanca, an ancient Roman city with Spain's oldest university, is surrounded by ranch land supporting excellent livestock. Zamora, with medieval castles patrolling the Portuguese border, is frontier land — and *garbanzo,* chickpea, country.

These provinces are all known as the *zona de los asados,* the region of roasts. Baby pig — called *cochinillo* or *tostón* — and baby lamb are the specialities. Split in half, they are basted with lard and roasted in huge brick ovens. Tender and succulent, such a meal is a memorable experience and would serve to put Castile on the touristic map even if no castles or cathedrals existed.

Not all pigs of Castile wind up in the oven at the tender age of three weeks. Many are fattened into tasty specimens and grow up to be the hams and sausages for which the region is famous. These pork products find their way into numerous dishes of the region, such as the *hornazo de Salamanca,* a flaky pastry filled with *chorizo,* roast meat and chopped egg.

Trout, from the Río Tormes and other fast-flowing, cold rivers, may be prepared simply wrapped in ham and grilled. Freshwater crayfish, *cangrejos de río,* cooked in a spicy sauce are a speciality of Burgos. All manner of game is taken in the area and dishes such as *pichones a la abulense,* pigeons Ávila style, and partridges stewed with vegetables, herbs and salt pork, are famous.

Other dishes of note are *ajo arriero,* mule-driver's style, which originated in the *posadas,* the "truck stops" of the old world, and is served with eggs, vegetables or codfish; lentils cooked with *chorizo; menestra de cordero a la leonesa,* a lamb stew; chicken in *pepitoria,* a sauce of ground almonds, and *arroz a la zamorana,* a Spanish rice dish without a trace of saffron.

Spain's most renowned wine, Vega Sicilia, is made in the region that now has the denomination Ribera del Duero. Also in Castilla y León are El Bierzo, Cigales, Rueda and Toro wines.

CATALONIA

Once a proud kingdom that extended into part of France, Catalonia today is an autonomous region with its own language and dynamic traditions. A seafaring nation, Catalonia has gathered from all over the world an eclectic mix of styles. It is, to pardon the culinary pun, the melting pot of Spain. There are pastas from Italy, rice dishes from Valencia, hearty country food from neighbouring Aragón, saffron-hued fish soups much like those of Provence. Catalonia assimilates it all, superimposing the contributions of other cultures on a very ancient culinary tradition. Catalans are extraordinarily proud of their cuisine, claiming it as the best in the country. And, with the sole exception of the Basques, they may well be right.

As far back as 1477, Ruperto de Nola wrote Spain's first cookbook — in Catalan — introducing the Italian cooking style to the nobility, for the Italians were the culinary masters of the era. By the 19th century, Barcelona was known for its restaurants and hostelries, some of the best of which were French and Italian. The versatile Catalans adapted foreign dishes to their own inimitable culture and dishes such as *canelones* today are not at all Italian, but truly Catalan.

Five sauces form the basis of many Catalan dishes: the *sofrito, samfaina, picada, alioli* and *romesco.* The *sofrito* is a tomato sauce flavoured with onions and garlic; the *samfaina* calls for aubergine, peppers and courgette as well; the *picada* is toasted almonds and hazelnuts ground to a paste with garlic and parsley; *alioli* is a garlic sauce; and *romesco* is a sweet pepper sauce.

Barcelona is a great and lively city, to which people have migrated from all over, adding individuality and variations on the indigenous genius. It offers an incredible variety of eating. There's pork loin served with white beans; codfish with *samfaina;* mussel soup spiked with anise; partridges packaged in cabbage leaves; *zarzuela,* a medley of fish and shellfish in a well-seasoned sauce; and *escudella i carn d'olla,* the Catalan version of the *cocido.*

Gerona, between the heights of the Pyrenees and the ruggedly beautiful Costa Brava, is one of the richest provinces of Spain. Here you find one marvellous seafood dish after another. Lobster appears in several preparations, including one combined with chicken in a herb-flavoured sauce that includes wine, anise, almonds, saffron, cinnamon and chocolate. *Suquets* is a seafood soup, not unlike bouillabaisse. Snails, *patarralada,* are grilled over coals and served with *alioli* or combined with rabbit. Gerona is famous for its poultry, chickens, ducks, turkeys and geese, many raised free-range and exceptionally flavourful. You can try *rostit,* roast chicken basted with lard, duck stuffed with apples, goose stuffed with pears, and truffled turkey, Pyrenees-style. Lamb is excellent and a favourite for country outings is *costellada,* lamb chops grilled on an open fire with *butifarra* sausage and served with *alioli.* Add to this game from the mountains, with many good ways of preparing it.

Neighbouring Lérida, the inland province of Catalonia, is a long province with a diverse geography, stretching from the French and Andorran borders in the Pyrenees, rich with game, to the river lowlands in the south, a very productive region for agriculture and livestock. Much of the food of Lérida is simple, hearty country fare, such as the *cassolada,* a vegetable stew, rice with codfish, broad beans with snails. The region produces fine local cheeses, *xolis,* a kind of sausage, and *confitat,* seasoned pork conserved in lard.

Back to the sea coast. Tarragona, today a small provincial capital, had more than a million inhabitants in Roman days. This province is crossed by the Ebro, which reaches the sea just south of the capital. It's an area famed for its seafood. Many dishes are simple fishermen's preparations, such as *pataco,* a stew of tuna, potatoes, courgettes and snails; *arros negre,* rice tinted black with ink fish; *rossejat,* rice cooked with fish and shellfish. The most famous culinary contribution of Tarragona is *romesco* sauce, a truly unique concoction, served with fish, chicken, meat and vegetables.

Catalonia produces most of the *cava,* sparkling wine, made in Spain plus superb table wines, both white and red. Of note are wines from the regions of Penedès, Costers del Segre and Priorat.

CASTILLA-LA MANCHA
The name La Mancha comes from the Arabic word, Al Manchara, meaning "dry land".

Toledo province most closely exemplifies the regional cooking of La Mancha; Ciudad Real edges off into Andalusia and Extremadura; Cuenca makes an abrupt transition into the Levant; Guadalajara is a throwback to a medieval civilisation. Albacete, once part of the kingdom of Murcia, shares rice-growing with that province.

La Mancha is the mother, the source of it all — from Don Quixote's windmills to the cliff-hung houses of Cuenca, to the jewel that is Toledo, to the lakes and hills of Guadalajara. The regional cooking of La Mancha is, too, the mother of them all, from the country's famous garlic soups to the many variations on the *cocido.*

A land of fierce winters and searing summers, La Mancha is a harsh land, but plentiful. There are great flocks of sheep and goats following the pastures, stretches of waving wheat fields, scrub brush of rosemary and thyme, partridge nesting in *arroyos.* The cooking is a direct reflection of the countryside, simple, direct, often fierce, the kind of food Spaniards call *fuerte.*

A famous dish of the region is *gazpachos.* The plural distinguishes the dish from the Andalusian cold gazpacho. Also called *galianos,* it is a classic shepherd's and hunter's dish, containing several partridges and rabbits. Lacking game, in the home the dish might be made with chicken and squab. An almost biblical dish, the game is fried with sliced onion, then flavoured with wine, garlic, saffron, cinnamon, rosemary, thyme. The soup is thickened with *torta,* a flat, unleavened bread baked on the hearth stone, very similar to Hebrew matzo. Another *torta* is used as a spoon and, in traditional times, everyone ate *gazpachos* from the pot in which it cooked.

Another country dish, open to wide variation, is *tojunto,* from *todo junto,* all together, so-called because all the ingredients are put to cook at the same time. This dish is said to be invented by the ladies of Almagro so as not to be interrupted from their lace-making to tend the dinner. The dish includes meat or rabbit and vegetables.

Another dish known throughout Spain is *pisto manchego,* a vegetable medley of tomatoes, peppers, courgette and aubergine, derived from the *alboronía* of the Moors, a dish still found in North Africa. Similar to the French ratatouille, the original dish incorporated tomatoes, peppers and squash after these vegetables found their way to Spain from the New World.

Guisado de trigo, whole-wheat grains stewed with *garbanzos* (chickpeas) and pig's foot and flavoured with onions and tomatoes, is a dish much appreciated in the eastern part of La Mancha and on into the Levant. *Migas* and *gachas* are staple peasant dishes throughout Spain, but most famous in La Mancha. *Migas* are simply dry breadcrumbs, moistened in water or milk, then fried in lard or olive oil with garlic, bacon and sausage. They may be served with sardines, with milk, with hot chocolate or with honey and grapes. *Gachas* is a thick porridge flavoured with garlic, salt pork, *chorizo*.

Other dishes of La Mancha are: *morteruelo,* a sort of pâté; roast lamb; salt cod cooked with onions, tomatoes and the anise brandy which is made here; *salpicón,* cold salad of chopped, cooked meat, eggs, onion, tomatoes, peppers, parsley dressed with vinaigrette; rice Toledo-style, with chicken, mushrooms and eels; hare stewed with beans; and dozens of different partridge dishes, for La Mancha is the partridge capital of Europe. Aubergine of Almagro is pickled with fennel; *hornazos* of Zamojón are rolls of ground lamb cooked in cabbage leaves.

Special mention must be made of the cheese, for Manchego cheese is Spain's most famous (see Chapter 2 for lots more about Spanish cheeses). Traditionally a ewes' milk cheese, cured in olive oil, it comes semi-cured and well-aged.

La Mancha also might be called the bodega of Spain, so great is its wine production. More than three-quarters of the province of Albacete is planted with vines. Of eight denominations, the wines of Valdepeñas and La Mancha are perhaps the best known. Restructuring and investment in the industry have led to new excellency in the wines.

MADRID

To talk about the cooking of Madrid is no simple matter. Unlike other regions, the cuisine of the capital is much more than a simple reflection of the produce of fields, mountains, rivers and sea.

The indigenous cooking of Madrid, to the extent that it still exists, is that of La Mancha, an area more pastoral than agricultural, rich in many kinds of game. Also native are the influences of Old Castile, the roast suckling pig and baby lamb, as natural to Madrid as to Segovia.

Had Madrid remained a peasant town on the plains of La Mancha no more would need be said of its culinary heritage. But at the end of the 1500s it became capital of a more or less united country. Kings and queens and wealthy aristocracy lived there and, except for a few religious fanatics, demanded food fit for kings. Chefs were imported from Italy and later France. The peasants and burghers of Madrid could hardly afford royal delicacies, but the influences slowly seeped down. Royalty wanted fresh seafood, so runners brought it in relays from far-away coasts. To this day Madrid is famous for seafood as fresh as that of Bilbao or Cádiz. Before modern transport, Madrid had snow from the high mountains to make ices, luscious fruits from Andalusia, the finest fresh vegetables from the Levant…these were the prerogatives of kings. All roads led to Madrid, opening up the centre of the country to produce from all over. Madrid became the source and the outlet, the supply and the demand.

Another factor contributing to the cuisine of Madrid was the early importance of restaurants. A capital city attracts visitors from everywhere who required all manner of services, from the lowliest *fondas* for traders to the poshest of hotels and dining-rooms for wealthy travellers. The cooking of Madrid was affected early by a lively restaurant trade — almost unknown in the rest of the country outside Barcelona.

Yet another influence was the influx of people from all the provinces of Spain, seeking work, culture and trade. They brought their individual cuisines with them and, to this day, in Madrid one can eat a *fabada* as good as Oviedo's, a gazpacho as good as Seville's or a paella as good as Valencia's.

The capital boasts a few famous dishes all its own. Certainly top of that list would be *cocido madrileño*. Though known throughout Spain with variations, Madrid's version is considered classic. Once a dish of only the wealthy, it later became the daily fare of working people. These days it is fast disappearing, being both too expensive and too time-consuming for every day.

Other specialities include: *callos a la madrileña,* stewed veal tripe, a speciality of Madrid's *tascas* (bars where food is served with a glass of wine); garlic soup; roast suckling pig; *judías blancas a lo tío Lucas,* white beans; *tortilla capuchina,* an omelette; asparagus from Aranjuez; anise brandy from Chinchón.

EXTREMADURA

Land of the *conquistadores,* this is the "far west" of Spain, on the Portuguese border, an almost forgotten land of rolling plains and wide open spaces, thick forests of holm and cork oaks and chestnut trees, fertile valleys and hillsides planted with olives and vines. It is a land of strong contrasts and few resources.

The basic dishes of the land present a similar contrast — shepherds' and peasants' simple dishes contrasted with the resplendent compositions of monasteries with a rich medieval tradition of good eating.

Some of these dishes entered the repertoire of French *haute cuisine*. The story goes that during the Napoleonic wars, the Benedictine monastery of Alcántara was sacked in 1807 by French troops on their way to Portugal. A cookbook manuscript was salvaged by General Junot, who sent it to his wife. It eventually wound up in the hands of the great French chef, Auguste Escoffier. This cookbook contained many extraordinary recipes, such as truffled pheasant and partridge, partially boned, stuffed with duck liver pâté with truffles, which, after marinating three days in port wine, is cooked and served with more truffles. Escoffier, who prepared it as pheasant *à la mode d'Alcantara*, pronounced the cookbook the only justification for the Napoleonic wars.

But where were those monks getting the truffles? They are a speciality of Extremadura. Called *criadillas de tierra* (earth balls), they're chopped, sautéed with garlic and finished off with a brown sauce thickened with egg yolk.

Most of the dishes of the region, however, are simple, country stews based on lamb, kid and pork, game, river fish. The pig reigns supreme here. This is the home of the *cerdo ibérico,* a breed of pig indigenous to the Iberian peninsula. The rough, viper-infested terrain is said to give the hams a special flavour. Feeding on wild acorns and aromatic herbs, they are the raw material for making *jamón ibérico*, the world's most delicious ham.

It's said that one of the best ways to learn the customs of a country is to partake of the local food and wines. This can lead to some curious culinary experimentations. You've heard of sheep's eyes and fried beetles and ants. But have you tried lizards?

In Plasencia the *lagarto* is consumed with gusto. I have to admit to never having tried them myself, but a culinary writer of some repute, Luis Antonio de Vega, tells of encountering in Extremadura a local man returning from the fields with a pole from which dangled a dozen or so lizards. The following day in the market he saw various women with tubs of water filled with a skinned, white-fleshed creature, which in no way could be confused with any kind of fish. The inveterate gourmet could hardly resist. He bought them and, on the advice of the lizard-vendor, took them to a nearby *taberna* to have them cooked. Then he invited his friends for lunch. The lizards came in a green sauce, lavish with parsley, and everyone declared the dish excellent. De Vega described the flavour of the lizard as somewhere between that of wild rabbit and frogs' legs. However, you will no longer find the lizards in the markets as they are now a protected species.

Dishes of more general appeal are: *caldereta,* lamb stewed in wine; potatoes Badajoz-style, cooked with pork; roast baby kid; *frita extremeña,* a lamb sauté; and partridge, rabbit and quail dishes. *Tenca,* tench, is one freshwater fish worth trying.

From Extremadura comes a special kind of paprika, *pimentón de la Vera,* widely used in cooking and in sausage-making. The sweet peppers are dried over smouldering holm oak fires before being ground to a powder.

LEVANT

The east of Spain, or the Levant, is actually made up of two kingdoms, the Comunidad Valenciana (which comprises the provinces of Castellón de la Plana, Valencia and Alicante) and Murcia. The Levant is famed for its popular tourist coast, the Costa de Azahar and the Costa Blanca. But it's also the land of paella. This fabulous rice dish — Spain's best-known culinary contribution — is native to the Levant.

On the low, coastal regions where water is abundant, rice has been a staple food for the many centuries since the Moors introduced its cultivation. Water means fecundity, and this area known as the "market basket" of Spain produces an extraordinary range of fine produce. There are the famous Valencia oranges but also peaches, apricots, melons, grapes, grapefruit, plums, pears, cherries, apples, asparagus, olives, garlic, capers, anise, saffron, onions, mushrooms, peas, broad beans, green beans, tomatoes, lettuce, cucumber, paprika.

The flat coastal strip, almost subtropical and well irrigated, is backed by rough sierra and small valleys which have more affinity with the scrubby inland regions of La Mancha. Though water is the life-blood and consuming passion of the region, with complex irrigation systems dating from the time of the Moors, parts of Alicante have an average annual rainfall lower than some regions of the Sahara desert.

Alicante offers a little of everything, from near-desert to irrigated fields, from the picturesque coastline of La Marina to the palm groves of Elche, from inland scrubland inhabited by rabbits, turtle-doves and partridge to some of Spain's best-known tourist resorts (Benidorm, Jávea, Calpe, Denia) which were once small fishing villages.

The gastronomy shows the same versatility: *conill i pollastre,* a rabbit and chicken dish; dates from Elche; *langostinos* of Santa Pola; meat pies of Orihuela; *arroz abanda,* a rice and seafood dish; *gazpachos,* plural, similar to that of La Mancha, with dove and rabbit. And, of course, *turrón,* almond nougat from Jijona and Alicante, a must at fiestas and Christmas time.

In Valencia, besides paella, you encounter *fideuá,* similar to paella, but made with vermicelli noodles, *arros rosetxat,* a rice dish with lamb. wild duck of the Albufera, and a wonderful assortment of seafood. Try *anguila,* freshwater eel, *llisa* or *mujol,* grey mullet, *dentón,* dentex, and *llobarro* or *lubina,* sea bass. And *mojama,* the "ham of the ocean", salt-cured tuna, thinly sliced and served as an aperitif.

Castellón boasts superb *langostinos,* big prawns, *robellons*, a wild mushroom the colour of ochre, and *empedrado,* a dish of rice, beans and codfish.

Murcia, with a strong Arabic tradition in cooking (even couscous is known here), enjoys a wealth of produce from fertile fields. Salads are a speciality of the region, including one made with wild greens and herbs, lightly blanched and dressed with olive oil and vinegar. The *mojete murciano* combines sweet green and red peppers, for which the area is famous, with sardines or cod. The mixture is eaten with chunks of bread instead of forks. The *pipirrana* or *rin-ran* is similar, with the addition of tomatoes, garlic and black olives. The *ensalada murciana* combines escarole, tomatoes and watercress.

The snails, as plump and delicious as those of Burgundy, are cooked with thyme, rosemary and fennel and sauced with tomato spiced with paprika, garlic, chili, cumin and mint. The *tortilla murciana* is an omelette with tomatoes, peppers, courgette, aubergine and ham. *Menestra,* like a miniature vegetable garden, is a stew which includes much of the land's produce in one pot. Another speciality is the *olla gitana,* gypsy pot, which besides vegetables includes fruit. It probably originated on the wayfarer's route as the cook plucked a pumpkin from one field, some tomatoes from another and pears from a nearby orchard, and can be freely varied to suit the available ingredients.

Dorada a la sal, a dish also appreciated on other coastlines, is a whole fish covered with coarse salt and baked. The skin comes off with the hard-baked salt and the flesh is served with a sauce of garlic, parsley and olive oil or a garlic mayonnaise.

Murcia is known for excellent wines of Jumilla and Yecla and Valencia for those of Utiel-Requena.

ANDALUSIA

At Almería, Spain turns a corner. This is the south of Spain, fabled Andalusia, the romantic, storybook image of Spain. Dark eyes and flamenco flounces, gypsies and bullfights; dazzling white, jewel-like villages, flowered patios and Moorish palaces; golden beaches, azure water, wide rivers and dusty hillsides. An enormous region, Andalusia includes a lot of Spain. Here are: the peninsula's highest mountains, the snow-capped Sierra Nevada above Granada; the golden beaches of the Costa del Sol, where thousands of holiday-makers throng; olive trees, citrus groves and avocado plantations; the bodegas of Jerez, where the world-famous sherry is made; Roman temples, Arabic mosques and Gothic cathedrals.

Andalusian food, like the culture, can be as subtle and refined as a cool *fino* served in the shade of a grape arbour; as brash and noisy as a tapa bar in the evening; as passionate as a red carnation, as simple and direct as the aroma of bread baking in wood-fired ovens. It is a far-ranging cuisine that takes in sardines grilled on spits over a driftwood fire on the beach to hams cured in the high mountains to partridge cooked in Málaga wine to spicy, Moroccan-style *pinchitos* or kebabs to the latest innovative creation for an international, sophisticated clientele which knows nothing of Spanish food.

Almería, Andalusia's most arid region, has some areas so dry and barren they look like a moonscape. Where there is water, there are lush fields with a year-round growing season which provides Spain and Europe with midwinter tomatoes and other vegetables. There is good seafood here and wheat dishes similar to those of Murcia and Albacete.

Granada is a lush paradise blessed with just about everything: a beautiful stretch of coastline, the highest mountain peak in mainland Spain, irrigated fields, rolling hills where olive trees thrive, wheat fields and that most special of cities, Granada, with its languorous memory of Moorish kings. Mountain hams flavour many local dishes, such as *habas con jamón,* broad beans stewed with ham, and *pollo granadina,* chicken cooked with wine and ham. Another famous dish is the *tortilla Sacromonte,* created at the monastery in the Sacromonte gypsy district. *Choto al ajillo* is baby kid braised in wine with lots of garlic.

Málaga, thriving port city of palm-lined avenues, is the gateway to the Costa del Sol. This is also the home of Málaga wines, sweet nectar of the muscatel grape which contains a year of sunshine in a sip. Cooks add it to sweets and to dishes such as partridge and chicken. *Fritura malagueña* is a mixed fish fry which usually includes fresh anchovies, rings of squid and a slice of a larger fish, all fried to crispy perfection. Excellent seafood soups include *sopa viña AB,* spiked with sherry, and *sopa de rape,* angler-fish soup tinted with saffron.

Cádiz province is Costa del Sol until it rounds the bend of Gibraltar and the Mediterranean becomes the Atlantic. Here is the southernmost point of Europe, the peninsula of Tarifa, that seems closer to north African villages just across the straits than it does to many places in Spain. Cádiz, the capital, is an ancient seafaring town on the Atlantic. Here and in the environs, seafood is fabulous: prawns, crab, clams, mussels, oysters, lobster and fish of many kinds. Specialities include: *abajá de pescado,* a fish stew; *lisa en amarillo,* saffron-tinted mullet; a "dog" soup, *caldillo de perro,* flavoured with bitter oranges; and a "cat" soup, *sopa de gato.* Not far away is the elegant town of Jerez de la Frontera, where sherry is made. The local cuisine is well spiced with this flavourful brew: *riñones al jerez,* kidneys in sherry sauce, *rabo de toro al jerez,* oxtail (or bull's tail, as this is also the region where fighting bulls are raised) braised in sherry.

Huelva is mountains and coast, renowned for the hams of Jabugo but also for excellent seafood. *Atún con tomate* is fresh tuna cooked in tomato; *pez espada* is swordfish, grilled or served in a saffron sauce; *chocos* are tiny squid, which may be cooked with broad beans; *merluza al vino blanco* is hake in a white wine sauce.

Seville, cosmopolitan heart of Andalusia, is magic. From the banks of the Guadalquivir to a tavern in the old quarter to the great cathedral to the promenades of the spring *feria,* where men wearing the handsome *traje corto,* bolero-topped riding breeches, and women in colourful ruffled dresses parade on prancing horses. Seville can somehow bring together the Gothic, the baroque, the rococo and the romantic, the ancient and the modern — and get away with it.

So, too, with the food. The Moorish influence, strong all over Andalusia, is noted here in the sweets and confections, such as *yemas,* candied eggs. Many of these delicacies are made in convents from recipes little changed for centuries. Special mention should be made of the olives of Seville, the plump *manzanillas,* so appreciated the world over. They're enjoyed with aperitif wine, in salads, and go into other dishes such as *pato a la sevillana,* duck with olives. Local dishes include *huevas,* fish roe crisply fried; *huevos de codorniz,* quails' eggs, and *huevos a la flamenca,* a very baroque dish of baked eggs garnished with asparagus, peas, *pimiento* (tinned or bottled peeled red peppers) and *chorizo. Callos a la andaluza,* savoury veal tripe, is a tapa bar speciality. Other meat dishes are *rollo de ternera,* veal stuffed with ham and braised in wine, and *solomillo de cerdo a la trianera,* pork fillet roasted with sherry.

Córdoba, once seat of the Moorish kingdom which ruled Andalusia, is all that is exquisite about this region. Surrounded by legions of olive trees, it is hot and heavy with jasmine in the summer, cool and airy in the Great Mosque with its candy-striped columns, ponderous with the memory of great philosophers, poets and emirs who once lived here when Córdoba was the cultural centre of the whole western world while the rest of Europe lived in the Dark Ages.

There are fine wines of Montilla and Moriles, made by the *solera* process, similar to sherry. From the rocky foothills of the Sierra Morena comes an amazing variety of game: venison, partridge, rabbit, boar. Such dishes as *conejo en salmorejo,* rabbit cooked in a marinade, and *pichones con aceitunas,* pigeons cooked with olives, are typical. A grazing region, Córdoba features excellent lamb and kid dishes such as *caldereta de cordero,* a lamb stew. The *cordobeses* have a way with vegetables, and artichokes, spinach, asparagus and beans are all treated with imagination. *Salmorejo* is a thick version of gazpacho, served as a starter.

Jaén, crossroads between Andalusia and Castile, sits with immense solemnity on the slopes of the Sierra Morena. The city has a decidedly Moorish flavour, with narrow streets that wind up to the

Castillo de Santa Catalina at the very top where there is a beautiful parador hotel. Vast stretches of the province are covered with row upon row of olive trees, ancient, gnarled sculptures against a stark blue sky. Wheat fields and rugged hills, grazing lands, and towns full of Renaissance mansions, Jaén is a surprising land. *Ajoharina* is a delicious way of preparing potatoes; *andrajos,* literally "rags", is a game dish with squares of pasta; walnuts are served in a cream sauce in Baeza; *pipirrana* is a concoction between a tomato salad and gazpacho, here garnished with the local ham.

BALEARIC ISLANDS

Islands are curious. Isolated from the mainstream of continental culture yet, as in the case of the Balearics, positioned to receive a confluence of influences, they are unique. The cuisine is all their own, but with flavours reminiscent of other places.

The island of Mallorca lies little more than 160 kilometres (100 miles) from the Spanish mainland, yet it isn't quite Spanish. It's a blend of ancient myth, fantasy paradise and crazy tourist industry.

The people and language are most akin to Catalonia, and so, too, are most of the dishes. But Italy and France are not so far away and their culinary influences are also apparent. Even before that, the Greeks (Hercules was said to have discovered the Golden Apples in Mallorca), the Romans, the Moors and the Barbary pirates made their way through Mallorcan history and left their imprint on the land and its customs.

The most recent invasion is, of course, by tourists arriving via charter jets. Palma and environs have sprouted with French, Italian and English restaurants to such an extent that the truly local cuisine is being lost.

Two Mallorcan specialities best known all over Spain are *sobrasada* and *ensaimada. Sobrasada* is a soft sausage of pork well-flavoured with sweet and hot peppers. The *ensaimada* is a sweet bread, traditionally made with *saim,* lard, and baked in spirals from the size of an ordinary bun to wagon-wheel dimensions. Pork has always been the primary meat in Mallorca and the charcuterie is justifiably famous. Baby pigs roasted in big ovens were, in the old style, stuffed with a *farce* of liver, heart, breadcrumbs, apples and prunes.

Mallorca has a special claim to fame when it comes to soups. Besides the usual liquid kind, there are "dry" soups. These are basic peasant fare, morning, noon and night and, besides vegetables, contain bread, once made of whole-wheat flour. There are also some fine liquid soups, *sopa de pescado,* a sister to bouillabaisse, and *sopa de cangrejos,* a seafood bisque.

Empanadas — pastry with savoury fillings, not unlike pizza — are famous in three areas of Spain: Galicia, Murcia and Mallorca. The Balearic version is filled with pork or lamb cooked with onions and spices and *sobrasada*. Though paella is quite at home in Mallorca, the natives prefer their rice dishes soupier and highly flavoured with saffron, as in the typical *arroz con pollo*, a chicken, rice and vegetable casserole. Seafood is excellent on the island. Some curious local specialities are tuna with chickpeas, squid stuffed with raisins and aubergine stuffed with fish. *Tumbet* is a casserole of aubergine and potatoes with either meat or fish.

The islands of the Baleares share similar foods, but Menorca has historical differences that make it unique. For nearly 80 years Menorca was ruled by the British (and, for a few years, by the French), who left a mark on the island's cuisine. For instance, Menorca still produces excellent English gin, English puddings and jams. Stuffed turkey is very reminiscent of English yuletide feasts and *maccarons con grevi* is macaroni with "gravy". It's made with the excellent local cheese, Mahón.

It's an old culinary quibble, but there are those who maintain that the famous sauce mayonnaise was invented in Mahón on the island of Menorca. It was supposedly discovered there in 1756 by the Duke of Richelieu, chief of the French invading forces, who either first ate it served by a lowly innkeeper or, possibly, by an illustrious Menorca lady who delighted the duke with the sauce as well as other things. He later popularised the sauce in Paris, calling it *sauce mahonnaise*.

Though it probably originated long before the Duke of Richelieu, mayonnaise was certainly a Spanish invention, if not Menorcan. To this day it is the one "French" sauce most thoroughly at home in Spain, a basic preparation known even in the simplest of kitchens. Whatever its origin, mayonnaise or *mahonnaise* is a lovely accompaniment to many foods in Spain.

Ibiza, smallest of the three main islands, has nearly lost its indigenous cuisine in the influx of tourism. *Burrida de ratjada* is ray fish in a sauce of garlic, almonds and egg; *langosta a la ibicenca* is lobster served with stuffed squid and *escupiñas,* a local shellfish; *sofrit pag'es* is a stew of chicken, lamb, salt pork, *sobrasada* and potatoes.

CANARY ISLANDS

The Canary Islands add a very exotic touch to the repertoire of Spanish cuisine. Located more than 800 kilometres (500 miles) from the European mainland, but only 110 kilometres (70 miles) from the coast of northwest Africa, the Canaries are said to be part of the lost Atlantis. The seven volcanic islands have a climate so mild that one can bathe in the sea in midwinter, making them a favourite tourist destination. Perpetual springtime also means produce unlike that of the rest of Spain. Besides bananas, which thrive here, tropical fruit such as mangoes, guavas, pawpaws, loquats, avocados, melons and yams are also grown.

According to the *conquistadores*, who made these islands a jumping-off point for travels to the New World, the original people of the Canaries, the Guanches, were a simple race, a strong people who lived on a mainly vegetarian diet of wild fruits and roots, native barley which they ground into flour, some fish, milk from goats and, occasionally, goat meat which they apparently consumed raw.

The native barley was ground into a meal, *gofio*, and eaten as a sort of bread. The arrival of the Spaniards, who took over the islands in the 15th century, changed things considerably. The Spaniards brought from Europe everything from wheat to oranges, and from the New World, everything from corn to tomatoes. Wheat and corn, first toasted, then ground, became the *gofio*, which country people carried to the fields in a goatskin and kneaded with water to make a doughy ball of bread. It is also eaten as a porridge, *escaldón*, or fried, *fritangos*, or sweetened as a pudding, *frangollo*.

Seafood is notably good in the Canaries, including some varieties peculiar to the area: *sama*, a type of sea bass, *vieja* and *burro*. A typical dish is *mojo palmero*, boiled fish with sauce. *Mojo colorado* is made with chili and paprika; *mojo verde* is made with coriander.

Frijoles con arroz, black beans and rice, is much like a Cuban dish and *puchero canario*, with beef, squash, corn and yams, could be straight from Argentina. Besides being shipped to Europe, bananas make a creamy sauce for roast chicken or cinnamon-flavoured fried cakes.

AT THE MARKET

What impressed me about Spanish food when I first came here to live was its freshness — fish harvested only a few hours earlier from the sea, eggs still warm from the hen, milk from the neighbour's goat, tomatoes fragrant from the vine, oranges I picked myself. Yes, even the meat — the pork chops that the day before I watched go squealing and grunting into the butcher's back patio.

I had olive oil from the trees that grew all around, wine from nearby vineyards, cheese made at a local farm, flour stone-ground by a water-powered mill and the bread baked just around the corner. Few village housewives owned a tin opener because there were almost no tinned products available. The shopkeeper would open the occasional tin of tuna or sardines for his customers. There were no refrigerated trucks, no freezers, no ice, no preservatives. Food in an Andalusian pueblo was very immediate.

Now, as then, the market is the best place really to appreciate the flavour of Spanish food. Bustling housewives, baskets in hand, throng counters heaped with glittering fish, looking for the day's best buy. Above the butchers' stalls hang freshly killed rabbits, chickens and partridge. There are wire baskets heaped with fresh country eggs and bowls of paprika-flavoured lard to spread on bread. Great slabs of beef share space with miniscule baby lamb chops.

The changing cornucopia of fruit and vegetable stalls is a cook's inspiration: ropes of garlic bulbs, branches of bay-leaves, strands of dusky dried chilies, vats of seasoned olives and string bags of nuts and dried fruits form a backdrop for the array of glistening fresh produce. The variety of fruits and vegetables available is astounding. Many markets also have a stall where spices and herbs are sold. From these treasure chests the vendor scoops pepper, cloves, cinnamon, allspice, aniseed, cumin and saffron, and herbs from the mountains, both culinary and medicinal.

In some markets you will also find a knife-sharpener, flower-sellers, stalls offering dried fruit and nuts, bread dispensary, toy shop, *ultramarinos* (literally, imports; usually means tinned foods), stalls selling nothing but frozen foods and others displaying exclusively cheeses and charcuterie. Near the entrance to the market there may be a wizened old lady selling sprigs of parsley or mint, a country man with bunches of wild asparagus or other wild greens, a vendor with a net bag full of snails, a gypsy selling brass mortars and ornaments and another with bunches of wild camomile and other herbs. The Spanish market is nothing if not lively and varied.

Besides the municipal markets, every town has neighbourhood *tiendas*, small shops where you can purchase staples, some fresh produce, usually milk, yoghurts, cheese, ham and sausages, household cleaning products, a few kinds of wine, and all but the tiniest villages usually have a *supermercado* or an *hipermercado* which will have, besides staples, fresh produce, meat and charcuterie, sometimes seafood as well, frozen foods, wines and liquors, dairy produce and much more. The largest of them, especially in big cities and those catering for up-market tastes, will have many speciality items as well, everything from imported caviar to English mustard powder to Chinese sesame oil to Scottish kippers to Indian relishes to rice wine with a lizard in the bottle, and much, much more.

Following is a bilingual marketing list of many of the foods you can expect to find in markets and shops in Spain.

FRUITS, VEGETABLES AND LEGUMES

Fresh produce is still a seasonal proposition, though modern transport and storage have made more out-of-season vegetables and fruits available to a wider market throughout Spain. In the following list, I've tried to give an idea of seasons, though this will vary throughout the country, with produce maturing much earlier in the south and later in the northern extremes. Produce at the height of its season in your own region will be the least expensive. You can expect to find out-of-season produce from the southern hemisphere (Chile, Peru) in local markets.

FRUITS

Apple *(manzana)*. Quite a few varieties, available year-round. New crop starts coming in midsummer through early autumn. Store apples in refrigerator crisper or in cool, dark place. Many brands of unsweetened apple juice are available.

Apricot *(albaricoque)*. My idea of paradise is to have a prolific apricot tree in the garden. This luscious fruit, of which there are many varieties, provides pop-in-the-mouth eating, wonderful compotes, conserves and jams, purées and elegant desserts. Apricots must be tree-ripened. Once harvested or purchased, keep them refrigerated and consume or conserve promptly — they neither keep well nor travel well. Available early summer through July. Some varieties are especially sweet and are best for eating. Others are tart, best for jam and cooked desserts. Taste before you buy in quantity. Apricots needn't be peeled, but if you wish to, dip them in boiling water briefly and skins will slip off. Dried apricots are *albaricoques secos,* also called *orejones.* Soak them in warm water for two hours. Apricot juice is usually sweetened, in which case it's labelled *nectar de albaricoque.*

Avocado *(aguacate)*. Though a native of the New World, the avocado has become naturalised in southern Spain, where great plantations of this fruit are grown. Most varieties mature through the winter months, but there are usually avocados available year-round. It is most appreciated for its buttery texture and nutty flavour that combine so well with seafood and salads. Both the smooth, green-skinned and dark, rough-skinned (Haas) avocados are available. Buy them firm and under-ripe and mature them, wrapped in paper or in a bag, in a slightly warm location. To test for ripeness, squeeze very gently in the palm of the hand — the flesh should feel soft. Store ripe avocados in the refrigerator. To prepare avocados for use, halve them lengthwise, twist gently to separate halves. Whack a sharp knife directly into the large seed and twist to lift it out. Avocados discolour quickly. Sprinkle cut fruit with lemon juice. To keep half an avocado, leave the pit in, sprinkle with lemon juice, cover with plastic wrap and refrigerate.

Banana *(plátano)*. The bulk of the banana crop comes from the tropical Canary Islands, where this favourite fruit grows very sweet, though some are grown in southern Spain, both for the decorative fronds and the fruit. Ripen them in a bag. Use green ones fried or diced and cooked. Available all year-round, so buy only what can be used within a few days of ripening. Refrigeration causes skins to blacken. Canary Island bananas are short and speckled and ever so sweet.

Blackberry *(zarzamora)*. These berries grow wild in many parts of Spain, are best in cold-weather regions where the brambly bushes get plenty of moisture. Good for jam-making, tarts.

Blueberry *(arándano)*. Seldom found fresh, jams are available.

Cherry *(cereza, guinda, picota)*. Different varieties carry different names. They vary from the deep red, almost black cherries to those that are yellow-orange, and in taste from very sweet to very sharp. Their season is early summer. Buy ripe, unblemished cherries and store them refrigerated. At a *ferretería*, hardware store, you can buy a pitter, useful for cherries, olives and other fruit with small stones. Candied cherries are *cerezas confitadas*, normally available around the Christmas season.

Coconut *(coco)*. Sold with nougat and candied fruits at *feria* stalls. Grated coconut, *coco rallado*, can be purchased in supermarkets. To make coconut milk, pour boiling water on to grated coconut, let sit for two hours and strain. The resulting liquid is coconut milk.

Currant *(grosella)*. Used for jams and juice. A delicious juice, the colour of red wine, is *grosella con uva*, currant and grape. Blackcurrants are used to make the appreciated cassis liqueur. Dried white currants — or Corinth raisins — are called *pasas de corinto*.

Custard apple *(chirimoya)*. Green, pear-shaped and faceted, this fruit looks like an over-sized hand grenade. Inside the flesh is white with shiny, black seeds randomly distributed throughout. It tastes like a creamy, lemon-pineapple pudding and has become a favourite with creative cooks for mousses, ices and puddings. It is quite delicious just spooned from the shell. Buy it under-ripe and firm, eat when it's soft to the touch. The *chirimoya* — cherimoya in the US — is available in the markets in late fall, early winter.

Date *(dátil)*. Fruit of the date palm, this super-sweet fruit is grown in Spain and also imported. Store dates refrigerated. Try serving them as hors-d'oeuvres, with salty foods such as ham, bacon, salt fish.

Fig *(higo)*. The fig tree is as much a part of the Spanish landscape as the olive. The ancient, gnarled, grey branches with broad, green leaves appear everywhere, on steep unirrigated hillsides, in tiny enclosed patios and growing, impossibly, out of rock crevices on vertical canyon walls. Its fruit is bountiful and sweet. The first figs appear in early summer. These are the *brevas*, plump, black figs which are sold at fancy prices. By late summer the ordinary variety ripens. Hard and green on the trees, they slowly turn a brownish-purple and are soft to the touch. Inside they are a luscious pink. Figs have to be ripened on the tree. Once picked, chill them. Ripe figs can be eaten as they are, skin and all. Or they may be peeled and sliced to be served as hors-d'oeuvres (with *serrano* ham) or dessert. Cooked fresh figs are lovely in compotes, tarts and puddings and make good jams and chutneys. To dry figs, pick ripe, unblemished fruit. Spread on a layer of palmetto leaves, tarp or newspapers in one layer on a flat surface where they will receive all-day sun. Turn them occasionally, bringing indoors in case of heavy dew, and discard any rotting or bug-infested ones. When fully dry, the figs are packed into baskets called *serretes,* sewn tightly closed and taken to the fig press. The pressing protects the fruit against bug and worm infestation. Small quantities, to be used within a few months, can simply be stored in tightly sealed containers. Soak dried figs in water to plump them or stew them for compotes.

Grapefruit *(pomelo)*. Available autumn to spring. Refrigerated, they keep a long time.

Grape *(uva)*. The Moors wrote paeans of praise to the Spanish grape, that delectable fruit of the vine. Today's invaders, the people of many nationalities who flock to this country to live in the sun, also enjoy the sweet nectar of Spanish grapes, sometimes plucked straight from the arbour which shades the terrace. Many varieties of grapes are grown, some specifically for the making of wines, from the sweet dessert wines of both Málaga and Jerez to the dry table wines of La Mancha, Rioja and Catalonia. Of the eating grapes, possibly the most famous is the muscatel, the Málaga grape.

Grapes come into the markets in late summer and last until New Year's Eve, when they are consumed, one at each of the midnight chimes, to assure 12 months of good fortune in the coming year. Store them in a cool but not cold place. Grapes are sun-dried to make raisins, *uvas pasas,* so appreciated for puddings and other sweets. To plump them for serving as dessert, soak for 10 minutes in warm water and dry well. If seeding them, dust raisins, fingers and knife with flour occasionally. The leaves of the grape-vine, if not treated with pesticides, can be used for *dolmades*, Middle Eastern stuffed vine leaves.

Guava *(guayaba)*. A tropical fruit grown in the Canary Islands, it is found in some supermarkets within Spain.

Kiwi. Imported from New Zealand or Spanish grown, available in many markets.

Lemon *(limón)*. This wonderfully scented fruit is essential in any kitchen, for its zest, verve and flavour, and is a favourite addition to gardens, where, besides providing ready fruit, its flowers perfume the air. Lemons are available year-round and some varieties bear fruit and flower at the same time. There are thick-skinned and thin-skinned types and some varieties come to market quite green. These are usually quite juicy and flavourful in spite of their colour. Store lemons in a cool place. Before juicing, roll the lemon on a board. Lemon juice is a potent anti-oxidant, preventing the darkening of other fruits and vegetables. It can be used in place of vinegar in any salad or sauce and, of course, is indispensable with fish and shellfish.

Lime *(lima)*. Not widely available. Substitute lemons.

Litchis. Available in some supermarkets.

Loquat *(níspero)*. A pear-shaped, plum-sized fruit of a deep yellow colour. The flesh is very sweet, slightly grainy. Buy them ripe. Season is late spring, early summer.

Mango *(mango)*. Another tropical fruit grown in the Canary Islands and in parts of the Málaga and Granada coasts.

Melon *(melón)*. Many varieties of superb melons are grown in Spain, from those with pale green flesh to deep orange flesh. The best variety, called *piel de sapo*, or "toad skin", is green-skinned and pale yellow-fleshed. It's ever so sweet. Sweet melons contrast nicely with salty ham or smoked salmon, so try them as hors-d'oeuvres as well as dessert. Everyone has a favourite method of picking a good melon: thumping, smelling, pressing, scraping. A slight give when pressed with the thumb at the blossom end is a good indication the melon is ripe; too soft, it's over-ripe. In any case, to be sweet, the fruit must be vine-ripened. Cut up non-sweet melons into salads as for cucumber. Chill the melon before serving. To store melons for eating during the winter, try suspending them by string from the ceiling in a cool pantry. Watermelon is called *sandía* (not *melón de agua*, as one dictionary-toting tourist in the market called it). Some market vendors will be willing to plug the watermelon to verify its ripeness. Chill and eat a plugged or cut watermelon promptly, as once the skin is broken it starts to ferment rapidly. In many places you can buy a half or quarter of a large watermelon. Look for the tiny ones, no bigger than a regular melon.

Nut *(nuez)*. First and foremost in Spain is the almond, *almendra*, widely grown. Spain is the world's second largest almond producer. They're available in the shell, shelled, blanched, toasted, salted. To blanch almonds, put them into boiling water, bring again to the boil and drain. While still warm, slip the skins off them. Almonds still green on the tree are edible and often used. Crack the outer casing, then the immature shell to get at the kernel. The other best-loved nut is not actually a nut, but an underground legume: the peanut or *cacahuete*. This is favourite nibbling food everywhere in Spain and is available roasted in the shells, raw and roasted shelled. Cashews are *anacardos;* Brazil nuts are *nueces de Brasil;* walnuts are *nueces de nogal;* pecans are *nueces americanas;* hazelnuts or filberts are *avellanas;* pistachios are *pistachos*. Chestnuts, *castañas,* come into the markets in the fall and vendors sell them roasted on street corners everywhere in Spain; a warm handful on a nippy evening. *Piñones* are the kernels of pine-cones with a subtle, resinous flavour much appreciated in poultry stuffings, sausages, vegetable dishes and sweets. They're very pricey and once you've gathered your own you'll understand why. The pine cones must first be heated till they open, then cracked to release the kernels. Then each tiny one must be cracked and the seed extracted.

Orange *(naranja)*. The Spanish name comes from the Sanskrit word for this beautiful fruit, *naranga,* which the Moors brought to Spain intact with the fruit. The first orange groves which proliferated in Spain during the rule of Islam (including those in the Great Mosque of Córdoba and the courtyards of the Alhambra) were bitter oranges, appreciated for their ornamental value and the aroma of the peel and blossoms. The juice was used as seasoning for meat and fish, and appears to this day as flavouring in some Spanish dishes. Portuguese travellers in the 15th century brought sweet oranges from China, and today most eating oranges are called *chinas* in Spain. Curiously, the variety known as

Valencia, the world's most popular orange, is little grown in Spain any more. Here, the navel orange, *washingtona,* easy to peel and seedless, has become the most popular, both on the domestic market and for export. *Clementinas* are the small, delightfully sweet tangerines.

Oranges are in season from fall through spring. My children said oranges were magic, because they always appeared in autumn in time for their first snuffly cold. We suddenly consumed quantities of oranges, fresh and juiced, and felt immune to the winter's cold germs. The season goes on until spring. Though available through the summer, the quality of the oranges is not usually very good. Oranges have to be fully ripe and sweet when picked — they will never ripen further. Green splotches on the skin do not indicate an under-ripe orange; skin colour is affected by night-time temperatures, and very warm nights can keep a fully ripe orange green. Store them in a cool place and they will keep for about a month from the time they were picked.

You may encounter another type of orange. Called *dulce,* sweet, it is without the tang and aroma that we expect of an orange. Rather insipid in flavour, the juice is very nice mixed with the sharp juice of *fuertes,* sour oranges.

The bitter orange, *agria* or *cachorreña,* is still grown extensively ornamentally and is used as root-stock for other varieties. So the bitter, Seville orange — essential for fine marmalade — is available, though seldom found in the markets. Shops carry fresh, pasteurised orange juice as well as many bottled and tinned juices, both sweetened and unsweetened. There is nothing more flavourful, though, than a tall glass of freshly squeezed Spanish orange juice, and some quality cafés and restaurants do provide it.

A few recipes, which certainly date from Moorish days, call for orange blossom water, *agua de azahar,* available in some speciality shops.

Peach *(melocotón).* Peaches are a fruit of full summer. There are both clingstone and freestone varieties and colours range from almost crimson to pale "peaches and cream" colour to fruit that is almost yellow. They must be tree-ripened; under-ripe ones will simply wither rather than sweeten and mature. Store fully ripe peaches refrigerated. To peel peaches in quantity, dip them into boiling water and skins slip off easily. Nectarines are a smooth-skinned variety of peach, usually available before peaches come in.

Pear *(pera).* A summer to early-winter fruit which seems to be available year-round. Pears come in an enormous range of colours — green, gold, russet — and sizes, from tiny ones the size of cherries, to some as big as grapefruit. Pears are usually picked when not quite ripe. They will ripen and sweeten at room temperature. Chilling tends to brown them. Some pears store well, other varieties are very perishable.

Persimmon *(caqui).* Looks like a small tomato when fully ripe. Grown in the south of Spain, this fruit comes into the markets in autumn. It must be allowed to mature, otherwise it's so astringent it puckers the mouth. Very soft to the touch when ripe. Eat with a spoon or use the pulp to confect sorbets, mousses and creams.

Pineapple *(piña).* The pineapple is the star of the fruit world. Besides flavour, it has presence. Grown in the Canary Islands, pineapples are available in mainland shops particularly at holiday times such as Christmas. A ripe pineapple should have a full, musky aroma. Inside the spiny exterior, the flesh should be pale yellow. Cut off the top and strip off the skin by cutting thin strips from the top to the bottom of the fruit. Cut out the "eyes" and slice the pineapple. Cut out the core, which is usually too pithy to eat. Fresh pineapple contains an enzyme which makes it a good digestive, but will prevent gelatine from setting. Either cook the pineapple for gelatine desserts or substitute tinned fruit.

Plum (*ciruela*). These fruit are like precious gems in their market crates, from the deep rubies to the golden topaz, the green jade to the amethyst. They last through the summer in the markets. Choose slightly soft ones; store refrigerated. The tartness is usually in the skins, with sweet flesh beneath. For jams and compotes, cook with skins to preserve flavour. *Ciruelas pasas* are dried plums, or prunes. The local ones tend to be more pit than fruit, but very good California prunes are available in supermarkets.

Pomegranate (*granada*). Pomegranates, which ripen in early fall, are not always available in the markets, though they grow widely in Spain. They look like a hard-skinned apple, blushed red and tufted. The fruit is filled with jewel-like red kernels. These are the seeds which are eaten, releasing a lovely, sweet-tart juice. The tiny "nut" of the seed can be swallowed or spat out. Pomegranates will keep quite nicely in a cool place. Serve them, quartered, with spoons for scooping up the juicy seeds (the juice will stain); use the seeds scattered on salads or other dishes as garnish; crush the seeds to extract the juice. Mix with other fruit juices or enjoy it plain. The juice freezes well.

Prickly pear (*higo chumbo*). This prickly cactus was once planted around isolated farms as a fencing, to keep outsiders out and domestic animals in. The fruit is pear-shaped, a rosy-yellow colour, and covered with a spiny skin. It is often sold by street vendors, who peel the fruit and hand you, untouched, the pristine, juicy inside.

Quince (*membrillo*). The quince looks like an over-sized, somewhat knobby, yellow apple. It's harder and grainier than an apple and, though it can be eaten fresh, is most often cooked. Quince comes into season in the fall. Bake it like apples, stew it or make *dulce de membrillo,* the amber-coloured quince jelly which can be bought in most food shops. For a typical Spanish dessert plate, combine a slice of quince jelly with *queso blanco,* soft, white cheese and a few walnuts or almonds — an inspired combination.

Raspberry (*frambuesa*). This fruit, which ripens in summer, grows best in cold-winter regions, but is now available throughout the country. Raspberries are delicate fruit which bruise and spoil easily, so handle them carefully. They must be ripened on the canes and their flavour should be tart-sweet. Buy in quantity when the price is lowest and freeze them, lightly sprinkled with sugar and packaged in plastic bags.

Strawberry (*fresa, fresón*). Strawberries are the first blush of spring, though new varieties and extensive plantings make this fruit available, if extravagant, very nearly the whole year. They should be fully sweetened when picked, for they won't ripen further. However, full red colour is not an indication of sweetness; some varieties are nearly white when fully ripe. Store strawberries, unwashed and unhulled, and loosely wrapped in the refrigerator or prepare them immediately for eating by washing, hulling, slicing, sugaring, and chill them, tightly covered, until serving time.

Tangerine *(mandarina)*. This dainty member of the citrus family is the first to appear in the markets in the fall and the last to finish the season, with the seedless *clementinas* in the spring. They seem to spoil more readily than oranges, so buy them fresh and use promptly. Chilled tangerine juice is a lovely drink.

Tiger nut *(chufa)*. Not a nut but a tuber. From it is made *horchata* or orgeat, now sold bottled all over Spain. It's a sweet, milky drink (which at home can be made with almonds) with overtones of coconut. The *chufa* can be eaten raw.

VEGETABLES

Artichoke *(alcachofa)*. An edible thistle, the artichoke is ostensibly a spring vegetable. In fact, it's available from early winter until almost summer. A perennial, the plant grows to around 1.2 metres (four feet). The frond-like leaves make it attractive for borders and, if you don't manage to eat all the buds — the artichokes — they will open into spectacular flowers. Buy artichokes with the leaves tightly closed and with no discolouration. Except for the very tiniest ones, only the heart and the fleshy pulp on the inside of the leaves and their bases are edible. Spanish ways with artichokes are, though delicious, less than dainty. The whole or halved vegetable is braised in its sauce, meaning messy fingers for the diner. Artichoke hearts or bottoms can be substituted in such recipes. To prepare artichokes for cooking, remove the first layer of coarse outer leaves. You can trim off the tips, cutting about one-third way down, or leave whole. Rub the artichokes with a cut lemon and drop into acidulated water so they don't darken. If preparing bottoms, continue snapping off leaves, leaving only their base and cut the artichoke top off just above the heart or core. Cook artichokes in enamel, glass or earthenware pots, as they will darken in metal pans. After cooking, the "choke" or fuzzy centre can be scooped out with a spoon. In case you're a novice at eating them, here's how: pull each leaf off with the fingers, dip it in sauce, and run it between the teeth to extract the fleshy goodness, then discard the leaf. When you get to the heart or base of the artichoke, eat it with knife and fork.

Asparagus *(espárrago)*. Harbinger of spring, the first stalks of wild asparagus poke up through damp earth in late winter, though the wonderful cultivated asparagus, both white and green, doesn't appear until almost Easter. Wild asparagus, called *espárragos trigueros* because it often grows beside fields of wheat, has thin, spindly stalks with a slightly bitter taste, much appreciated in *tortillas,* omelettes. It should be freshly cut or it can be woody and excessively bitter. Fresh green and white asparagus is usually cooked whole, removing the tough butt ends and, if desired, shaving off the thin outer skin right up to the tips.

Aubergine *(berenjena)*. Americans know this gorgeous, deep purple vegetable as "eggplant". A summer vegetable, aubergines range from tiny plum-sized ones to big globes. The colours, too, can vary, from purple-black to violet striations to white. Aubergine lends itself to numerous delicious dishes — stuffed, fried, stewed and incorporated in omelettes. It can be cooked peeled or unpeeled. After slicing or dicing, it is usually sprinkled liberally with salt and left to drain in a colander for about an hour. This removes excess water so the vegetable absorbs less oil in frying.

Bean, green *(judía verde, habichuela)*. Available year-round, beans are considerably less costly in the summer. There are quite a few varieties — skinny ones, wide and flat ones and plump ones. Beans that are young and tender and freshly picked seldom need stringing. If they do, cut off tops and tails and remove strings.

Bean, broad *(haba, fava)*. Plump, pale green beans inside big pods, they very much resemble the American lima bean but are actually a relative of the pea. Their season is springtime. Very small and tender ones can be cooked *con calzones* ("with their breeches on"), unpodded. Otherwise, remove the beans from shells immediately before cooking so they don't darken and harden. Each bean is covered with a thick skin, usually left on. However, if the beans have been sitting around the market or pantry too long, this skin can be tough, in which case they may be blanched, the skins slipped off and the beans cooked according to recipe. Cook broad beans in ceramic, enamel or glass pans to prevent their turning dark.

Bean, dry. See PULSES.

Bean sprout *(brote)*. Available fresh and bottled in many supermarkets.

Beet *(remolacha)*. Red beets, a winter vegetable, are mainly used in Spanish cooking as an ingredient in *entremeses* and salads. Beet greens can be cooked exactly as for spinach and are quite delicious.

Broccoli *(brócoli, brécol)*. Winter to spring. Choose broccoli with dark green, compact heads.

Brussels sprout *(col de Bruselas)*. Winter to spring.

Cabbage *(col, berza, repollo; lombarda is red cabbage)*. Always available, but at its best in the winter, cabbage is a fairly standard ingredient in many Spanish *pucheros* and *cocidos,* the regional variations of boiled dinner. Green cabbage, red cabbage, Chinese celery-cabbage, curly cabbage, are all to be found. Cabbage seems particularly good when slowly braised, especially with pork, ham and sausages, as in many Spanish preparations for this vegetable. But it's also good and more nutritious if steamed only about 10 minutes until just barely tender, or served raw in slaw salads.

Cardoon *(cardo)*. A relative of the artichoke. The stalks are peeled and cooked as for asparagus. It is a typical dish on Christmas Eve. The thin stalks of the golden thistle *(tagarnina)* which grows wild are also enjoyed as a vegetable or in omelettes.

Carrot *(zanahoria)*. A few carrots usually go into the daily *puchero*. They also make a very acceptable marmalade. Carrots are available year-round. Store refrigerated.

Cauliflower *(coliflor)*. A most versatile vegetable, cauliflower turns up raw, cooked in salads, soups and puddings as well as fried, sauced and casseroled. Choose heads with white, compact florets. If the cauliflower is yellowish or has a fuzzy look, it has been stored too long.

Celery *(apio)*. Appreciated for its crunch when served raw and its herbal flavour when cooked. There are several types of celery available: the knobby root, known as celery root, celeriac or *céleri-rave,* which commands very high prices; the white or pale green type, and a spindly, woody type with an especially aromatic flavour, good for flavouring stews and soups. Celery, available through all the cool months, is usually sold by the bunch, or *manojo*.

Chard *(acelga)*. Also called Swiss chard or white beet, this vegetable, which looks like a celery stalk topped with a spinach leaf, is, in fact, a member of the beet family. It's grown extensively in Spain and is worth getting acquainted with. The ribbed, white stalks can be cooked, then sauced or batter-dipped and fried. The broad, green leaves can be cooked exactly as for spinach. They taste very much the same, if a little coarser in texture. The smaller stalks are less stringy than the big ones.

Chicory *(achicoria)*. See endive.

Corn *(maíz)*. Sweet corn on the cob has only recently become available in Spain, especially in regions where foreigners live. However, the Canary Islanders have been using corn for centuries as an ingredient in some stews.

Courgette, small marrow *(calabacín)*. Americans call this vegetable by its Italian name, *zucchini*. This member of the squash family, a summer vegetable, looks much like a cucumber, though some specimens grow considerably larger (good for stuffing). Select firm ones with unblemished skin. Wash them well, but they don't need paring. If very mature, it may be necessary to scoop out seeds in the centre.

Cucumber *(pepino)*. Cool cucumbers, though available year-round, are a real summer-time vegetable, a basic ingredient in salads and gazpacho. The skinnier ones usually have less-developed seeds than thick ones. If you happen to get a bitter one (due to lack of moisture when it was still on the vine), peel it, slice, and sprinkle liberally with salt. Let drain in a colander for an hour, wash in running water and pat dry. The bitter flavour disappears with the liquid. Cucumbers make an interesting cooked vegetable, lightly sautéed.

Endive *(endibia)*. Called chicory by the English, Belgian endive is shaped like a small white, elongated cabbage, with overlapping leaves tapering to a point. It can be eaten raw in salads or braised and sauced. Endive is available through the winter months. To confuse the issue, curly endive, a frizzy, slightly bitter-tasting "lettuce" is also called chicory and, in Spanish, mistakenly called *escarola*. Powdered chicory for giving coffee a rich taste is called *achicoria,* available in many supermarkets. It is the dried root of endive.

Fennel *(hinojo)*. The bulbous root of the cultivated fennel, to be found in many Spanish markets, can be eaten raw or cooked. It has a very subtle anisette flavour and is much appreciated with seafood. Wild fennel grows on hillsides everywhere in Spain. It's used in the curing of olives and flavours some soups and potages. Try putting a few stalks of fresh fennel on top of the coals when grilling fish.

Garlic *(ajo)*. Read about this favourite seasoning ingredient under the section on spices and herbs.

Leek *(puerro)*. A member of the onion family, these look like fat, overgrown scallions. Favoured for soups and stews, they can also be cooked as a vegetable in their own right. Cut off most of the green tops and discard. Wash very well to get the grit out from between the layers.

Lettuce *(lechuga)*. The most common type of lettuce in Spanish markets is the loose-leaf type, dark green leaves branching from a single stalk. Iceberg lettuce *(crispilla)*, a compact head lettuce, is also found, as are romaine *(lengua de burro)*, long sheaves of leaves, escarole *(escarola)*, similar to endive but not as frizzy, and the aforementioned curly endive. Lettuce is available year-round, but is most expensive in the winter. Loose-leaf lettuce is often especially gritty. Wash individual leaves under running water or separate the leaves and let them soak briefly in a basin of water.

Mushroom *(champiñón, seta, hongo)*. The first of the Spanish names, taken from the French, is used only for the cultivated white mushrooms found in markets everywhere. The second name means every other kind of mushroom, mainly wild ones. The last word means "fungus", which is what all mushrooms are, but is used for a few varieties. Add to this the dozens of regional names for particular varieties and the names for "mushroom" go on and on. Collecting wild mushrooms is a sport with passionate devotees, especially in Galicia, the Basque country and Catalonia. Some of the "wild" varieties are often found in the markets and certainly contribute to the culinary spectrum. The most usual are: *boleto,* the boletus, also known as *cèpe;* the chanterelle or *Cantharellus cibarius,* known as *seta amarilla, saltxa-perratxiku,* or *rossinyol;* the *Russulas cyanoxanta* and *virescens,* called *gibeludiñas* by the Basques or *carbonera;* and the *Lactarius deliciosus,* the ochre-coloured *rovellon* or *níscalo,* saffron milkcap, also available tinned. Store unwashed mushrooms in a basket or string bag in a cool, dry place. Discard any which are mushy or soft and discoloured. Rotting mushrooms probably cause more toxic reactions than the consumption of actually poisonous mushrooms. Some mushrooms can be dried. Thread them in a strand and hang in a dry place. Reconstitute by soaking in warm water. A few speciality shops import dried Chinese mushrooms. Truffles, *trufas,* are available tinned, very rarely fresh.

Olive *(aceituna)*. Strictly speaking, these are a fruit, not a vegetable. They are not, by the way, edible straight from the tree, a fact of which I was unaware the first time I saw a real, live olive tree laden with ripe fruit, and popped one in my mouth. Incredibly bitter, the fruit must be soaked, cured and fermented (see Chapter 4 for how to do it). Olives in Spain come in an incredible variety — pitted and stuffed with anchovies, almonds, red peppers, onions; green, black and purple; seasoned with garlic and herbs, tangy with vinegar, red with paprika and zingy with chili pepper. They are sold from open stock, dipped from vats, in bottles, tins and plastic envelopes.

Onion *(cebolla)*. How could we cook in any language without this pungent member of the lily family? In Spain it's used in many guises. Raw spring onions, washed and topped, are munched with typical soups; chopped onions go into many salads, and sautéed they are essential to many dishes, in particular the *sofrito,* a sauce of fried onion and tomato. The best onions are the sweet, yellow Spanish onions. There are also red ones; tiny ones, called *cebollas francesas;* green onions, usually harvested a little bigger and more bulbous than scallions, and, where available, shallots, *chalotas* or *escalonia.* Chives, which can be grown from seed, are *cebollina.* Onions come into the market in early summer, full-sized globes, but with their tops still on. Store them in a cool, dry, dark place. Ready-dried onions keep for several months unless the pantry is too warm or humid. To remove the odour of onions from hands, rub with salt and lemon juice, then rinse in soapy water.

Palm heart *(cogollo de palmito)*. These are usually only found tinned, an exotic addition to salads. However, they are sometimes sold by street vendors, who gather the wild variety and pare them down to the woody heart for consumption raw. The leaves are peeled off, rather as one eats an artichoke, and the fleshy part eaten and the leaf discarded.

Parsnip *(chirivía)*.

Pea *(guisante)*. Available winter through spring. Peas are best when very freshly picked, before the natural sugars turn to starch. Snow peas, mangetouts *(guisante de tirabeque)*, are sporadically available.

Pepper *(pimiento)*. Red and green, big and small, sweet and hot, peppers come in an enticing variety. Red peppers, the mature version of the green ones, are sweeter and milder. Bell peppers and the smaller, narrower Spanish pepper can be used more or less interchangeably. The first are fleshier with a tougher skin; the second are crisper and thin-skinned. *Pimientos de piquillo*, available in tins, are favourites for stuffing. They have a pointy tip and a bit of a bite. Peppers are commonly roasted to facilitate peeling them. Tinned, peeled red peppers are pimientos *(pimiento marrón)*, much used for garnish. Hot *(picante)* chili peppers are affectionately called *guindillas*. The tiny red ones are the most fiery; thumb-sized and plum-sized ones are medium-hot. They come into the market in the early fall, threaded on strands, still fresh in brilliant reds, oranges and yellows. Once dried, they keep for many months. Also dried are sweet peppers, *ñoras*, or *pimientos choriceros*. Substitute paprika if unavailable.

Potato *(patata)*. It's a good thing Columbus discovered the Americas, else the other half of the world would never have had this remarkable tuber. Spanish explorers brought the potato from South America around 1540 and it was cultivated in Spain long before it became popular in the rest of Europe. The French, in fact, considered it suspect until Parmentier began his potato rehabilitation campaign in 1771. The nicest thing about the potato is its versatility. It makes a fine foil for any meat, fish or fowl, adds body to soups and stews and can even stand alone when times are lean. Oil and butter enhance it; garlic doesn't hurt it; spices, herbs, milk, eggs are absorbed by it. The potato probably appears on Spanish dinner tables more frequently than any other food except bread. The favourite preparation is, of course, *patatas fritas* (chips or, as Americans call them, fries). The most common potato is the white, which has a golden-brown skin. Red potatoes are also grown. New potatoes come into the markets in springtime. They are least starchy, have a higher moisture content and tender skins which needn't be peeled. Store potatoes in a cool, dark, dry place. Discard any which are sprouting or are green as they can be toxic.

Pumpkin *(calabaza)*. A member of the squash family, this hard-skinned variety is harvested in the summer, but keeps well through the winter. Some of them grow to enormous size and are sold in the markets by the piece. Spanish pumpkins are usually green-skinned (orange-skinned ones are sometimes found). The flesh ranges from pale yellow in the immature and recently harvested ones to bright orange in the big ones. Scoop out the seeds and fibrous flesh surrounding them and peel the pumpkin before cooking. The seeds can be dried and toasted for snacking. Store cut pumpkin in the refrigerator. The bland, slightly sweet flesh of pumpkin can go sweet or savoury, though in Spain it is most often used as a vegetable in hearty potages with beans and sausages.

Radish (*rábano*). These come in all sizes, from tiny, cherry-sized ones to big, turnip-sized. Conserve in refrigerator crisper with tops removed; crisp in ice water before serving in salads.

Spinach (*espinaca*). Spinach is a cool season crop, available from autumn to spring. Fresh spinach needs thorough washing to remove all grit. Wash it in a basin of water, let it sit five minutes so sand and earth sink, scoop the leaves off the top and wash again in running water. Drain well and store it, loosely wrapped in a plastic bag in crisper, or steam it immediately, then refrigerate for later use. Spinach can be cooked with only the water clinging to the leaves. If very mature and likely to be bitter, blanch in boiling water, drain, then cook in fresh water. Spinach leaves can also be eaten raw as a salad green.

Squash (*calabaza, calabacín*). These vegetables, summer and winter varieties, have been covered under courgette and pumpkin. Occasionally other types are found in the market. If the skins are soft, like courgette, they are summer squash and can be cooked skin, seeds and all. If hard-skinned like pumpkin, they are winter squash, can be baked, steamed, or fried and the skin and seeds are not eaten.

Sweet potato (*batata, boniato*). This sweet-tasting, orange-fleshed vegetable appears in the market in time for All Souls' Day, when it is eaten with chestnuts, lasts through November when Americans enjoy it for Thanksgiving, and disappears shortly after Christmas. Buy firm ones and use them promptly as they do not store well. They can be boiled, then peeled and puréed, or baked and served like jacket potatoes. Americans often mistakenly call sweet potatoes yams. Real yams, *ñames*, a starchy root, are grown and eaten in the Canary Islands, much the same as in West Africa.

Tomato (*tomate*). It just wouldn't be Spanish cooking without the tomato. This is not to say that there aren't many, many dishes which contain no tomatoes at all, but its use is so pervasive that it's considered a basic ingredient. How in the world did the people of Spain eat before the discovery of America? No gazpacho, as it is known today; no *sofrito,* the basic tomato sauce; no *ensalada mixta* with great chunks of vine-ripened tomato. Tomatoes are absolutely a summer crop. However, in Spain's southern regions and the Canaries they are grown year-round in protected places and in hothouses, both for the domestic market and for export. Spanish cooks prefer the slightly green, under ripe tomatoes for chunking into salads. The dead-ripe ones are selected for gazpacho and tomato sauces. Green tomatoes will ripen on the kitchen counter in a few days. Once ripe, store them refrigerated, but use promptly. To peel a single tomato, rub across the skin with the edge of a knife, then pull the skin off. To peel several tomatoes, dip them in boiling water for a few seconds and the skins slip off easily.

Turnip (*nabo*). Most often used as a flavouring ingredient in *cocidos,* turnips are also eaten raw and cooked. Try them puréed with carrots for a tasty treat. In Galicia, *grelos,* which are the flowering stems of the turnip, are stewed with cured pork shoulder and beans for the well-known dish, *lacón con grelos.*

PULSES

Pulses, legumes *(legumbres secas),* include all the dried beans, peas and pulses much used in Spanish cookery. All of them are an excellent source of protein, albeit incomplete. However, combined with small quantities of meat, eggs, dairy products or grains, they form whole protein. This helps explain how some of the heavy stews of beans or chickpeas have sustained peasant people who eat little meat.

Black-eyed pea *(chícharo, figüelo, judía de careta).* Unlike the other real beans, which are native to the Americas, this one comes from Africa. It looks like a white bean but with a black belly-button. Can be substituted in any recipe calling for dried beans. Makes an excellent vegetable side-dish to accompany meat dishes, particularly pork and ham.

Chickpea *(garbanzo).* The *garbanzo* is a basic ingredient in Spain's national dish, the *cocido.* With long, slow cooking (or a pressure cooker) it is quite toothsome, though never as tender as most beans. It has a delicious, nutty taste and seems to have a special affinity for some of the strong flavours of Spanish cooking — salt pork, strong garlic sausage, black pudding, tomatoes, cabbages and onions. *Garbanzos* must be soaked before cooking. However, you can often buy them *en remojo,* soaked, at meat and poultry stalls in the market. Drain the soaked beans and put to cook in boiling water. Pueblo cooks advise not adding salt to the *garbanzos* until they are at least half-cooked. Though cooking time varies with quality, I find that two hours produces tender ones.

Dried beans. These are *alubias secas,* but they have a host of other names: *habichuela, judía seca, lingote, bolo, faba, fesol, fréjol, fríjol, frisuelo, pocha, mongete...* And they come in various colours: *pintada,* pinto, which are speckled, brown ones; *negra,* black; *roja,* red; and *blanca,* white. The fat, white beans for the Asturian *fabada* are called *fabes* (where these are not available, use dry lima beans or butter beans).

Lentil *(lenteja).* Most shops carry at least two varieties of lentils, the tiny, dark ones and the larger, greenish-brown discs. A few supermarkets might have yellow lentils or peas.

Lima bean *(alubia de Perú).* Though fresh lima beans are uncommon in Spain, the dried variety, also called butter beans, can be found occasionally. They should be briefly soaked to prevent the skin splitting during cooking.

Lupin *(altramuz).* Edible seed served as snack food in Spain.

Soy bean *(alubia de soja).* Available in some supermarkets and health food stores. These never get as tender as other beans. Mung peas for making bean sprouts are usually found in the same shops which carry soy.

Split pea *(guisante mondada).* Great for soups.

FISH AND SHELLFISH

A visit to the fish market is among the most quintessential of Spanish experiences, whether it's the raucous wholesale market, where fish are unloaded at quayside, or the shoppers' market in town. Here the fish in their incredible variety attest to the fact that the country's hundreds of kilometres of coastline provide much more than a sunbather's paradise.

For many newcomers to Spain this variety is both perplexing and just a little intimidating. When I landed on these sunny shores — direct from Midwest America, where seafood came frozen and packaged — I had never bought, cleaned and cooked a fresh fish in my life! My first fish, bought at the village market, was an especially large, ugly and scaly specimen. The maid showed me how to scale it, clean and fillet it. I baked it with butter and lemon and it was delicious. I was impressed by the freshness.

The fishmongers can be more or less helpful and more or less straightforward, depending on how business goes. For instance, if not too pressed, a vendor may well tell you exactly how to prepare a good dish of *almejas a la marinera* (clams sailor style); he may be more than pleased to fillet your sole or scrounge around to find some tasty trimmings for the cat. Another day, he'll tell you the *lisa* is *lubina*, when you know better; that the sole is fresh, when it's obviously thawed; that he hasn't time to fillet the John Dory, and that it's not his problem if the price has doubled since last week.

You'll get better value if you know your way around the market, know what's a *lubina* and what isn't, what it's worth, whether it's fresh and how to clean it yourself.

Select fresh fish. All seafood starts to lose in flavour and goodness as soon as it leaves the water. Careful treatment and storage will keep the fish in top quality for a longer time. Look for bright and bulging eyes. Sunken eyes are a dead give-away for a fish that's been around too long. The skin should be shiny, not dull, and scales tightly adhered to the skin and free of slime. The flesh should feel firm and springy. Poke the fish with a finger; it should leave no indentation. The gills should be moist and red. The sniff test should reveal no offensive odours, just a fresh sea tang. Check that the tail and other fins are intact. Brittle, broken or jagged tails may indicate fish was frozen and thawed. Fillets or fish steaks should show no discolouration or dryness around cut edges which also might indicate defrosted pieces.

It is permitted to sell defrosted frozen fish, but it must be marked accordingly. Most markets have a frozen fish section. Though the varieties are more limited, the prices are generally less than for fresh fish. Freezing processes (usually done at sea) and warehousing have greatly improved in recent years, but frozen fish just doesn't taste as good as fresh fish. Never refreeze fish that has already thawed.

Unless you are going directly home with your catch, ask the fishmonger to gut the fish (*quitar las tripas*). If you also want it scaled (*descamado*) or filleted (*en filetes*), he's usually willing to do this. If possible, avoid washing the gutted fish until immediately before cooking. Water just hastens the deterioration of very delicate flesh. Don't stash the fish in a plastic bag, which speeds spoilage. Wrap it in newspaper or put it in a loose string bag. If the day is warm or you've far to go before your finned friend sees a refrigerator, take an insulated ice chest on your market fishing expedition.

Once home, refrigerate the drawn fish immediately. Don't wrap the fish directly. Either place it in a covered refrigerator dish or on a plate and cover the plate with plastic wrap. Store in the coldest part of the refrigerator, but use it promptly while flavour and texture are still intact. Fatty fish, such as mackerel and sardines, spoil quickest. In no case should you keep a refrigerated fish longer than three days.

Shellfish are highly perishable. Most molluscs (clams, mussels, oysters, scallops) are sold in the shell and should still be alive to guarantee freshness. Shells should be tightly closed. Pitch any that are cracked or open. Don't store them in the refrigerator but place in sea water or fresh water to which one-third cup salt to four litres of water has been added. Besides staying fresh, this gives the shellfish a chance to pump out sand inside the shells. If you have to keep them more than half a day, cook them and refrigerate covered in some of the liquid.

Crustaceans (prawns, lobsters) should smell sea-fresh and show no sign of broken tails, claws or feelers, which indicates frozen seafood that has been thawed. Store refrigerated and use within a day, or cook immediately and then refrigerate until needed.

Following is a listing of fish and shellfish most commonly found in Spanish markets, some of which are unknown in other waters. The list is loosely grouped by families of fish. For a really definitive guide to Spain's seafood, consult *The Tío Pepe Guide to the Seafood of Spain & Portugal*, by Alan Davidson (Santana Books).

BLUEFISH

Albacore (*bonito del norte*). White-meat tuna.
Amberjack (*pez de limón*). A really excellent fish, suitable for grilling or baking. Fillets may be poached and sauced. It's a pretty blue fish with a yellow streak from cheek to tail.
Anchovy (*boquerón, anchoa, bocarte*). Fresh anchovies are a speciality of Spain's southern coasts. Crisply fried, these very small fish can usually be eaten bones and all. This silvery fish has a protruding upper jaw, from whence it gets its Spanish name, "big mouth". The anchovy is easy to fillet: cut off the head and grasp the top of spine between knife blade and fingers and pull it down sharply across

the belly. Cut it off at the tail, leaving the two fillets attached at tail. They can then be "cured" in vinegar or dipped in batter and fried.

Bonito. Bigger than a mackerel and smaller than a tuna, its name means "pretty". A big, meaty fish which seems to have less wastage than any other, it's wonderful grilled or baked. A very good buy.

Bluefish (chova). A meaty fish, somewhat like mackerel. Good grilled or baked.

Horse mackerel or **scad** (jurel, chicharro). A greenish-blue back with a pronounced lateral line, this fish, which is not really a mackerel, is common in pueblo markets where it is usually cheap. It's often fried whole; large ones can be baked.

Mackerel (caballa). A beautiful blue fish with dark wavy lines across its back and a silvery-blue belly. This is a very oily fish and weighs in at 177 calories per 100 grams. The high fat content helps keep it moist while cooking. Very good grilled or baked, or Spanish style floured and fried. Any leftovers get marinated en escabeche, in vinegar, onion and herbs, for a stunning cold appetiser. A very economical fish. Estornino, Spanish mackerel, is interchangeable with caballa. The wavy lines are not so pronounced and it is more spotted and mottled.

Pompano (palometa blanca, lecha, palometón, caballo). Very good fish. Can be prepared as for bonito or mackerel.

Salmon (salmón). Some wild salmon is taken in northern rivers of Asturias, but the salmon found in Spanish markets is farmed and imported from Norway. Salmon trout is trucha asalmonada, trucha del mar or reo.

Sardine (sardina). Grilled on a driftwood fire on the beach, fresh sardines are a wonderful treat, with little similarity to the tinned fish of the same name. The silvery-blue sardines, usually about 15 centimetres (six inches) long, have black spots just behind the gills. Grilling is the best treatment for sardines, but they can also be fried or casserole-baked with wine and potatoes. Of the same family as herring, the sardine can be substituted for that fish.

Tunny or **Tuna** (atún). A real treat when found fresh. Usually sold in steaks, the flesh of the tuna is darkly grained and firm textured like meat, with a flavour that's very good. The best meat comes from the belly section. Grill it, bake it, braise it or pot-roast in wine just like veal. Fresh tuna can be used in any way suitable for tinned tuna: salads, sandwiches, casseroles. The albacore tuna is known as bonito del norte.

SEA BREAM

Dentex (dentón). An excellent bream. Silvery-blue with reddish tints. Good grilled. Others of this family also found in markets are breca, pargo, urta, zapata, sargo, boga, chopa, salema and oblada. The smaller ones tend to be bony, though are quite suitable for fish soups. Add to court-bouillon, then strain and pick the flesh from the bones to return to the soup.

Gilt-head (dorada). Probably the best — and most expensive — of a variety of sea breams to be found in Spanish markets. Weighing a kilo or more, the dorada is a pinkish-gold colour and marked with gold spots on the cheeks and between the eyes. The flesh is firm and moist. It's delicious baked whole and is the fish most often cooked *a la sal*, encased in coarse sea-salt. Also good grilled. Fillets can be grilled, baked or poached. Gilt-head from fish farms comes to market in smaller sizes and at good prices.

Red bream *(besugo)*. One of Spain's favourites. It's typically charcoal-grilled, but is prepared in numerous other ways. *Besugo* is a traditional Christmas Eve speciality. It's a pinkish-grey fish with a large black spot on the shoulder.

Pomfret, Ray's bream *(palometa negra, japuta)*. Very good. Prepare as for bream or fillet and pan fry.

Redfish, Bluemouth, Norway haddock *(gallineta)*. This is not a bream — it's related to the rascasse family — but can be treated as one. A ruddy colour with bulging eyes. A firm-fleshed fish very good grilled or baked. Relatives of the redfish are the rascasses, essential to bouillabaisse, but good eating in their own right: *cabracho*, scorpion fish, is armoured in coppery red; and *rascacio* or *cabra*, grey with a pink belly. All of the rascasses can be cooked as bream and are excellent choices for fish soup.

FLAT-FISH

These are divided into two groups which help to identify them in the market — sinistral and dextral. Sinistral doesn't mean a fish of evil character, it simply means one with eyes on the left side. The other side is blind and usually a much paler colour.

Angler or **monkfish** *(rape)*. This is one of the least attractive specimens in Spanish markets, but very, very good eating. A grey colour and without scales, the angler fish has a huge head and slim tail, a little like an enormous tadpole which never got around to turning into a frog. The flesh is firm and sweet-flavoured and can readily be substituted in recipes which call for lobster. Slices from the tail are very good grilled or braised with sauce. Head and trimmings make wonderful soups.

Brill *(rombo, rémol)*. An excellent fish, similar to turbot in appearance, but without the knobby protuberances. Cook as for turbot or sole.

Flounder *(platija)*. This fish, which makes excellent eating, is usually dextral, but sometimes sinistral. It's an olive-drab colour and may have orange spots and a row of spiny protuberances.

Halibut *(fletán)*. Not found in Spanish waters, but is imported fresh.

John Dory *(pez de San Pedro, gallo)*. Though not actually a flat-fish, I have included it here because the flesh can be separated easily into four bone-free fillets, much resembling those of sole, which can be prepared as for flat-fish. Called St. Peter's fish in Spanish, French and Italian (for the so-called fingerprints the saint left on either side of the fish), it is a big-headed, spiny-finned creature with very tasty flesh. Head and trimmings make good additions to fish soup or fumet.

Lemon sole *(limanda)*. Not found in the Mediterranean, but occasionally in northern markets. Rough-scaled, brownish colour. Can be cooked as for true sole.

Plaice *(solla)*. A very good-tasting fish. Dextral, it is a brownish-grey with obvious red blotches or spots. It may have a crest on the head of small-bony protuberances.

Scaldfish *(peluda, serandell)*. Looks very much like sole, but is left-handed. And not nearly as good.

Sole *(lenguado)*. Chances are fish vendors will call *"lenguado"* any flat-fish that vaguely resembles a sole. As noted above, some of them are very good indeed, and others definitely are not. The fish the English call Dover sole and the Spanish *lenguado,* doesn't hang out exclusively around Dover but is found from the warm Mediterranean to the far north. It is not, however, found in American waters — fish called sole there is either another variety or else imported from Europe. The sole is dextral and is usually a smooth brown or greyish-tan colour. The flesh is very delicate, delicious poached, sautéed or grilled. Unless purchased frozen, the vendor will usually skin it and often will fillet the fish as well. Keep the heads, bones and trimmings for making a fumet in which to poach the fillets. Other members of the sole family, also quite good, are: the *tambour* or *tigre,* tiger sole, with distinctive dark spots; the *sortija* or French sand sole, which may be lighter in colour and flecked with spots; and the *suela,* which has a black rim on the fins.

Turbot *(rodaballo)*. One of the most expensive fish in the market because it is scarce and so highly esteemed (although farmed turbot are fairly reasonably priced). A sinistral fish, it has dark spotted back with hard protuberances. The flesh is white, delicate and very slightly gelatinous. The fillets are usually poached and sauced.

Whiff, megrim *(gallo)*. Fishmongers regularly hawk this one as sole — though it should cost about half the price of real sole. However, the *gallo* or similar *llisera* is sinistral and the sole is dextral. This fish is a yellowish-grey and the flavour is very bland and dry. It can be cooked as for sole, whole or in fillets, but is best with sharp seasoning.

MULLET

Red mullet *(salmonete)*. A superb fish. It is very rosy in colour and has a chin barb. Very small ones are mostly fried; larger ones are usually grilled whole. The flesh is firm, moist and beautifully flavoured.

Grey mullet *(lisa)*. A pretty, silvery fish with dark striations, the *lisa* is sometimes sold as *lubina,* sea bass, which its colouring somewhat resembles. However, the grey mullet is not nearly so pricey as the bass. A fairly oily fish, the grey mullet lends itself to grilling and baking, and can also be poached. It has good flavour if fished in clean waters and is easy to bone. It is quite good smoked as for trout or mackerel. Other grey mullets, all good, are *pardete, galupe, corcón, mújol* and *capitón.*

SEA BASS

Sea bass *(lubina)*. One of the finest fish to be found in Spanish markets — and priced accordingly. Firm-fleshed, fine flavour, free of bones, it is wonderful grilled, baked, poached, hot or cold. It is a lovely silvery fish with a white belly and darker markings on the back. Wild sea bass is very pricey, but the farmed specimens are fairly reasonable. The *baila* is very similar to the *lubina*, but with small, dark spots on the back and sides, and is usually less expensive. Another member of the bass family is the *cherna,* the wreckfish or stone bass. Darkly coloured and with a much thicker body than the bass, it can be prepared in the same manner.

Meagre, croaker *(corvina)*. White-fleshed, good eating. Prepare as for sea bass, or cut into slices, flour and pan fry.

Grouper *(mero)*. Sometimes called sea perch, this is a delicious fish, lean and flaky. It has a ruddy colour with darker mottling, but is more frequently encountered in the frozen food section than fresh on the market slab. An excellent fish for grilling, baking, poaching. Two lesser members of this family are the *serrano* and *cabrilla,* comber.

HAKE AND ITS RELATIVES

Hake *(merluza, pijota)*. This must certainly be the favourite fish all over Spain, and for good reason. Its white, fine-flavoured, flaky flesh makes it a good choice for many different preparations. It's delicious floured and fried, poached and sauced, grilled or baked. A beautiful silver fish, it usually weighs in around a kilo, though smaller ones, called *pescadilla,* are very common, often seen in the markets with their tails between their teeth. Hake which is hooked on a long line, *anzuelo,* is pricier — and in better condition — than that caught in a net.

Cod *(bacalao)*. Cod is not found in Spanish waters, but the far-ranging Spanish fishing fleet brings cod to northern ports where it is salted and dried. In this form it is a staple food, basis of many tasty dishes, throughout Spain. Frozen or fresh cod is available in some areas.

Coley, saithe, coalfish *(carbonero)*. Similar to cod.

Forkbeard *(brótola)*. Very lean, bland fish, excellent for making fish balls or stuffings.

Haddock *(eglefino)*. Not generally available fresh, though imported smoked haddock can be found in many supermarkets.

Whiting *(merlán)*. Very bland, light and digestible. Fish similar to whiting are the ling, *arbitán, escolano* or *maruca;* and the excellent rockling or *lota. Bacaladilla is* blue whiting.

Pollack *(abadejo)*. Lean and flavourful.

OTHER FISH

Chanquetes. Tiny, transparent fish of the goby family, somewhat similar to whitebait. Long a Málaga culinary trademark, these fish have nearly disappeared from local waters and their fishing is now prohibited in order to prevent the larvae of other species being sold as *chanquetes*. A different species is imported from China as a substitute for these tiny fish.

Dogfish *(cazón, galludo, pintarroja)*. These small sharks, euphemistically called "rock salmon", make excellent eating. They are usually sold in steaks, except for the very small ones, which are marketed whole. The flesh is white, firm and somewhat dry. *Cazón en adobo*, a favourite tapa bar speciality, are chunks of dogfish marinated in vinegar and herbs, then batter-dipped and deep fried. The *pez ángel* or *angelote*, angel fish, is another member of the shark family which is good to eat. Others which are sometimes found are *cailón, alitán, musola, pez martillo* and *mielga*.

Eel *(anguila)*. These are usually brought to market alive, then skinned and cut into chunks for sale. Tiny baby eels, sold frozen, *angulas,* are very popular in Spain, sautéed with lots of garlic. So scarce are the little elvers that imitation ones are made from surimi fish paste (look for them under the Gulas trademark). *Congrio* is the conger eel. The top half is very bony, but can be used in fish stocks. *Morena* is the moray eel. Much appreciated by some connoisseurs, it can be used in fish soups or braised with wine and herbs.

Gar, needle fish *(aguja)*. Very good eating, in spite of a curious appearance, long and skinny with a needle for a snout and a spine that turns blue-green when cooked. Cut in chunks, batter-dip and fry, or stew in a tomato-based sauce.

Gurnard *(perlón, rubio)*. Quite an ugly fish with an odd-shaped head, of a flamboyant red colour. It is quite tasty at table. Grill or bake, whole or filleted, and baste it well as flaky flesh tends to be dry. Other rosy cousins often found in local markets are the: *armado,* with a snout like a tank; *garneo* or piper; *bejel,* tub gurnard; *borracho,* grey gurnard; and *arete,* red gurnard.

Rosada. Widely marketed in Spain, this fish is never found fresh, but only frozen or thawed. It is ocean wolf-fish or cusk-eel *(genpyterus capensis)*, taken in the South Atlantic and frozen at sea. A versatile and economical fish, let's just keep its nice Spanish name: *rosada*.

Skate, ray *(raya)*. This is usually found in the market already dressed, as the wing flaps are the edible part. Somewhat strong in flavour, skate responds nicely to well-flavoured sauces or poaching in a vinegar court-bouillon.

Swordfish *(pez espada, emperador)*. This giant often comes to market whole, where it is cut into steaks. Though expensive, there is very little wastage. The firm-textured, almost meaty flesh is most often grilled, but can be baked or pot-roasted. It is only medium fatty and needs basting while cooking to prevent it drying out.

Weever *(escorpión, araña, víbora)*. "Scorpion", "spider" and "viper" — they sound like a nasty lot. Weevers have poisonous spines which are removed before they get to market. They are, despite name and appearance, good to eat, lean and flavourful. Filleted and fried, braised or added to fish soup. A related but non-poisonous fish of especially ugly demeanor is the *rata,* or star-gazer, so-called because its eyes are set at the top of its head.

Wrasse *(bodio, gayano, maragota, tordo, merlo, doncella).* Some of these are spectacularly coloured with combinations of royal blue, yellow and red. They are all good for fish soups and large specimens may be fried, whole or filleted.

RIVER AND FRESHWATER FISH

Trout *(trucha).* Trout hatcheries in many regions of Spain provide a good supply of delectable rainbow trout. Wild trout are fished in many regions, usually catch-and-release.

Tench *(tenca),* carp *(carpa),* pike *(lucio)* and barbel *(barbo)* are fished in rivers and lakes throughout Spain, but are seldom seen in markets.

CRUSTACEANS

Prawn *(gamba).* Used generically, the word "gamba" includes all of what the English call prawns and Americans call shrimp. The common prawn might also go by the name of *quisquilla* or *camarón;* the enormous, scarlet-coloured ones are *carabineros.* The big, pinkish-tan prawns so appreciated for grilling are called in Spanish *langostinos,* which are not the same thing as what the French (and often the British, too) call *langoustine* (see *cigala,* below).

Prawns range in size from tiny to jumbo. The tiny ones, a chore to peel, are often added, unshelled, to paella and soups, where they impart flavour. In the Cádiz area, tiny live shrimp, *camarones,* go into a fritter batter. The bigger the prawns, the higher the price. Some prawns at the market are frozen ones which have been defrosted for sale. These, often, are imported from fisheries in Asia and Africa. Fresh prawns appear more limpid, transparent and softer than the frozen, which have a slightly "cooked" look. Frozen ones can be excellent as long as they were properly stored at sufficiently low temperatures all along the way. It is safer to buy them frozen and thaw them yourself. Frozen *langostinos,* most of which are imported, are graded by size. Supermarkets also carry packages of frozen shelled prawns. When buying unshelled prawns, allow approximately a half-kilo for three servings. Store refrigerated and use promptly. Never refreeze those which have been frozen. Most prawns change from grey to pink or red when cooked. Best-known Spanish prawns are those from Sanlúcar de Barrameda, Vinarós and Guardamar. They are very expensive — but worth the cost.

Dublin Bay prawn *(cigala).* This is known as the "Norway lobster", the French *langoustine,* the Italian *scampi,* and what Americans call sea crayfish. Like miniature lobsters, these creatures have small pincers and a tougher carapace than prawns. They are a lovely coral colour with white tipping and do not change colour when cooked. Frozen ones, unfortunately, are not so good. Fresh, they are exquisite, but very expensive.

Lobster *(langosta, bogavante).* The *langosta* is the spiny lobster or rock lobster which has no claws, but long antennae appended from the head. The sweet, succulent meat comes from the tail. They are a reddish-brown colour before cooking. The *bogavante* is the true lobster, the French *homard*, with heavy claws containing good meat. It is a mottled greenish-black. Lobsters should be purchased live. Check to see if the legs are moving and that the tail curls under when picked up. The smell should be fresh. Buy approximately one lobster of a half-kilo or so per person. Frozen lobster tails are sold in some speciality shops.

Crab (*cangrejo, centolla, buey, nécora*). Crab is much-prized for the sweet-tasting flesh inside the armour. Unfortunately, a good-sized crab weighing about a half-kilo doesn't really provide a lot of meat. The *centolla* is the spider crab, whose shell is covered with knobby protuberances; the *nécora* is a tiny crab, often served as a finger-food tapa or cooked in soups. Buy crabs live, picking those which seem heavy for their size. They're alive if the legs are moving. They should have no disagreeable odour. Cook immediately, then store refrigerated.

Crayfish (*cangrejo del río*). Freshwater crayfish are a real delicacy. Once netted wild in rivers, now they are farmed. Crayfish look rather like dark red prawns, but they have little claws. Buy them live and wiggling; cook immediately.

MOLLUSCS

Bi-valves are the ones with two hinged shells, gastropods have a single shell, cephalopods — which include squid and octopus — have their "shell" on the inside in the form of a cartilage stiffener.

Oyster (*ostra*). As oyster beds proliferate, this wonderful mollusc has become more widely available — and a little less pricey. The Portuguese oyster, *ostión,* longer and flatter than the regular oyster, is a speciality near Cádiz. Oysters, by the way, are safe to eat any time of the year. The old adage about not consuming them during months spelled without an "r" stems from the fact that in some areas oysters spawn during warm months and are thus not so plump and tasty. Buy oysters alive with shells tightly closed. Allow six per person. Store them refrigerated, but consume while still pristine fresh.

Clam (*almeja*). These range from tiny ones to those as big as a two-euro coin. Their colour varies from grey to tan and they are lightly ridged. They're all quite delicious if great care is taken not to overcook them. Shells should be tightly shut or should close when tapped. Discard broken and open ones. A half-kilo of clams provides two good servings. Don't refrigerate clams. Put them to soak in a pot with sea water or salted water (1/3 cup salt per 4 litres of water). Change the water every 45 minutes to replenish the oxygen. During this soak, the clams pump water through, eliminating sand inside the shells. If you need to keep them more than a day, steam them and store, refrigerated, covered with their own liquid.

Cockle (*berberecho*). Rounder and bigger than clams, with deeply ridged shells. Purge them as for clams, then serve raw or steamed.

Venus shell (*concha fina*). Beautiful smooth shells, the colour of mahogany. Buy them live. They can be soaked in salt water as for clams. Serve raw with lemon, as cooked they become quite rubbery, though they can be finely minced and added to soup.

Wedge shells (*coquinas*). Tiny, wedge-shaped shells, brown-yellow-beige. Absolutely delicious. Prepare as for clams.

Razor-shell (*navaja*). Long gold-brown rectangle, looking like a pen-knife. These can be eaten raw or steamed open. They're very good.

Mussel (*mejillón*). Sometimes called the poor man's oyster, these black-shelled bivalves make very good eating. They're highly nutritious and very digestible. Because the shells are so thin, a kilo of mussels provides more food than a kilo of clams or oysters. Mussels sold commercially are harvested from non-polluted waters in Galicia and are safe to eat all year round — as long as they're alive. Shells should be tightly closed or close upon being tapped. Throw out any cracked or open ones or any that float. Chip off encrustations on the shell and wash them well. If it's necessary to keep mussels more than a day, clean them, steam them open, then refrigerate covered in their liquid.

Scallop (*vieira, concha peregrina*). Also called pilgrim shell and *coquille St. Jacques*, this shellfish has a beautiful scalloped shell, which makes a serving dish for its contents. It was the symbol for the pilgrims to Santiago de Compostela, the shrine of St. James (Santiago, St. Jacques), patron saint of Spain. The name *vieira* comes from Galicia, where the scallop is most abundant and appreciated. Scallops are available in southern markets only during the winter months. Because scallop shells don't close as tightly as clams or mussels, this shellfish doesn't stay alive as long after leaving the water. If most of the scallops in the market heap are closed, you can figure the few open ones are also fresh as long as their odour is sweet. Scallops seem to be especially gritty and, after opening, may need to be rinsed in running water. For a first-course serving, such as the richly sauced *coquille St. Jacques*, allow at least three scallops per person; for an entrée, fried or sautéed, allow from six to eight. Both the white, marshmallow-shaped muscle or eye and the red coral "foot" are edible.

Sea snail or **whelk** (*caracola, búsano*). They come from tiny to pretty good-sized. Wash well, soak in salt water, cook in a court-bouillon about 45 minutes and extract the dollop of flesh with a pin or toothpick.

Barnacle (*percebe*). People do eat the strangest things. These are much enjoyed. Because they are so difficult to harvest — from cliffs overhanging the sea — they are always expensive. Wash in running water. Cook in boiling salted water for five minutes, turn off heat and let them cool in the liquid.

Sea urchin (*erizo de mar*). These hedgehogs of the sea, whose spines are always getting lodged in children's feet, are not commonly found in the markets. Alive and fresh, cut in half, the coral (roe) is extracted to eat raw with lemon, cook in omelettes or make an attractive sauce to serve with fish.

Squid (*calamar*). Not the sort of thing your normal Englishman or North American would even consider eating — until tasted one day, perhaps by accident in a Spanish tapa bar, piping hot and crisply golden. After which, this odd creature can get to be an addiction. They're delicious in many different ways, as Mediterranean peoples and the Japanese have known all along. High in protein and other nutrients, squid are about 98 per cent edible, so a good buy for the money. Squid are available both fresh and frozen. They are one of the few shellfish that don't seem to suffer from freezing. They have a long, slender body pouch from which protrudes a head with short tentacles. Tiny squid are sometimes called *chipirones* or *chopitos,* though that name may also refer to small cuttlefish. Squid is very quick cooking, can be fried, braised or poached.

Cuttlefish *(jibia, sepia).* A related creature, the cuttlefish body is much rounder than the squid. Its ink is the "sepia" of antiquity. Not as tender as squid, cuttlefish is usually braised or stewed in a sauce.

Octopus *(pulpo).* The skin-diver's favourite bounty along Spanish coasts, the octopus is quite edible. Freshly caught, it's usually beaten against a stone to tenderise it. Home from the market, Spanish housewives usually resort to the pressure cooker. Freezing the octopus also tenderises it. Otherwise it takes several hours of slow simmering. Once cooked, it can be sauced or diced into salads. The octopus has a bulbous head and eight long tentacles lined with a double row of suction cups.

POULTRY AND GAME BIRDS

Poultry is usually sold in the same shops and market stalls that sell butcher's meat, though there are some shops which specialise in poultry *(aves)* and eggs.

Chicken *(pollo).* Spanish chickens are excellent — plump, tender and flavourful. They are battery-raised and come to market fresh and well-plucked and at a price that makes chicken a very economical choice. Their weight can vary between one-and-a-half and two-and-a-half kilos, or more or less what would be called a roaster. The butcher will weigh the bird whole — with head and feet still attached — then cut it up for you.

Big supermarkets offer chicken parts — legs, breasts, wings — weighed and packaged. Generally the price per kilo will be more for part of a chicken than for a whole one. If you have freezer space, it's economical to buy two or three chickens at a time, especially when the price goes down, and have them cut into parts for freezing. Usually you must buy at least a quarter of the bird, so, for instance, if you ask for the breast, *pechuga,* you also get the wing; if you want the leg and thigh, *muslo,* you also get part of the back. The butcher will bone the breast if you wish.

A whole chicken may contain all the giblets and viscera (though the livers are sometimes removed and sold separately). For some dishes, such as paella and chicken fried with garlic, it is customary to hack the chicken into small pieces. Though this makes for quick cooking, it also makes for nasty bone splinters.

Many stores sell ready-boned chicken breasts *(filetes de pechuga)* and boned legs, *muslos deshuesados.* Store fresh chickens loosely wrapped in the refrigerator. Don't hold more than a couple of days.

Very small spring chickens are called poulets. Capons, large and tender, are available in some markets at Christmas time. Boiling fowl, *gallina,* is usually available where chickens are sold.

Turkey *(pavo)*. Native of the New World, this flavourful fowl has been naturalised in Spain since the 16th century, when a recipe for its preparation is mentioned in one of the earliest cookbooks. Turkey is favourite holiday fare in Spain and shortly before Christmas it will be found in all the markets, fresh, frozen and "on the hoof". Many supermarkets carry fresh turkeys year-round or can obtain frozen ones to order. The preferred size seems to be between three and four kilos and it often takes some searching to find a really big turkey. Free-range turkeys, usually sold fresh, should be selected only when they're quite small or they will tend to toughness. The battery-raised turkeys are plumper and more tender. Turkey is the most economical of the fowl, providing more meat to bone than chicken or duck. Allow about 350 to 400 grams per serving.

Duck *(pato)*. Frozen duckling is available in most poultry shops. Fresh duck breast, *magret*, comes from speciality producers. Duck has a much heavier bone structure and higher fat content than chicken, so allow about 500 grams per serving. Wild ducks, taken in marshy regions, are often fish-feeding. Their flavour can be strong and they are usually prepared in pungent sauces such as *pato con aceitunas*, duck with olives.

Goose *(oca, ganso)*. Not widely appreciated in Spain, perhaps because on one memorable day in the 16th century Queen Elizabeth was eating roast goose when news arrived that the Spanish Armada had been repelled. Like duck, it has heavy bone structure and is very fatty. It must be quite young to be good.

Guinea fowl *(pintada)*. This fowl, which originates in Africa, is available in some speciality markets and appears on the menus of gourmet restaurants. Its flesh, which is very lean, somewhat resembles pheasant or partridge and can be cooked as for either of those birds.

Quail *(codorniz)*. These tiny game birds are now farm-raised and readily available, both fresh and frozen, in poultry markets all year-round. They can be spit-roasted, grilled over charcoal or braised in a casserole, but need frequent basting as they are quite lean. The beautiful speckled eggs, which look like beach pebbles, are also available in many supermarkets. Serve them poached, on a crouton of fried bread, in a steaming bowl of *sopa de ajo* (garlic soup) or hard-boiled with aperitif wines.

Partridge *(perdiz)*. Spain is known as the partridge capital of Europe and, during the winter hunting season, it's quite usual to see men returning to the village with several of these handsome birds tied to their belts. Partridge must be young, otherwise they need long, slow braising. Partridge are also farm-raised, so they reach the market while still tender. The flesh is very lean, so requires barding or basting to keep it from being dry.

Pheasant *(faisán)*. Not nearly so widely found as partridge, pheasant is taken in some areas of Spain and can often be ordered through butchers and poultry dealers who specialise in luxury products.

This bird is very lean, should be young to be tender and profits from being hung for a few days.

Squab, pigeon, dove (*pichón, palomita*). Though battery-raised, these are not available everywhere. Young and tender, they are quite tasty.

Small wild birds. Neither size nor song matters to the hunter of tasty morsels. Thus *pajaritos*, tiny birds hardly amounting to a mouthful, used to be a speciality of many tapa bars. *Zorzales* are thrushes, *alondras* are larks, *becadas* are woodcock, *tórtolas* are turtle-doves.

Rabbit (*conejo*). No, it's not bird, but it's frequently found at poultry shops, so is included here. Wild rabbit is taken, by gun and by trap, all over Spain, but most rabbit found in the market is domestic. They are usually young and small, weighing under two kilos. They are skinned, but weighed whole. You can usually buy half a rabbit, split lengthwise. Rabbit can be cooked in many of the ways suitable for chicken, such as *al ajillo* and in paella, or in the many preparations for wild rabbit and hare, *liebre*, which often call for marinades and wild mountain herbs.

MEAT

The Spanish butcher shop can be a bewildering experience for the uninitiated — chunks of red meat, pink meat, fatty meat, bony meat, often with not even an indication of its source, and seldom named by cut. Nor is butchering here comparable with British or American methods, so you won't find a piece of meat that looks like, for instance, a silverside or porterhouse. With a little knowledge, however, you can choose meat that comes from roughly the same part of the beast as the familiar cut.

Meat to be sold commercially must be slaughtered in an approved *matadero*, where it is veterinarian-inspected to ensure it derives from healthy animals. The carcasses will carry a stamp of inspection approval. After slaughtering, carcasses are split lengthwise (*en canal*), cleaned of viscera and organ meats. They are then delivered to butcher shops, where they will be cut up with more or less finesse. It is not unusual to see a whole side of beef or pork displayed, cut to order as the customer wishes. In supermarkets increasingly the meat is cut up and may even be weighed and packaged.

Freshly killed meat does not make good eating — it is hard, dry and flavourless. All meats profit by a period of refrigerated storage which softens tissues before cooking. The larger the carcass, the longer the meat can be held, two weeks being about maximum for beef. Spanish consumers don't much appreciate aged meat, so most meat is sold within 72 hours.

Meat is graded or classified according to its weight for age of animal, colour of meat and fat, water content. The wholesale price depends on this grading. Though the consumer may never know what grade meat he or she purchases, this system explains why prices of the same cut of meat can vary in different butcher shops in the same area.

Meat prices are based on a percentage mark-up over the cost of the animal "on the hoof", so will fluctuate with supply and demand. Lamb and young veal are the most expensive meats; beef is next and pork the least expensive. Goat meat is cheaper still, though baby kid commands prices similar to baby lamb.

Cut also determines price, depending on degree of tenderness and the proportion of meat to bone. Those with the most connective tissue and gristle and bone are the cheapest, though their nutritional value is the same as costlier cuts. The cheapest cuts are not always the most economical — this depends on the proportion of edible meat to bone and wastage. In general, allow about 150 grams per serving of boneless meat; 225 grams of meat with some bone (such as chops); and 450 grams for a serving of bony meat (such as spare-ribs).

Most butchers sell one or more minced meat mixtures, *carne picada* or *molida,* as well as ready-made *hamburguesas,* which may be all pork, pork and beef, or all beef. Ground meat may contain flavouring or colouring additives and more or less fat. Any butcher will be willing to grind the meat of your choice. You can request that the selected meat, after weighing, be trimmed of all fat, sinew and connective tissue before grinding or, for very lean meat, have it ground with additional fat. Most butchers are happy to make up a mixture for *albóndigas,* meatballs, by grinding meat, ham, onion, garlic and parsley, but not all are willing to grind liver, which requires cleaning the machine before the next order. Butchers usually will prepare a selected piece of meat according to your needs — boned, rolled, barded and tied for oven roasting.

The art of butchering has improved enormously and most vendors really know their meat and can give you sound advice about what to buy.

In general, the younger the animal, the more tender the meat (less exercise means less fibrous meat) and the older the animal, the more flavourful the meat. When buying meat, beware of any with discolourations, sliminess, slipperiness, or strong odours. Cut meat shouldn't exude more than a little beading of moisture — if it's sweating a puddle, it can indicate either meat which was frozen and thawed or which comes from animals fed on hormones (prohibited in Europe).

Store meat, loosely wrapped, in the refrigerator. Large pieces can be kept longer than small ones (up to four days). Minced meat, cubed meat and organ meats should be consumed within 24 hours of purchase, as they are the most perishable. Meat should not be kept in the freezer longer than eight months as it begins to deteriorate in flavour and texture. Never refreeze meat once it has thawed.

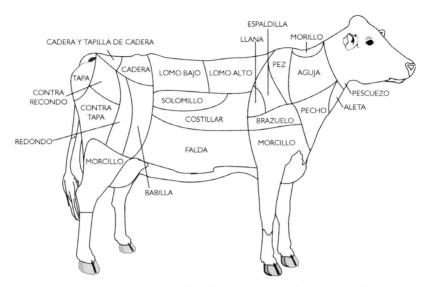

Beef, veal *(carne de vacuno, buey, ternera)*. Beef in Spain is excellent, but it didn't use to be. New breeds introduced into Spain in recent years and crossed with the indigenous strains have produced cattle adaptable to local conditions, and also better producers of quality meat. The fact remains that cattle-raising requires grazing lands and feed crops, something that much of Spain, with fiercely hot and dry summers, cannot provide. Much of the beef comes from the top third of Spain. Let's start with nomenclature, which can be confusing. Asking for a slice of *vacuno* unfortunately won't get you a steak. And asking for *ternera*, veal, won't necessarily get you a scallop of pale pink, milk-fed veal. Generally, beef cattle in Spain are slaughtered at from one to two years, whereas what is called beef in the United States, England or France comes from an animal from three to five years. This is why beef in Spain is often called *ternera*, veal, though it is more correctly labelled *añojo* or yearling. In many regions *carne de buey, or vacuno menor,* signifies meat from an animal between two and five. The younger the animal, the paler the flesh; the older, the deeper and more scarlet its colour.

Age makes a big difference in the quality of the meat. The younger animal makes tender eating, but the flavour is more insipid than full-grown beef. It will have much less fat layering, so will be less juicy than that from an older animal. Meat from an older animal will have more real-beef flavour. In the Basque Country, the best steaks served at an *asador*, grill restaurant, come from eight-year-old dairy cows.

Bull meat from animals fought in the *corridas* is called *carne de lidia* and a butcher is not allowed to sell it in the same place as other beef. It is a very deep red-black colour.

If what you want is real veal, not young beef, then look for *ternera lechal* or *ternera de Ávila,* named for the breed and the province where much of it is raised. This is meat from a milk-fed calf between three and 12 months. The flesh should be a rosy-pink, not red.

Each beef carcass is divided into cuts which are price-categorised depending on degree of tenderness and proportion of meat to bone. The most expensive cuts are *extra,* which includes the *solomillo,* fillet or tenderloin, and boneless pieces of the *lomo bajo,* sirloin or loin. The fillet is the most tender part of the whole animal and can be roasted or grilled whole or cut into smaller pieces *(Chateaubriand, tournedos, filet mignon).* In many butcher shops you must specially order the fillet in advance and are often required to buy the whole piece. In butchering veal the fillet is usually not removed and chops are cut across the loin and fillet, called *chuletas de solomillo.*

The next best cuts, usually boneless, are *lomo alto,* the widest part of the loin, and the *lomo bajo,* which narrows to the hip. The contra filet or eye of sirloin can be grilled or roasted as for the fillet. Entrecotes, "between the ribs", can be cut from the *lomo alto* or *bajo* and make excellent steaks. *Chuletas* are bone-in rib steaks from the *lomo alto.* A rack of them makes a standing rib roast.

The remaining part of the hindquarter *primera A,* first category, includes the *cadera* or hip, which corresponds roughly to the rump or US sirloin. It can be grilled or roasted, though will be less juicy and less tender than cuts from the loin. Several cuts of *primera* category are taken from the leg. The *redondo* or round is a long, thin muscle from the back of the leg. From the sides of the leg are cut the *tapa* and *contratapa* and, from the inside, the *babilla.* Any of these pieces can be rolled, barded, tied and labelled *"rosbif"* or "roast beef". They can be successfully roasted, though should be removed at rare to medium, so the meat does not become too dry. Any of these cuts, which are quite lean and close-grained, can be braised, pot-roasted, stewed or ground for hamburger.

Meat from the forequarter, above the loin section, is generally coarser and stringier, best for braising and stews. These are classed as *primera B,* cheaper than *primera A.* They include the *espaldilla,* shoulder, good for *cocido* or pot-roasting; the *pez,* a long, narrow piece adjoining the shoulder which is quite juicy and flavourful; the *aguja* or chuck which, adjoining the *lomo alto,* makes medium-quality steaks, and adjoining the neck, for pot-roasting, *culata de contra* and *rabillo de cadera.*

Cuts classed as *segunda,* second category, are *morcillo,* the shin or shank meat, especially flavourful and appreciated for stocks and soups; the *llana,* from behind the shoulder, which is sometimes cut with the grain into *filetes* or steaks, but is better for stew meat or braising; the *aleta,* a strip attached to the brisket, good for pot-roasting and mince meat; *brazuelo,* like the shin, excellent for the stock pot, and *morillo,* below the neck, also good for the *cocido.*

Costillas (ribs), *falda* (skirt or flank), *pecho* (brisket), *pezcuezo* (neck), *jarrete* (shin bone) and *rabo* (tail) are sold, with bones, as *tercera,* third category. Often the flank and brisket will be boned, presenting a thin slab of meat quite acceptable for braising or mincing, and priced as *segunda.*

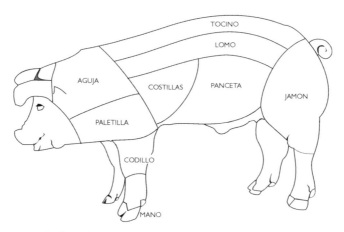

Pork *(cerdo).* Years ago, before there was municipal rubbish collection, refuse was dumped into a nearby *arroyo* or over the back patio wall. Being ecologically-minded, I gave table scraps and vegetable peelings to my neighbour for the pig she was fattening. Come butchering day, I received a few links of well-flavoured sausages in return. Though pigs today are fattened on commercial feeds and not hand-raised in village back patios, their meat is still of excellent flavour and quality. With prices approximately a third less than beef, pork is an economical as well as tasty choice.

The pig has long been the monarch of meat in Spain, ever since the Reconquest and Inquisition, when Muslim and Jewish converts to Christianity substituted pork, forbidden in their religions, for the lamb and kid of their traditional dishes. Also, unlike other animals which require good grazing land, the pig is not particular about what it eats, and can be raised on scraps. A fat hog for a poor family was like money in the bank, food for the winter, and the *matanza,* or hog slaughtering, was an occasion for an annual pig-out, when several families would get together to feast while making the sausages, hams, blood puddings, salt pork which would see them through many months.

Pork is divided into fewer cuts than beef, but the pricing is similar. *Solomillo,* pork fillet, and *lomo,* boned loin, are known as *extra;* bone-in loin chops, *chuletas,* and cuts from the leg or ham, *pierna* or *jamón,* are *primera* (here the *babilla* and *tapa* are especially good cuts for pork roasts); *segunda* is from the shoulder section, the *paletilla* or *brazuelo;* and *tercera* includes the spare-ribs, *costillas* (allow about a half-kilo per person) and hocks, *manos*. Some typical Spanish dishes call for the ear (*oreja*), tail (*rabo*) and everything but the squeal. Because pork is fattier than beef, it is virtually self-basting and almost any cut can be successfully roasted or grilled. Choose meat which is pink — the redder the pork, the stronger its flavour. Suckling pig, *cochinillo,* is found in many meat markets around Christmas. It is a year-round speciality in Madrid and Castile. The Ibérico breed of pig, which is fattened on acorns, is prized for ham-making. Fresh Ibérico pork can be bought in many shops. *Presa* and *secreto*, cuts from the top of loin and shoulder, because of the marbling of fat, are as juicy and satisfying as the best beefsteak.

Lamb *(cordero)*. Spain raises excellent lamb. Rocky uplands, unsuitable for crops or cattle pasturage, provide fine grazing for huge flocks of sheep, from which come wool for clothing, skins for rugs, milk (especially esteemed for cheese-making, from Manchego to Basque Idiazábal) and very fine meat. Aragón, Navarre, Castile, La Mancha, Extremadura and Murcia are the prime sheep-raising regions, though the meat is generally available in markets throughout the country.

Most familiar to English and American consumers is spring lamb, *cordero pascual,* butchered between three months and a year, after the animal has begun grazing. It is flavourful and succulent meat, rosy-coloured with a thin layer of white fat. The lamb is cut into sections and sold, bone-in. The leg (*pierna*) and chops (*chuletas*) are the most expensive cuts. The shoulder (*espaldilla* or *paletilla*) is considerably cheaper, but has a large proportion of bone to meat. The breast of lamb (*pecho*) and ribs (*costillas*) are least costly. These can be cut into riblets and cooked much like pork spare-ribs. With any of these bony cuts, allow about a half-kilo per person. For trimmed, boneless meat, about 150 grams per serving.

Considered a delicacy in Spain and available in most butcher shops is tiny, baby lamb, *cordero lechal.* They are butchered between one and three months, before they have been sent to pasture. The meat, almost white in colour, has very little fat and is very delicate in flavour. It's sold either whole or split lengthwise. Country-style, the meat would be hacked into evenly-sized pieces for evenness of cooking. However, to avoid bone splinters, it's best to have the meat cut into joints. The chops can be cut separately, allowing about six per person, as each one provides only a tiny morsel of meat.

Mutton, *(carnero)* is meat from sheep older than a year. The flavour is stronger, the meat coarser and its colour darker. Mutton is butchered similarly to lamb, or may be sold in smaller pieces.

Kid *(choto, chivo, cabrito)*. Kid is much appreciated, especially at Christmas. Its flesh is pale and without fat, very similar to baby lamb. Older goat meat (*carne de cabra*) is seldom found in butcher shops any more. It is coarse, and can be cooked like mutton.

Offal, organ meats and other edible parts *(despojos)*. Many, if not all, of these variety meats can be found in the butcher shop. Liver is *hígado,* and can be of veal, beef, pork or lamb. Pork liver is much appreciated in Spanish dishes, often flavoured with pungent sauces and herbs. Kidneys, *riñones,* are most delicate from veal and lamb, but pork and young beef kidneys are also consumed. *Mollejas* are sweetbreads, the thymus gland from young animals, usually veal or lamb. Brains are *sesos;* tongue is *lengua;* cheeks are *carrillos;* heart is *corazón. Criadillas* is kitchen terminology for the testicles of beef, lamb, veal or pork. *Callos* is tripe, a tapa bar speciality in many regions of Spain. Rennet, a substance taken from the stomachs of suckling animals, used for cheese-making, is also sold at the butcher shop. It's called *cuajo para queso.* A tiny piece, about 30 grams, is sufficient for a small cheese. *Redaño* is caul or mesentery, fatty membrane used to wrap skewered meat.

No longer widely used for human consumption, but available in meat markets for pet food are lung, *pulmón,* and blood, *sangre.* Fresh pork fat is *tocino;* lard is *manteca;* beef suet is *sebo.* Bones are *huesos;* marrow is *tuétano.*

Game *(caza).* Quite a few types of game are taken in Spanish hunting preserves. *Jabalí* is boar; *rebeco* is chamois; *corzo* is a roe-deer and *ciervo* is deer. Only venison, *venado,* and boar are likely to be found in speciality butcher shops. (See Poultry for more about small game, both furred and feathered.)

Cured meats *(chacinería, charcutería).* Salting, smoking, drying and curing are ancient ways of preserving meats, without the benefit of refrigeration, from one season to the next. Today the many varieties of cured meats are enjoyed as much for their flavour as for keeping qualities. In Spain there are many types of hams, sausages and *fiambres,* or pressed meats, some of them common everywhere and others which are particularly regional. Many are still made on a very small scale by local butchers or by country folk on the occasion of a *matanza,* or pig butchering. Others have been industrialised and are available by brand-name all over the country. The finest of Spanish hams and sausages, which are very costly, are best served on a platter of *entremeses,* hors-d'oeuvres, or as tapas with aperitif wines. Others are meant for slow simmering in the *olla,* where they give flavour and body to the typical *cocidos,* or boiled dinner containing meats, sausages, ham bone, chickpeas and vegetables.

Though much of today's cured meats are pork products, there are still *salazones,* salt-cured meats made from lamb, kid and beef. In grazing regions, a lamb might be split and flattened like an enormous codfish, salted and dried. This *tasajo* is eaten like ham or stewed with beans and *garbanzos* in hearty country stews. *Cecina* is dry, salt-cured beef or venison.

Ham *(jamón).* The most typical Spanish ham, called *jamón serrano,* or mountain ham, because traditionally it was cured in cold mountain regions, is salt-cured and aged from seven months to several years. It is thinly sliced and served raw as an aperitif. The colour is deep red to scarlet and the texture is chewy and more or less dry, depending on age.

Ham made from pigs of the *Ibérico* breed, which are raised exclusively in western Spain where they feed on acorns, is extraordinary, the best ham in the world. *Jamón ibérico* is considerably more expensive than *jamón serrano*. *Serrano* and *ibérico* hams are traditionally hand-sliced lengthwise, with the grain of the meat. However, most supermarkets and *charcuterías* today also sell boned *serrano* ham, which can be machine-sliced across the grain. If you are buying a whole ham, look for the metal stamp, the producer's guarantee. Some hams have *denominación de origen*, or guaranteed denomination of origin.

If, instead of the hind leg or ham, the front leg, hand or shoulder of the pig is cured, it is called *paletilla*, *paleta* or *lacón*. These pieces are cheaper than ham, are coarser in texture and contain more bone.

In addition to salt-cured, air-dried *jamón serrano*, there are several types and qualities of cooked ham, *jamón cocido*, and hand or shoulder, *paleta cocida*. Colour of the label indicates quality (based on proportion of lean to fat, gelatine, water, etc.), with red indicating *extra*; green, *primera*; yellow, *segunda* and white, *tercera*. With ham and shoulder, the yellow label usually indicates *fiambre de jamón*, pressed ham, which can contain fillers and thickeners. *Magro de cerdo cocido* is similar to ham, but made of a piece of meat of undefined cut; *fiambre de lomo* is the pork loin, salted, seasoned and cooked. Any of these pieces can additionally be smoked, *ahumado*, for flavour.

Spanish sausages (*embutidos*) come in many shapes, sizes and colours. Probabaly the best known everywhere is *chorizo*, a semi-hard sausage of pork and pork fat tinctured with paprika. Varying amounts of garlic, black pepper and chili pepper flavour the mixture, which, once packed into sausage casing, can be tied into short segments or long ones. *Chorizo* is dry-cured and can be consumed without cooking. *Chorizo de Pamplona* is similar in flavouring, but the mixture is more finely chopped and homogenous in texture. *Chorizo* can be sliced and served with bread and on sandwiches. The soft ones which have a high proportion of fat are excellent for cooking. Try a few links added to a pot of lentils during the last 30 minutes of cooking.

Morcilla is black pudding or blood sausage. Its confection varies from one region to another, but may contain rice, pine-nuts, cloves, anise and cinnamon. In Asturias, where it is indispensable for a real *fabada*, bean casserole, the *morcilla* is hung in huge chimneys to smoke, which gives it an especially rich and robust flavour. *Butifarra* is the famous Catalan sausage. The white ones confected of cooked pork, are plump links, especially appreciated for grilling and frying. *Butifarra negra* is black pudding. In the Balearics, where the pig reigns supreme, a soft sausage flavoured with paprika is called *sobrasada*. It can now be bought all over continental Spain.

Salchichas are fresh pork sausages, usually in short links. Their seasoning varies from quite bland to very spicy. They are not cured, must be refrigerated and cooked before eating. *Salchichón* is cured sausage, quite hard, the Spanish equivalent of salami (which is also widely available, of a finer grind than *salchichón*). It is usually speckled with peppercorns and may be smoked. Long skinny ones are called *longaniza*. *Lomo embuchado* is whole pork loin which has been seasoned and cured in sausage casing. *Lomo adobado* is loin which has been marinated with garlic, paprika, oregano and vinegar and may also be smoked. It is, however, fresh meat, not cured, and must be thoroughly cooked. Any of these speciality items can also be made with meat from the *Ibérico* pig, *cerdo ibérico*, especially appreciated for its flavour.

Bacon is variously called *bacón* or *beicon* and may be smoked, *ahumado*. It is machine-sliced to order and also comes sliced and packaged. *Panceta* is uncured belly bacon consisting of fat streaked with lean. Pork fat, *tocino*, can be fresh or salt-cured. In regions where they are appreciated, salt-cured ribs, ears, tails may also be available at butchers' shops, as are the powerfully scented old ham bones, called *añejo* or *rancio*. If you've wondered about red-coloured stuff on sale in tins, it is *manteca colorada*, rendered pork fat seasoned with paprika. It's used as a spread for bread.

A wide selection of prepared luncheon meats, *fiambres*, and pâtés are also found at the supermarket's *charcutería*. Some of these, such as *mortadela*, are also sold in packets. In a cafeteria, a hot dog is called, literally, a *perrito caliente*, but at the supermarket, you'll find the package labelled *salchicha de frankfurt*.

DAIRY PRODUCTS

Except in the lush pastures of Galicia and Asturias, dairy cattle have never been extensively raised in Spain. Nor are dairy products part of the gastronomic heritage. Olive oil and lard are more widely used in cooking than butter; cream has only recently been used in confecting or garnishing desserts. Many of the regional cheeses, including the best-known Manchego, are made from goats' milk or ewes' milk.

Milk *(leche)*. Pasteurised, homogenised cows' milk is sold in supermarkets everywhere. It is dated. Store refrigerated and use before date indicated. Also widely sold and especially useful because it requires no refrigeration is sterilised milk, *leche esterilizada* or UHT. It is treated at higher temperatures than pasteurised milk, which effectively destroys all bacteria, allowing the milk to be stored without refrigeration for many months. Once opened, keep it in the refrigerator. This milk is available whole *(entera)*; skimmed *(desnatada* or *descremada)*, and partially skimmed *(semidesnatada)*. Powdered milk *(leche en polvo)*, also comes whole and skimmed. Evaporated milk *(leche evaporada)* and sweetened condensed milk *(condensada con azúcar)*, are available everywhere. Pasteurised goats' milk is available in many supermarkets.

Fresh raw milk, whether from cow, goat or sheep, is always boiled before use in order to destroy bacteria.

Cream *(nata)*. Available in many supermarkets fresh, pasteurised or sterilised. This is heavy whipping cream. If a lighter cream is desired, it can be thinned with milk. There is also tinned, sterilised cream, which will not whip. Frozen food sections may have cartons of ready-whipped cream. These contain stabilisers.

Yoghurt *(yogur)*. Many brands, many flavours, also made with skimmed milk. A different kind of cultured milk, *kefir*, is sold in some health food stores.

Butter and margarine *(mantequilla, margarina)*. Butter comes unsalted, *sin sal*, and salted, *con sal*, and so do margarines. Most margarines are made with hydrogenated vegetable fats, though several brands contain animal fats, so it's wise to read the label. There are also "light" margarines, which have more liquid, less fat. Many margarines consist of trans-fats, now considered to be a health risk. Best to switch to olive oil.

Cheese *(queso)*. Manchego cheeses, crumbly and mildly pungent, are somehow reminiscent of rocky hillsides and strong sunshine. They make you think of crusty bread, tangy olives, dark red ham and strong wine. What few people realise is how many different cheeses are produced in Spain — a catalogue of Spanish cheeses published by the Ministry of Agriculture lists almost 100, of which 15 have protected denomination of origin. They include cheeses of ewes', cows' and goats' milk. If the local supermarket only stocks three or four of these many cheeses, it's because most are still products of *artesanía*, handcrafted on such a small scale that they seldom reach markets beyond the immediate region. Like other local crafts, the cheeses are worth seeking out when you travel through these regions. Some of them are available in speciality stores and can be ordered through gourmet selection clubs.

Cheese may be produced from raw or pasteurised milk. Most commercially produced cheese nowadays is made from pasteurised milk. The pasteurisation process destroys any possibly dangerous bacteria, but it also does away with natural bacteria which produce natural fermentation. In many cases ferments must be reintroduced. Artisanal cheese is made from raw milk. Fresh, unaged cheeses are made from pasteurised milk. Ageing cheese more than two months eliminates bacteria. Supermarkets here have a range of cheeses as international as their clientele, with imported varieties as well as copies of other types manufactured in Spain.

Besides moulded cheeses, some of which are consumed fresh and some of which are aged, there are several types of soft cheeses, usually marketed in cartons or small pots. *Cuajada*, which just means curd, is mild-flavoured and of custard consistency. Sweetened, it is the same as junket or rennet pudding. *Requesón* or *queso fresco* is like a smooth cottage cheese. It can be made with skimmed milk, but may have cream added to it for richness.

Following is a listing of Spanish cheeses. Those marked with DO have *denominación de origen*, or protected regional status.

Afuega el pitu: The name means "choke a rooster", supposedly because to test the cheese's readiness, a piece was fed to the barnyard cock: if he gagged, the cheese was declared *en su punto*. Small, cone-shaped cheese, very dry in texture, pungent in aroma and flavour. Not available outside the Asturian region of Montaña de Morcin, Oviedo, where it is made.

Anso: Named for the valley of Huesca where it is produced, from milk of the Pyrenean sheep. White and creamy, good with white wine.

Alicante: A soft, white goats' cheese, not aged.

Armada: A unique cheese made from cow's colostrum in the province of León. Semi-hard, sharp and lightly bitter in flavour. Keeps two or three years.

Beyusco: Made in Beyos de Ponga, Asturias, of a mixture of ewes' milk and goats' milk. Hard, amber skin if aged or soft and creamy if fresh. Pleasant aroma, sharp flavour, lightly smoked.

Burgos: Widely available and much appreciated. A soft, but compact cheese of ewes' milk, round and completely white, with no rind. It is not fermented, but after forming in moulds, the cheeses are submerged in a brine for 24 hours. Good dessert cheese with honey, nuts, fruit. A Spanish expression says: *"Miel y queso saben a beso* (honey and cheese taste like a kiss)."

Cabrales (D.O.): Spain's indigenous Roquefort, a real gourmet cheese. Made from cows' milk, sometimes mixed with small quantities of sheep's and goats' milk, produced at Cabrales (Asturias). Also called *picón, tresviso* or *cabraliego*. The skin is dark grey, but the cheese is encased in leaves. The flesh is off-white veined with blue-green. The flavour is strong, more acidic than Roquefort, with a lovely creamy consistency. These cheeses are aged in natural mountain caves where certain bacteria cause the veining. This is one of the cheeses now being produced commercially and available all over Spain.

Cádiz: Fresh, white goat cheese, full of *ojos,* tiny holes. Made in a number of localities of Cádiz province. Strong in flavour but pleasant, good with sherry wines, which are also produced in this region.

Camerano: Fresh goat cheese from the area around Logroño (Rioja). Ball-shaped and marked by the wicker basket in which it is moulded. Flavour is pleasant, lightly acidic.

Cebrero: An excellent, tangy cheese made in the mountains of Cebrero (Lugo) from cows' milk. It is mushroom-shaped, with a semi-hard skin and smooth, white flesh.

Cervera: A fresh, unaged cheese made in Cervera (Valencia) from sheep's milk with a little cows' milk. White and mild; doesn't keep.

Gallego: Also called Ulloa, this cheese is made in Galicia, of cows' milk. It has a mild flavour, is pale yellow inside with yellow skin in the shape of a slightly flattened ball. Keeps well.

Gamonedo (D.O.): Made in Cangas de Onís (Asturias) of a mixture of cows', ewes' and goats' milk. The cheese is smoked for 10 to 12 days before being placed in natural caves to mature for about two months. The rind is yellow, but the cheeses are wrapped in fern leaves. The flesh is white with blue veins, with tiny, oval "eyes". The flavour is rather more *picante* than Cabrales or Roquefort.

Gorbea: From the Gorbea mountains in Vizcaya. A ewes' milk cheese with large *ojos,* holes. Strong aroma and flavour. Dark yellow rind, creamy yellow flesh, flat bottom, rounded top.

Grazalema: From the mountains of Cádiz. A ewes' milk cheese very similar to Manchego. It is marketed fresh, semi-cured and well-aged. Pleasant flavour, hard rind, pale yellow flesh with tiny holes throughout.

Ibores. (D.O.) : Made from raw goats' milk in Cáceres (Extremadura). It has a dark rind and a buttery, wild herb flavour.

Idiazábal (D.O.): Made in the provinces of Guipúzcoa and Navarre of ewes' milk, and sold fresh, semi-cured and hard. It has a dark, hard rind and light yellow flesh with an excellent flavour. The cheese is smoked during initial curing, giving it an extra taste dimension.

L'Alt Urgell (D.O.): A cows' milk cheese from the Catalan Pyrenees. Amber skin, mild and creamy flesh.

León: Cows' milk cheeses from mountain regions. Well-aged ones are crumbly and strong; keep well. Brown rind, yellow flesh.

Mahón (D.O.): Made in the Balearic Islands, particularly Menorca, usually of cows' milk, though may include sheep's milk. It is consumed both fresh and aged, in which case it becomes a very hard cheese of strong aroma and flavour. Shape is usually a rounded square. It has amber, oily skin and pale yellow flesh. Interestingly, this cheese is produced in greater quantity than any other in Spain, but a great part of it is used in the production of the many types of *queso fundido,* processed cheese.

Málaga: White goat cheese moulded in esparto forms, traditionally preserved in earthenware vats of oil.

Majorero. (D.O.): From the Canary Islands. Usually rubbed with oil and paprika. Acidic, a little piquant, but buttery.

Manchego (D.O.): Native of La Mancha, the high central plateau of Spain, where sheep have long been raised for wool, meat and milk. Originally a cheese handmade by shepherds, usually in small quantities, it is now produced both artisanally, of raw milk, and industrially, of pasteurised milk. Real Manchego comes from the milk of the Manchega breed of sheep and is aged a minimum of 60 days, often much more. The cheese is a pale yellow colour with a hard, straw-coloured rind, or sometimes black if the cheeses aren't cleaned of mould after fermentation. The rind shows the striations of the braided esparto forms used to mould the curds, now replaced by high-tech plastics. Semi-cured cheeses have a little bite, are quite well-rounded and smooth. Well-aged Manchego cheese is dry and should splinter when cut. It has a tantalizing sharpness; needs a good red wine to set it off nicely.

Morella: Small goat cheeses from Castellón, mild in flavour.

Orduña: Sheep's milk cheese from Álava, very strong, with a bite. Hard skin of dark yellow, pale yellow inside. Keeps well for two years.

Oropesa: Sheep's milk cheese similar to Manchego, made in Puente del Arzobispo and Talavera de la Reina (Toledo). The cheese is yellow, full of tiny holes and strong in flavour.

Pasiego: Made from cows' milk, occasionally with addition of ewes', in the southwest of Santander.

The curd is white, firm with a creamy consistency and a pleasant bite. Also made *sin prensar,* without pressing, in which manifestation it is the main ingredient of the *quesada,* a Santander cheesecake.

Pedroches: A sheep's milk cheese made in the province of Córdoba. Light yellow outside and in, with a strong aroma and a salty, tangy flavour. Keeps well for months, longer if conserved in olive oil.

Puzol: An unfermented ewes' milk cheese from the Valencia area, similar to Burgos cheese. A white, fresh cheese, very mild, meant to be eaten fresh, with a conical indentation left from the mould.

Quesucos (D.O.): Also called Liébena, this is a smoked cheese made from a mixture of cows', ewes' and goats' milk in Santander. Smoky yellow rind, pale yellow inside with "eyes". Mild in flavour.

Roncal (D.O.): One of the most highly regarded cheeses of Spain, but made in limited quantities. Made with ewes' milk or mixture of ewes' and cows', in the Roncal valley of Navarre. Hard rind the colour of leather; inside hard and full of tiny holes. Aroma and flavour are sharp but mellow.

San Simón: Made in San Simón de la Cuesta (Lugo) of cows' milk. Looks like a plump, amber-coloured pear, shiny on the outside from exuded oil. The cheese is smoked over herbs and oak wood and keeps well up to two years. The creamy inside has a mild, smoky flavour with a pleasant tang.

Serena (D.O.): Sheep's milk cheese from Badajoz. One of the few cheeses made with a vegetable coagulant, the pistil of the wild cardoon flower, instead of the more usual animal rennet. Both semi-cured and cured, it is mild with a slight bite; golden skinned, pale, very soft curd.

Soria: Goats' milk cheese made in the province of Soria. White skin and curd. Aroma of fresh milk, lightly salty flavour.

Tetilla (D.O.): Named for its shape, a rounded cone, reminiscent of a breast. Made of cows' milk in the province of Pontevedra. Yellow on the outside, paler on the inside, smooth consistency, salty, tangy flavour.

Torta de Casar (D.O.): A soft, runny cheese with a slight bitter taste. To serve, the top rind is opened and the cheese scooped out with a spoon.

Tronchón: Ewes' milk cheese made in Teruel and Castellón de la Plana. Yellow skin, whitish-yellow inside. Domed shape with an indentation. Very mild flavour.

Villalón: Also called *pata de mulo,* mule's foot, for its shape, a long cylinder. A very bland, white cheese, made from sheep's milk, often recommended for delicate stomachs. It is sold *con sal* and *sin sal,* with or without salt. Made in Tierra de Campos (Valladolid). Like Burgos cheese, it is good with honey and fruits.

SPICES, HERBS, SEASONINGS AND CONDIMENTS

The spice sellers in Spanish markets with their bags of spices and herbs, sweet and pungent, dull and bright, so reminiscent of more Eastern markets and oriental cuisines, are tantalizingly exotic.

Though the use of spices and herbs in Spanish cookery is subtle — few dishes could be described as "spicy" — it is a constant. Saffron to colour rice dishes, aromatic wild thyme in the rabbit stew, nutmeg in the meatballs, a sprig of fresh mint in the consommé…the touch of flavouring is what makes a dish special. Generally, spices and herbs are purchased whole and freshly ground in the mortar as needed for use in a dish. Ground spices are sold in supermarkets. Their flavour diminishes rapidly and should be replaced within a year. Wild herbs are free for the picking all over Spain and many people enjoy growing them on patios.

Allspice *(pimienta de Jamaica)*. A spice from the New World that combines the flavours of cinnamon, nutmeg and cloves. The whole berries are somewhat larger than peppercorns.

Aniseed *(matalahuga)*. Extensively used in Spanish sweets and fried pastries, often in combination with cinnamon and lemon peel. Seeds are usually used whole or may be ground in the mortar. They are sometimes toasted or fried in olive oil which is then incorporated. Aniseed also flavours a clear brandy, *aguardiente,* both sweet and dry, which is used in cooking. Try a dash of it with fish and shellfish.

Basil *(albahaca)*. Pots of sweet basil adorn many Spanish kitchens, where it is said to freshen the air. Young girls might pluck a sprig for wearing in the hair, as young men are said to be attracted by the sweet fragrance. In spite of such popularity, the lovely herb is never used in traditional Spanish dishes. It can be bought dried and, in the spring, pots of it are to be found in flower markets.

Bay leaf *(laurel)*. Essential to many stews and potages. Bay is usually added whole to the pot, but is sometimes fried crisp, then pulverised in the mortar.

Cardamom *(cardamomo)*. Remove the black seeds from the hull. Good in breads, fruit compotes, curry mixtures. If the spice vendor doesn't have it, try the *herboristería,* herbalist or health food store.

Chili pepper, cayenne *(pimiento chile, cayena, guindilla)*. The chili is used with great moderation in Spanish cuisine. Whole hot peppers come fresh or dried, usually strung in *ristras*. They are a colourful adornment in a kitchen, though few families could consume so many fiery peppers. Generally, the larger the pepper, the milder the flavour. The tiny ones are the hottest. There are also dried sweet peppers, *ñoras* or *pimientos choriceros*. These can be rehydrated by soaking in water or ground to a powder and used like paprika. Ground chili pepper is called cayenne. Chili powder, the Mexican-type seasoning, is a blend of ground chili, cumin, coriander, oregano, paprika and garlic.

Caraway seed *(alcaravea)*. Not widely used in Spanish cooking, except in La Mancha. Try caraway with breads, potted cheese, cabbage, aubergine and cauliflower.

Celery *(apio)*. A leafy stalk of bitter celery is used in a bouquet garni to flavour soups. Stalks of celery or celery root can be used either raw or cooked. Both the seed *(semilla de apio)* and celery salt *(sal de apio)* can be purchased in jars from spice vendors.

Chervil *(perifollo)*.

Chive *(cebollina)*. Grow this member of the onion family from seed.

Cinnamon *(canela)*. This sweet spice comes ground and in sticks. It is much loved in sweets and puddings, but is also used in some meat and poultry dishes.

Clove *(clavo)*. The word in Spanish means a nail, which the whole spice resembles. It goes into everything — soups, stews and sauces — usually crushed in the mortar with whole peppercorns. Use sparingly, as the flavour is strong.

Coriander *(cilantro)*. One of the ingredients in *pinchito* spice and curry powder. The seeds can be bought whole or ground. Sprout them to grow the herb for its leaves, which resemble parsley. Sometimes called Chinese parsley or Mexican parsley, it is widely used in these cuisines as well as in nearby Morocco. Freshly cut, the herb has a sharp, acrid smell, which diminishes after addition to food. It is appreciated in salads and seafood cocktails, with beans, lentils and *garbanzos*, and as a garnish for purée soups.

Cumin *(comino)*. This is one of the exotic spices brought to Spain by the Moors that really caught on here. Cumin is often used in tomato sauces and even in gazpacho, though always in very small quantities. Like coriander, it is one of the basic spices of North African cookery. Buy the seeds whole and grind in the mortar or purchase the spice ground.

Curry powder. This is a blend of spices and can be bought in Spain, both imported and mixed here.

Dill *(eneldo)*. Not an ingredient in Spanish food, but the seeds can be purchased. Plant them to grow the fresh dill, so necessary for pickles and many Scandinavian dishes.

Fennel *(hinojo)*. Grows wild throughout the countryside, a tall, rangy plant with ferny leaves. The young sprouts are added to soup and are good with fish. The seeds which form after the yellow flower, can be used in any way dill is used, with vegetables, fish and breads. Fennel is added to home-cured olives. Cultivated fennel, grown for the root bulb, can be found in markets.

Garlic *(ajo)*. The spice of Spanish life. Garlic is sold in the markets by the head, *cabeza*, or plaited into strands, *ristras*. A single clove of garlic is a *diente* or "tooth". Select bulbs which feel firm and store in a cool, dry place. Fresh garlic is harvested in the spring and summer and keeps, refrigerated, for many months.

Ginger *(jengibre)*. Ginger root is available fresh, in bulb form and powdered. Can be grown from rhizome starters.

Juniper berry *(enebro)*. A few of these dried berries impart a nice flavour to marinades for game.

Marjoram *(mejorana)*. Similar but slightly sweeter than the much more common oregano.

Mint *(hierba buena, menta)*. In Spanish it's called "the good weed". Next to parsley, this is probably the favourite home-grown herb in Spanish kitchens and is usually available fresh in vegetable markets. It turns up in the most unexpected places — in a fish soup, in a saffron-flavoured noodle casserole, even in gazpacho.

Mustard *(mostaza)*. Available in seed *(en grano)*, both black and yellow; powdered, and prepared.

Nutmeg*(nuez moscada)*. A very versatile spice, it goes in custards and a number of meat and chicken dishes. Whole nutmeg best preserves the flavour; is quickly grated fresh. Also available ground. **Mace**, *(macis)*, found ground, is the thin outer shell of the nutmeg.

Oregano *(orégano)*. The Mediterranean herb. Used in meat stews and in most marinades with vinegar.

Paprika *(pimentón)*. As with chili pepper, a type of capsicum pepper. It is sweet rather than hot, and is dried and ground. Comes both strong, *fuerte*, and sweet, *dulce*. Beloved for its strong red colour as much as for its flavour, in Spanish cookery it is an integral ingredient — not a sprinkle or garnish — in many dishes, from sausage to paella.

Paprika that is smoke-dried, *Pimentón de la Vera*, has its own designation of origin. Smoked *pimentón* can be sweet, bittersweet or hot.

Parsley *(perejil)*. Ubiquitous, it goes into just about everything but sweets. The Spanish housewife grows it on her patio, a mild, flat-leafed variety. Sold fresh at vegetable stalls. Handfuls, finely chopped, go into salads and marinades; crushed in the mortar with spices, it flavours sauces; a few stems and leaves in a bouquet garni for soups and stocks; combined with chopped garlic and lemon in a dressing for grilled fish.

Pepper *(pimienta)*. Pepper is most fragrant when freshly ground. Spanish style, it is crushed in the mortar. Buy whole peppercorns, *en grano*, and crush in mortar or in pepper mill. White pepper is *pimienta blanca*. Tinned green peppercorns are *pimienta verde de Madagascar*.

Pinchito spice *(especia para pinchitos)*. Pinchitos are skewered meat, very similar to the brochettes of Morocco. A blend of spices, with cumin and coriander predominating, is used to marinate the meat before charcoal grilling. Buy the spice at Spanish markets or, if not available, substitute a curry powder, and add cumin and coriander.

Rosemary *(romero)*. Grows wild on the mountainsides, an attractive shrub with violet flowers. Its powerful, resinous aroma and flavour is milder when the herb is dried. Still used to fuel wood-burning stoves and bread ovens, rosemary is little used in Spanish cookery.

Saffron *(azafrán)*. The queen of spices in Spain, legacy of the Moors. The word comes from the Arabic, *zafran*, meaning yellow. Though grown in Spain this precious spice is expensive. It takes the stigmas of 75,000 *Crocus sativus* to make a single pound of the dried herb. Besides paella, it colours and flavours many typical Spanish dishes. In fact, *la comida amarilla*, the yellow meal, is so loved that powdered yellow colouring, *azafrán de color* or *colorante*, is often used instead of, or in addition to, pure saffron. Real saffron is sold in "threads" or *hebras*, the whole stigma. A wonderful souvenir of Spain.

Sage *(salvia)*. Grows wild in many parts of Spain, though not widely used in Spanish cooking. Try it with pork, poultry, rice and vegetables.

Sesame seed *(ajonjolí)*. Used in holiday pastries such as *mantecados* and *polvorones*. When not available where spices are sold, try the pastry shop.

Tarragon *(estragón)*. Used to flavour vinegar, this lively herb lends an interesting piquancy to everything from chicken to beans to eggs. Best when fresh, so worth growing.

Thyme *(tomillo)*. Several varieties of this aromatic herb grow wild on rocky hillsides. A wonderful flavour with poultry, rabbit, meat stews, stuffings, pâté. It is a standard ingredient in the home-curing of olives, lending a wild taste of the countryside and sierra.

Turmeric *(cúrcuma)*. A basic ingredient in curry powders, turmeric imparts a bright yellow colour and a pungent flavour. Also used in Moroccan spice blends. Available in powdered form. Not a substitute for saffron, as the flavour is very pronounced.

Vanilla *(vainilla)*. In 1510 Moctezuma served it in chocolate to Cortés in Mexico. Our word comes from the Spanish *vaina,* meaning "pod". Available in pods, the vanilla "bean" can be steeped in milk to flavour puddings, and also is bottled as vanilla extract.

Herbal teas *(infusiones)*. These are very popular in Spain, for their flavour and medicinal properties. Hundreds of different ones are found at the health food stores and herbalists. Some are packaged in tea-bags for easy preparation. The most usual ones are chamomile, *manzanilla,* both bitter and sweet; mint with pennyroyal, *poleo-menta;* linden flower, *tila;* lemon verbena, *hierba luisa;* and hibiscus flower, *malva.*

Condiments *(condimentos)*. Most of the usual condiments and bottled sauces are to be found on the shelves of supermarkets: ketchup, Worcestershire, steak sauce, bottled dressings, prepared mustards, Tabasco and soy. Capers are *alcaparras;* pickles are *pepinillos en vinagre;* horseradish is *rábano blanco picante.*

Vinegar *(vinagre)*. Most used is wine vinegar. Its colour varies between amber (white wine vinegar) and pink (red wine vinegar). Gourmet vinegar produced from sherry wine can be found in speciality food shops and good supermarkets and is worth looking for when visiting Jerez. Although mellow from cask ageing, it is more acidic than ordinary wine vinegar. Herb-flavoured vinegars and cider vinegar also are available. Bottled lemon juice used to dress salads, *limón para adereza,* is found with the vinegars. Pickled foods are *encurtidos;* those in a vinegar marinade are *en escabeche,* a favourite preparation for tinned tuna and sardines.

Salt *(sal)*. Not all table salts are the free-flowing type. Check the label. Sea-salt, available in health food shops, is *sal marina;* iodised salt is *con yodo.* Rock salt for ice cream-makers can be found in many supermarkets and at ice factories in ports where seafood is packed for shipping.

Sugar *(azúcar)*. Sugar-cane is grown in many areas of southern Spain and sugar refineries and rum distilleries are quite common. Confectioners' or icing sugar, *azúcar tamizado,* can be found in some supermarkets and in bakeries which make pastries. It should be sifted before using, as it tends to be lumpy. Brown sugar, *azúcar moreno,* is a light brown sugar. Demerara sugar is not so widely available. Health food shops carry other sugars: dextrose, fructose, lactose. Sugar substitutes are also sold in pharmacies. Molasses or treacle, called *miel de caña* or *melaza,* a favourite baking sweetener, can be found in supermarkets and health food shops.

Honey *(miel)*. Spain is a paradise for the honey connoisseur, with different regions specialising in single-flower honeys. Especially appreciated are those from bees kept in the sierra where they feed on wild thyme flowers *(miel de tomillo)* and from orange groves where orange blossoms flavour the honey *(miel de azahar)*. The traveller in Spain can find wonderful selections of natural honey at roadside stands — a very special souvenir. Store honey, tightly covered, at room temperature. Natural honey will crystallise — set the jar in a pan of hot water to restore its fluidity.

Jarabes are fruit-flavoured sugar syrups which can be used for making drinks or ices. There are strawberry, blackberry, lemon and pineapple, but probably the most widely known is *granadina,* grenadine, made with pomegranate juice.

Leavening ingredients *(levadura).* Baking powder is *levadura en polvo.* Baking soda is *bicarbonato sódico.* Both are the same as those found in English or American shops. Yeast *(levadura)* can be purchased from bread bakeries. Most widely available is *levadura prensada,* fresh, pressed yeast. Store it refrigerated for a week or keep it in the freezer. Many supermarkets now carry dry yeast, *levadura en polvo,* which can be stored in a tightly covered jar without refrigeration. You can also purchase bread starter dough, *masa de levadura,* from a *panadería.*

Chocolate *(chocolate).* This is chocolate as a cooking ingredient. There is a big assortment of bon-bons, filled chocolates and chocolate bars for eating, for which the chocoholic needs no guidance. Unsweetened baking chocolate is not to be found in Spanish shops; substitute semi-sweet chocolate and decrease sugar in recipe. Some chocolate bars are meant for making a thick chocolate drink, *chocolate a la taza,* and contain a thickening ingredient. This is not suitable for baking, so read labels carefully. *Cacao* is cocoa powder, and there are some unsweetened, non-instant ones, very useful for baking and desserts.

Gelatine *(gelatina).* Gelatine for making sweet and savoury moulds comes in two forms: imported, powdered gelatine and leaf gelatine, *cola de pescado.*

GRAINS, CEREAL AND FLOUR

Wheat is the grain of Spain, but rice, which is grown in several regions, runs a close second. Almost every cereal can be bought here in some form — if not available in supermarkets, check in a health food store.

Wheat *(trigo).* As in many western countries, highly refined, white wheat flour is much appreciated in Spain for breads. That, unfortunately, it sacrifices much of the nutrient value of the whole grain wheat is seldom considered. Stone ground, whole-wheat flour *(harina integral)* is available directly from mills where it is freshly ground, and from health food stores. More and more bread bakeries also provide whole grain breads. Some few produce bread from unbleached white flour. Whole grains should be stored in a cool place (preferably refrigerated) to guard against rancidity and tightly covered against insect infestation.

Available at health food shops and some supermarkets are wheat germ, *germen de trigo;* bran, *salvado;* wheat flakes, *copos de trigo,* and whole-wheat pastas. Couscous, Moroccan cracked wheat, can be found in many supermarkets, as can semolina for making porridge. Durum wheat is not widely available, except from manufacturers of pasta products. Buckwheat, *trigo sarraceno,* can be found in health food shops.

Wheat flour, *harina de trigo,* is plain, all-purpose flour. *Harina para repostería,* cake flour, is finer milled and *harina para rebozar,* for breading fish to be fried, is coarser. To substitute for self-raising flour, add two teaspoons baking powder to a quarter-kilo of plain flour.

Rice *(arroz)*. Spanish rice, which is extensively grown in the lowland coastal regions of the Levant, is plump, medium to short-grained rice with a slightly sticky consistency once cooked. A proper paella cannot be made with any other type of rice. Rice dishes are often slightly undercooked and left to sit for 15 minutes before serving in order to prevent their being gummy. Long-grained rice or pilaff-style grain, *grano largo* or *variedad americana,* is extensively grown in southwestern Spain, predominantly for the export market. Brown rice, which preserves the bran and germ, is *arroz integral,* available in health food shops and many supermarkets. It is also a short-grained variety, but takes considerably longer cooking time to become tender. Converted rice, quick cooking, is costlier than regular rice.

Maize *(maíz)*. Maize flour (corn meal), *harina de maíz molido,* is used for breads (especially in Galicia), porridge and polenta. Finely ground cornstarch, or cornflour, for thickening sauces and breading is *harina fina de maíz, almidón de maíz,* or, named for one if its brand names, Maizena. Popcorn is *maíz de flor* or *palomitas. Gofio canario* is a corn meal made from the toasted grain.

Oats *(avena)*. Packaged porridge oats are *copos de avena,* oat flakes, some of which are quick cooking. Oat bran is *salvado de avena.*

Rye *(centeno)*. Grown in cooler regions of Spain, rye breads are appreciated in some parts of the country.

Barley *(cebada)*. Sold in polished grain and in flakes.

Millet *(mijo)*.

Alfalfa *(alfalfa)*. These tiny seeds make wonderful sprouts.

Soy *(soja)*. Soy flour, beans and other products, available at health food shops, make high-protein additions to many dishes.

Breadcrumbs *(pan rallado; migas)*. Packaged fine breadcrumbs for breading foods to be fried. Migas is a dish made by frying cubes of stale bread with garlic and bacon.

COOKING OILS, FATS AND SHORTENING

When I bought a plot of land in Spain I acquired a small olive grove of 20 trees and built my house in their midst. Each autumn a family would come to pick the ripening fruit. I received an owner's percentage, which, depending on the harvest, is between 10 and 25 litres of pure olive oil. I love it for salads, tomato sauces, stews, pasta, soups, frying and for any dish I want to give an authentic Mediterranean flavour.

For those who didn't grow up on the Mediterranean, olive oil probably wasn't a staple in the pantry. Bland vegetable oils, hydrogenated vegetable fats, butter, margarine and lard have always been the preferred fats in lands where the olive doesn't grow. However, in recent years olive oil has acquired gourmet status.

For much of Spain, where lack of grazing land meant no animal fats, olive oil has flavoured cooking ever since Roman times. The Spanish word for the olive tree, *olivo*, comes from Latin, but the word for oil, *aceite*, comes from the Arabic, meaning "juice of the olive". Spain produces more olive oil than any other country in the world. About 75 percent of it comes from Andalusia, which has an estimated 165 million olive trees.

Olive oil is the only oil which, extracted by mechanical and physical processes, can be consumed without any further refining. This is known as virgin oil or *aceite de oliva virgen,* a completely natural product containing all the flavour, aroma, vitamins and other nutritional attributes of the fruit from which it derives. Virgin oil can vary enormously in colour and flavour depending on variety of olive, region, time of picking, transport and processing times. Hand-picked olives that are pressed immediately produce the fruitiest, most delicate oil.

Select oil from different varieties of olive for different uses. Arbequina olives produce a very delicate, almondy oil, good with fish and vegetables. Cornicabra oil is sweet and buttery, with ripe pear overtones. Use for sauces such as mayonnaise. Empeltre oil, good for marinades and vinaigrettes, is best used fresh and uncooked, as it is not very stable. Hojiblanca olives make a very stable oil, excellent for frying and sautéing. Its sweet taste makes it a good choice for olive-oil pastries. The Picual, representing almost half of all oil olives produced in Spain, is a high-yield variety, producing fruity oil with a distinctive bitterness. With a high degree of mono-unsaturates, it is a very stable oil, as acceptable for frying as for finishing gazpacho. Picudo makes a delicate oil, best for salads. Verdial, somewhat unstable, is sweet and fruity, luscious on vegetables. Many oils on the market are blends of two or more varieties, so that, for example, Verdial might add sweetness to the slightly bitter, but ever-so-stable Picual.

Virgin oil is classified by degree of acidity (percentage of oleic acid). *Extra virgen* is allowed an acidity of not more than 0.8 per cent; while virgin oil cannot exceed 2 per cent. Virgin oils with greater acidity, *lampante*, are generally considered too strong-tasting and are treated with refining procedures.

Olive oil produced in designated geographic areas and meeting stringent quality regulations can qualify for denomination of origin status (D.O.). These are Baena and Priego de Córdoba (Córdoba); Sierra de Cazorla, Sierra Mágina and Sierra de Segura (Jaén); Montes de Toledo (Toledo); Bajo Aragón (Teruel and Zaragoza); Les Garrigues (Lérida), and Siurana (Tarragona).

Oil labeled simply "Olive Oil," or *aceite de oliva,* is a mixture of virgin oil and refined olive oil. This may not exceed an acidity of 1 per cent. It still has the real olive flavour, but without the fruitiness so prized in virgin oil. Because it derives from refined oil, it does not have the full range of health benefits of virgin oil. It is, however, considerably more economical than virgin.

All other vegetable oils are extracted by means of chemical dissolvents, followed by a distillation process to remove the dissolvents. None is edible at this point and must undergo refining. This consists of neutralisation, bleaching, deodorisation and winterisation. Each step, especially the ones involving heat, changes the composition of the oil and destroys natural vitamins and antioxidants, which must be replaced as additives. Most other vegetable oils are cheaper than olive oil, which, because of labour-intensive cultivation and picking, will never be price-competitive.

All oils contain the same number of calories, nine per gram, and none of them contains cholesterol (which animal fats do). Most vegetable oils are poly-unsaturates which lower total blood cholesterol levels. Olive oil is a mono-unsaturate which lowers "bad" cholesterol and raises "good" cholesterol. Chemical analysis has further shown that olive oil is more stable at higher temperatures, making it the best frying medium.

After olive oil, the most extensively produced oil in Spain is sunflower, *aceite de girasol,* a New World plant which was introduced into Europe by Spaniards, just as it was Spanish explorers who carried the olive tree to the New World. The sight of vast fields of sunflowers, great yellow heads nodding, is as beautiful in its way as the hillsides dotted with silvery olive trees. Safflower oil *(aceite de cártamo),* so widely used in other countries, is little found in local markets. Buy it in health food shops. Peanut oil, *aceite de cacahuete,* and soy oil, *aceite de soja,* are available. Corn oil, *aceite de maíz,* has become very prevalent, but is by no means cheap. Rapeseed oil, *aceite de colza,* is little used as a cooking oil.

Though cooking oils today are marketed in plastic containers, for storage it is advisable to keep virgin olive oil in either glass or metal tins, tightly covered and always protected from heat and light.

WINES AND SPIRITS

Spain is one of the greatest wine-producing countries of the world and has been since Roman times. Even the Moors, whose religion forbade alcoholic beverages, were known to let their grape juice ferment during their centuries-long sojourn on Spanish soil. Wine is produced in almost every region of Spain and is consumed before meals, during meals, after eating and between meals. It is probably, along with olive oil, the most distinguishing flavour of Spanish cooking, in the casserole as well as at the table.

One of the pleasures of travelling in Spain is trying out the local dishes accompanied by the wines of the region, many of which are not commercially available further afield. My travel memories are well-flavoured with such brews: a slightly fruity Jumilla red with a roast lamb in Murcia; an amber brew that warmed one from the inside consumed in the mountains of the Sierra Nevada with slices of the local ham; a superb Rioja *reserva* served with fillet of beef — utter simplicity; a Montilla *fino* the colour of sun-baked earth with a plate of thyme-scented olives; rabbit stew at a country *venta* paired with a straightforward Valdepeñas, served in an earthenware jug; a perfumed and fruity Penedés white, light as air, with seafood on the beach near Barcelona; dry sherry with the world's freshest shellfish at Puerto de Santa María, where wineries flank one side of the port and the fishing wharves the other; fountains of sparkling *cava* in the village plaza at midnight on New Year's Eve, bottles passed from hand to hand to accompany the 12 grapes of good luck; and sweet nectar of Málaga sipped to the dulcet tones of baroque music played by a classical guitarist.

A winery, where wine is produced, is called a bodega, which means cellar (or, in Catalán, *celler*).

Following is a survey of the principal wine regions of Spain that have *denominación de origen* (D.O.), or controlled quality appellation. D.O. wines specify vintage only if the wine is from a single year's harvest (sherry, for example, is not). Some wines are aged, *de crianza,* in oak barrels; others are consumed fresh. *Reservas* are wines that profit by ageing and have been kept in wood and bottles for several years before marketing. Names of specific wines or bodegas (wineries) are not listed. You will have to taste to find your favourites.

Andalusia

Sherry (Jerez-Xérès-Sherry and Manzanilla-Sanlúcar de Barrameda). Possibly the best known of Spanish wines and exported all over the world. The English word, sherry, is a corruption of the name Jerez, a beautiful town in Andalusia where this wine is made. Sherry, which varies from dry aperitif wines to velvety-smooth dessert wines, is made by a very special process, the *solera* method of blending. New wines are added to the top barrels and, after a proper rest, are introduced into casks of slightly older wine. Fully-matured wine, after several such blendings, is drawn off from the bottom casks. Sherries have a higher alcoholic content than most table wines (between 15 and 20 per cent). The dry ones, *fino, manzanilla* and *amontillado,* vary from the colour of pale straw to topaz. Their flavour is nutty without a trace of sweetness and their aroma is golden. Enjoy them with aperitif foods, olives, nuts, shellfish, some soups. With a hint of sweetness on the edge of their rich palate are the *olorosos* and *palos cortados,* old gold in colour and velvety in texture. These are also appreciated as aperitif wines. The sweet sherries are mahogany in colour with a pleasant sweetness, good with biscuits for afternoon tea or with coffee after a meal. Most Spanish brandy is also produced by the Jerez bodegas. It is, in general, not as dry as a French brandy, but a very pleasing after-dinner drink.

Montilla-Moriles. Produced in the province of Córdoba, like sherry, by the *solera* method. Montilla *finos* are a little sharper than sherry, with a pleasantly bitter background. They are also considerably less expensive.

Condado de Huelva. Young, white table wines and fortified aperitif wines.

Málaga. This is produced primarily from the Pedro Ximénez and Muscatel grapes which give a wine with a high sugar content and a high alcoholic content (as much as 23 per cent). The colour varies from a rich, burnished gold to deepest amber, and the flavour, from sunny fruit to intense raisin. Why the wine with the highest alcohol should be considered a lady's wine, I'm not sure, but it is. Lovely with a selection of pastries or, after dinner, with fresh fruit and cheeses.

Aragón

Calatayud. Producers of bulk wines, with tendency to modernisation. Predominantly Garnacha (Grenache) variety of grape.

Campo de Borja. Full-bodied reds, primarily of Garnacha grapes.

Cariñena. The wine of Aragón, dark and solid as ancient castles, high in alcohol, the perfect accompaniment to the region's *chilindrones*, lamb and chicken stewed with peppers, is gradually being modernised.

Somontano. Vanguard of wine-making, with use of "foreign" varietals such as Chardonnay, Cabernet Sauvignon and Gewürztraminer as well as classic Spanish grapes such as Tempranillo.

Balearic Islands

Binisalem, Mallorca. Interesting local grape varieties, red Mantonegro and white Prensal Blanc.

Pla i Llevant. Mallorca. Experimentation with foreign varietals.

Canary Islands

Abona, El Hierro, La Gomera, Gran Canaria, La Palma, Lanzarote, Monte Lentiscal, Tacoronte-Acentejo, Valle de Güimar, Valle de la Orotava, Ycoden-Daute-Isora. Variety of vineyards and *terroirs*. Interesting wines of Listán Blanco, Listán Negro and ancient Malvasía, or malmsey.

Castilla-la Mancha

Almansa. Experimentation with Monastrell grape together with Tempranillo.

La Mancha. A vast area of vineyards. Wineries range from huge cooperatives to single-estate operations. While Airén white grape still predominates, the red Tempranillo is the star. A lot of investment in this region's wineries is producing new-style, delicious, fruity wines at very affordable prices.

Manchuela. Bobal the principal grape, but experimenters abound. Keep tasting.

Méntrida, Mondéjar, Ribera del Júcar. If a little rough, these wines go just fine with many Spanish dishes not ashamed of their peasant roots. In general, they lack the tannin and body that make them improve with age. Drink them young and enjoy their simplicity and low cost.

Valdepeñas. A pocket within the huge La Mancha region, making impressive Tempranillo reds. A very old wine district that has seen a lot of restructuring.

Castilla y León

El Bierzo. A lot of interest in the Mencía grape, native to this region.

Cigales. Old-style *clarete*, has been replaced with well-made wines of Tinto del País.

Ribera del Duero. Maybe the finest wines in all of Spain come from this D.O., with exceptional wineries making extraordinary wines from Tempranillo, Tinto Fino and Cabernet Sauvignon grapes. Legendary Vega Sicilia bodegas are in Ribera del Duero. High ratings mean high prices.

Rueda. Best known for fruity white wines from the Verdejo grape, while new plantations of Sauvignon Blanc are producing crisp new-style whites.

Toro. Classic big wines from Tinta de Toro grapes. Modernising trends here.

Catalonia

The wines of this region are as diverse as the people and the landscape. Though there are some very fine red table wines, the region's climate and varieties seem to favour white wines, which are among the finest in Spain. Most of the *cavas,* the Spanish word for sparkling wines made by the champagne method (fermented in the bottle) are made at Sant Sadurní de Noya. Choose *cavas* from *brut* and *seco,* dry, to *semi-seco* and *semi-dulce,* sweet and fruity.

Alella. Wines from this district, white and rosé *(rosado),* tend to be slightly sweet and spicy.

Conca de Barbera. A spin-off from *cava*-making, with Macabeo and Parellada grapes predominating.

Costers del Segre. Chardonnay, Pinot Noir and Cab shine in this region.

Empordà-Costa Brava. Cabernet Sauvignon and Merlot are moving up on traditional wines made from the Cariñena grape. Best known for rosé *(rosado)* wine.

Montsant. Borders the Priorat region. The Tempranillo grape variety is known as Ull de Llebre.

Penedés. Overlaps with *cava*-producing country. From Penedés come wonderful crisp white wines, light and dry with a delicate perfume, from Xarel.lo, Macabeo and Parellada grapes. Juicy reds make this a wine region for all seasons.

Pla de Bagés. Exquisite white wines from the Picapoll grape.

Priorat. Old vines on vineyards of low production and visionary wine-making have turned this region into the block-buster of the 21st century. High prices, sumptuous wines.

Tarragona. Known for long-aged semi-sweet wines called *rancio.*

Terra Alta. Traditional wines such as *rancio* and *mistela.*

Extremadura

Ribera del Guadiana. Varietals and styles for every taste.

Galicia

The top northwest Atlantic corner of Spain, with winemaking in the provinces of Pontevedra, Vigo, Ourense and Lugo. White wine country.

Rías Baixas. Crisp, fresh and fruity white wines from the Albariño grape are, arguably, Spain's best whites. Vineyards are situated on the banks of *rías*, estuaries, that open out to the Atlantic ocean.

Monterrei, **Ribeira Sacra**, **Ribeiro** and **Valdeorras**. Some interesting wines are being made in these smaller D.O.s of Galicia, in particular with the native Mencia, Treixadura and Godello grapes.

Madrid

Vinos de Madrid. Madrid is the capital city, but it's also the name of an autonomous region or province, the Comunidad de Madrid. That's where the vineyards are. Some excellent Tempranillo reds.

Murcia

Bullas. A tiny D.O. with a few quality wines.

Jumilla. New-style wines concentrate on fresh fruit flavours. Monastrell grape makes for juicy, silky reds. Blended with newer varieties, such as Cabernet Sauvignon and Merlot, they produce some outstanding wines. A region to watch. And taste.

Yecla. Monastrell is the important grape variety in this small D.O.

Navarra

Contiguous with La Rioja, this region shares many of the characteristics of its wines. It is famous for its rosé (*rosado*) wines made principally from the Garnacha grape. Sample stylish new red wines made with blends of Tempranillo, Cabernet Sauvignon and Merlot and Chardonnay whites.

Pais Vasco (Basque country)

The province of Álava belongs to D.O. La Rioja. In the provinces bordering the Bay of Biscay, Vizcaya and Guipúzcoa, *txacolí*, a zingy, very acidic white wine is produced from the varieties Hondarribi Zuri and Hondarribi Beltza. **Txacolí de Getaria**, **Txacolí de Vizcaya**, **Txacolí de Álava**.

La Rioja

This region situated in northern Spain brings together excellent growing conditions with a long tradition of dedication to wine-making. The result is Spain's finest table wines, both red and white. Divided into three distinct regions, Rioja Alta, Rioja Baja and Rioja Alavesa, the region produces fairly diverse wines, from the young and fruity to the smooth and oaky. Reds based on the Tempranillo grape, often with the addition of Mazuelo, Graciano and Garnacha, are especially suited for ageing, reaching a peak of smoothness and maturity after several years. Whites are dry and pleasant, predominantly based on the Viura grape. Alongside the classic Rioja style of oak-aged wines are modern wines that point up the fresh fruit flavours and are best consumed fairly young and fresh.

Valencia

The Comunidad Valenciana comprises the provinces of Alicante, Valencia and Castellón. Wine is made in both Alicante and Valencia provinces. **Alicante**, **Utiel-Requena** and **Valencia**. New winemaking tendencies have shown the attributes of old varieties such as Bobal and Monastrell. Lots happening in these regions.

Asturias

Almost no wine is produced. The local drink is *sidra,* apple cider, naturally fermented. Bottled cider can be bought everywhere in Spain, and makes a good summer drink when well-chilled.

BUYING WINE

How wine is transported and stored from bodega to supermarket to your home affects its quality and flavour when uncorked at table. Buy from reputable stores and, if you should ever get an "off" bottle, return it courteously. In the home, store wines on their sides (so the cork stays moistened) in a cool place away from direct light.

You can also order wines direct from bodegas, often saving money. Wine clubs turn up some interesting wines not to be found in supermarkets, and at good prices. Search for these on the Internet.

If you live outside Spain, a visit to your favourite wine shop will show you that many excellent Spanish wines are being exported, and at very competitive prices. Though the enormous variety won't be available, Spanish wines abroad make a fine introduction.

LIQUORS

The word *aguardiente* means any distilled liquor — as in *aguardiente de caña,* rum. However, in much of Spain, "*aguardiente*" refers specifically to an anise-flavoured brandy, both dry and sweet. In Galicia, *aguardiente de orujo,* is a potent brew that packs the punch of molten lava, distilled from the last pressings of grapes. It is a little like French *marc* or Italian *grappa,* clear, dry and with a grape taste. The word *licor* usually means liqueur, a sweetened and flavoured after-dinner drink. Spanish brandy, much of which is produced in Jerez by the makers of sherry wines, is excellent. It has a rich, mellow taste, but is never as dry as French Cognac. If today whisky has become the preferred drink in middle-class society, not so many years ago the properly accoutered bar would have a silver tray with decanters of good brandy, dry anise *aguardiente* and Málaga wine for the ladies, and tiny crystal *copitas* in which to serve them. A favourite Spanish digestive is *pacharán,* subtly flavoured with anise and sloe berries. Serve it over ice.

All of the world's best-known liquors can be found in Spain — whisky, gin, vodka, rum, tequila, aquavit, saki, bourbon, rye, Irish. Some of these are produced inside Spain as well as imported. So "whisky español" is Scotch-type whisky, made in Spain. It's considerably cheaper than imported whisky. Best-known liqueurs are also found here, many produced inside Spain.

IN THE KITCHEN

TOOLS AND UTENSILS

Mortar and Pestle. The music of the brass mortar and pestle, the *almirez,* has been a call to good food in Spain since time was. Such love is there for the sound of the *almirez* that it is used as a musical instrument in some festivities. Whole, unground spices and herbs are crushed and ground in the mortar, then dissolved in a little liquid before addition to the pot. This is especially important with saffron, for its taste and colour will be spotty if simply sprinkled into the pan. When producing a blend in the mortar, begin with the small, hard ingredients, such as cloves and peppercorns. Then add saffron and garlic, next such items as almonds, and last, bulkier items such as bread. Dissolve the paste in a little water, wine or stock before adding it to the pot.

The mortar is still the most convenient utensil for preparing a small quantity of spices and garlic. However, when a quantity of almonds or vegetables for gazpacho or other purées is to be made, the electric blender or food processor saves time and energy. Machines are used today for many of the chores once done manually in the mortar and for making mayonnaise, chopping vegetables or fruits, mixing of batters, whipping of egg whites.

Paella pan. The cook who wants to produce paella at home, whether in Spain or abroad, needs a proper paella pan big enough to serve the assembled guests (46 cm to serve 12). Curiously enough, this is not a standardised utensil. Some swear by the earthenware *cazuela,* which holds the heat and finishes the cooking after removal from the fire. Others prefer a two-handled, high-sided pan, *perol,* blackened from many uses on a fast-burning wood fire. Then there is the shallow two-handled pan, a true paella or *paellera,* in which all the ingredients cook in a single layer. Brought beautifully garnished to table, it makes a stunning presentation. Though usually made of hammered metal, these can also be purchased with non-stick surfaces. The metal ones should be well-scoured, then stored with a thin film of oil or dusting of flour to prevent rusting. A flat-bottomed Chinese wok makes an excellent stand-in for a paella pan.

Earthenware. Bowls, crocks and casseroles of earthenware are indispensable in the kitchen. Many foods which are discoloured by metal cookware can be safely cooked in earthenware which holds heat wonderfully. Clay casseroles for cooking should be either unglazed, in which case the porous surface becomes "seasoned" with flavours, or glazed only on the inside. They can be used on direct heat as well as in the oven. Bring them up to temperature very gently or use a heat-diffusing pad beneath. Treat new earthenware by soaking overnight in water before the first use. Do not store acid foods or beverages in earthenware.

In this book, the word "casserole" refers to an earthenware cooking vessel. If not available, any heat-proof casserole or ordinary cooking pan can be used.

Pots and Pans. The most commonly used pots and pans in Spanish kitchens are enamelware, a porcelain, glass-like finish bonded to metal pans, though all types of cookware are to be found in stores. In addition to the basic saucepans in graduated sizes, every household needs an *olla*, the characteristic tall Spanish pot with a narrow bottom, thick middle and narrow top, perfect for long-cooking meals like the *cocido*. Deep, long-handled frying pans of rolled steel and high sides are useful for turning out Spanish *tortillas*, omelettes, and for frying foods. They do rust, however, and must be kept seasoned with a film of oil after scouring. Other pots, pans and utensils can be added as needed: custard cups for *flan*-making; apparatus for *churro*-making; olive-pitters; a *plancha*, griddle for grilling fish; ham-slicing board, and other speciality items.

KITCHEN HOW-TO

The recipes in this book are written for people who already know how to cook, know what to do if the recipe says sauté, blanch, poach or simmer. However, there may be some few techniques peculiar to Spanish cooking which need explaining. Here are several.

Garlic. There are quite a few different ways of cooking with garlic — none of which calls for a shake of garlic salt — ranging from the subtle to the sublime. In its raw state, garlic is at its most powerful. Chopped, raw garlic might be used in marinades or sprinkled liberally over some salads. The quantity can be adjusted to personal tastes. Cooking diminishes the bite of garlic, but infuses other foods with its flavour. It might be included in a bouquet garni to flavour soups, stews and stocks, wrapped in cloth and later removed; slivers of it can be inserted in meats to be roasted; it can be sautéed or poached. A typical Spanish preparation calls for whole, peeled garlic cloves to be fried in olive oil until golden (don't let them burn) then crushed in the mortar with spices, dissolved in water or stock, then added to the food to be cooked.

Yet another method is char-roasting, usually done with a whole bulb of garlic, which gives a mild, nutty flavour. **To roast garlic:** grasp the head of garlic with kitchen tongs or spear it on a fork and hold it over the gas flame or place under grill. Turn it slowly until well charred and blackened. Separate the cloves and either add them whole to the cook pot or peel them.

Raw garlic cloves are easy to peel if given a light blow with a wooden mallet or pestle, not enough to crush them, but sufficient to break the skin, which then peels off in one piece.

Garbanzos and dry legumes, pulses. These should be soaked overnight in water to cover before cooking. Only lentils, *lentejas,* and black-eyed peas, *chicharritos,* can be cooked without previous soaking. Chickpeas *(garbanzos)* need two hours to cook, and never get as soft as other legumes. (Spanish cooks like the pressure cooker for reducing cooking time.) If your water is very hard, use bottled or filtered water to cook pulses. Do not add salt to *garbanzos* until they are about half-cooked, as salt tends to toughen them. Leftover cooked *garbanzos* and beans, drained, make wonderful salad ingredients and can also be puréed for thickening soups.

Cooking oil. In these recipes, "oil" always means olive oil, the most basic ingredient in Spanish cooking. You may substitute other vegetable oils, if preferred, though in many dishes, such as gazpacho and garlic soup, olive oil is essential for the flavour. The golden, crisp, fried foods so typical of Spain depend on the right oil heated to the right temperature. Though olive oil is absolutely the best for fried foods — including sweets — many people prefer other vegetable oils, both for blander flavour and lower cost. Do not mix two kinds of oil in cooking, for heat can cause release of possibly toxic material, though mixing raw for salad dressing and mayonnaise is fine.

Olive oil for frying can be used for several fries. Keep separate jars of oil for frying fish and oil for frying potatoes and other foods. After use, let the oil cool, then strain it through a dampened cloth. For oil in which fish was fried, dampen the cloth with diluted vinegar or lemon juice or gently heat the oil with a thick slice of lemon until all but the rind disintegrates, then strain and store. Discard oil after two or three uses.

If using a thermostatically controlled deep-fryer, heat oil to 180 to 190 degrees C or just below the "smoking" level (the lower temperature for olive oil). If you're not using an electric fryer, heat the oil until hot enough to brown a bread cube in 30 seconds. The idea with crisply fried foods is to immerse them in oil hot enough to seal the outside so no fat is absorbed, but without browning too quickly while the interior cooks. Don't crowd food. Let oil reheat between each batch. The exception to this rule in Spanish cookery is *patatas fritas*. Fried potatoes in Spain are not equivalent to British chips, American French fries or French *pommes frites*. They're not supposed to be crisp, and in fact are often added to a sauce after they have been fried. For frying potatoes Spanish-style, fry them slowly in olive oil. They will slowly get crisp and, surprisingly, absorb hardly any oil.

Sauces. Spanish cuisine has lots of foods *con salsa*, saucy, but not so many authentic sauces, in the French sense. All this means is that foods are usually cooked in their sauce. The sauce is not a separate preparation. For example, chicken *en pepitoria* or *en samfaina* is chicken cooked in its sauce, which occasionally is made separately and served separately. Any of these sauces can be made on its own and added to other foods.

A basic sauce in much of Spanish cooking is the *sofrito* or fried tomato mixture (see recipe in Chapter 12). Though it is sometimes served separately as a sauce, for instance to accompany a *tortilla* or the meats from the *cocido,* it would more likely be added to a food while it is cooking. The *sofrito* can be sieved for a perfectly smooth texture or left roughly chopped. *Tomate frito* is a tinned tomato sauce which can be used instead of *sofrito.*

Thickening ingredients. There are not very many flour-thickened sauces in Spanish cuisine. Occasionally, a gratin dish is coated with a béchamel or cream sauce, and a thick béchamel is the basis of the beloved *croqueta.* Sauces are more usually thickened either by slow cooking and reduction or by the addition of bread or ground nuts (almonds, hazelnuts and walnuts being the most common). The usual procedure is to fry a slice or more of crustless bread until crisply golden on both sides, then crush it in the mortar (or processor) with spices and garlic, then dilute in water, wine or stock before adding to the cooking pot. For some dishes, such as gazpacho, the bread is not fried, but soaked in water and then squeezed out. Use only "real" bread (such as Spanish country loaf); packaged, sliced bread contains texturising additives which prevent it from turning into a doughy mass for dissolving in a sauce. Some recipes call for finely ground *galletas,* plain biscuits, to thicken a sauce.

Stock and consommé. Typical Spanish home cooking is not based on fortified stocks, though, of course, restaurant chefs do use this flavour-adding basis for many dishes. The Spanish housewife, if she wants to enrich a sauce or stew, would use the *caldo,* broth, from the *cocido,* which is usually highly flavoured with chicken, meat bones and ham bone. This broth, which is not the same as a clear, defatted consommé, is the starting point for several soup variations. Packaged soups and stock cubes are also used for their quick flavour boosts. When a recipe calls for stock, use any home-made broth, store-bought stock or water that has been boiled with a little wine, carrot, onion and bouquet garni.

Pimiento. A favourite garnish for paella and other dishes and basis for several salads are sweet red peppers, roasted and skinned. Tinned red pimiento can be used, but the flavour is better if freshly made. To roast peppers, spear them on a fork or hold with tongs over gas flame or place under grill, turning the peppers until the skin is charred. While still warm, peel off the blackened skin. Remove stem and seeds and cut the peppers into strips.

Wine in cooking. One of the nicest things about cooking in Spain is that you can afford to experiment with wine-based dishes that in other countries would be an expensive luxury: fillets of sole in white wine sauce, beef in a red wine marinade, sherry-laced soups, wine-spiked fruit cup…all can be added to the culinary repertoire for not much money and the twist of a corkscrew.

Sweet wines, such as Málaga muscatel and cream sherries, are mainly used for puddings and sweets but, in discreet quantities, are an interesting addition to savoury foods as well. Avoid sweet wines with fish, however, as they tend to emphasise the fishiness rather than point up the delicacy. Sparkling wines are good with delicate sauces. As the bubbles get dissipated in cooking, this is a good way to use up the tag ends of a bottle of *cava.*

Aperitif wines, sherry and Montilla in particular, are good cooking wines. Another one to try is dry vermouth. With a herb-based flavour, it can be substituted for white wine in cooking.

Spanish recipes often call for *vino rancio,* aged, mellow wine. If not available use an *amontillado* sherry. The tried and true guidelines — red wine with red meat and white wine with light meat and fish — are not so definite in the kitchen as at the table. For instance, a white wine which could never stand up to a hearty beef dish might, in the cooking pot, add just a hint of piquancy. Or a strongly flavoured fish stew, which has already been coloured by onions and tomatoes, might get just the oomph it needs with a good splash of red wine. Rosé wine, less used in cooking, can add interesting colour contrasts to otherwise bland dishes.

What wines to choose? The alcohol content in wine is completely evaporated within a few minutes of cooking, leaving only the flavour. The better the wine, the better the finished dish. Don't pick the cheapest wine for cooking, but neither do you need to select the finest *reserva* vintages. Of the red wines, the moderately-priced ones are excellent for cooking. The equivalent white wines don't stand up to cooking as well. They tend to be a bit thin and can give a finished dish a sort of tinny taste instead of mellow silver. With whites, a higher-priced wine or a more full-bodied one is best. An insignificant wine, red or white, can be given a boost in the cooking stages by the addition of a tablespoon or two of brandy.

Don't cook with wine in aluminium pots and pans. The acidity can cause discolouration and off-tastes. When marinating food in wine — a most flavourful and tenderising procedure — use glass or enamel utensils. Under-salt dishes cooked with wine and taste before serving. Natural salts and minerals in wine, especially when reduced, can make for excessive saltiness.

MENUS AND MEAL SERVICE

Not so many years ago, before many village people owned cars, at midday women would carry food to their men folk working in the fields or on construction sites several kilometres from town. No simple sandwich, but an *olla* of hot food. Though the pace of life has changed incredibly everywhere in Spain, the midday dinner is still an important part of life. Even in cities, where fast-food restaurants proliferate, many working people will return to their homes for a proper meal, and, in hot weather, enjoy the leisure of a siesta before returning to work in the late afternoon.

The day starts with *desayuno,* breakfast, *café con leche,* coffee with lots of milk and sugar, and bread, toast or *churros,* fritters sprinkled with sugar. At first glance this seems too small to sustain a body until lunch. However, almost everyone eats a second breakfast between 10 and 11:30, which might be coffee with a sweet roll such as a *suizo* or *ensaimada; a tostada,* which is a whole roll split and toasted on the grill, served either with butter or with olive oil and salt for dipping; a *bocadillo,* sandwich with sausage, tuna; or a chunk of *tortilla,* omelette.

To further fortify oneself until the main meal between two and three, there is always the tapa bar, from which, around 1pm when shops and offices close, waft tantalising smells. Here, a crisply-fried anchovy or croquette, a small pile of prawns, perhaps a few slices of ham with a *copita* of sherry help to stave off hunger until the main meal.

The *comida,* or midday dinner, consists of at least three courses, a starter, main course and *postre,* dessert. The first course might be soup, *potaje,* an egg dish, a vegetable dish or salad, followed by a main course of meat or fish, probably accompanied by potatoes. Fresh fruit, in a country where it is astonishingly good, is the most customary dessert, but there are some excellent puddings to be had as well.

Late afternoon — any time from 5 to 7pm — is the hour of the *merienda,* a light lunch or snack. *Pasteles, bizcochos, tartas* and *galletas,* pastries, cakes, tarts and biscuits, with coffee or tea are typical. In the evening, the tapa bars fill up again as shops close around 8pm. Supper, *cena,* comes any time from then on, though it tends to be somewhat earlier in winter than summer. In Madrid and other major cities, supper can be as late as 11pm. Unless dining out, most people would make this a lighter meal than the midday one, for example, soup followed by an omelette and fruit for dessert.

Many holidays and local fiestas feature special foods or menus. For instance, *bacalao,* salt cod, is consumed everywhere during Semana Santa, Holy Week. Christmas customs vary. Usually the feast is served on Christmas Eve. Almond soup, grilled fish and stuffed turkey are Christmas favourites. No holiday meal is complete without the typical *turrón,* nougat candy, marzipan confections and other sweets.

You needn't plan a whole Spanish meal in order to enjoy the dishes in this book. Any of them could fit quite comfortably into your regular menu planning — gazpacho is a wonderful prelude to fish and chips, paella can become a side-dish to accompany grilled fish or chicken, and *tortilla* is every bit as good for breakfast, even if that's not traditional breakfast food in Spain.

SUBSTITUTIONS, ADAPTATIONS AND VARIATIONS

The recipes in this book are intended to be an introduction to traditional Spanish cooking, authentic and typical dishes, many of which are still to be found today. But they're also a starting point, the inspiration, for ways of combining foods, of spicing and seasoning, which are quite out of the ordinary.

In my own kitchen I often make substitutions, adaptations or variations, either for reasons of practicality or for those of inventive cookery. Though the pueblo *abuela* (grandmother) would never dream of putting chopped basil in a typical vegetable *pisto* (a delicious addition) or a dollop of cream with the stewed chard or a bit of chili pepper in the *escabeche* of marinated fish, it doesn't mean *you* can't. Take a fresh look at the typical. You'll enjoy Spanish cooking most if you adapt these dishes to your own menus.

For those of us who live here, cooking in Spain is a two-way proposition, adapting familiar dishes from our homelands to produce available here as well as learning the cuisine of our adopted country. For those who live abroad, Spanish cooking sometimes presents the problem of finding necessary ingredients. Again, don't be afraid to change and adapt recipes to suit yourself. For example, if you can't find squid to go in the paella, try substituting frozen scallops — it won't change the nature of the dish. However, don't try to substitute corn oil for olive oil and long-grain rice for short-grain rice and still make a real paella. Likewise, if you don't like so much oil in the *gambas al ajillo* (sizzled prawns), it's quite all right to decrease the quantity of oil and even sprinkle the prawns with a favourite herb. But if you use butter instead of olive oil and omit the garlic, don't call it *ajillo*. Likewise, gazpacho isn't gazpacho without extra virgin olive oil.

CONVERSIONS

"First you beat a few eggs together with some sugar. Then you add your wine, a little oil and the cinnamon. Then you work in as much flour as it will admit. Form the *roscos* and fry them in plenty of olive oil."

This is a translation of one of my authentic village recipes. How many eggs? How much wine and oil? How much flour will it admit? These recipes are like cryptograms — unless your mother and grandmother had been making that recipe for ever and ever, you wouldn't have the slightest idea how to proceed. It wasn't until I had helped my village friend make *roscos*, fried doughnuts, and weighed and measured the ingredients that her recipe meant anything.

An experienced cook works more by taste, smell and feel than by measuring. Few cooks will slavishly follow the dictates of a recipe — a little more wine here, a little less garlic there, three tomatoes instead of four, omit the aniseed. It's such creativeness that makes cooking and eating fun. Most cooks can get by with very rough conversions. For example, a recipe that calls for a chicken of 1 1/2 kilos to be cooked in a half-litre of wine would be equally successful with a 3lb chicken cooked in 1 pint of wine. We can even ignore the fact that the US pint and the British pint are not the same.

But with some cooking, especially baked goods, quantities are important and for the novice cook, or even the experienced one working with a new cuisine, a fairly precise formula is a necessary starting point.

In Spain, foods are bought and measured in grams and litres, so that is how these recipes are written. Whether you are British and still accustomed to pre-metric recipes in ounces and pints, or a North American who's never weighed a cup of flour, **I suggest you immediately buy an inexpensive one-kilo set of scales and a one-litre measuring cup.** It's much simpler than trying to convert these recipes back to familiar measures.

Americans measure volume as well as liquid in standardised measures, so flour, sugar, rice and butter are all measured in cups, not on the scales. As all the rest of the world measures dry ingredients on scales, which, by the way, give more accurate results than the cup-volume method, that is how these recipes are written.

The American quart, pint or cup is 5/6 the quantity of the British Imperial quart, pint or cup. The American tablespoon equals 14.2 millilitres; the British tablespoon equals 17.7 millilitres. Where the measure "cup" is used in this book it means a Spanish breakfast cup, 250 millilitres. or about 9 fluid ounces. A tablespoon means a Spanish tablespoon or 15 millilitres.

Following is a table of approximate equivalents of commonly used foods (based on ingredients in Spain).

	American Standard Measure	Avdp Weight	Metric Weight
Butter, Margarine	1 tbsp 7 1/2 tbsp 1/2 cup	1/3 oz 3 1/2 oz 3 2/3 oz	13 g 100 g 105 g
Cheese, grated	3/4 cup	3 1/2 oz	100 g
Cornstarch	1 tsp 1 tbsp	 1/3 oz	3 g (5 ml) 10 g (15 ml)
Flour (all purpose)	3/4 cup 1/4 cup 1/2 cup 1 cup 3 3/4 cups	3 1/2 oz 1 1/4 oz 2 1/4 oz 4 1/2 oz 1 lb 2 oz	100 g 35 g 65 g 130 g 500 g
Gelatine	1 tbsp	1/4 oz	7 g
Rice	1 cup	7 oz	200 g
Salt	1 tbsp	1/2 oz	15 g
Sugar (granulated)	1 tbsp 1/4 cup 9 tbsp 1 cup	1/2 oz 2 oz 3 1/2 oz 6 oz	15 g 55 g 100 g 175 g

For those who use Spanish cookbooks, here are some common measuring terms. The cups are filled to one centimetre of container rim; the spoons are level.

Copa (sherry glass or brandy snifter) 100 ml
Copa vino (wine glass) 150 ml or 1 1/2 decilitres
Taza (breakfast cup) or *vaso* (water glass) 250 ml or 1/4 litre
Cucharadita (teaspoon) 5 ml
Cucharada (tablespoon) 15 ml
Cucharón (soup ladle) 100 ml
Un dedo de grueso (one finger thick) 1 centimetre
Un dedo de largo (one finger long) 6 centimetres
Arroba 11.3 kilos (25 lb)

The calculator in the kitchen. At the back of this book you will find a conversion table, giving metric, British and American measures. For weights and measures beyond those on the chart, here is an easy-to-follow rule for converting. Get out the calculator — sometimes the decimals make a difference. When calculating grams, centimetres or millilitres, you can round off decimals to the nearest whole number, but with kilos, metres or litres, don't round them off. For instance, 50.4 millilitres is close enough to 50 millilitres, but 1.4 kilos is 1 kilo 400 grams. Where a second decimal appears, round it off. Thus 1.48 kilos becomes 1.5 or 1 1/2 kilos.

FLUID MEASURE

To convert from	To	Multiply by
Millilitres	Fluid ounces British	0.035
Litres	Fluid Ounces British	35.0
Millilitres	Fluid Ounces US	0.034
Litres	Fluid Ounces US	33.8
Litres	Pints British	1.75
Litres	Pints US	2.1
Ounces, US Fluid	Litres	0.03
Ounces, US Fluid	Millilitres	29.6
Ounces, US Fluid	Ounces, British Fluid	1.04
Ounces, British Fluid	Ounces, US Fluid	0.96
Ounces, British Fluid	Litres	0.028
Ounces, British Fluid	Millilitres	28.4
Pints, US Fluid	Litres	0.47
Pints, British Fluid	Litres	0.57
Pints, US Fluid	Pints, British Fluid	0.83
Pints, British Fluid	Pints, US Fluid	1.2
Quarts, US Fluid	Litres	0.95
Quarts, British Fluid	Litres	1.14

LINEAR MEASURES

To convert from	To	Multiply by
Centimetres	Inches	0.39
Inches	Centimetres	2.5

WEIGHTS

To convert from	To	Multiply by
Ounces (Avdp British & American)	Grams	28.3
Grams	Ounces	0.035
Kilograms	Ounces	35.2
Kilograms	Pounds	2.2
Pounds	Kilograms	0.45
Pounds	Grams	453.6

TEMPERATURE

To convert from	To
Fahrenheit	Celsius: subtract 32, multiply by 5, divide by 9.
Celsius	Fahrenheit: Multiply by 9, divide by 5, add 32.

WEIGHT EQUIVALENTS

Metric	**Avoirdupois – US and British**
250 grams (g) = 1/4 kilogram (kg)	4 ounces (oz) = 1/4 pound (lb)
500 grams = 1/2 kilo	8 ounces = 1/2 pound
750 grams = 3/4 kilo	16 ounces = 1 pound
1000 grams = 1 kilo	

FLUID EQUIVALENTS

US (also used for volume)	**British**
3 teaspoons = 1 tablespoon = 1/2 fluid ounce	5 fluid ounces = 1/4 pint
4 tablespoons = 1/4 cup = 2 fluid ounces	10 fluid ounces = 1/2 pint = 1 cup
4 fluid ounces = 1/2 cup	20 fluid ounces = 1 pint
8 fluid ounces = 1 cup	40 fluid ounces = 2 pints = 1 quart
16 fluid ounces = 2 cups = 1 pint	4 quarts = 1 gallon
4 cups = 2 pints = 1 quart	
4 quarts = 1 gallon	

Metric
100 millilitres (ml) = 1 decilitre (dl) =1/10 litre = 100 cubic centimetres (cc)
250 millilitres = 2 1/2 decilitres = 1/4 litres
500 millilitres = 5 decilitres = 1/2 litres
750 millilitres = 7 1/2 decilitres = 3/4 litres
1000 millilitres =10 decilitres =1 litre =1000 cc

The following chart lists some (very approximate) equivalents.

FOOD	QUANTITY	WEIGHT
Almonds, other nuts	40	50 grams
Breadcrumbs	8 tbsp (!/2 cup)	50 grams
Capers	4 tbsp	50 grams
Mussels	2 1/2 dozen	1 kilo
Olives	20 (pitted or stuffed)	50 grams
Onion	1 medium	150 grams
Peas	1/2 kilo	1 1/2 cups shelled
Potatoes	7-8 medium	1 kilo
Tomatoes	4 large	1 kilo
Tomato sauce	2 tbsp	30 ml

TAPAS, APPETISERS AND SALADS

The tapa bar or *tasca* is a very special part of Spanish life. Here wine, sometimes from the barrel, is dispensed along with a huge variety of foods, both hot and cold, which are usually consumed standing up. After enjoying several small portions of food, lots of people go on to eat a whole meal. Others make a meal out of tapa food. They are a great introduction to Spanish cooking.

Besides the usual finger foods, olives, nuts, crisps, one can order plates of sliced cheese, ham and sausages, croquettes and fried foods, as well as many more substantial dishes — tiny, breaded pork cutlets, prawns sizzled in garlic, rabbit stew, chicken in tomato sauce — and a variety of cold salads, plus fish and shellfish. A tapa portion, usually served on a tiny plate with a chunk of bread, really is just a nibble. A larger serving is a *ración*.

Many of these appetiser foods make great selections for parties. Except for the *fritos*, fried foods which must be served piping hot from the oil, most can be made in advance and reheated to serve.

Sometimes a plate of appetiser foods is served at table as a first course, *entremeses*. Such a plate might contain a mound of potato salad garnished with *pimiento* (tinned or bottled peeled red peppers) and olives, asparagus dressed with mayonnaise, pickled beets, sliced *serrano* ham and sausages, fried sardines, a slice of omelette, a few prawns and olives. A platter of *entremeses* makes an agreeable luncheon dish on its own.

Under the heading of "salads" falls a wide variety of cold dishes. Many are commonly served as a tapa, others make elegant starters and yet others can serve as garnish or accompaniment to the main dish.

FRIED TAPAS

Fritos are fried foods such as croquettes, fritters, pastry puffs and batter-dipped foods, all wonderful with aperitifs, but also nice supper dishes. Use any vegetable oil —preferably olive — for deep frying. The oil should be deep enough to completely cover the pieces of food. Use a heavy pan with high sides or an electric deep fryer which has a basket for lowering food into the oil. Heat the oil until just short of smoking. If not hot enough, the food will soak up the oil before it cooks; if too hot, the surface will brown before the food is cooked. Don't crowd the pieces of food. Remove when golden and drain on absorbent paper. Serve sizzling hot and crispy. Salad garnishes are good with fried foods or you can invent a zippy dipping sauce.

Clockwise from bottom left: Fresh Tomato Relish with Shellfish (*Pipirrana*), page 109; Olives (*Aceitunas*), page 105; Marinated Fresh Anchovies (*Boquerones al Natural*), page 106; Croquettes (*Croquetas*), page 100, and sliced Ibérico ham, page 66.

BATTER-DIPPED PRAWNS
Gambas rebozadas

Shell the prawns, wash and de-vein them. Spear each one on a toothpick and set aside. In a mixing bowl, beat the egg with the water. Add the salt and baking soda, then gradually beat in the flour, making a thick batter. Let it sit for an hour.

Heat oil in deep fryer. Dip the prawns, toothpicks and all, into the batter, and fry until golden. Serve hot with lemon.

1/2 kg fresh or frozen prawns
wooden toothpicks
1 egg
80 ml water
1/2 teaspoon salt
1/4 teaspoon bicarbonate of soda
65 g flour
vegetable or olive oil for frying

CROQUETTES
Croquetas

Heat the oil or butter in a saucepan and sauté the minced onion until transparent. Do not let it brown. Stir in the flour and let it cook briefly, then whisk in the milk. Cook, stirring constantly until this sauce thickens. Season it with nutmeg, salt and pepper. Stir in the cooked and chopped filling — any choice of cooked meat, fish or vegetables can be used, as long as it is very well drained of all liquid. Spread the mixture in a dish and refrigerate it until solid.

Place the beaten eggs in a dish, the breadcrumbs in another. With moistened hands, form the croquette mixture into balls, cylinders or cones. Dip each croquette first in breadcrumbs (or flour), then in beaten egg, then again in breadcrumbs, taking care that they are well covered. Allow to dry in a cool place for 30 minutes.

Heat oil in deep fryer and fry the croquettes, a few at a time, until golden — about three minutes.

3 tablespoons olive oil or butter
1/2 small onion, minced
4 tablespoons flour
1/4 litre milk
1/8 teaspoon grated nutmeg
1/2 teaspoon salt
400 g finely chopped cooked chicken,
    ham, tuna or fish
2 eggs, beaten with a little water
200 g fine breadcrumbs
olive oil for frying

FRITTERS
Rebozadas

These delectable titbits are also called *buñuelos*. All kinds of food can be prepared in this manner — small bits of *chorizo* sausage, dried salt cod which has been soaked overnight, pieces of cooked cauliflower, artichoke hearts or aubergine as well as shellfish such as mussels, scallops and oysters.

If using salt cod, soak it overnight in water to cover, changing the water at least once. Then remove all bones and skin and cut it in small chunks. In a bowl mix the minced onion, minced garlic, parsley and crushed saffron with the egg yolk. Beat in the water, salt and baking soda. Beat in the flour and enough water to make a thick batter which will adhere to the food. Let the batter rest for an hour.

Before frying, beat the egg white until stiff and fold it into the batter. Dip the food into the batter and fry it in deep, hot oil, a few pieces at a time. Drain and serve hot.

1/2 small onion, minced
1 clove garlic, minced
1 teaspoon chopped parsley
1/4 teaspoon crumbled saffron
1 egg, separated
160 ml water (approximately)
1/2 teaspoon salt
1/2 teaspoon bicarbonate of soda
140 g flour
300 g salt cod, *chorizo*, etc.
olive oil for frying

HAM ROLL-UPS
Flamenquines

Top slices of cooked ham with slices of cheese. Roll them up and secure with a toothpick. Dredge the rolls in flour, then beaten egg, then fine breadcrumbs and fry in deep, hot oil until golden and crisp. Serve with salad garnish.

FRIED PIES
Empanadillas

Place the flour and salt in a bowl and cut the butter or lard into it until crumbly. Add the wine, mix quickly into a ball and turn out on to a floured board. Knead very briefly, adding only enough additional flour to make a dough that doesn't stick to the hands. Form into a ball, cover with plastic wrap and refrigerate for at least two hours.

Mix all the ingredients together. Roll out the chilled dough on a floured board and cut it into rounds about 10cm in diameter. Place a spoonful of filling on each round and fold over the dough to make half-circles. Crimp the edges together with the tines of a fork.

Fry the pies, a few at a time, in deep, hot oil. Drain and serve hot or cold. The pasties may also be baked in a medium-hot oven. Makes about two dozen.

FOR THE DOUGH:
270 g flour
100 g butter or lard
1/2 teaspoon salt
100 ml white wine

FOR THE FILLING:
200 g tuna or any cooked meat, chicken, fish, prawns or ham, finely chopped
3 tablespoons tomato sauce
1 hard-boiled egg, chopped
1 tablespoon parsley, chopped
1 tablespoon brandy
salt and pepper
20 red pepper-stuffed olives, chopped
1 tablespoon chopped onion
olive oil for frying

SHRIMP FRITTERS, CÁDIZ-STYLE
Tortillitas de camarones a la gaditana

Camarones are tiny shrimp, sold live and jumping like leaf-hoppers in Cádiz markets. The unshelled shrimp are stirred into a batter and fried until crisp. If shrimp are not available, use peeled prawns chopped into small bits.

Mix the minced onion and chopped parsley with the shrimp. Add the flour and baking powder, then stir in the water and wine to make a heavy batter. Season with salt and a dash of cayenne. Cover and let the batter sit for three hours, refrigerated.

1/2 onion, minced
2 tablespoons parsley (or seaweed)
1/4 kg shrimp or tiny prawns (125 g shelled)
1/4 kg flour
1/4 teaspoon baking powder
1/2 litre water
50 ml white wine
1 teaspoon salt
dash of cayenne
olive oil for frying

Heat oil about 2cm deep in a frying pan. Drop spoonfuls of the batter into the oil and press to make a small pancake. Fry until golden-brown, turning to fry the other side. Remove and drain on paper towelling and serve hot. Makes about three dozen.

CHEESE PUFFS
Buñuelos de queso

Put the water, oil and salt in a saucepan and bring it to the boil. Remove from heat and add all the flour, beating hard with a wooden spoon. Return to a low heat and beat the dough until it forms a ball. Remove from heat and beat in the eggs, one at a time, beating hard after each addition. Then mix in the grated cheese.

Drop the dough by spoonfuls, a very few at a time, into deep, hot oil. They should rise to the surface and puff up quite a bit. Turn them over once in the oil and remove with a skimmer when golden-brown. Drain and serve hot. Makes about two dozen.

200 ml water
80 ml olive oil
1/2 teaspoon salt
130 g flour
4 eggs
150 g Manchego cheese, grated
olive oil for frying

FRIED CHEESE
Queso frito

Cut slices of semi-cured Manchego cheese into triangular slices about 1cm thick. Dredge in flour, dip in beaten egg, then in breadcrumbs and fry in a little olive oil, turning to brown both sides.

ENTREMESES

In Spain, much appreciated are *entremeses con apellido* — hors-d'oeuvres with surnames — meaning you don't serve just any old *jamón serrano* or sliced sausage, but a particular one from a particular place. See page 65 for more about Spanish ham.

HAM WITH MELON OR FIGS
Jamón con melón o higos

Salt-cured *serrano* or mountain ham is served very thinly sliced and accompanied by chunks of bread. Another delicious presentation contrasts the salty ham with fruit.

With melon, remove the seeds from well-chilled Spanish melon and cut into slices. With a sharp knife cut the flesh from the skin, leaving it in place. Then cut crosswise slices. Push pieces alternately to one side and the other. Drape thinly sliced ham over the top of the melon slices and serve.

With figs, arrange sliced ham on salad plates. Peel well-chilled ripe figs and cut them in quarters. Arrange decoratively around the ham.

QUAIL EGGS
Huevos de codorniz

Serve hard-boiled (about five minutes) quail eggs in a bowl accompanied by a mixture of salt, ground pepper and ground cumin to sprinkle on them after peeling.

TOASTED ALMONDS
Almendras tostadas

Blanch almonds in boiling water very briefly, drain and slip off skins while still warm. Dry well on paper towels. Spread the almonds on a baking tin. Drizzle with olive oil, sprinkle with salt and a little paprika and toast in a hot oven, stirring frequently, just until slightly coloured. They may also be toasted in a little olive oil in a frying pan.

OLIVES
Aceitunas

Many types of olives are to be found in Spain and always accompany hors-d'oeuvres. Some of the best don't come bottled but are home-cured. Because so many people living in Spain have their own olive crop, two recipes for their preparation are included here.

Method 1: This is similar to the process used for commercial olives and works well with whole, green manzanilla olives. Pick through the olives and remove any bruised or blemished ones. Wash them thoroughly and place in an earthenware, glass or plastic vat. Add water to cover, *measuring it as you fill the container.*

In a separate container, dissolve 100 grams of soda-lye (*sosa cáustica,* sold in *droguerías*) for every five litres of water that you have added to the olives. Be careful with the lye, as it can burn the hands. Add the solution to the olives, mix well and leave for 24 hours.

Pour off the lye solution and wash the olives in running water. Cover them with clear water. The following day, wash and change the water again. Repeat this procedure for eight days.

Prepare a strong brine — about seven tablespoons of salt for every litre of water. Place the drained and washed olives in the brine, cover the vat and leave for two weeks. They are now ready to eat. They can be additionally flavoured as in the following recipe.

Method 2: Use for green olives, such as hojiblanca or morisco varieties. Remove any bruised or blemished olives. Using a stone or mallet, crack the olives lightly, just to split open the fruit (wear old clothes, as you'll be spattered with olive juice).

Wash them and place in an earthenware, glass or plastic container. Cover completely with water. Change the water every few days for several weeks, or until the olives, when tasted, are no longer bitter. This will take about a month.

Prepare a brine (see preceding recipe) and place the olives in it along with cloves of garlic, quartered lemons, and sprigs of thyme and fennel. The lemons (oranges can also be used, giving an interesting flavour) keep the olives from darkening. Other herbs can be used, or the olives can be spiced with paprika or hot chili peppers. Cover the olives and let them sit for at least a week. They are then ready to eat. Replenish the brine as necessary and the olives should keep for several months. (If mould forms on top, skim it off. It will not hurt the olives).

MARINATED FRESH ANCHOVIES
Boquerones al natural

Remove heads of the fish. Grasp the top of the backbone with knife tip and finger, give it a sharp jerk down across the belly and the bone will come free. Cut it off, leaving the two fillets attached at the tail. Wash them and place in a single layer in a shallow dish. Add enough vinegar to cover and the salt. Marinate from 12 to 24 hours, or until the fillets are white and solid — they are "cooked" by the vinegar.

Drain the anchovies, rinse in cold water and arrange on a bed of shredded lettuce on a serving plate. Sprinkle with olive oil, minced garlic and parsley. Garnish with sliced lemon.

1/2 kg fresh anchovies *(boquerones)*
vinegar
1 teaspoon salt
shredded lettuce
50 ml olive oil
2 cloves garlic, minced
2 tablespoons chopped parsley
lemon

MARINATED FISH
Escabeche de pescado

This recipe originated as a way of preserving fish without refrigeration. However, it is such a good hors-d'oeuvre it's worth making for its own sake. Mackerel, *caballa,* is most commonly used, but *escabeche* can also be made with tunny, bonito, sardines, herring, bluefish, amberjack or trout.

Clean the fish and cut it into crosswise slices or fillets. Dust the pieces with flour and fry them in just enough olive oil to cover the bottom of the pan. Remove as they are cooked and let them cool, then place the fish in glass jars or bowl.

Add the remaining oil to the pan and in it heat the peeled cloves of garlic with the bay-leaves, thyme, oregano, cloves and peppercorns. Remove from

2 kg mackerel
flour
100 ml olive oil
1 head garlic
4 bay-leaves
1 sprig thyme or 1 teaspoon dried
1 sprig oregano or 1 teaspoon dried
2 cloves
10 peppercorns
2 teaspoons paprika
1/4 litre vinegar
1/4 litre water
1/4 litre white wine
2 teaspoons salt
1 dry chili pepper (optional)
onions, tomatoes and red bell pepper to garnish

heat and stir in the paprika. Add the vinegar, water, wine, salt and chili to the oil mixture and bring to a boil. Let the marinade cool slightly and pour it over the fish. Cover and marinate, refrigerated, for at least 24 hours.

Serve at room temperature, garnished with sliced onions, tomatoes and peppers. Serves six as a first course.

VEGETABLE DIP
Porra antequerana

This dish, from the town of Antequera (Málaga), is traditionally made in a wooden bowl and served as a starter, eaten as a thick soup with a spoon. In Córdoba it is called *salmorejo*. It also makes a wonderful party dip with crisps or bread sticks. Or use it as a cold sauce for grilled fish, poultry or meat.

Cut the bread into chunks and sprinkle it with water or the juice of a sour orange and set aside to soften.

In a blender, food processor or wooden bowl with a pestle, purée the tomatoes, peppers and garlic. Add the pieces of bread and process until you have a smooth paste. Add the olive oil to the mixture, pouring it in slowly with the processor running. Then add vinegar and salt to taste.

Serve the *porra* either garnished with chunks of tuna, julienne pieces of ham and sliced egg, or serve them separately as accompaniments, along with chopped tomatoes and onions, for each person to add to his serving.

1/2 kg bread, crusts removed
200 ml olive oil
3 large, ripe tomatoes, peeled and chopped
3 green peppers, seeded
6 cloves garlic
50 ml white wine vinegar
1 teaspoon salt
1 large tin tuna
300 g serrano ham
4 hard-boiled eggs
chopped tomatoes
chopped onions

STUFFED EGGS
Huevos rellenos

Hard-boil the eggs, plunge them in cold water and peel them. Cut them in half lengthwise, remove the yolks and set aside.

In a small bowl mix the flaked tuna or chopped prawns with the chopped olives, part of the red pepper, chopped finely, the salt and pepper and lemon juice. Fill the egg whites with this mixture.

Arrange the eggs on lettuce leaves on a serving dish. Top each egg with a dab of mayonnaise and garnish with a strip of remaining red pepper. Sieve the egg yolks and sprinkle over the eggs.

8 eggs
200 g tinned tuna or cooked and peeled prawns
8 green olives, chopped
1 small tin peeled red peppers
1 teaspoon lemon juice
salt and pepper
100 ml mayonnaise

PRAWN AND AVOCADO COCKTAIL
Aguacate con gambas

Arrange lettuce on six salad plates. Cut the avocados (widely grown commercially in southern Spain) in half lengthwise. Whack a knife into the pit and twist to remove it. Use a large spoon to scoop out the flesh of each half in one piece. Slice the avocado and divide the slices between the plates. Arrange the prawns on top.

In a small bowl whisk the mayonnaise, olive oil, lemon juice, onion, brandy and cayenne. Add salt to taste. Spoon the dressing over the prawns. Garnish the plates with tomatoes and olives. Serves six.

shredded lettuce
3 ripe avocados
3 dozen cooked and peeled prawns
150 ml mayonnaise
50 ml extra virgin olive oil
4 tablespoons ketchup
4 tablespoons lemon juice
1 tablespoon minced onion
1 teaspoon brandy
pinch of cayenne
salt to taste
sliced tomatoes and olives for garnish

TOMATOES STUFFED WITH RUSSIAN SALAD
Tomates rellenos con ensaladilla rusa

Cook the whole, unpeeled potatoes with the carrot, peeled and cut in pieces, in water to cover until just tender. Cook the peas until tender.

Peel the potatoes and cut them into small dice. Add the diced carrots, peas, chopped pepper, parsley and salt. Stir the vinegar into the mayonnaise and blend into the potato mixture.

Cut the tops off the tomatoes and scoop out the seeds and pulp. Drain the shells and fill with the potato mixture. Place on lettuce leaves to serve. Serves four.

2 medium potatoes
1 large carrot
60 g shelled peas
1 red pepper, chopped
1 teaspoon chopped parsley
1/2 teaspoon salt
75 ml mayonnaise
1 teaspoon vinegar
4 large tomatoes
lettuce

FRESH TOMATO RELISH
Pipirrana

This salad-relish, which in North Africa is seasoned with chopped coriander instead of parsley, is a wonderful accompaniment to fried fish. Finely diced cucumber may also be added. If cooked prawns or other shellfish are added, the salad is called *salpicón* and is a tapa bar favourite.

Chop the tomatoes, onions and green peppers and mix together in a bowl. Finely mince the garlic and add to the salad with the salt. Separate the yolks and set aside. Chop the whites into the salad. Mash the yolks in a bowl and beat in the oil, drop by drop, then beat in the vinegar. Add the dressing to the salad and toss lightly. Serve garnished with chunks of tuna or ham, or both.

6 medium tomatoes
1/2 onion
2 green bell peppers
1 clove garlic
2 hard-boiled eggs
1 teaspoon salt
6 tablespoons olive oil
50 ml vinegar
2 tablespoons chopped flat-leaf parsley
tinned tuna
diced serrano ham

ORANGE AND COD SALAD
Remójon

In some places this is called *salmorejo*. In Málaga, an unusual version of the salad is made with oranges, tomatoes, cod, and potatoes. If you don't want to use salt cod, substitute tinned tuna or julienne strips of *serrano* ham. The salad is a festive starter for holiday meals.

Toast the salt cod by holding it, skin side up, over a gas flame or place under a grill (broiler) for a few minutes until it has an evenly browned surface and is softened. Leave it in a bowl of water while preparing the other ingredients.

Chop the peeled tomato and combine with the chopped onion, olives and minced garlic. Peel the oranges, separate into sections and chop them into the bowl. Drain the codfish and remove all skin and bones. Shred it and add to the salad. Drizzle with oil and vinegar and toss the salad. Add the chili pepper, if desired. Serves four.

1/4 kg dried salt cod
   (or 1 tin water-packed tuna)
1 medium tomato, peeled,
   seeded and chopped
6 scallions or 1 onion, chopped
50 g pitted olives, green or black
1 clove garlic
2 sour oranges
2 tablespoons extra virgin olive oil
1 tablespoon vinegar
pinch crushed red chili flakes (optional)

POTATO SALAD
Ensaladilla de patatas

Cook potatoes in their skins in water until tender. Drain well, peel and dice into a bowl (Chilling them first facilitates dicing.)

Clean the onions and chop into the potatoes. Chop the tomato finely and add to potatoes. Sprinkle with parsley. Squeeze juice of lemon (to taste) over the potatoes and drizzle with olive oil. Toss lightly. Flavour improves if the salad marinates, covered and refrigerated, for two hours.

Shape the potato salad into a mound on a serving plate and coat it with a thin layer of mayonnaise. Garnish with egg slices, strips of red pepper and green olives. Serves six.

1 kg potatoes
4 scallions or 1 small onion
1 large tomato, peeled and chopped
1 lemon
50 ml extra virgin olive oil
2 tablespoons chopped parsley
100 ml mayonnaise, thinned
2 hard-boiled eggs, sliced
1 small tin peppers
12 pitted olives

CATALAN SALAD
Amanida

Where the Catalan sausage, *butifarra blanca*, is not available, bratwurst or frankfurters might be substituted. Use a Catalan arbequina olive oil for this salad.

Wash and drain the escarole and place the cut-up leaves in a salad bowl. Add the diced celery, chopped scallions and diced ham. Mince the anchovies and add to the salad.

In a bowl mix the mayonnaise with a clove of crushed garlic, the vinegar and salt. Toss the dressing with the escarole and garnish with sliced egg and pieces of *butifarra* sausage.

1 escarole
3 stalks celery, diced
6 scallions, chopped
100 g cooked ham, diced
1 small tin anchovies, rinsed and drained
100 ml mayonnaise
1 clove garlic
1 tablespoon vinegar
salt
2 hard-boiled eggs
150 g *butifarra* (Catalan white sausage)

TARRAGONA SALAD
Xato

No tarragon in this recipe, a salad from the Catalan city of Tarragona.

Wash and drain the lettuce, tear it into pieces and place in a salad bowl with the chopped celery and artichokes.

Roast tomato and garlic under broiler/grill until tomato is softened and garlic somewhat charred. Peel them. Soak the dried *ñora* pepper and chili in a little water. (If sweet dry pepper, *ñora*, is not available, use a spoonful of paprika made into a paste with a little water.)

In a mortar (or processor or blender) crush the peeled tomato and garlic with the drained peppers, the parsley, the blanched and skinned almonds and the hazelnuts. When this is a smooth sauce, beat in the olive oil, then the vinegar and salt. Thin with a little water.

Pour the dressing over the salad and let it macerate for an hour before serving. Serves six.

2 lettuces
2 stalks celery
4 artichoke hearts cooked and quartered
   (optional)
1 ripe tomato
4 cloves garlic
1 dried *ñora pepper* or 1/2 teaspoon paprika
1 piece chili pepper (optional)
1 bunch flat-leaf parsley
50 g almonds, blanched
10 hazelnuts
50 ml olive oil
2 tablespoons vinegar
salt

ROASTED PEPPER SALAD
Ensalada de pimientos asados

A classic recipe. If an equal quantity of onions is roasted with the peppers, then cut into strips, the dish becomes *mojete*, a Murcia salad. If aubergine and peppers are roasted, the dish is *escalibada*, a Catalan speciality. The roasted pepper salad makes a good side dish, but it can also be heaped on toasted bread and served as a tapa.

Wash and dry the peppers. Roast them under the broiler/grill, turning frequently until charred on all sides. Remove and wrap them in a towel, just until cool enough to handle. (Peppers can also be speared on a fork and roasted over a gas flame, or laid on a charcoal grill, which gives a wonderful flavour.)

Peel the skin from the peppers, cut out stems and remove seeds. Tear the peppers into strips and put on a serving plate. Mix the minced garlic, olive oil, vinegar, chopped parsley, salt and pepper. Drizzle the peppers with this and toss lightly. Serve at room temperature as an appetiser or as an accompaniment to grilled meat or poultry. Serves six.

1 kg bell peppers, red and/or green
2 cloves garlic, minced
50 ml extra virgin olive oil
3 tablespoons vinegar or lemon juice
2 tablespoons chopped parsley
salt and pepper

BEAN SALAD
Ensalada de judias verdes

Make this salad also with leftover cooked broad beans, chickpeas, black-eyed peas or white beans.

Remove strings from beans if necessary, but leave them whole. Cook the beans and the unpeeled potato in boiling salted water until just tender. Rinse in cold water and drain. Peel the potato and slice it.

Arrange the beans on a serving platter with layers of sliced potatoes between. Sprinkle the minced onion over the top. Whisk together the olive oil, vinegar, minced garlic, salt and pepper and cumin and drizzle this over the salad. Sprinkle with finely chopped fennel leaves and garnish with quartered eggs. Serves six.

1/2 kg green beans
1 medium potato
1 tablespoon minced onion
6 tablespoons extra virgin olive oil
salt and pepper
1/2 teaspoon cumin
2 tablespoons vinegar
1 clove garlic
1 sprig fresh fennel leaves (or parsley)
2 hard-boiled eggs

RICE SALAD
Ensaladilla de arroz

Fluff the rice with a fork. Add to it the minced onion, pepper, garlic, parsley and olives. Season to taste with salt and pepper. Drizzle with olive oil and vinegar and toss with a fork to blend.

Arrange mounds of the salad on lettuce leaves. Garnish with strips of red pepper and arrange quartered tomatoes around the edge. This salad also makes a good filling for stuffed tomatoes. Cooked prawns can be added to the mixture. Serves four to six.

400-500 ml cooked, chilled rice
1 small onion, minced
1 green pepper, minced
1 clove garlic,
2 tablespoons chopped parsley
20 black or green olives, pitted and chopped
salt and pepper
6 tablespoons extra virgin olive oil
3 tablespoons vinegar
minced red pepper
lettuce
tomatoes
anchovy fillets (optional)

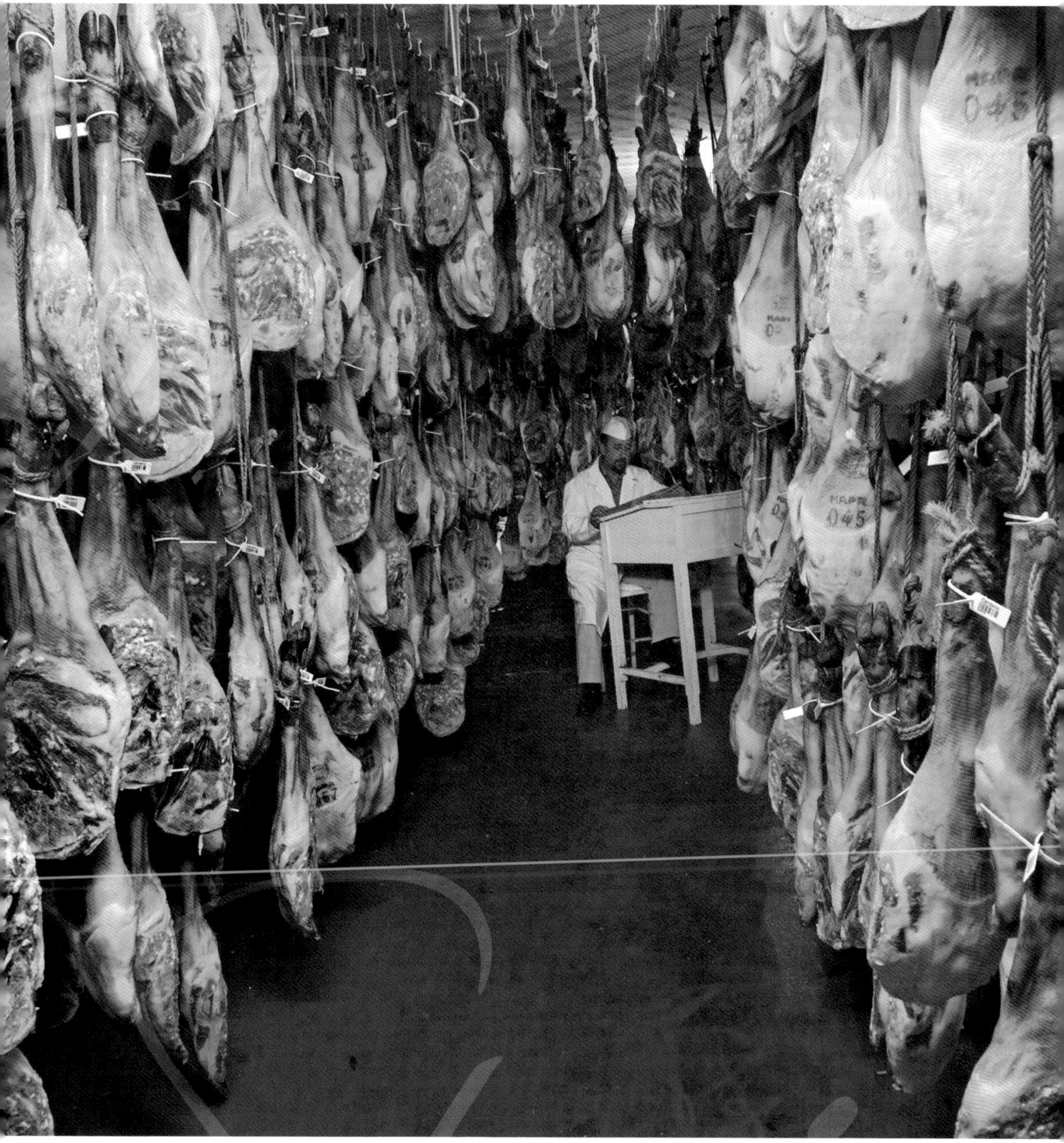

SOUPS AND GAZPACHO

Soup is a big category in any language, but in Spanish it's enormous. And it's as basic to life as bread. In fact, quite a few Spanish soups are little more than bread and water gruel which, besides sustaining people through poor times, are surprisingly tasty. Of these, *sopa de ajo*, garlic soup, in its myriad variations, even turns up on restaurant menus, a peasant dish in sophisticated surroundings.

Though visitors to Spain immediately think of gazpacho when they think of soup, this concoction — a sort of liquid salad — is a genre all by itself.

Naturally enough in a country surrounded by the sea, fish soups are among the best. Some are rich medleys containing four or five kinds of fish, clams, prawns and squid, not unlike the French bouillabaisse. Others are smooth bisques.

The basic soup in Spain is the broth from the *puchero* or *cocido*, interchangeable words for the Spanish boiled dinner of chicken, beef, sausages, chickpeas and vegetables. On the first serving it would contain rice or thin vermicelli noodles *(fideos)*. For a second meal, perhaps supper the same day, the broth forms the basis of a new soup.

Then there are the *potajes* and *cazuelas*. *Potaje*, meaning pottage or potage, is a thick soup, usually containing chickpeas or pulses, vegetables and small bits of meat or sausage. Though often served as a first course for the main meal, it is certainly substantial enough to stand alone. A *cazuela* is an earthenware cooking dish and these meals are, quite simply, casseroles, similar to the *potajes*.

Within these various categories there is a soup for every taste and every season. Gazpacho is light summer fare; the *potajes* make sturdy winter eating; the seafood soups are delicious any time; the garlic soups make satisfying family meals.

Clockwise from left: Andalusian Vegetable Pot *(Berza de Acelga)*, page 140; Gazpacho with Accompaniments, page 118, and Seafood Soup *(Sopa de Pescado)*, page 124.

GAZPACHO

Gazpacho, in one form or another, is nearly as old as these hills. Some say it derives from the *alboronía* of the Moors, which certainly didn't include tomatoes until after the discovery of the New World. The name probably derives from the Latin *caspa*, meaning fragment or little piece, and refers to the breadcrumbs which are such an essential ingredient. Gazpacho was and still is basic fare of the Andalusian peasant.

It was little appreciated by the upper classes until not so long ago when both vitamins and tourism were "discovered". We learned that this poor man's soup was extraordinarily nourishing and tourists decided that, furthermore, it was delicious as well as *tipico*. Between that and the invention of the electric blender, gazpacho was soon out of the fields and on to the restaurant tables.

Here's my tried and true recipe for Andalusian gazpacho: take a hot August afternoon at a little *finca* deep in the countryside. Pick the reddest, ripest tomatoes, sweet-smelling off the vine, a few green peppers, a cucumber, and dip them all in the cool water of a spring to rinse off the sun's heat. In the deep shade of a carob tree, start mashing all these ingredients in a big wooden bowl, adding a bit of garlic and onion stored under the straw in the shed. Pick a lemon from a nearby tree and add its tang to the gazpacho. Olive oil, bread and salt — brought from home in a cloth bag — complete the gazpacho. From the earthenware jug add cold water. Serve immediately and follow with a siesta!

ANDALUSIAN LIQUID SALAD
Gazpacho

Garnishes: Typically, gazpacho is accompanied by small bowls of chopped tomatoes, chopped onions, chopped peppers, small croutons of toasted bread, diced, chopped hard-cooked eggs, chopped cucumbers. Not so typical but quite acceptable garnishes: chopped mint, chopped olives, strips of red pimiento, diced apples, pears, melon or peeled grapes.

Serving suggestions: As a "soup" course, serve gazpacho in wooden or ceramic bowls. Glasses or mugs might be used for serving as an aperitif. A chilled Thermos of gazpacho is wonderful picnic fare — serve into paper cups. Store it in the refrigerator in a glass jar or pitcher with a lid and have a gazpacho "pick-up" any time of the day (try

2 slices bread, crusts removed (75 g)
4 large ripe tomatoes, peeled (1 kg)
2 small green peppers or 1 bell pepper
1/2 cucumber
1/2 onion
2 cloves garlic
70 ml extra virgin olive oil, preferably
    Hojiblanca or *Picual* from Andalusia
2 teaspoons salt
1/4 teaspoons ground cumin
5 tablespoon vinegar or lemon juice
1/4-1/2 litre water
Garnishes: chopped tomatoes, onions,
    peppers, toasted bread, chopped hard-
    cooked eggs, chopped cucumbers.

it for breakfast!). Leftover gazpacho can be used as dressing for lettuce salads, made into aspics with the addition of gelatine, or turned into a sauce for rice or pasta. Concoct a *maría sangría* by thinning gazpacho with vodka; serve over ice with a cucumber stick.

Adaptations: If you don't have a blender or processor and don't fancy the effort it takes to make gazpacho in the mortar, use a food mill, or a sieve, or finely chop the vegetables, add the bread and oil mixture, then water. This is really quite authentic.

Variations: Try green tomatoes instead of red ones with cucumber and a little onion, finished with dill and a dollop of sour cream or yoghurt; experiment with other seasonings — paprika, oregano, parsley, basil, chili powder, chopped chili peppers, coriander leaves. Whatever variation you choose, be sure the basic gazpacho is made with olive oil.

Put the bread to soak in water to cover. Cut the peeled tomatoes into chunks and put them in blender or food processor with the seeded peppers, cucumber and onion, all cut in pieces, and the garlic. (If blender container is too small, process in two batches if necessary.) Whirl until the vegetables are puréed and strain them into a large bowl or tureen.

Squeeze the water from the bread and purée in a food processor. With the motor running, add the oil in a slow stream until incorporated into the bread. Then add the salt, cumin and vinegar. Ladle some of the tomato back into the processor, then mix it with the tureen of tomato purée. Stir in the water (more may be added for a thinner gazpacho) and correct the seasoning, adding more salt and vinegar to taste. Chill the gazpacho until serving time. Serves 6.

WHITE GARLIC SOUP WITH GRAPES
Ajo blanco con uvas

This sensational summer soup is better than the sum of its ingredients might indicate. Try it.

Soak the bread in water until softened, squeeze it out and put in blender or food processor with the almonds and peeled garlic. Blend to a smooth sauce (adding a little water if necessary). Then, with the motor running, add the olive oil in a slow stream, then the vinegar and salt. Beat in some of the water, then pour the contents of the container into a pitcher, wooden bowl or tureen and add the remaining water. Taste for seasoning, adding more salt or vinegar if necessary.

Serve garnished with peeled and seeded grapes. Serves six.

3 thick slices bread (about 200 g), crusts removed
100 g almonds, blanched and skinned
3 cloves garlic
150 ml extra virgin olive oil
5 tablespoons vinegar
2 teaspoons salt
1 litre water
200 g muscatel grapes

HOT GAZPACHO (TOMATO SOUP)
Gazpacho caliente

In a soup pot combine the onion, pepper, tomatoes, garlic and olive oil and let them stew for 10 minutes. In a mortar crush the saffron and mix with the cumin, pepper and salt. Add to the pot with the water or stock. Bring to the boil and cook for 10 minutes more.

Serve garnished with croutons of toasted bread. (Clams, prawns and pieces of fish can be added to this soup.) Garnish with mint and serve with figs and pieces of green pepper and raw onions, or apples, grapes or diced cucumber. One unusual version includes snails.

1 medium onion, chopped
1 green pepper, chopped
2 large tomatoes, peeled, seeded and chopped
1 clove garlic, minced
50 ml olive oil
1/4 teaspoon saffron or paprika
1/4 teaspoon cumin
1/4 teaspoon ground chili pepper (optional)
1 teaspoon salt
1 litre water or stock
4 slices bread, toasted and cubed
mint for garnish
figs to accompany

SEAFOOD SOUPS

From the elegant to the homely, seafood soups in Spain are wonderful. Take advantage of the lower-priced fish at the daily market for these soups, which are usually subtly flavoured with saffron, garlic and other spices. Choose firm-fleshed fish that won't disintegrate in cooking: *rape*, angler; *lubina*, bass; *corvina*, meagre; *mero*, grouper; *congrio*, eel; *breca* and *besugo*, bream; *palometa*, pompano; *lisa*, grey mullet; *rubio*, gurnard; *gallineta*, redfish; *cabracho* or *rascacio*, scorpion-fish; and any of the tiny fish, from which the bones can be easily picked after the fish has cooked. Seafood soups also make tasty use of inexpensive frozen fish.

Try several kinds of fish and shellfish in the same soup, but allow different cooking times depending on their texture. For instance, *merluza*, hake, will disintegrate if left to simmer too long, and prawns need little more than two minutes. Clams and mussels to be added to soup are best prepared by steaming them in a saucepan with a little water just until the shells open. Strain the liquid and add to the soup then add the clams or mussels at the very last instant. A very Spanish touch is to leave them unshucked, though they're certainly easier to eat if shelled.

Enrich any fish soup by first preparing a good stock (fumet) as a basis for the soup. Simmer head and trimmings of any white fish, prawn shells, etc., with a quarter of an onion, a bouquet garni of herbs, a carrot, stalks of celery and a good swallow of white wine or sherry. Cover with 1 1/2 litres of water; boil, skim, and simmer for 45 minutes. Strain the stock through a fine sieve. Keep stock in the freezer handy for making quick soups with bits of leftover fish and shellfish.

SHERRIED FISH SOUP
Sopa Viña AB

Famous in Málaga, this soup is named for a type of sherry that is added. A simpler version, without the seafood and sherry, is called *gazpachuelo*.

Place the egg in a blender. With the motor running, add the olive oil in a slow stream until it is emulsified. Blend in the lemon juice. Heat the water or stock in a soup pot, reduce to a simmer and add the potatoes and cook them 10 minutes. Add the cleaned fish, peas, ham, pepper and sherry. Bring to a boil and add the prawns.

1 egg, at room temperature
120 ml olive oil
4 tablespoons lemon juice
1 1/2 litres water or fish stock
250 g peeled, diced potatoes
1/2 kg cleaned fish (angler or hake), cut in
    bite-size pieces
1/4 kg prawns, shelled
100 g peas, shelled
50 g *serrano* ham, diced
1 tinned red pepper, diced
50 ml dry sherry
salt and pepper

With the blender running, ladle some of the hot soup into the emulsion in the blender. Remove the soup from the heat and whisk the emulsion into the soup. Serve immediately. The soup can be reheated, but do not boil. Serves six.

FISH SOUP WITH ORANGE PEEL
Cachorreñas

This soup is named for the sour orange (the real marmalade orange) grown everywhere in Andalusia. It can also be made without fish, a winter-time gazpacho. A similar soup in Cádiz is called *caldo de perro*, dog soup. (Cádiz also has a "cat soup" — see *Sopa de Ajo.*) If sour orange is not available, use the peel of a sweet orange and vinegar instead of orange juice.

Bring the water or stock to the boil in the soup pot with the tomato, pepper and onion. Peel the orange in a spiral and add the skin and its juice. Boil the broth for 15 minutes, then strain into another pot.

Soak the bread in water, squeeze it out and add to blender or food processor with the cooked tomato, pepper, onion, peppercorns, cumin, parsley, garlic, paprika, olive oil and salt. Whirl until smooth, then beat in some of the hot broth. Add this mixture to the soup pot with the cleaned clams and sliced or filleted fish. Cook just until fish is done, about eight minutes. Skim out the fish into soup bowls. Top with a thin slice of orange and fill the bowls with the broth.

1 1/2 litres water or stock
1 medium tomato
1 green pepper
1/2 onion
1 sour orange
2 slices bread
6 peppercorns
1/4 teaspoon cumin
1 tablespoon chopped parsley
2 cloves garlic
1 teaspoon paprika
4 tablespoons olive oil
3 teaspoons salt
300 g clams
1/2 kg *pescadilla* (small hake, or
    other white fish)
1 orange for garnish

SEAFOOD SOUP
Sopa de pescado

This five-star soup changes somewhat from one region to another and is freely varied depending on the day's catch. It starts with an aromatic fish stock to which tomato sauce or *sofrito* (Chapter 12) is added. It's flavoured with a touch of saffron and is usually slightly thickened with bread. I like to use at least two different kinds of fish: one, like angler, which keeps its firm texture in cooking and one more delicate, like hake, which disintegrates in the soup, giving it more body.

There are several ways to prepare the fish. Sometimes it is cut in slices and cooked in the stock and each person removes the bones at table. An easier method is to have the fish vendor fillet the fish, saving all the heads, bones and trimmings. Cut the fillets into chunks, removing any remaining bones, and set aside. Shell the prawns or slice the halved lobster, remove from shell and hack the shell and head into pieces. Scrub the clams, mussels, etc., and steam them open over a high heat in a covered pan. Remove from shells and discard these. Strain the liquid and reserve it.

Put all the fish trimmings and crustacean shells into a large pot with the water, white wine, salt and pepper, onion, carrot, celery and herbs. Bring to the boil, skim the froth and simmer, partially covered, for an hour. Meanwhile, in another pot or deep casserole heat the olive oil and sauté the minced onion and garlic. Add the pieces of fish and sauté them, then add the peeled prawns or pieces of lobster and the reserved clams or mussels (they may be chopped).

2 kg fish
1 kg crustaceans, prawns, langostinos, crab
— lobster for a luxury version
1 kg clams, mussels, scallops or other bivalves
1 squid, cleaned and diced (optional)
2 litres water
100 ml white wine
salt and pepper
1/4 onion
1 carrot
1 stalk celery
herbs — bay, thyme, parsley and fennel
4 tablespoons olive oil
1/4 onion, finely chopped
1 clove garlic, minced
50 ml brandy
100 g bread, toasted or fried
1/2 teaspoon saffron
10 peppercorns
cayenne
200 ml tomato sauce
parsley

Pour the brandy over (it can be flamed if desired). Crush the toasted bread in mortar or blender with the saffron, pepper and cayenne. Dissolve in some of the fish stock and add to the fish with the tomato sauce. Strain the prepared stock and add about 1 1/2 litres of it to the fish. Simmer the soup for 10 minutes. Serve with chopped parsley and triangles of fried bread. Makes six servings.

FIFTEEN-MINUTE SOUP
Sopa al cuarto de hora

Heat the olive oil in a soup pot and sauté the chopped onion. Add the peeled and chopped tomato, the fish stock, crushed saffron, diced ham, sherry, rice and peas and bring to the boil. Cook on a lively fire for 10 minutes, then lower heat and add the clams and prawns. Season with salt and pepper and cook five minutes more.

Serve with a sprinkling of chopped parsley and the chopped egg. Serves six.

50 ml olive oil
1 small onion, chopped finely
1 tomato, peeled and chopped
1 1/2 litres water or fish stock
1/2 teaspoon crushed saffron or paprika
100 g diced ham
50 ml dry sherry
150 g rice
100 g shelled peas
1/4 kg clams, cleaned
1/4 kg prawns, shelled
salt and pepper
chopped parsley
2 hard-boiled eggs, chopped

ANGLER FISH SOUP
Sopa de rape

Have the angler fish cleaned and the head separated. Put the water to boil in a pot with the herbs, onion and salt and pepper. Add the head and any trimmings from the fish and cook for 30 minutes on a hot fire. Reduce to a simmer and add the rest of the fish. Poach it for 10 minutes and remove from heat. Strain the stock and reserve.

Cut the cooked fish from the bone into small pieces and reserve it, discarding head and bones. Heat the olive oil in a soup pot or deep casserole and in it fry the almonds, hazelnuts, peeled garlic, sliced bread and sprig of parsley, just until almonds, garlic and bread are toasted. With a skimmer, remove them to mortar or blender. In the same oil, fry the chopped onion just until translucent. Add the tomatoes and fry for 15 minutes. (This *sofrito* can be used as is or puréed in a blender or passed through a sieve.)

In a mortar or blender, purée the toasted almonds, etc., with the saffron, nutmeg, cinnamon, pepper and salt, adding a little of the reserved stock to make a smooth paste. Stir this into the tomato mixture, add the stock and bring to the boil. Simmer for 10 minutes, then add the pieces of cooked angler fish and simmer another few minutes. Makes six servings.

1 angler fish, about 2 kg
2 litres water
herbs — bay leaf, oregano, thyme and celery
salt and pepper
1/2 onion
4 tablespoons olive oil
20 almonds, blanched and skinned
10 hazelnuts
3 cloves garlic
3 slices bread
1 sprig parsley
1/2 onion, chopped
2 tomatoes, peeled and chopped
1/4 teaspoon saffron
grating of nutmeg
1/8 teaspoon cinnamon
1/4 teaspoon pepper
2 teaspoons salt

MUSSEL SOUP
Sopa de mejillones

Clean the mussels very well and steam them open in the water, covered, over a very hot fire, shaking the pan while they cook. Remove from heat the instant they open. Shuck the mussels, discarding the shells. Chop the mussels coarsely and reserve. Strain and reserve their cooking liquid.

Heat the olive oil in a soup pot or earthenware casserole. In it sauté the onion. Add the puréed tomatoes. Fry for 15 minutes until the tomatoes are reduced to a sauce. Add the crushed garlic, parsley and cinnamon, then the anise brandy (if unavailable, use anise-flavoured drink such as Pernod). Add the strained liquid to the tomato mixture. Bring to the boil, then reduce to a simmer and add the chopped mussels. Cook five minutes and serve.

Garnish with toasted croutons and chopped parsley or fennel. Makes four servings.

3 dozen mussels
1/2 litre water
3 tablespoons olive oil
1 small onion, finely chopped
4 tomatoes, peeled, seeded and puréed
   (or use tomato paste)
2 cloves garlic
1 tablespoon chopped parsley
1/4 teaspoon cinnamon
2 tablespoons *aguardiente* (dry anise brandy)
salt and pepper
fennel or parsley
50 g bread, toasted or fried

CONSOMMÉS, GARLIC SOUPS, VEGETABLE SOUPS AND PURÉES

Authentic consommé — a thin, clarified broth — is rare in Spanish cookery. The *caldo* or broth from the *puchero* is usually served, unclarified, with the fat from a stewing hen floating on the top, embellished with rice, pasta or bread and a garnish of chopped herbs. The *consommé madrilène* (*caldo madrileño*) of classic cookery calls for sieved tomato pulp or juice to be added to a clarified and reduced chicken broth and fortified with a dash of dry sherry. It can be served hot or cold, garnished with chopped parsley and very finely diced sweet red peppers.

GARNISHED BROTH
Sopa de picadillo

This is what happens to the leftover broth from the *puchero* or *cocido*, a rich brew of chicken, beef and ham bone. The soup appears as a light evening meal or a first course for a different dinner the following day. When real *puchero* broth is not available, substitute any good chicken broth or tinned consommé, boiled briefly with a piece of ham, ham bone or even bacon.

In the bottom of a soup tureen put croutons of fried bread, chopped and fried ham and chopped, hard-boiled eggs. Add the hot, strained broth, a dash of sherry and serve the soup garnished with a sprig of mint. Rice, thin noodles or chopped potatoes can be used instead of the croutons.

GARLIC SOUP
Sopa de ajo

Here is the perfect example of a poor man's soup — nothing more than bread, olive oil, garlic and water and is now found on sophisticated restaurant menus everywhere in Spain. Garlic soup, like gazpacho, is better than the sum of its parts, a category to itself, a unique contribution to the world's culinary delights. Every province has a variation on garlic soup. In some places it is called *oliagua* (garlic water), and might additionally contain onion, tomato and peppers, or *sopa de gato*, "cat soup" typical of Cádiz, with the addition of grated cheese. You can use an aromatic stock for this soup, but plain water is just fine.

Heat the olive oil in a soup pot or heat-proof casserole and add the chopped garlic and bread cubes. Fry until lightly golden, then stir in the paprika. Immediately add the boiling water and salt. Cover and simmer slowly for 5-10 minutes. The bread should almost dissolve in the broth.

Place the soup in four individual earthenware bowls and add one egg per bowl. Poach the eggs in the soup (in oven or on top of stove) and serve with a garnish of chopped parsley. Alternatively, the eggs can be beaten together and stirred into the pot of hot soup, letting it cook just until the eggs have set, thickening the soup. Serves four.

6 tablespoons olive oil
6 cloves (or more) garlic, chopped
6 slices bread, cut in cubes (300 g)
1 teaspoon paprika
1 3/4 litres boiling water or stock
2 teaspoons salt
4 eggs
chopped parsley

MALLORCAN CABBAGE SOUP
Sopa de col mallorquina

This is one of the "dry" soups of Mallorca, so-called because a quantity of bread is added to soak up the broth. Instead of the cabbage, you can substitute broccoli, cauliflower, spinach, chard, asparagus or other vegetables. This "soup" can also be allowed to set and served at room temperature.

Cut the bread into thin strips. In a casserole or soup pot heat the olive oil and fry the strips of bread. Remove them when browned and set aside. In the same oil, sauté the chopped onions until softened, then add the peeled and chopped tomatoes, the minced garlic, chopped peppers and chopped cabbage. Sautée the vegetables on a high heat for a few minutes, then add the chopped parsley, paprika, salt and pepper.

Add the boiling water or stock to just cover the vegetables. Bring to the boil and simmer for 10 minutes. Then add the fried bread. Cover the casserole and simmer until the liquid is absorbed, another 10 minutes. Serve with a sprinkling of chopped parsley. Makes four to six servings.

400 g wholewheat bread

100 ml olive oil

2 onions, chopped

2 tomatoes, peeled and chopped

3 cloves garlic, minced

2 small peppers, chopped

1 medium cabbage, chopped

2 tablespoons chopped parsley

1 teaspoon paprika

salt and pepper

1 litre approx, boiling water or stock

PORK AND VEGETABLE SOUP
Garbure navarro

Other vegetables — cauliflower, leeks, spinach, carrots, lettuce — can be added instead of, or in addition to, the ones given.

Cut the pork loin into cubes and put in a soup pot with the piece of ham bone and the salt pork or bacon, cut in dice. Add the broad beans and peas. Cover with water and bring to the boil. Skim the froth, then simmer, covered, until the broad beans are tender, about 40 minutes.

Remove strings from green beans and cut them into short lengths. Peel and dice the potatoes. Wash the cabbage and chop it. Add these three vegetables and the pork sausage links, diced, to the soup with salt and pepper to taste. Simmer another 40 minutes, or until all the vegetables are very tender.

Remove the ham bone and serve the soup. Makes four servings.

150 g pork loin
1 piece ham bone
150 g salt pork or bacon
150 g broad beans, shelled
2 litres water
150 g peas, shelled
150 g green beans
2 large potatoes
1 small cabbage
150 g pork sausage links
salt and pepper

ALMOND SOUP
Sopa de almendras

This savoury brew hints at its Moorish ancestry. It is typically served for Christmas dinner, and a delightful starter it makes, light, yet so full of flavour. In this dish the flavour of real olive oil is essential. There are numerous versions of this soup. This savoury one, typical of Granada, is flavoured with saffron and cumin, whereas in Castile a sweetened version contains cinnamon, mint and lemon juice and is served for pudding.

Heat the olive oil in a soup pot and in it toast the almonds, saffron, garlic and bread. Remove them when just golden and place in blender, food processor or mortar with the peppercorns, cumin and salt, reserving a few of the croutons of fried bread for garnish. Purée these ingredients, adding a little of the broth and the vinegar.

Heat the broth in the same soup pot, stir the puréed almond mixture into it and bring to the boil. Simmer for 15 minutes and serve hot, garnished with chopped parsley and the reserved bread cubes. Serves six.

50 ml extra virgin olive oil
200 g blanched almonds
1/4 teaspoon saffron
2 cloves garlic
100 g bread, diced
10 peppercorns
1/4 teaspoon cumin
salt
1 1/2 litres chicken broth
1 teaspoon vinegar
chopped parsley

KIDNEY BEAN SOUP
Puré de San Juan

Soak the beans in water to cover overnight. Put them to cook in fresh water with the quartered onion, carrot, garlic, bay leaf, thyme, ham bone, salt and pepper. Bring to the boil, then simmer until the beans are tender. Remove bone and herbs.

Purée the beans and vegetables in a blender, food processor or food mill and return to the pot. Thin with water if desired. Serve, garnished with the chopped olives, eggs and parsley. Serves four.

1/4 kg kidney beans
1 1/2 litres water
1 onion, quartered
1 carrot
6 cloves garlic
1 bay leaf
1 sprig thyme
1 piece ham bone
salt and pepper
50 g olives, pitted and chopped
2 hard-boiled eggs, chopped
chopped parsley

COCIDO

The usual English translation of this meal-in-a-pot — boiled dinner — hardly does justice to this fantastic dish. It's more like an elaborate theatre production in three acts, with plenty of drama, fabulous costumes and saucy interludes. Though you seldom find *cocido* on restaurant menus, it is the real national dish of Spain. It's hardly a set piece, however, as each region stages it a little differently. It is variously called — besides *cocido* — *puchero, pote, olla, escudella*. Mostly they are named for the pot in which they cook.

The original *cocido* in Spain was the *adafina* of the Spanish Jews, a dish nearly identical to today's. It was left to cook very slowly overnight during the Sabbath (when work was forbidden by Mosaic law) to be ready to eat at midday. After the Reconquest, Jews who chose to be baptised added pork and sausage.

Olla podrida, much appreciated centuries ago by Don Quijote and his sidekick Sancho Panza, was a similar dish. Literally translated as "rotten pot", it might have been so called because the ingredients were allowed to cook to nearly a mush. At first it was a dish of the upper classes and might have contained chicken, beef, mutton, bacon, doves, partridge, pork loin, sausages, hare, beef and pork tongues, cabbages, turnips and other vegetables. The *garbanzo*, or chickpea, was added early on and remains today a standard ingredient. By the 18th century, the potato from the New World got thrown into the pot too.

With the accession of the Bourbons to the Spanish throne, the *olla podrida* disappeared from aristocratic tables and passed on to the bourgeois and lower classes. It was much simplified in the process. The *cocido* today is still standard fare in pueblo homes, where the housewife puts the *olla* to cook while going about household chores. In fast-moving cities, however, the *cocido* is becoming nostalgia food. For one thing, the ingredients, once locally produced and cheap, have become increasingly expensive. And fewer people have the time and patience to tend the slow cooking of the *cocido*. Packaged soups, ready in minutes, and quick-cooking *filetes* of pork and beef are replacing the traditional *cocido*.

The *cocido madrileño* is certainly the most representative of all. It is made with beef, ham, salt pork, stewing hen, sausages, black pudding, chickpeas, potatoes, cabbage, carrots. The broth is strained out and cooked with fine soup noodles to provide the first course, then the vegetables and chickpeas are served on one platter and all the meats, cut up, on another.

The Catalan *escudella i carn d'olla* ("soup with meat of the pot") includes the *pelota,* a huge dumpling of minced pork seasoned with garlic, cinnamon and parsley, and *butifarra* sausages, both white and black. The first-course soup is cooked with rice or noodles or, for special occasions, might be *de galets,* with huge tubes of pasta.

The *puchero* or Andalusian *cocido* usually contains a wider range of vegetables — pumpkin, courgette, green beans and other seasonal vegetables are allowed to make an appearance. The whole might be flavoured with garlic, paprika and saffron or a *sofrito,* tomato sauce. The *cocido vasco,* Basque version, adds red kidney beans, cooked separately with the *chorizo* and black pudding. The soup is made up of the broth from both pots. Then follow four platters: chickpeas and potatoes, red beans, cabbage and other vegetables and the meats, served with sauces of tomato and peppers. The *pote gallego,* "Galician pot", includes *grelos* and *nabizas,* turnip leaves and flowers. *Sopa y bullit mallorquín,* the Mallorcan version, adds lamb and *sobrasada,* the local soft sausage. In the Canaries, both corn and sweet potatoes are included. The *puchero de las tres abocas* of Valencia substitutes lamb for the beef.

I like to make *cocido* as a full-scale production for at least six guests with good appetites (whereas the *potajes* which follow I consider more as homely, family meals), using the finest ingredients and serving the platters heaped with the different foods, each cooked to perfection. It's a most impressive meal.

You will need two or three large soup pots. Remember to soak the chickpeas in water for at least 12 hours. The flavourful broth can be used for making other soups (see *sopa de picadillo*). Leftover meats and sausages can be finely minced, bound with egg and breadcrumbs and made into dumplings for the soup. Leftover vegetables can be puréed with some of the broth, seasoned with nutmeg and served garnished with chopped ham and hard-boiled eggs.

SOUP, MEAT AND VEGETABLES IN A POT
Cocido

Put the water to boil in a very large *olla* or soup pot. When it is boiling, add the beef, beef bone, trotter, salt pork and ham. Keep the water boiling and skim off the froth as it rises to the surface. When no more froth boils up, reduce the liquid to a simmer and add the chickpeas, drained of soaking water. Add the carrots, peeled and halved lengthwise, the turnip cut in quarters, the leeks and the celery cut in half. Cut the onion in half and stick a clove in each and add to the pot with the chicken. Keep the liquid at a good simmer, cover the pot and let it cook for an hour. Then add the salt. Cook another 30 minutes.

In a separate pot, using some of the broth from the *cocido* or with additional water, cook the cabbage, coarsely chopped, with the two kinds of sausage. This operation is done separately to avoid flavouring the soup broth with the cabbage and colouring it with the red *chorizo*. Those who enjoy this flavour and colour can add these ingredients directly to the cooking pot. When they have cooked for 30 minutes, drain, reserving the liquid if desired. Heat the olive oil in a frying pan, sauté the garlic and add the cooked cabbage to it. Sautée for five minutes.

Meanwhile, add the potatoes, peeled and cut in half, to the main cooking pot and simmer another 30 minutes, or until all the ingredients are tender and chickpeas (*garbanzos*) are cooked. Now strain some of the broth into another pot, bring it to the boil and cook in it the thin noodles or the rice. If bread is to be used instead, remove crusts

3 litres water
500 g stewing beef
1 beef marrow bone
1 salted pig trotter (optional)
100 g salt pork
200 g ham (or ham bone)
1/2 kg chickpeas, soaked overnight
2 carrots
1 turnip
2 leeks
1 stalk celery
1 onion, halved
2 cloves
1/2 large boiling fowl (stewing hen), about 2 kg
2 teaspoons salt
6 medium potatoes
1 small cabbage
150 g *chorizo*
150 g *morcilla*
2 tablespoons olive oil
1 clove garlic
200 g fine noodles, rice or bread
parsley or mint
tomato sauce

135

and cut it into strips and place in six soup plates. Ladle the broth into the soup plates, garnish with a little chopped parsley or mint and serve as the meal's first course. The broth from the cabbage and *chorizo* can be combined with this broth if desired.

Drain the chickpeas and place them on a serving platter accompanied by the carrots, turnip, leeks, celery, onion, potatoes and cabbage. Cut all the meats, sausages, salt pork and ham into serving pieces and serve them on a second platter. Serve separately a tomato sauce which can be mixed with the meats and vegetables in any combination. Serves six to eight.

SOUP AND VEGETABLES, CANARY ISLANDS-STYLE
Puchero canario

Where available *morcilla dulce*, black pudding sweetened with sugar and almonds, would be added to this dish.

Put the water to boil in a large pot with the soaked beans, the pork and salt pork. Cook until beans are partially cooked, about 30 minutes.

Add the washed and chopped chard, watercress and courgette. Season with salt and pepper. Cut the corn kernels from the cobs and add to the pot with the potatoes, peeled and cut in chunks. Continue cooking the soup until everything is quite tender.

In another pot heat the olive oil and sauté the chopped onion until softened. Add the peeled and chopped tomatoes and the garlic, and fry until tomatoes are reduced to a sauce. Stir in the *gofio* or cornmeal, then add the strained broth from the soup pot. Cook this soup for five minutes.

Serve the soup first, garnished with chopped parsley or coriander. Then serve a platter of the beans, vegetables and meat, cut into individual portions. Serves four.

3 litres water
1/4 kg white beans, soaked overnight
1/2 kg pork
150 g salt pork
4 stalks chard
1 bunch watercress
1 courgette, diced
salt and pepper
3 ears corn (or 1 tin sweetcorn)
2 potatoes or sweet potatoes, peeled
3 tablespoons olive oil
1 small onion, chopped
2 tomatoes, peeled and chopped
2 cloves garlic, chopped
4 tablespoons *gofio* (toasted maize flour, or cornmeal)
parsley or coriander leaves

POTAJES and CAZUELAS

These are among my very favourite Spanish dishes — such rich and satisfying flavours for a small expenditure of money and effort. Most contain legumes or pulses (beans, chickpeas or lentils) and, though not exactly soups, they're somewhat soupy. Typically, these potages and casseroles would be served as a first course, but many are substantial enough to make an informal supper accompanied by salad and good bread. They are different from the *cocidos* in that the broth is not strained out to make a first-course soup.

ASTURIAN HAM AND BEANS
Fabada

This is Spain's most famous bean dish, wonderfully flavoured, robust food from the northern regions. The *fabes* are big, fat white beans which cook up soft without disintegrating. Where unavailable, substitute the bigger dried lima beans or butter beans, or any large white bean. The *morcilla* and *chorizo* should be, if possible, from Asturias, where they are oak-smoked. *Lacón* is cured pork hand. If not available, use ham. Salt beef, salt-cured pig trotters and hard *longaniza* sausage are also used.

The day before: put the beans to soak in plenty of water. Put the *lacón* or ham to soak overnight in hot water. Blanch the salt pork in boiling water for five minutes.

The following day: wash the sausages to eliminate excess smokiness. Drain the beans and put in an earthenware casserole or large cooking pot and cover with water to a depth of two fingers. On a hot fire, bring to the boil and skim off the froth.

Crush the saffron in a mortar and dissolve in a little water and add to the beans. Add the *lacón*, ham and salt pork to the casserole, pushing them to the bottom of the beans. Cover and cook five minutes and skim again. Now add the *chorizo* and *morcilla*, boil five minutes and skim. Add bay leaf, cover and cook very slowly, two to three hours. Add cold water occasionally just to keep the beans barely covered so they don't dry out and split. Do not stir, but shake the casserole from time to time.

When beans are quite tender, let them sit for 20 minutes to blend and mellow the flavours. If too

1/2 kg *fabes* (dried white beans)
400 g Asturian smoked *morcilla*
400 g Asturian smoked *chorizo*
400 g cured pork hand (shoulder) or ham
100 g streaky salt pork
1/2 teaspoon saffron
1 bay leaf

much liquid remains, purée some of the cooked beans in the blender and add them to the casserole to thicken the sauce. Serves four.

GALICIAN SOUP
Caldo gallego

In Galicia this soup is made with *grelos*, the flowering stems of a sort of turnip. Substitute any greens, such as chard, for the *grelos*.

Put the soaked beans, desalted pork ribs (or substitute any meaty pork bone) and the stewing beef to boil in the water. Skim the froth, then add the pork fat. Cover partially and simmer for two hours.

Wash and chop the *grelos* or other vegetable and add to the pot with the potatoes, peeled and cut in small pieces, and salt and pepper to taste. Cook another hour, or until the contents are all very tender.

Remove some of the potatoes, beans and pork fat to the blender and purée with the garlic and paprika. Stir into the soup to thicken it. Cut the beef into small pieces. Serve in soup bowls. Serves six.

1/4 kg white beans, soaked overnight
300 g salt-cured spare ribs, soaked overnight
200 g stewing beef
3 litres water
50 g lard or salt pork
1/4 kg *grelos* (or use chard or collards)
3 medium potatoes
salt and pepper
1 clove garlic
1 teaspoon paprika

ANDALUSIAN VEGETABLE POT
Berza de acelga

Of the hundreds of Spanish recipes I have collected over the years, this one is the most stained, the most used. It is straightforward pueblo food and its earthiness and simplicity appeal to me on a gut level. In village homes, chard would be used in winter months, green beans in their place in the summer. Other more unusual vegetables, such as cardoons, carrots, artichokes, lettuce, broad beans, might be added in addition or in their place. Though the chard is trimmed to include only the stalks — the deep-green leaves being saved to cook as spinach — I prefer to add the leafy part as well as the stalk to the *berza*. This potage is sometimes made with both chickpeas and white beans. Black-eyed peas can be used in place of either. Add quartered firm pears or other fruits to the *berza* and you can call it *olla gitana,* gypsy pot.

If using both the *garbanzos* and beans, drain and put the *garbanzos* to cook first with the salt pork, piece of fresh pork and water. After 30 minutes, add the soaked beans. Let all simmer for about one and a half hours.

Add the chard, or green beans, which have been cleaned and chopped, and the *chorizo* and *morcilla*. In the mortar crush cloves and peppercorns with the garlic, salt and paprika and add to the *berza*. When meat and *garbanzos* are nearly tender — about two hours total — add the potatoes and pumpkin, both peeled and cut in small chunks. Cook another 30 minutes.

Cut the pork and sausages into small pieces (kitchen scissors work well for this) and serve into soup bowls. Serves six.

400 g chickpeas *(garbanzos)* and/or white beans, soaked (separately) overnight
100 g salt pork or bacon
200 g pork or meaty pork bone
2 litres water
1/2 kg chard and/or green beans
1 *chorizo*
1 *morcilla*
2 cloves
8 peppercorns
3 cloves garlic
2 teaspoon salt
2 teaspoons paprika
4 medium potatoes
1/4 kg pumpkin

MOORS AND CHRISTIANS
(BLACK BEANS WITH WHITE RICE)
Moros y cristianos

Put the beans to cook in the water with the quartered onion, sliced carrot and celery, crushed garlic and bay leaf. Bring to the boil, skim, then simmer, partially covered, until the beans are nearly tender, about one hour.

Mix together the paprika, olive oil, salt, pepper and cayenne and stir into the beans with the juice of one orange and finish cooking. Let the beans sit for 15 minutes. Ladle them with a skimmer into a serving bowl.

Meanwhile cook the rice with salt just until done. Pack it into an oiled bowl or ring mould, let it rest 10 minutes, then unmould on to the black beans. Garnish with parsley, and the sliced onion, orange and eggs. Serves six.

400 g black beans, soaked overnight
2 litres water
1 onion
1 carrot
1 stalk celery
10 cloves garlic, peeled and crushed
1 bay leaf
1 teaspoon paprika
3 tablespoons olive oil
2 teaspoons salt
pepper
dash cayenne
1 orange
300 g rice
parsley
sliced onion
sliced orange
sliced hard-boiled eggs

LENTIL POT
Cazuela de lentejas

Rice instead of, or in addition to, the potatoes can be cooked with the lentils. Pumpkin, peeled and cut in chunks can also be added. *Chorizo* can be added during the last 30 minutes, instead of, or in addition to, the pork sausage.

Bring the lentils to the boil in the water, turn off the heat and let them soak for two hours.

Add the olive oil, the whole tomato, quartered onion stuck with cloves, whole pepper cleaned of seeds, bay leaf, roasted garlic cloves, salt. Bring to the boil, then simmer slowly for one hour.

Meanwhile in the mortar crush the cumin, paprika and pepper together with the cayenne. Add to the pot with the potatoes, peeled and chopped, and the sausage, scissor-cut into short pieces. Cook the lentils another 30 minutes until they and the potatoes are quite tender. Makes six servings.

1/2 kg lentils
2 litres water
50 ml olive oil
1 medium tomato
1 medium onion, quartered
1 green pepper
1 bay leaf
1 head garlic, roasted (instructions below)
1 tablespoon salt
2 cloves
2 large potatoes, chopped
1/4 teaspoon cumin
1/2 teaspoon paprika
1/4 teaspoon ground pepper
dash cayenne
200 g spicy pork sausage links

TO CHAR-ROAST A WHOLE HEAD OF GARLIC

Spear the head of garlic on a fork or grab it with tongs (protect your hands with an oven mitt) and hold over a gas flame or put under the grill. Turn the garlic until it is charred on all sides. Peel the garlic cloves and rinse in water.

UNCLE LUCAS'S BEAN POT
Judias a lo Tío Lucas

Heat the olive oil in a soup pot and in it fry the salt pork or bacon, cut in small dice. Add the soaked beans, the onion, roasted garlic, bay leaf, paprika, cumin and parsley. Cover with approximately two litres of water, bring to the boil and simmer for an hour. Season with salt and pepper and continue cooking until beans are quite tender, about 30 minutes more.

Ladle into soup bowls and serve hot. Makes six servings.

50 ml olive oil
200 g salt pork or bacon
1/2 kg dried white beans, soaked overnight
1 onion, quartered
1 head garlic, roasted (instructions above)
1 bay leaf
1 teaspoon paprika
1/4 teaspoon ground cumin
1 sprig parsley
salt and pepper

CHICKPEAS AND SPINACH POTAGE
Potaje de garbanzos con espinacas

This dish, especially typical during Lent, might have salt cod, soaked overnight, cooked with the chickpeas. For non-Lenten dishes, lard, salt pork and ham might be included.

Put the chickpeas (*garbanzos*) to cook in the water with the carrot, 1 onion, parsley and bay leaf. Bring to the boil and simmer, partially covered, for one hour. Then add 2 teaspoons salt and 2 tablespoons olive oil and continue to cook the chickpeas until tender.

Meanwhile, clean the spinach and chop it. Add it to the *garbanzos* to cook. In a frying pan heat remaining oil and in it sauté the other onion, chopped, and garlic. Add the peeled and chopped tomatoes and continue frying until reduced, about 15 minutes. Season with paprika and salt and pepper.

Skim the *garbanzos* and spinach into a casserole and add the tomato sauce and enough of the cooking liquid to make it just saucy. Cook another 10 minutes and serve garnished with chopped hard-boiled eggs. Serves six.

1/2 kg chickpeas, soaked overnight
2 litres water
1 carrot
2 onions
1 sprig parsley
1 bay leaf
1/2 kg spinach
80 ml olive oil
2 cloves garlic, chopped
2 tomatoes, peeled and chopped
1 teaspoon paprika
salt and pepper
hard-boiled eggs

COOK'S NOTES:

TORTILLAS AND OTHER EGG DISHES

Years ago, in the pueblo where I once lived, the most familiar sounds on a sleepy afternoon were the cackling of hens and the chorusing of cocks as they perched on high patio walls. I would put the olive oil to heat in the frying pan and go next door where my neighbour reached under the chattering hens and handed me two, three or four eggs. They were so fresh and delicious that I liked making them the starring dish for lunch — scrambled with mushrooms; baked flamenco style, with bright strips of pepper and peas; or bound with potatoes in a fat omelette.

Today I buy fresh eggs at the supermarket, but I continue to enjoy them prepared Spanish-style, for luncheon and supper. Though a Spaniard might eat a boiled or fried egg for "elevenses", the mid-morning snack, eggs are seldom consumed for breakfast. They're most likely to appear as starter for the main meal or as a main course for a light supper. *Tortillas* are classic tapa bar fare. A good deal of imaginative flavourings are combined with the simple egg.

Certainly the most popular egg dish on Spanish tables is the *tortilla española*. A Spanish *tortilla* is a kind of omelette — not related to the Mexican *tortilla* (a flat bread made out of maize flour), and only a distant cousin of the French omelette. Omelette, Spanish style, is served round and flat, not folded, and contains potatoes or bits of meats, vegetables, seafood, mushrooms or herbs. It may be cooked in a huge disc, which is sliced like a pie, or in small, individual portions. For tapa servings, the *tortilla* is cut into small squares, a perfect nibble. No train journey or excursion is complete without a hamper of ample provisions, always including a *tortilla* or two.

Tortilla-making is not as simple as it looks. My first ones were disasters — sort of potato scrambled eggs — though they tasted just fine, washed down with the local wine. I advise you not to invite guests to sample your first attempt. But don't be scared off, either. The *tortilla* is a quick and easy meal from ingredients almost always to hand.

The type of frying pan contributes much to the success of the *tortilla*. You need a lightweight pan to facilitate the tricky flipping of the omelette. I still use an old-fashioned rolled steel pan with a long handle and high, sloping sides. It has to be kept well-seasoned and free of rust or the omelette tends to stick. Plenty of Spanish housewives today use frying pans with non-stick surfaces. A four-egg *tortilla* should be cooked in a pan with a bottom diameter of 20cm (8in) or smaller so that it comes out quite thick, about 4 or 5cm (2 in). The outside should be golden-brown, the inside, still juicy.

Olive oil makes the best frying medium and you're going to need quite a bit of it to keep potatoes and other ingredients from sticking (less, if you use a non-stick pan). The following instructions for the classic potato omelette can be adapted for any type of *tortilla*.

Spanish Omelette (*Tortilla Española*), page 148.

SPANISH OMELETTE
Tortilla española

All sorts of other ingredients may be incorporated in the *tortilla*, either instead of or in addition to the potatoes. It's a good catch-all for leftover bits of meat, ham, sausage, seafood and vegetables. Try green beans, peas, mushrooms, spinach, prawns, chicken livers, sweet peppers, asparagus, etc. One of my favourites is made with *habas,* broad beans, which look like pretty green gems when the *tortilla* is sliced. Allow two to three cups diced, cooked vegetables, meats, etc. Favourite additions to the omelette are chopped onion, ham, parsley and garlic, though you can certainly experiment with other seasonings.

Peel the potatoes and either cut them in dice or, for a layered effect, into very thin slices. Heat the oil in the frying pan until very hot and add the potatoes, and onions if desired. Stir them into the oil to completely coat and seal them, then reduce the heat slightly and continue frying without letting the potatoes brown, stirring frequently. With the edge of a metal spatula or skimmer, keep cutting into the potatoes, dicing them as they cook.

When potatoes are quite tender (about 25 minutes) place a plate over the frying pan and drain off the olive oil into a heat-proof container. Place the potatoes in a bowl. Beat together the eggs and salt until very well combined and stir the eggs into the potatoes and mix well.

Return the oil to the frying pan and let it reheat. Now pour in the egg and potato mixture. Let it set on the bottom, regulating the heat so it doesn't brown too fast. Use the spatula to firm the edges of

1 kg potatoes
3 tablespoons chopped onion (optional)
50 ml olive oil
4-5 eggs
1/2 teaspoon salt

the *tortilla* all around its circumference. Shake the pan frequently to keep it loose on the bottom.

When the eggs are set, about five minutes, place the plate over the pan, drain off the oil and turn the *tortilla* out on to the plate. Return the oil to the pan, adding a little more if necessary and slide the *tortilla* back in to cook on the reverse side. Remove the *tortilla* when it is golden by sliding out on to a serving plate. Serves two as a main dish or four to six as an appetiser or first course.

SPINACH OMELETTE
Tortilla de espinacas

This omelette is thinner than the classic *tortilla*. It can be served individually or several of them stacked, a tomato sauce poured over, and sliced to make individual servings.

Drain the spinach well, chop it finely and mix with the minced onion, salt and pepper and beaten eggs.

Heat the olive oil in a small frying pan and pour in the spinach-egg mixture. Let it cook on the bottom without browning, then, with a spatula, flip it over to cook the other side. Serve sprinkled with the cheese. One serving.

6 tablespoons cooked spinach (about 80 g)
2 teaspoons minced onion
salt and pepper
2 eggs, beaten
1 tablespoon olive oil
grated cheese

CAPUCHINE OMELETTE
Tortilla capuchina

Cut the potatoes into dice and fry them with the onions, in 2 tablespoons of the olive oil. When potatoes are tender, stir in the breadcrumbs and asparagus. Fry all for a few minutes.

In a bowl, combine the potato mixture with the chopped parsley, salt and beaten eggs. Add remaining oil to the frying pan and pour in the mixture. Cook on both sides. Serves six as starter.

400 g potatoes (2 large)
1 onion, sliced thinly
50 ml olive oil
100 g fine breadcrumbs
100 g asparagus tips, cooked
1 tablespoon chopped parsley
1/2 teaspoon salt
6 eggs, beaten

MURCIA OMELETTE
Tortilla murciana

This dish is even better if the sweet red peppers are roasted and peeled before they are fried with the tomatoes and aubergine.

Prepare the peppers by cleaning them of seeds and cutting in strips. Heat part of the olive oil in a frying pan and fry the prepared tomatoes, peppers and aubergine together for 15 minutes.

Meanwhile beat the eggs and salt together in a bowl. Mix the fried tomato mixture into the eggs. Add remaining oil to the pan and pour in the egg mixture. Cook on both sides. Cut into six slices.

3 tomatoes, peeled, seeded and chopped
4 sweet red peppers
50 ml olive oil
1 small aubergine, peeled and diced
1/2 teaspoon salt
6 eggs

SCRAMBLED EGGS
Revueltos de huevos

Scrambled eggs are just shapeless omelettes. Any of the previous combinations of foods can be used for scrambled eggs, and any of the following can be just as well turned into omelettes. Scrambled eggs should be cooked on a very low heat and removed from the fire before the eggs are set. Serve them very soft and creamy.

SCRAMBLED EGGS
WITH CHANTERELLES
Revuelto de setas

This Basque combination — so simple — makes a wonderful supper dish. If chanterelles are not available, use any other wild or cultivated mushroom.

Clean the mushrooms carefully of all grit; wash and dry them. Cut them into small pieces. Sautée them in a frying pan in the olive oil with the minced garlic.

Break the eggs one by one into the pan with the mushrooms. Use a wooden spoon or spatula to stir the whites into the mushrooms. As the whites are scrambled and set, break the yolks and stir them into the mushrooms. Sprinkle with the chopped parsley, salt and pepper. Continue stirring the egg mixture until it is just set. Serves two.

150 g chanterelles
2 tablespoons olive oil
1 clove garlic
4 eggs
1 tablespoon chopped parsley
salt and pepper

TOMATO SCRAMBLED EGGS
Revoltillo de huevo con tomate

This makes a very nice brunch dish, especially when topped with *riñones al jerez*, sautéed kidneys in sherry.

Heat the olive oil and fry the chopped onion until soft. Add the tomatoes and salt. Fry until the tomatoes are reduced to a smooth sauce, about 15 minutes.

Beat the eggs with another pinch of salt and pepper and stir them into the tomato mixture. Stir constantly on a low fire until the eggs are just set. Serve on triangles of fried bread. Serves four.

3 tablespoons olive oil
1 medium onion, chopped
2 large tomatoes, peeled seeded and chopped
1 teaspoon salt
pepper
4 eggs
triangles of fried bread

SCRAMBLED EGGS WITH ASPARAGUS
Huevos revueltos con espárragos

If desired, peeled prawns can be added to the asparagus.

Blanch the asparagus tips in boiling water (or, if using tinned ones, rinse them and drain).

Heat the oil in a frying pan and sauté the asparagus and ham for several minutes. Then add the eggs, beaten with salt and pepper, and stir over a low heat until the eggs are soft-set. Serves two.

100 g asparagus tips
100 g diced *serrano* ham or bacon
2 tablespoons olive oil
4 eggs, well beaten
salt and pepper

FRIED EGGS

Huevos fritos

The fried egg, in Spanish, really *is* a fried egg, using a cooking technique quite unlike a typical English or American fried egg. The egg should emerge from its immersion in olive oil with the white a little crackly around the edges — *estrellada* — and the yolk still unset. The procedure is more like poaching, only the medium is olive oil, not water.

The eggs must be very fresh and at room temperature. In a small frying pan heat enough olive oil to almost cover the egg until it shimmers, just short of smoking. Break the egg on to a saucer and slip it into the hot oil. Use the skimmer to baste the top of the egg with the oil. Remove it to drain and continue frying eggs, one at a time.

The eggs may be served with pieces of ham or *chorizo*, slices of bread and chopped garlic, all fried in the same olive oil. One of the best ways to serve Spanish fried eggs is atop garlic-flavoured croutons (see *migas*). A very heart-warming meal, whether you call it breakfast or supper.

EGGS, MOUNTAIN STYLE

Huevos serranos

Cut the tomatoes in half crosswise and scoop out the seeds. Finely chop the ham and divide it among the six tomato halves. Place them in an oiled baking tin. Season with salt and pepper and put them in the oven for five minutes, just until hot.

Place a fried egg in each tomato half, sprinkle with grated cheese and dust with paprika. Serve hot. Serves six as a starter.

3 large tomatoes
100 g ham
salt and pepper
6 eggs, fried in olive oil
100 g grated cheese
paprika

FRIED EGGS, CÓRDOBA STYLE
Huevos a la cordobesa

Peel the potatoes and cut them in thin slices. Heat the olive oil and fry the potatoes, adding the sliced onions. When tender, remove to a serving platter.

Adding more oil if necessary, fry the peppers, seeded and cut in thin strips, in the same pan. Place them on top of the potatoes. Then fry the eggs, season with salt and pepper and place them around the potatoes. Cut the *chorizo* in six slices and fry it very briefly. Add to the platter and serve immediately. Serves six.

750 g potatoes (4 large)
50 ml olive oil
1 small onion, sliced
2 sweet red peppers
1 small dry red chili pepper (optional)
6 eggs
salt and pepper
150 g *chorizo*

BAKED EGGS
Huevos al plato

Eggs baked in earthenware *cazuelas*, whether individual or casserole-size, might do nicely as breakfast or brunch, but I like them best for supper, when they seem quite special, but light.

FLAMENCO EGGS
Huevos a la flamenca

Heat the olive oil in a frying pan and sauté the chopped onion and garlic and half of the diced ham. When onion is soft, add the tomatoes, peeled, seeded and chopped. Season with salt, pepper and paprika and cook on a medium fire until reduced to a sauce, about 15 minutes.

Oil four individual earthenware ramekins. Divide the sauce between them. With the pestle or back of a spoon make two indentations in the sauce and carefully break an egg into them. Sprinkle each ramekin with some of the cooked peas. Cut the pepper into strips and arrange it decoratively over the eggs. Cut the artichoke hearts in half and place them around the eggs. Sprinkle with salt and pepper and chopped parsley. Put in a medium-hot oven just until the whites are set, the yolks still liquid, 10 minutes. Serve immediately with triangles of fried bread.

50 ml olive oil
1 small onion, chopped
1 clove garlic, minced
100 g ham, diced
600 g tomatoes (3 large)
1/2 teaspoon paprika
8 eggs
75 g cooked peas
1 small tin red pepper
8 cooked asparagus tips
100 g *chorizo*
2 artichoke hearts, cooked or tinned
salt and pepper
chopped parsley
fried bread to accompany

EGGS IN POTATO NESTS
Huevos en nido de patatas

Peel the potatoes, cook them in boiling, salted water until tender, and drain well. Purée the potatoes, adding one tablespoon of the butter, the egg yolk, salt, pepper and nutmeg.

Butter an oven dish or individual ramekins and either spread the potatoes in it or pipe them in with a pastry gun. Make four indentations — nests — in the potatoes. Dot the potatoes with butter and put them in a hot oven or under the grill and let the potatoes brown very lightly.

Remove from oven and break an egg into each nest. Sprinkle with grated cheese, dot with butter, sprinkle with salt and pepper and return to the oven. Bake just until the whites are set. Sprinkle with chopped parsley and paprika. Good served with pork sausage links or with sautéed chicken livers. Serves four.

1/2 kg potatoes (4 medium)
3 tablespoons butter
1 egg yolk
salt and pepper
grating of nutmeg
4 eggs
50 g grated cheese
chopped parsley
paprika

EGGS BAKED IN SPINACH NESTS
Huevos en nido de espinacas

Finely chop the cooked spinach and season it with salt and pepper, nutmeg and grated onion. It should be hot, so if not freshly cooked, reheat it. Spread the spinach in a buttered baking dish.

Make four indentations in the spinach and break an egg into each. Cover the eggs with the bechamel sauce and top with grated cheese. Dot with butter and bake in a medium oven until the whites are set and yolks still liquid, about 15 minutes. Serves four.

400 g cooked spinach
salt and pepper
grating of nutmeg
1 tablespoon grated onion
butter
4 eggs
100 ml bechamel sauce
50 g grated cheese

TOMATO CUSTARDS
Flan con tomate

This savoury custard makes an interesting starter. Once unmoulded, surround it with one of the following: asparagus tips, cooked crayfish or prawns, artichoke bottoms, sliced ham, sweetbreads or chicken livers.

Beat the eggs in a bowl until frothy. Beat in the milk and the tomato sauce. Season with salt and pepper, nutmeg and cayenne.

Butter four custard cups and divide the egg mixture between them. Set them in an oven dish, add boiling water to half their depths and place in a medium oven until the custards are set. Test them by inserting a toothpick — when it comes out clean, they are done, about 30 minutes. Let them sit a few minutes, then unmould on to individual plates and garnish. Or chill the custards, then unmould. Serves four.

6 eggs
200 ml milk
250 ml tomato sauce
salt and pepper
grating of nutmeg
dash of cayenne
butter

VEGETABLES

Vegetable dishes in Spain get preferential treatment, often enhanced with inspired sauces. Many are designed to stand on their own, being quite substantial. Though they can certainly be served as an accompaniment to a meat, poultry or fish dish, try them as starters or as light luncheon entrées.

Though Spaniards traditionally prefer their vegetables very well cooked, they almost always incorporate the cooking liquid (with all the vitamins and minerals) into the accompanying sauce. For instance, in preparing vegetables *salteadas*, sautéed, the chopped, raw vegetable is fried in olive oil with garlic and often chopped ham, then just enough water is added to keep them from scorching as they cook until tender. Modern cooking techniques have given us a taste for crisp, lightly cooked vegetables. Certainly these recipes can be adapted if so desired. See Chapter 2 on marketing, for many tips on selecting, storing and preparing vegetables.

The recipes selected for this section emphasise those vegetables and ways of cooking them that are not so likely to be found in ordinary British or American cookbooks.

ARTICHOKES

ARTICHOKES WITH MAYONNAISE
Alcachofas con mayonesa

One of the simplest possible preparations, and my very favourite. Cut off stalks and remove outer leaves from artichokes (allow one large artichoke per person). Rub each with a cut lemon and drop into water to which the juice of a lemon has been added.

 When all are prepared, add salt, bring to the boil and simmer until the artichokes are tender (when a leaf pulls off easily), from 20 to 30 minutes, depending on size. Drain them well upside-down. Place upright on salad plates and gently pull open the leaves. When the choke (the fuzzy centre) is exposed, scoop it out with a spoon and discard. Fill the centre with mayonnaise and serve. Similarly, artichokes can be served with a vinaigrette sauce.

To eat artichokes, pull off the leaves one by one and pull them through the teeth, scraping off the tender, fleshy part, then discard the leaf. When you get to the heart, the bottom, cut into bites. It's all edible.

Clockwise from left: Garlic-Sizzled Mushrooms (*Champiñones al Ajillo*), page 185; Cauliflower, Mule Driver's Style (*Coliflor al Ajo Arriero*), page 180; Sautéed Artichokes with Ham (*Alcachofas Salteadas con Jamón*), page 160.

MARINATED ARTICHOKES
Alcachofas aliñadas

Serve these artichokes at room temperature as an hors-d'oeuvre or reheat to serve as a vegetable dish. Very nice as a garnish with cold cuts, smoked meats and sausages.

Wash the artichokes well and remove the tough outer leaves. Leave them whole or cut in halves or quarters, rubbing all cut surfaces with a cut lemon. Place them immediately in a saucepan with the olive oil, 225 ml water and wine. Add the juice of the lemon, and the salt. Bring to the boil and simmer about 15 minutes.

Meanwhile, in the mortar crush the cumin, peppers, clove, saffron and garlic. Blend in the flour, then add remaining water to form a smooth paste. Add this to the artichokes, stirring until the liquid is slightly thickened. Cook until artichokes are completely tender, then remove from heat and let them cool in the sauce.

16 small artichokes
1 lemon
75 ml olive oil
275 ml water
225 ml white wine
1 teaspoon salt
1/4 teaspoon ground cumin
10 peppercorns
1 clove
1/4 teaspoon saffron
1 clove garlic
1 tablespoon flour

SAUTÉED ARTICHOKES WITH HAM
Alcachofas salteadas con jamón

Trim the artichokes of outer leaves and cut them about 3-4 cm (1 1/2 in.) from the bottom. Cut these pieces in half and rub all the surfaces with a cut lemon. Cook in boiling water to cover to which the lemon juice and salt have been added. When tender, drain well.

In a frying pan or shallow casserole heat the olive oil and sauté the diced ham and garlic. Scoop out chokes from drained artichokes and fill cavities with

12 artichokes (or 1 package frozen
    artichoke bottoms)
2 teaspoons lemon juice
1 teaspoon salt
3 tablespoons olive oil
100 g *serrano* ham, diced
2 cloves garlic
2 tablespoons red wine
salt and pepper

the ham. Sauté on a medium heat without letting them actually brown. Add the wine, the salt and pepper, and cook just until wine has evaporated. Serve immediately. Serves six.

ARTICHOKE AND POTATO CASEROLE, CÓRDOBA STYLE
Alcachofas a la cordobesa

Trim the artichokes to bottoms or hearts, rubbing them with lemon. Leave them in a bowl of acidulated water.

Heat the olive oil in an earthenware casserole or frying pan. Fry the cloves of garlic until toasted and remove. Crush in a mortar with the saffron. Dissolve the saffron in the vinegar and stock.

Drain the artichokes and add them to the oil with the potatoes which have been peeled and left whole if small. Sauté them for five minutes, then stir in the flour. Let cook another few minutes, then add the stock and mortar mixture. Cover and cook until the artichokes and potatoes are tender. Garnish with sprigs of mint. Serves four as a starter.

12 artichokes (or 1 package frozen
   artichoke hearts)
lemon
50 ml olive oil
2 cloves garlic
500 g small new potatoes
1/4 teaspoon saffron
1 teaspoon salt
1 tablespoon vinegar
100 ml stock or water
1 tablespoon flour
mint sprigs

STUFFED ARTICHOKES
Alcachofas rellenas

Remove tough outer leaves from the artichokes, rub them with lemon and put to cook in boiling salted water. Cook only about 10 minutes — they will not be quite tender. Drain well.

Open the leaves carefully. Cut out the cone of leaves at the centre; scoop out and discard the fuzzy choke. Set the artichokes aside.

Season the minced meat with the garlic, parsley and salt and pepper and let it sit for 15 minutes. Heat the olive oil in a frying pan and sauté the chopped onion. Then add the meat and ham. Let it brown, then add the wine and cook until wine is reduced. Remove from the heat and add the egg.

Stuff the artichokes with this mixture, topping each with a spoonful of the prepared tomato sauce. Place the artichokes in an oiled oven dish. Drizzle with olive oil, sprinkle with breadcrumbs, cover the dish and put in a medium oven for about 10 minutes. Remove the cover and cook another five minutes. Serves six.

18 artichokes
lemon
200 g minced meat (pork or beef)
50 g ham, finely chopped
1 clove garlic
1 tablespoon chopped parsley
salt and pepper
3 tablespoons olive oil
2 tablespoons finely chopped onion
50 ml white wine
1 egg, beaten
250 ml tomato sauce
olive oil
breadcrumbs

ASPARAGUS

ASPARAGUS, ANDALUSIAN STYLE
Espárragos a la andaluza

This is usually made with the thin, slightly bitter, wild asparagus, but it's quite good with cultivated asparagus as well. Choose thin stalks.

Cut off and discard the woody ends of the asparagus. Chop the stalks into short lengths and blanch them in boiling water for two minutes and drain well.

Heat the olive oil in a heat-proof earthenware casserole or frying pan and fry the garlic and the bread until toasted. Remove them to mortar or blender and crush with the paprika, cumin, vinegar, a little of the water and salt and pepper.

Add the drained asparagus to the oil in the pan and sauté for five minutes, tossing with a fork. Add the mortar mixture and more water, cover and simmer the asparagus until tender, about 15 minutes, adding water as necessary. The sauce should be thick, but should not cook dry.

The asparagus can be served as it is. Or beat two eggs with the spoonful of water, salt and pepper and paprika. Pour them into the casserole and cover. Cook on a low heat just until the eggs are set. Serve the casserole with pieces of fried bread. Alternatively, one egg per person can be placed on top of the cooked asparagus and the casserole placed in the oven until the eggs are set. Serves four as a starter or light entrée.

500 g asparagus
50 ml olive oil
2 cloves garlic
1 slice bread, crusts removed
1 teaspoon paprika (or 1/2 teaspoon saffron)
1/2 teaspoon cumin
1 teaspoon vinegar
150 ml water
salt and pepper
2 eggs
1 tablespoon water
pinch of paprika

ASPARAGUS AU GRATIN
Espárragos gratinados

Snap off the butt ends of the asparagus spears. With a vegetable peeler or sharp knife shave off the thin outer skin of the stalks almost to the tips. Tie them in bundles and cook in plenty of salted water until tender, about 10 minutes. Remove and drain well. Place them in a buttered oven dish.

In a saucepan melt the butter, and sauté the chopped onion and ham for a few minutes. Stir in the flour, then the milk and let it cook, stirring, until thickened. Season with salt and pepper. Spoon the sauce over the asparagus and top with grated cheese. Put in a hot oven or under grill just until top is browned and cheese bubbly. Serves six.

1 kg white and/or green asparagus
3 tablespoons butter
1 tablespoon chopped onion
50 g chopped ham
2 tablespoons flour
220 ml milk
salt and pepper
50 g grated cheese

AUBERGINES (Eggplant)

AUBERGINE MOUSSE
Pastel de berenjenas

The mousse can also be made with other vegetables — carrots, leeks, spinach, broccoli, asparagus. The vegetable pulp can be combined, or baked in three layers, using one egg white and 80 ml of cream for each 230 ml of vegetable pulp.

Roast the aubergines, onion and pepper under the broiler/grill until aubergines are soft when pierced with a knife and peppers are charred. Scoop the aubergine pulp from the skins and chop it with the onion fairly finely (can be done in a food processor). You should have about 700-750 ml of vegetable pulp. Season it with minced garlic, lemon juice, salt, nutmeg and cayenne. Peel the peppers, cut them in strips and set aside.

3 aubergines
1 onion
1 sweet red pepper
1 clove garlic
3 tablespoons lemon juice
1 teaspoon salt
grated nutmeg
dash of cayenne
2 egg whites
1/4 litre cream

When the aubergines and onion mixture is completely cool put it in a food processor with the egg whites and whip the mixture. With the motor running, pour the cream into it in a slow stream. Pour half this mixture into a well-oiled loaf pan. Lay the strips of red pepper on top of it and fill the pan with the rest of the vegetable mixture.

Set the pan in a larger receptacle and add boiling water to half the depth of the pan. Cover the mould with foil and bake in a medium oven until a knife inserted in the centre comes out clean, about 1 1/2 hours. Let the mousse cool for a few minutes in the pan, then unmould it on to a serving platter.

After setting, pour off accumulated liquid in the dish, cover the loaf and chill. Serve it hot or cold with a tomato or garlic sauce. Serves 8 to 10 as a starter.

FRIED AUBERGINES
Berenjenas fritas

Fried aubergine is often served as a tapa drizzled with just a little honey. The salty vegetable contrasts so nicely with sweet honey.

Peel and slice the aubergines thinly. Layer the slices in a colander, sprinkle liberally with salt and let them drain for an hour. Rinse in running water, drain, then pat the slices dry.

Dredge the aubergine slices in flour, then fry them in a frying pan in a small quantity of olive oil (enough to cover the bottom of the pan), adding more oil as needed. Drain on absorbent paper, sprinkle with salt and serve hot, drizzled with honey, if desired.

PICKLED AUBERGINES
Escabeche de berenjena

If aubergines are very tiny (4cm), pierce them with a knife and leave whole. Otherwise cut them in half or quarters and pack into a saucepan. Pour over the olive oil. Add the slivered garlic, sliced onion, lemon, vinegar, water, paprika, oregano, fennel, parsley, salt, pepper and bay. Bring to the boil, reduce heat and cook, covered, until aubergines are tender, 15 minutes.

Remove from heat and let them cool in the liquid. Place in jar or other non-reactive vessel, cover and marinate, refrigerated, for at least 24 hours. Garnish with chopped fennel or parsley.

10 tiny aubergines or 6 small ones
150 ml olive oil
3 cloves garlic, slivered
1 onion, sliced
1 sliced lemon
100 ml vinegar
200 ml water
1 teaspoon paprika
1/2 teaspoon oregano
1 teaspoon chopped fennel leaves
3 tablespoons chopped parsley
1 teaspoon salt
freshly ground pepper
1 bay leaf

AUBERGINES, CATALAN STYLE
Berenjenas a la catalana

Good with grilled and roast meats and a delicious accompaniment to fried eggs.

Peel the aubergines and cut into cubes. Put in a colander, salt them and let them sit for an hour. Rinse, drain and pat dry.

Heat the olive oil in a heat-proof casserole and fry the walnuts or hazelnuts and remove with a skimmer. Add the aubergine to the casserole and sauté it a few minutes. Add the chopped onion and garlic and continue frying. Then add the prepared tomatoes.

Crush the toasted nuts in the mortar or blender to a smooth paste and dissolve it in the stock. Add this to the casserole with salt and pepper and continue

3 medium aubergines
6 walnuts (or 15 hazelnuts)
50 ml olive oil
1 onion, chopped
2 cloves garlic, chopped
2 medium tomatoes, peeled,
　　seeded and chopped
50 ml stock or water
salt and pepper
parsley

cooking until the aubergines are tender. Serve in the same casserole sprinkled with chopped parsley.

BAKED AUBERGINES
Berenjenas al horno

If you use tinned tomato sauce, be sure to flavour it well with crushed garlic, a pinch of cumin and paprika and a dash of cayenne, and chopped parsley or another herb, such as oregano.

Peel the aubergines, cut them in slices, salt and let them drain for an hour. Rinse, drain and pat dry. Dredge them in flour and fry the slices in olive oil, turning once to brown both sides.

Oil an oven casserole and arrange a layer of the fried aubergines in it. Cover with a layer of tomato sauce and grated cheese, then repeat with another layer of aubergines, sauce and cheese. Top with breadcrumbs and dot with butter.

Put in a medium hot oven until bubbly and lightly browned on top, about 20 minutes. Serves six as a side dish.

3 aubergines
salt
flour
olive oil
400 ml tomato sauce
100 g grated cheese
30 g fine breadcrumbs
15 g butter

STUFFED AUBERGINES, MALLORCA STYLE
Berenjenas rellenas a la mallorquina

Cut the aubergines in half lengthwise. With a sharp knife cut out the pulp, leaving the shells about a centimetre thick. Either stew the shells in olive oil until they are soft or place them on a baking tin, brush with oil and bake until soft or boil in water until soft.

Chop the pulp and reserve it (food processor does it quickly). Heat three tablespoons olive oil in a frying pan and sauté the minced meat and chopped ham. Add the chopped onion and aubergine pulp and continue frying a few minutes. Add the tomato, cinnamon and wine. Cook until liquid has evaporated and the mixture is dry.

In a saucepan heat the remaining tablespoon of oil, stir in the flour, then whisk in the milk. Stir this sauce until thickened. Season with a grating of nutmeg and salt and pepper. Add the meat mixture to the sauce and then add one of the eggs, well beaten.

Arrange the aubergine shells in a casserole. Spoon the stuffing mixture into them. Beat the remaining egg and spoon a little of it over each, top with breadcrumbs and drizzle with olive oil. Put in a medium-hot oven for 15 minutes. Makes four main course servings or eight starters.

4 aubergines
4 tablespoons olive oil
200 g minced beef or pork
50 g chopped ham
1 onion, finely chopped
1 tomato, peeled, seeded and chopped
50 g fine breadcrumbs
1/4 teaspoon cinnamon
50 ml white wine or water
1 tablespoon flour
100 ml milk
grating of nutmeg
salt and pepper
2 eggs

MOORISH AUBERGINES
Berenjena a la morisca

Bake or grill the whole aubergines until they are fork-tender. When cool enough to handle, peel them and cut in dice. Place in a bowl and toss with the lemon juice. Add the chopped onion, chopped parsley, oregano, cumin, salt, minced garlic, pepper, minced chili. Drizzle with the olive oil and lemon juice. Serve at room temperature. Serves eight.

4 small aubergines
3 tablespoons lemon juice
1 small onion, finely chopped
1 tablespoon chopped parsley
1/2 teaspoon oregano
1/2 teaspoon cumin
1 teaspoon salt
1 clove garlic, minced
freshly ground pepper
minced chili or dash cayenne
4 tablespoons olive oil
1 tablespoon vinegar or lemon juice

BEANS

CASTILIAN GREEN BEANS
Judías verdes a la castellana

Use either wide, flat green beans or skinny haricots for this recipe.

Snap the ends off the beans and remove strings if necessary. Put them to cook in boiling water until tender. Drain them and keep warm.

While they are cooking, roast the peppers under the broiler/grill until they are charred on all sides. Remove, wrap in a towel until cool enough to handle, then peel them. Remove seeds and cut the flesh into strips.

Heat the olive oil in a frying pan and sauté the diced salt pork or bacon, and add chopped garlic. Add the beans, the strips of pepper, the parsley, salt and pepper. Toss for a minute or two and serve. Makes six servings.

500 g green beans
3 sweet red peppers
3 tablespoons olive oil
50 g salt pork or bacon (optional)
3 cloves garlic
1 tablespoon chopped parsley
1/2 teaspoon salt
freshly ground pepper

GREEN BEAN AND SAUSAGE CASSEROLE
Cazuela de judías verdes con chorizo

Snap the beans into regular size pieces, remove any strings and cook them in boiling water with the bay leaf. When tender, drain, saving the liquid.

Meanwhile peel the potatoes and cut them in thin slices. Heat the olive oil in a heat-proof casserole and fry the potatoes slowly, sprinkling them with the salt. When nearly tender, add the *chorizo*, cut in slices. Fry for a few minutes more, then remove to another plate.

In the same oil fry the chopped onion until softened and add the minced garlic. Stir in the flour, tomato sauce and about 50 ml of the reserved bean liquid. Stir until thickened and return the potatoes, *chorizo* and green beans to the casserole. Season with salt and pepper and simmer another 10 minutes, adding a little more liquid if necessary. Makes six servings.

500 g green beans
1 bay leaf
5 medium potatoes
50 ml olive oil
1/2 teaspoon salt
3 *chorizo* sausages
1 medium onion, chopped
2 cloves garlic, chopped
1 tablespoon flour
3 tablespoons tomato sauce
salt and pepper

SHELLED BEANS, RIOJA STYLE
Pochas a la riojana

These are freshly-shelled beans, harvested when the shells are too dry to be edible, but before the beans have been spread to dry. Use flageolet beans or substitute dried beans — white, pinto or black — soaked before cooking. (For other recipes for dried beans, see the section on *potajes* in Chapter 5.)

Heat half of the lard in a frying pan and sauté the chopped onion and garlic until softened. Stir in the

1 kg shelled beans
350 g lambs' tails or lamb riblets, cut in very
   small pieces
100 g lard or olive oil
1 large onion, chopped
2 chopped cloves garlic
1 teaspoon paprika or 1/2 teaspoon saffron
3 tablespoons chopped parsley
freshly ground pepper
1 teaspoon salt
1 *chorizo* (optional)

paprika or saffron, which has been crushed, and the parsley.

Melt the rest of the lard in a heat-proof casserole and brown the pieces of lamb. When very well browned add about 50 ml of water and part of the sautéed onion mixture. Cover and cook until meat is tender.

Meanwhile, put the shelled beans in a pot, add the rest of the fried onion mixture, the salt and pepper, the *chorizo* if desired, and cold water to cover. Bring to the boil and simmer until nearly tender. Using a skimmer, add the beans to the meat in the casserole with a little of the liquid and cook them together another 15 minutes. Cut the cooked *chorizo* into pieces and use it to garnish the top of the casserole. Serves six.

BROAD BEANS AND HAM
Habas con jamón

Shell the beans. Heat the olive oil in a heat-proof casserole and add the beans, ham and garlic. Fry them on a high heat very briefly, then reduce the flame and let the beans stew in the oil until they are quite tender, about 20 minutes. A little water can be added if needed.

2 kg broad beans
100 ml olive oil
150 g *serrano* ham, diced
4 cloves garlic, chopped
salt and pepper
chopped parsley, fennel or mint

Season with salt and pepper to taste and serve with a sprinkling of one of the chopped herbs. This dish can also be made omitting the ham and using a chopped onion.

BROAD BEANS, CATALAN STYLE
Habas a la catalana

Shell the beans. Heat the lard in a soup pot or heat-proof casserole. Cut the piece of salt pork into six or eight pieces and brown in the lard. Add the chopped scallions or onion and the chopped garlic. Let them brown, then add the shelled beans and the two kinds of *butifarra* sausage.

Season with salt and pepper and add the herbs tied with a thread. Add the sherry or *vino rancio*, the anise brandy and enough water or stock to just cover the beans. Cook them, covered tightly, until very tender, about 35 minutes. Discard the bouquet garni. Cut the sausages into pieces and arrange on top of the beans. Sprinkle with chopped parsley. Makes six to eight servings.

4 kg broad beans
2 tablespoons lard
6 scallions or 1 onion, chopped
3 cloves garlic
200 g *butifarra* (white Catalan sausage)
200 g *butifarra negra* (Catalan
   black pudding)
150 g streaky salt pork
salt and pepper
bouquet garni of thyme, bay, rosemary,
   mint and cinnamon stick
60 ml medium-dry sherry or a *vino rancio*,
   if available
2 tablespoons dry anise brandy
chopped parsley

BROAD BEANS, ALICANTE STYLE
Faves al tombet

Wash the lettuce and chop it. Mix with the shelled beans. Heat the olive oil in a flame-proof casserole and fry the bread and the garlic. When toasted, remove to mortar or blender and mash with the water, vinegar and paprika.

Add the beans and chopped lettuce to the same oil and sauté for several minutes. Then add the bread paste and salt and pepper and a small quantity of water. Cover the casserole and cook the beans very slowly until tender, about 25 minutes. Serves four.

800 g shelled broad beans
2 lettuces
4 tablespoons olive oil
1 slice bread
3 cloves garlic
50 ml water
1 tablespoon vinegar
1 teaspoon paprika
salt and pepper

CASSEROLE OF BROAD BEANS, GRANADA STYLE
Cazuela de habas a la granadina

Trim the artichokes (they are easier to manage in the finished dish if cut down to the hearts only, or substitute frozen artichoke hearts). Blanch in boiling water for five minutes. Shell the beans and blanch for five minutes. Drain and reserve.

Heat the olive oil in a heat-proof casserole and fry the bread and garlic until toasted. Remove and set aside. Add the chopped scallions to the same oil and fry until slightly browned. Add the blanched beans and artichokes and sauté a few minutes more. Add the prepared tomatoes and the bouquet garni. Add enough water to barely cover. Cover the casserole and simmer.

Meanwhile, in mortar or blender crush the saffron, cumin and peppercorns with the fried bread and garlic. Dilute with a little of the liquid from the vegetables and add this mixture to the casserole. Season to taste with salt and cook until beans are quite tender.

Break eggs on top of the vegetables and put the casserole in a hot oven just until the whites are set (can also be spooned into individual casseroles). Garnish with a little chopped parsley or chopped mint. Serves six.

12 artichokes
3 kg broad beans
60 ml olive oil
1 slice bread
3 cloves garlic
6 scallions or 1 onion, chopped
2 tomatoes, peeled, seeded and chopped
bouquet garni of bay, parsley and mint
1/4 teaspoon saffron
1/2 teaspoon cumin
6 peppercorns
salt
6 eggs

BROAD BEANS IN THEIR BREECHES
Habas con calzón

Use very young, tender broad beens (fava) for this dish, which is prepared without shelling the beans.

Snap off the ends, remove any strings and break the beans in half. Put them to cook in water to cover with the potatoes, quartered onion, 3 tablespoons of olive oil and ham bone. Cook until beans are tender.

Drain and place in a serving bowl, discarding the bone. Heat remaining oil in a small frying pan and fry the chopped garlic with the diced ham. Toss with the beans, season with salt and pepper and serve garnished with chopped parsley or mint. Serves four to six.

1 kg small broad beans
3 medium potatoes
1 onion, quartered chopped
3 tablespoons + 50 ml olive oil
1 piece ham bone
2 cloves garlic
salt and pepper
parsley or mint
100 g ham (optional)

CABBAGE

WHITE CABBAGE WITH GARLIC SAUCE
Col blanca con ajoaceite

Cut white cabbage into wedges and boil in salted water to which two tablespoons of vinegar have been added. When tender, drain, saving some of the liquid, and place in a serving bowl.

Meanwhile, crush two cloves garlic and mix them into 125 ml mayonnaise (or make *alioli* page 352). Beating constantly, add a little of the hot, reserved cabbage liquid to the sauce to thin it. Pour over the cabbage and serve. Potatoes can be cooked with the cabbage if desired.

CABBAGE, VALENCIA STYLE
Repollo a la valenciana

Chop the cabbage and cook in boiling salted water until tender. Drain. In a casserole, heat olive oil and in it sauté two chopped cloves of garlic. Add the cabbage and sauté for a few minutes. Then add pitted and chopped olives and capers. Toss the cabbage and serve.

CABBAGE ROLLS, SEVILLE STYLE
Liadillos sevillanos

To remove the leaves from the cabbage, cut all around the core with a sharp knife, then put the whole cabbage into a pot of boiling water for one minute. Remove it and drain. The leaves should easily separate from the head. (Save inner leaves for another dish.) Return the leaves to the boiling water and blanch them for about three minutes. Drain and set aside.

In a frying pan sauté the minced meat in the oil until browned. Add the salt pork or bacon, chopped, and the ham, diced. Season with salt and pepper and nutmeg. Remove from heat and add the chopped parsley, minced garlic and chopped olives. Add one beaten egg to the mixture.

Spread out a cabbage leaf, place a spoonful of the filling on it and roll it up, securing with a pick or string. When all the leaves are rolled, dredge them in flour, dip in beaten egg, then breadcrumbs, and sauté until browned in olive oil or lard. Serves four.

12 large cabbage leaves
2 tablespoons olive oil
200 g minced meat
50 g salt pork or bacon
50 g ham
salt and pepper
grating of nutmeg
1 tablespoon chopped parsley
1 clove garlic, minced
15 black olives, pitted and chopped
flour
2 eggs
breadcrumbs
olive oil or lard

STUFFED CABBAGE
Col rellena

This is one of my favourite supper dishes, so satisfying on a chilly winter's night. There are several ways to stuff a cabbage. The one I like best is to remove all the leaves from the head of cabbage (as in preceding recipe). Place them on a clean, dampened cloth or towel in layers with the filling, keeping the "construction" as round as possible. Then tie the corners of the cloth together, making a round ball. Cook, and remove the cloth to serve.

The second way is to cut out the core and some of the inner leaves, leaving a hollow in the cabbage (works best with tight-leafed head of cabbage). Fill the hollow with stuffing and cover with one or two large leaves.

The third way, which is nice with the loose-leafed curly cabbage, is to stuff each leaf. First blanch the whole head of cabbage briefly and drain well. Gently spread apart the leaves. Starting in the centre, spread a little stuffing mixture on each leaf and press it closed. Continue until all the leaves have been stuffed. Tie with string to keep the stuffing in place.

Prepare the cabbage for stuffing as described above. Season the minced meat with one clove of garlic, finely minced, and the salt and let it sit for 15 minutes.

In a frying pan heat three tablespoons olive oil. Chop one of the onions and sauté it with one clove of minced garlic. Then add the meat and brown it. Add the prepared tomatoes, chopped green pepper and parsley. Fry for a few minutes, then add the wine and cook until liquid has evaporated. (Finely chopped, leftover cooked meat can also be used.) Beat the egg and add to meat.

Stuff the cabbage with this mixture in one of the ways described above. In a large pot heat the remaining oil and brown the cabbage (unless you are using the method in which cabbage is tied in cloth). Add the remaining onion, cut in quarters.

1 large cabbage
300 g minced meat
3 cloves garlic
1 teaspoon salt
75 ml olive oil
2 onions
2 tomatoes, peeled, seeded and chopped
1 small green pepper
2 tablespoons chopped parsley
50 ml white wine
1 egg
150 g ham or bacon
3 carrots
1/2 litre stock
salt and pepper

In the mortar crush the remaining clove of garlic with the parsley. Dissolve in a little of the stock and pour over the cabbage. Dice the ham or bacon and add to the pot with the carrots, peeled and cut in short lengths.

Add the stock, bring to the boil and simmer the cabbage, covered, for about an hour and a half. Remove the cooked cabbage to a serving platter, removing the string or cloth. Sieve the remaining juice and thicken it slightly with one tablespoon of flour. Scatter the carrots and pieces of ham around the cabbage and pour some of the sauce over it. Serves four.

RED CABBAGE, CASTILIAN STYLE
Lombarda a la castellana

This dish is served in many parts of Spain on *Noche Buena*, Christmas Eve. In some regions the Christmas Eve dinner, before taking communion at midnight mass, is a "fasting" meal, with no meat. In other places it is definitely a "feast" and the red cabbage would accompany stuffed turkey or other meats.

Shred a large red cabbage and put it to cook in salted water with a few spoonfuls of olive oil, an onion stuck with two cloves and a bay leaf. Cook for 10 minutes and drain. In a casserole heat three tablespoons of olive oil, add one chopped clove of garlic, one apple, peeled and diced, two tablespoons chopped parsley and the cooked cabbage. Sauté for several minutes, seasoning with salt and white pepper. Add 50 ml white wine and cook until liquid is absorbed. Serve hot. Serves eight.

CARDOONS

CARDOONS
Cardos

If you were to cross an artichoke with celery, you would have a cardoon. *Cardo*, a thistle, is related to the artichoke and can be prepared as for artichokes or asparagus. The outer leaves are stripped off, the stalk is peeled and rubbed with lemon juice to prevent its darkening. Cook in acidulated water for an hour. Drain and serve with a bechamel sauce or the following garlic-almond sauce.

Heat the olive oil in a saucepan and sauté the chopped garlic. Stir in the flour, let it cook until lightly coloured, then add the white wine and about 150 ml of the liquid in which the cardoons cooked. Cook, stirring constantly, until the sauce is thickened.

Crush the almonds in mortar or blender with the peppercorns. Season with salt and dissolve in a little liquid. Add to the sauce. Return the cooked cardoons to the sauce and heat thoroughly.

3 tablespoons olive oil
2 cloves garlic, chopped
1 tablespoon flour
50 ml white wine
100 g almonds, blanched and
    peeled
5 peppercorns
salt

CARROTS

CARROTS BRAISED IN MÁLAGA WINE
Zanahorias con vino de Málaga

Peel the carrots, slice them and cook in boiling, salted water until almost tender, about 10 minutes. Drain.

Heat the olive oil in a frying pan and sauté the carrots very gently, turning them with a fork so

1 kg carrots
4 tablespoons olive oil
2 tablespoons stock
100 ml Málaga wine
salt and pepper

they brown very lightly. Add the stock, wine, salt and pepper and cook until the liquid is partly evaporated and carrots are very tender, about 20 minutes. Serves six to eight.

CAULIFLOWER

CAULIFLOWER WITH GARLIC SAUCE
Coliflor al ajiaceite

Cut the cauliflower into flowerets. Where stalks are especially thick, slice into them almost to the flower head so they will cook quicker. Bring salted water to the boil and add the cauliflower. Cook without covering until just tender, about 12 minutes. Drain and rinse with cold water.

In the mortar or blender crush the garlic with the parsley and celery leaves. Drizzle the bread with the vinegar, then add enough water to cover. Soak briefly, then squeeze out and discard the liquid. Add the bread to the garlic and crush to a paste. Add the olive oil, drop by drop, beating hard until it is all incorporated. Season with salt and pepper and thin, as desired, with a little water.

Place the cooked cauliflower in a serving bowl and pour the sauce over. Garnish with parsley and strips of red pepper. Serves eight.

1 large cauliflower
2 cloves garlic
1 sprig parsley
1 sprig celery leaves
1 slice bread, crusts removed
2 tablespoons vinegar
100 ml olive oil
salt and pepper

CAULIFLOWER, MULE DRIVER'S STYLE
Coliflor al ajo arriero

Cook the cauliflower as in the recipe for cauliflower with garlic sauce. Drain, reserving a little of the cooking liquid, and place the cauliflower in a serving bowl.

In a frying pan heat 75 ml olive oil and in it sauté four cloves of chopped garlic. Remove from heat and stir in one teaspoon paprika, one tablespoon vinegar, two tablespoons chopped parsley and two tablespoons liquid. Pour this sauce over the cooked cauliflower.

CHARD

Chard, *acelga,* is a wonderfully versatile vegetable because it can go white or green or both. The stalks can be prepared in any way suitable for cooked celery, leeks or asparagus (very nice *au gratin*), and the leaves in any way in which spinach is cooked.

FRIED CHARD STALKS
Acelga frita

Fried chard makes a good garnish for meat dishes and is also good as an appetiser, served with lemon wedges or a dipping sauce. Sometimes chard stalks are sandwiched with ham and cheese, then breaded and fried.

Cut off the green leaves and save them for another use (cook as for spinach). Remove strings from chard stalks and cut them into short lengths, about 5cm. Cook in boiling, salted water until just tender, but not limp. Drain and pat dry.

Dredge the pieces in flour, dip in beaten egg, then coat in breadcrumbs. Fry in hot olive oil, turning the pieces once, until crisply golden. Remove and sprinkle with salt. Serves six.

1 dozen chard stalks
flour
1 egg, beaten
breadcrumbs
olive oil
salt

CHARD, MÁLAGA STYLE
Acelgas a la malagueña

Chop the chard, both stalks and leaves, removing strings. Cook the chard in boiling, salted water until tender, about 25 minutes. Drain well and set aside.

Meanwhile, in a frying pan sauté the chopped garlic in the olive oil. When golden, add the raisins and cook briefly, then add the cooked chard. Toss it and season with salt and pepper and serve hot, sprinkled with toasted pine-nuts, if desired. Serves six. Spinach can be prepared in the same manner.

1 1/2 kg chard
3 tablespoons oil
3 cloves garlic, chopped
100 g Málaga raisins, seeded
salt and pepper
pine-nuts (optional)

COURGETTES (Zucchini)

STUFFED COURGETTES
Calabacines rellenos

This version of stuffed courgette, which contains no meat, makes an admirable accompaniment to a simple main course such as roast chicken, or might serve as a light luncheon dish. For a more substantial preparation, prepare as for stuffed aubergine. The usual manner of stuffing a courgette is to split it lengthwise and scoop out the pulp. However, a very attractive way is to split the courgettes crosswise into pieces of about 8cm. Serve them upright on a plate.

Wash the courgettes and cook them whole in boiling water just until they can be easily pierced with a fork, about 10 minutes. Drain and cut them in half lengthwise. With a spoon hollow out the pulp.

Heat the olive oil in a frying pan and sauté the chopped onion and chopped green pepper until onion is soft. Add the tomatoes and the pulp of the courgettes, finely chopped. Crush the garlic in a mortar with the parsley and add to the pan with the paprika, brandy, salt and chopped egg. Cook the mixture until liquid has evaporated, about 10 minutes.

Spoon the mixture into the courgette shells and place in an oiled oven dish. Sprinkle with grated cheese and bake in a hot oven until the cheese is melted, about 10 minutes. Serves six to eight.

2 large courgettes (zucchini)
3 tablespoons olive oil
1 onion, chopped
1 green pepper, chopped
3 medium tomatoes, peeled, seeded and chopped
2 cloves garlic
1 tablespoon parsley
1/4 teaspoon paprika
2 tablespoons brandy
1/2 teaspoon salt
1 hard-boiled egg
50 g grated cheese

SEPHARDIM-STYLE COURGETTE TIMBALE
Fritada de calabacín sefardí

Grate the courgettes and place in a colander. Sprinkle with the salt and let sit 10 minutes to drain.

Squeeze the courgette pulp, then place in a bowl and mix with eggs, butter or olive oil, breadcrumbs and grated cheese. Season with salt and pepper to taste. Pour into a greased baking dish and bake in a medium oven until set, about one hour. Serves six.

1 kg courgettes
1 teaspoon salt
3 eggs, lightly beaten
3 tablespoons melted butter or olive oil
2 tablespoons fine breadcrumbs
75 g grated cheese
salt and pepper

BAKED COURGETTES
Calabacines al horno

Cut the courgettes into crosswise slices. Dredge them in flour and fry in olive oil, turning to brown both sides. As they are cooked, arrange in layers in an oven dish.

In the remaining oil fry the chopped onion and garlic until soft. Add the prepared tomatoes, parsley, salt and pepper. Cook for about 15 minutes, until reduced to a sauce. Purée this mixture in a blender or sieve and pour it over the courgettes. Top with the grated cheese and bake in a medium oven until the cheese is melted, 10 to 15 minutes. Serves six to eight.

3 or 4 small courgettes
50 ml olive oil
flour
1 onion, finely chopped
2 cloves garlic, chopped .
2 large tomatoes, peeled,
    seeded and chopped
2 tablespoons chopped parsley
salt and pepper
75 g grated cheese

LEEKS

STEWED LEEKS
Purrusalda

This Basque dish is usually made with *bacalao,* salt cod. However, it's a delicious preparation on its own, as an accompaniment to any other fish or poultry dish. It can be served "soupy" or "dry".

Clean the leeks very well and slice them, including a little of the green part. Heat the olive oil in a saucepan and fry the garlic just until toasted, and remove. Add the sliced leeks to the oil and sauté very gently. Peel the potatoes and cut into pieces similar in size to the leeks. Add to the oil with the bay leaf, salt and pepper.

Add the water or stock (it can be poultry or fish stock or, if using *bacalao,* the liquid in which the codfish cooked). In the mortar crush the fried garlic with the paprika and add to the vegetables. Cook slowly for about 35 minutes, or until the leeks are very tender and the potatoes almost disintegrated. Serves four to six.

3/4 kg leeks (about 8)
50 ml olive oil
2 cloves garlic
1/2 kg potatoes
1 bay leaf
salt and pepper
1/2 teaspoon paprika
1/4 litre water or stock

MUSHROOMS

GRILLED MUSHROOMS
Rovellons a la brasa

This simple preparation can be used for any kind of mushroom, wild or cultivated. Wipe the *rovellons* clean, but do not wash them unless they seem very dry. Put them whole on to a hot griddle or a grill over charcoal and drizzle with olive oil. Turn them after five minutes and grill the reverse side. Sprinkle with more oil, a few drops of water and chopped parsley and garlic if desired.

GARLIC-SIZZLED MUSHROOMS
Champiñones al ajillo

Clean the mushrooms. Slice them if they are large or quarter them if small. Heat the olive oil in a frying pan or earthenware casserole and sauté the mushrooms, adding the chopped cloves of garlic after a few minutes and the chili pepper if desired.

When mushrooms are cooked, about 10 minutes, season with salt and pepper and sprinkle with parsley. Serve hot. Serves four as a starter or side dish.

1/2 kg mushrooms
100 ml olive oil
1 head garlic
1 dry red chili pepper (optional)
1/2 teaspoon salt
freshly ground pepper
2 tablespoons chopped parsley

MUSHROOMS WITH SHERRY
Setas al jerez

Clean the mushrooms well and cut into regular-sized pieces. Heat the olive oil in a frying pan or casserole and put in the mushrooms. Fry until they stop sweating out liquid (some wild mushrooms, such as the boletus, will need about 20 minutes or more of cooking).

Add the chopped onion and garlic. When browned, add the sherry, salt and pepper, and simmer for 10 minutes. Serve sprinkled with chopped egg and parsley. Serves six.

500 g mushrooms
50 ml olive oil
1/2 onion, chopped
2 cloves garlic, chopped
125 ml dry sherry
salt and pepper
1 hard-boiled egg
chopped parsley

EARTH BALLS (TRUFFLES), EXTREMADURA STYLE
Criadillas de la tierra a la extremeña

Brush the truffles (they are found in Extremadura, Catalonia and Castellón), clean off grit, wash and dry them. Chop very finely. Heat lard or olive oil in a frying pan and sauté in it some finely sliced onion and minced garlic. Add the chopped truffles and sauté for a few minutes. Add meat stock to cover and simmer for a few minutes more. Skim the truffles out and reserve.

Beat two egg yolks with one tablespoon vinegar for each 1/4 litre of stock. Stir this into the stock and cook, stirring, until the sauce is thickened. Pour over the truffles and serve.

ONIONS

GRILLED SPRING ONIONS
Calçotada de Valls

A Catalan speciality, this is a fine addition to a barbecue. The grilled onions would traditionally be served with grilled pork chops and *butifarra* sausage.

The onions should be 2-3 cm thick and 15-20 cm long. Lay them on the grill over hot coals and cook until charred. To eat, peel back the charred skin with the fingers, dip the roasted onion into sauce and eat. Serve with a *romesco* sauce and *alioli* (Chapter 12).

BRAISED ONIONS
Cebollas guisadas

Peel outer skins from the onions. If small, leave them whole, otherwise cut in halves or quarters. Put them in a saucepan with the whole garlic cloves, olive oil, bay leaf, peppercorns and clove. Put on a medium heat and toss them in the oil, without letting the onions brown.

Add the paprika, salt and wine, cover the pan and cook slowly until the onions are quite tender, about 25 minutes, shaking the pan from time to time to prevent the onions from scorching. Serves four.

1/2 kg tiny onions (about 2 dozen)
3 cloves garlic
3 tablespoons olive oil
1 bay leaf
5 peppercorns
1 clove
1/2 teaspoon paprika
1/2 teaspoon salt
50 ml white wine

PEAS

PEAS, VALENCIA STYLE
Guisantes a la valenciana

Shell the peas. Heat the olive oil in a saucepan and add the peas, the chopped onion and one clove of garlic. Sauté briefly, then add the wine, anise and herbs. Cover and simmer until the peas are nearly tender.

Meanwhile crush the other clove of garlic in the mortar with the saffron and cumin. Dissolve in a little water and add to the peas with the salt and pepper. Simmer until peas are tender. Serve garnished with strips of red pepper and chopped parsley. Serves six.

1 kg peas
3 tablespoons olive oil
1 onion, chopped
2 cloves garlic
100 ml white wine
1 tablespoon anise brandy
bay, thyme and parsley
1/4 teaspoon saffron
1/4 teaspoon cumin
salt and pepper
strips of red pepper

PEPPERS

FRIED PEPPERS
Pimientos fritos

Make these with skinny green frying peppers or with *pimientos de Padrón*, small green peppers famous in Galicia. The peppers are picked up by the stems and eaten whole, discarding the stem and seeds. They are usually served as a *tapa,* but make a nice side dish with meat or poultry.

Wash and dry the peppers. Cut a slit in the bottom end of each and rub a pinch of salt inside each one. Fry slowly in the olive oil, turning to ensure both sides are cooked. Serve when very tender.

16 small green peppers (not bell peppers)
salt
100 ml olive oil

STUFFED PEPPERS
Pimientos rellenos

Roast the peppers under the broiler/grill until skins are charred, and remove. Cover with a cloth and let sit until cool enough to handle. Then carefully peel the skins off and cut out stems and seeds.

Season the minced meat with finely minced garlic and let it rest 15 minutes. Heat three tablespoons of the olive oil in a saucepan and sauté all but one tablespoon of the chopped onion until soft. Add the prepared tomatoes and fry for five minutes. Add two tablespoons chopped parsley, 50 ml white wine and salt and pepper and cook until the sauce is reduced, about 15 minutes. Sieve or purée in the blender.

Heat the remaining two tablespoons oil in a frying pan and add the meat and spoonful of chopped onion. Fry until meat is browned. Meanwhile, soak the bread slices in water or milk until spongy. Squeeze out and add bread to the meat, mashing it with the back of a fork. Season with salt and pepper and nutmeg. Stir in remainder of the wine and cook the mixture, stirring to prevent it sticking, for several minutes. Remove from heat and stir in one beaten egg and the rest of the parsley. (A more homogenous stuffing is made by chopping the mixture in the processor.)

Spoon the mixture into the prepared peppers, taking care not to split them. Dip the stuffed peppers in beaten egg, then in flour and fry in hot olive oil until browned. Place in an oven dish and pour over the sieved sauce. Bake the peppers for 20 minutes in a medium oven. Makes six servings.

6 medium bell peppers
1/2 kg minced meat (pork and/or beef)
1 clove garlic
5 tablespoons olive oil
1 onion, chopped
3 tomatoes, peeled, seeded and chopped
3 tablespoons chopped parsley
80 ml white wine
2 slices bread (75 g) crusts removed
salt and pepper
grated nutmeg
2 eggs
flour
olive oil

PIQUANT PEPPERS STUFFED WITH FISH
Pimientos de piquillo rellenos con pescado

These peppers are smaller than bell peppers, with a pointy bottom and a slight "bite" or piquancy. They are purchased already roasted and peeled, in tins. Although salt cod is the most traditional filling, the peppers are delicious with any fish or shellfish.

Heat the butter or olive oil in a saucepan and sauté the minced onion and garlic until softened, about two minutes. Stir in the flour and cook, stirring, a further two minutes. Whisk in the milk and season with nutmeg, salt, pepper and cayenne. Cook, stirring constantly, until sauce is thickened, about eight minutes. Set aside about five tablespoons of the sauce. Add half the sauce to the cooked fish or shellfish, flaked or chopped.

Drain and rinse the peppers. Very carefully fill them with the fish mixture and place in an oiled oven dish. Stir the reserved sauce with the white wine and paprika and cook five minutes. Pour over the stuffed peppers. Cover and bake in a medium oven for 15 minutes or until heated through.

8 peppers (460 g)
300 g cooked fish or shellfish
3 tablespoons butter or olive oil
1/2 onion, minced
1 clove garlic, minced
3 tablespoons flour
1/2 litre milk
grating of fresh nutmeg
salt and pepper
dash of cayenne
8 tablespoons white wine
1 teaspoon paprika

POTATOES

Visitors to Spain dining only in restaurants might surmise that the ubiquitous *patatas fritas* (chips or fries) and an occasional boiled potato are the only way potatoes are ever cooked here. These two preparations are the most usual garnishes for main-course dishes. However, dozens of delicious potato dishes in the Spanish repertoire seldom turn up on restaurant menus. Many are meant to stand on their own two feet — as a first course in place of a soup or vegetable dish, or a main course for a light meal. These are among my favourites.

POTATOES, RIOJA STYLE
Patatas a la riojana

Peel the potatoes and cut them in chunks or thick strips. Heat the olive oil in a pan and fry slowly, without letting them brown. Cut the pork loin in pieces and add to the potatoes and continue frying.

In the mortar or blender crush the garlic, peppercorns, chili pepper, paprika and salt. Dissolve in the water and add to the potatoes. *Chorizo*, cut in slices, may also be added. Cover and cook until potatoes are tender, about 30 minutes. Let sit 10 minutes before serving, garnished with chopped egg. Serves four. Try this dish, without the pork, served alongside grilled pork chops.

1 kg potatoes (7 medium)
100 ml olive oil
1/4 kg pork loin
2 cloves garlic
10 peppercorns
1 small dry red chili pepper
1 teaspoon paprika
2 teaspoons salt
150 ml water
chorizo (optional)
hard-boiled eggs

GRANNY'S POTATO CASSEROLE
Cazuela de papas a la abuela

This *pueblo* dish often has pieces of fish and shellfish added to it, in which case it makes a main course. *Papas* are an endearing term for potatoes. This dish is also called *ajo pollo*.

Heat the olive oil in a pan and fry the almonds, two cloves garlic and bread until golden and toasted. Remove and set aside.

In the same oil fry the chopped onion and green pepper until softened. Add the chopped tomato and fry until reduced to a sauce, about 15 minutes. Meanwhile, in mortar or blender crush the peppercorns, cloves, saffron, fried garlic and one clove raw garlic, almonds and fried bread. Dilute in some of the water and add it to the pot with the remaining water, salt, bay leaf and paprika.

50 ml olive oil
40 g almonds, blanched (about 25)
3 cloves garlic
1 slice bread, crusts removed
1 small onion, chopped
1 small green pepper, chopped
1 tomato, peeled, seeded and chopped
6 peppercorns
2 cloves
1/4 teaspoon saffron
1/2 litre water
1 teaspoon salt
1 bay leaf
1/2 teaspoon paprika
1 1/2 kg potatoes

Peel the potatoes and cut them in chunks and add to the pot. Simmer until the potatoes are tender, but not mushy, about 30 minutes. Let them sit for 10 minutes before serving. Liquid should remain. If fish and shellfish are to be used, add the pieces of fish during the last 10 minutes of cooking. Garnish with sprigs of parsley. Serves four to six.

POTATOES IN GREEN SAUCE
Patatas en salsa verde

Peel the potatoes and cut them in thin slices. In a pan or casserole, heat the olive oil and add the sliced potatoes, turning them so they don't brown. Add the chopped garlic and onion and continue frying. Stir in the flour, mixing it well.

Add two tablespoons parsley and the water or stock and wine. Bring to the boil, then reduce to a simmer. Season with salt and pepper and cook until the potatoes are tender. Do not stir the potatoes, for they will break up, but shake the pan occasionally to prevent sticking. Garnish with lots of chopped parsley and a little chopped egg. Serves six.

1 kg potatoes
100 ml olive oil
6 cloves garlic, chopped
2 tablespoons chopped onion
1 tablespoon flour
chopped parsley
200 ml water or stock
50 ml white wine
salt and pepper
hard-boiled egg

POTATOES WITH MUSSELS
Patatas con mejillones

Heat the olive oil in a pot or casserole and sauté the onions. Peel the potatoes and cut them into chunks and add to the onions with the tomatoes, frying for several minutes. Add the wine, water, salt and pepper, bay leaf and thyme and simmer until potatoes are nearly tender.

Meanwhile, scrub the mussels well, put in a pot and cover them. Place over high heat, shaking the pan, until the shells open. Remove from heat. Discard the shells, adding the mussels to the potatoes with the vinegar. Strain their cooking liquid through a fine sieve on to the potatoes. Cook for a few minutes more and serve, lavishly sprinkled with parsley. Serves four to six.

3 tablespoons olive oil
1 onion, finely chopped
1 kg potatoes
1 tomato, peeled and chopped
50 ml white wine
150 ml water
salt and pepper
1 bay leaf
pinch of thyme
2 dozen mussels
chopped parsley
1 teaspoon vinegar

WRINKLED POTATOES
Patatas arrugadas

Cook small, unpeeled potatoes in very little water with coarse salt until they are tender and all the water is boiled away. The potato skins will wrinkle. Serve the potatoes with *mojo verde* or with *alioli* (Chapter 12).

BOLD POTATOES
Patatas bravas

Parboil potatoes. Drain, peel and cut in 3cm cubes. Deep-fry or sauté in hot olive oil until browned and crisp. Drain and serve immediately, sprinkled with salt.

For the sauce, combine 175 ml tomato sauce with four tablespoons mayonnaise, one clove crushed garlic, one tablespoon vinegar, one teaspoon paprika, half a teaspoon ground cumin and enough chili pepper or cayenne to make the sauce *picante,* spicy-hot. Spoon the sauce over the potatoes, or serve separately for dipping.

POOR MAN'S POTATOES
Patatas a lo pobre

Peel the potatoes and slice them fairly thinly. Peel and slice the onions. Cut peppers in strips. Pour a little of the olive oil into the bottom of a flame-proof casserole and arrange the potatoes, peppers and onions in layers in it. Sprinkle with the garlic, finely chopped, the chopped parsley and the bay leaves broken into pieces, and sprinkle with paprika. Pour over the rest of the oil.

Place on a medium flame until potatoes start to sizzle. Add the wine and water. Season with salt and pepper. When the liquid comes to the boil, cover the casserole with foil and put in a medium oven until potatoes are tender, about 30 minutes. Let the casserole rest for a few minutes before serving. Serves six to eight.

2 kg potatoes
2 onions
2 small green peppers
150 ml olive oil
3 cloves garlic
3 tablespoons chopped parsley
2 bay leaves
1/2 teaspoon paprika
100 ml white wine
100 ml water
salt and pepper

POTATOES STEWED IN GARLIC SAUCE, JAÉN STYLE
Ajoharina de Jaén

Soak the dried pepper in boiling water to cover. Either mash it well in the mortar or scrape the flesh from the skin. (If not available, use a little paprika.)

Heat the olive oil in a pan and fry the potatoes, peeled and sliced, very slowly without browning. Add the paprika, salt and the water. In the mortar, crush the garlic with the peppercorns and flour. Dissolve in some of the liquid from the pan. Stir this mixture into the potatoes and continue cooking until tender. Let sit a few minutes before serving. Serves four to six. Serve the *ajoharina* also with spinach.

1 dried pepper (*ñora, choricero*)
50 ml olive oil
1 kg potatoes (7 medium)
1 teaspoon paprika
salt
1/4 litre water
2 cloves garlic
8 peppercorns
1 tablespoon flour

PUMPKIN

"FRIED" PUMPKIN
Calabaza frita

Peel the pumpkin and cut into large dice. Heat the olive oil in a pan and fry the slices of bread and the garlic until golden and crisped. Remove them. Add the prepared pumpkin to the same oil and sauté for a few minutes.

Cover the pot and let the pumpkin stew in the oil. In the mortar mash the fried garlic and bread with the vinegar and oregano, salt and pepper. Add to the pumpkin and continue cooking until tender, adding just a little water if necessary. Serves four. Very good served with pork.

1 kg pumpkin
50 ml olive oil
2 slices bread, crusts removed
3 cloves garlic
1 tablespoon vinegar
1 tablespoon oregano
salt and pepper

STEWED PUMPKIN
Calabaza guisada

Peel the pumpkin and cut in thin slices. Layer it in a pan or casserole with the peppers, cut in strips, sliced onions, sliced tomatoes. Sprinkle with the chopped garlic, cumin, salt. Add the bay leaf, broken into a few pieces, and drizzle the olive oil over all. Add the water. Bring the vegetables to a simmer, cover the pan and stew or bake until very tender.

Serve as a vegetable dish, or add stock and serve as a soup, or purée the mixture and use as a sauce (good with stuffed aubergines, meatballs, fritters). Serves six to eight.

1 kg pumpkin
2 red or green peppers
1 onion
2 tomatoes
2 chopped cloves garlic
1/2 teaspoon cumin
1 teaspoon salt
1 bay leaf
4 tablespoons olive oil
1/4 litre water

SPINACH

SPINACH, CÓRDOBA STYLE
Espinacas a la cordobesa

Wash the spinach well, trim off stems and cook in just a little water until it is limp. Drain very well.

In a frying pan heat the olive oil and fry the chopped onion and garlic. Remove from heat when soft and stir in the paprika, vinegar, cinnamon and salt. Add the spinach to the sauce and reheat it very briefly, mixing well. Serves four.

1 1/2 kg spinach
50 ml olive oil
1/2 onion, finely chopped
2 cloves garlic, chopped
1 teaspoon paprika
2 teaspoons vinegar
1/4 teaspoon cinnamon
1/2 teaspoon salt

CATALAN SPINACH PASTIES
Panadons amb espinacs

Cook the spinach in just a little water until wilted. Drain well and chop finely.

In a frying pan heat two tablespoons olive oil and add the chopped garlic. Toss the chopped spinach in the olive oil, adding the seeded and chopped raisins and the pine-nuts. Season with salt and set aside.

Place the sifted flour in a bowl and mix with half a teaspoon salt. Drizzle in remainder of the oil and mix with the flour. Then add just enough water to make a pliable dough. Knead it very briefly to mix, and chill the dough.

Roll out on a floured board. Cut into rounds of about 10cm. Place a spoonful of the spinach on each round. Fold over and twist the edges together to seal. Brush the pasties with beaten egg and bake in a medium oven until browned.

250 g frozen spinach
100 ml olive oil
2 cloves garlic
25 g Málaga raisins, seeded
25 g pine-nuts
salt
175 g sifted flour
water (about 2 tablespoons)
1 beaten egg

SPINACH FRITTERS
Fritos de espinacas

Wash and trim the spinach and cook in a very little water until limp. Drain well and chop finely.

Heat two tablespoons olive oil in a frying pan and sauté the chopped onion and garlic until softened. Add the spinach and fry until heated. Beat three of the eggs and mix into the spinach, cooking as a *tortilla* until set. Season with salt and pepper and let cool.

Cut into squares and dip them in beaten egg and flour. Fry in hot olive oil, turning to brown both sides. Serve hot with lemon wedges.

1 kg spinach
olive oil
2 tablespoons chopped onion
2 cloves garlic
salt and freshly ground pepper
4 eggs
flour

MIXED VEGETABLES

MIXED VEGETABLE MEDLEY
Menestra de verduras

Typically, this casserole is made with vegetables in season at the same time — artichokes, broad beans and peas in the spring, green beans, potatoes, courgettes and pumpkin in the summer. It's also a good way to prepare frozen vegetables.

Cook each of the vegetables separately until tender, and reserve.

Heat the olive oil in an earthenware *cazuela*, casserole, or frying pan and in it fry the chopped onion and garlic. Add the diced ham and the chopped pepper and fry a few minutes more. Add the cooked and drained vegetables and sauté briefly.

Sprinkle with the flour, season with salt and pepper and paprika and stir in the tomato sauce and water. Cook on a medium heat for 10 minutes and serve garnished with a sprig of parsley or mint. Serves four to six.

1/4 kg shelled peas
1/4 kg artichoke hearts
1/4 kg shelled broad beans
50 ml olive oil
1/2 onion, chopped
2 cloves garlic, chopped
200 g serrano ham, diced
1 red pepper
1 tablespoon flour
salt and pepper
1/2 teaspoon paprika
3 tablespoons tomato sauce
100 ml water
parsley or mint

STEWED SUMMER VEGETABLES
Pisto

This is the French *ratatouille,* the Catalan *samfaina,*
the *tumbet* of the Balearics and La Mancha's *alboronia,*
which is what the Moors called it some centuries
ago before there were tomatoes and peppers to
make it so piquant. In Spain, it may be served on its
own, cool as an hors-d'oeuvre or salad, or hot as a
vegetable, or accompanied by fried eggs for a light
supper dish. It's also a flavourful cooking medium
for fish, meat and poultry. Try fresh tuna with *pisto,*
pork or chicken stewed in *pisto.* I particularly like
pisto with the addition of chopped, fresh herbs
(oregano, thyme or basil) and served with simple
grilled foods. The vegetables can be prepared very
coarsely — large chunks, or slices — or quite finely
diced. Whichever way they are cut, take care not to
overcook so the vegetables become mushy.

Heat the olive oil in a pan or heat-proof casserole.
In it sauté the onions, green peppers and garlic. Add
the aubergine, peeled and cut in dice, and continue
frying until much of the oil has been absorbed.

Season with salt and pepper and add the prepared
tomatoes and courgettes. Cook, covered, on a
medium heat until vegetables are tender, about
15 minutes. Remove cover and cook to evaporate
liquid.

One or two beaten eggs can be added to the
vegetables and cooked on a very low heat until
set. Or break one egg per person on top of the
vegetables and put in a medium oven until set.
Variations: potatoes or pumpkin can be added to
the *pisto.* Diced ham, bacon or salt pork are other
frequent additions. In Albacete, a version that
includes tuna is garnished with pine-nuts.

50 ml olive oil
1 large onion chopped or sliced
2 green peppers, chopped or cut in strips
1 clove garlic, chopped
1 large aubergine
1 teaspoon salt
pepper
6 tomatoes, peeled, seeded and chopped
2 courgettes, sliced or diced
eggs (optional)

PIMIENTOS
1'00 €
KILO

ZUMO
KILO= 0'40
3=KILOS
1'00 €

VER

RICE, PASTA AND BREAD DISHES

I sometimes wonder how many paellas are served up along the sunny coasts of Spain on a single summer's day. It must be thousands, as tourists, residents and Spaniards alike dig into Spain's favourite food.

Paella is native to the area around Valencia, where rice is grown extensively. But it's equally at home in Madrid, Mallorca, Murcia and Málaga. Each region has made adaptations to the original — a fairly simple dish of rice, eels, snails and beans — so today there are dozens of versions, some of them quite luxurious.

Like pasta in Italy, paella rice is frequently served as a first course, to be followed by a main dish. In this case it would contain only small bits of meat, chicken and seafood. But it's most likely to be served as the main event for a gathering of friends and family on Sundays or holidays.

The basic ingredients of paella are rice, olive oil and saffron. Beyond that a wide variety of meat, poultry, fish, shellfish and vegetables can be included. Some paellas are truly baroque extravanganzas, with a wild assortment of everything from sea, land and sky. Others show an almost Zen-like simplicity — flavourful yellow rice and a few clams strewn with strips of red pepper.

An all-seafood paella, sometimes called *arroz a la marinera,* might include prawns, clams or mussels, squid and chunks or slices of fish or eel. Snails are typical in Valencia paellas. Some cooks add a sprig of rosemary to paella instead of the herbaceous snails. The Catalans invented paella with no bones, the *parellada.* Rabbit frequently is substituted for chicken. Though a combination of pork, chicken and seafood is typical, pork sausage links or slices of *chorizo* sausage might be used as well. Chicken livers are another favourite addition, instead of or in addition to poultry. In Valencia, paella usually includes wide, flat green beans and dried lima beans. Elsewhere, the usual vegetables are peas, peppers and tomatoes, but others in season can be used as well. Broad beans, green beans, artichokes, asparagus and mushrooms are all authentic additions. (I make a delicious vegetarian paella, using all these vegetables and parboiled brown rice. It is well-flavoured with olive oil and saffron and even Spanish friends enjoy it.)

Spanish paella is by no means an exclusively indoor affair. It's favourite picnic fare for excursions on San Juan's day in June or at *romerías,* fiestas held at sanctuaries in the countryside, where hundreds of paellas might be sizzling over wood fires at the same time. Hunting parties cook up a paella on the spot using some of the day's catch — rabbit and small birds.

Paella needs a hot, fast-burning fire. Well-dried grape-vine prunings, twigs of wild rosemary and

Spanish Rice with Chicken
and Seafood (*Paella*), page 204.

thyme, almond shells, pine-cones and boughs can all be used. Even a charcoal grill on the patio, with some fast-burning wood added, is great for paella-making. In fact, you may find the grill far more effective than the kitchen cooker, as a big paella pan never cooks evenly when placed on a single gas flame. Families that have frequent paella parties usually buy special gas cooking rings big enough to accomodate a huge paella pan.

The paella pan is a shallow, two-handled pan of rolled steel. A similar, but deeper pan is favoured in some localities—but then it's not called a paella. Some cooks swear by earthenware casseroles for cooking rice, but then it's a *cazuela*, not a paella. Earthenware has the advantage of holding the heat for a long time, so the rice keeps cooking even after it is removed from the heat.

Spanish stores also sell paella pans with non-stick finishes. Choose a paella pan 40cm in diameter (about 16 inches) to serve eight people. If you don't have a paella pan, try making paella in two or three frying pans or in a flat-bottomed Chinese wok. Though it's permissible to use more than one pan in the preparation, the paella rice is always served in the same pan in which it cooks.

Paella is seldom oven-cooked (until recently, few Spanish homes had ovens), though it can be put in a low oven for its 10-minute settling time, essential for the rice to finish cooking and flavour to develop. It is cooked uncovered.

Use medium/short-grain rice for paella. It is starchier than long-grain pilaff rice and absorbs the flavours of the food in which it cooks much better. Because it is so easy to overcook into a sticky mess, paella is usually removed from the heat before the rice is completely cooked and left to finish cooking from the heat of the pan. Good olive oil is essential for a real paella and you can't cut down the quantity very much. Besides flavour, the oil provides an "insulation" to each grain of rice, keeping it from getting sticky.

Curiously enough, saffron is not always used in paella. Because of its cost, powdered yellow colouring is substituted in many of the paellas which are served up in beachside *chiringuitos*. Paprika is also used, to augment the colour or in place of saffron for those who don't appreciate its particular flavour. But don't substitute yellow turmeric, which has its own distinct flavour. By the way, if you brown large quantities of chicken or meat in the oil in which the paella is to cook, you'll wind up with a muddy-yellow paella. Brown these ingredients in a separate pan.

Though not a difficult dish to make, your first paella is likely to be a hectic experience. Mine was. With all the chopping, mincing, mashing, frying, stirring and heart-thumping, I completely forgot to add the salt. Prepare all the ingredients beforehand. Clean the squid, steam the mussels, peel the prawns, peel and chop the tomatoes, cut up the chicken and assemble everything in the order you're going to need them. Once this is done the total cooking time is only about 40 minutes: 20 minutes to sauté all the ingredients for the *sofrito* and another 20 minutes to cook the rice once the liquid has been added.

Cut up all ingredients so they cook in the time it takes the rice to cook. Chicken, for instance, is usually hacked into very small pieces, which unfortunately makes for bone splinters. If you're using whole chicken pieces, partially cook them in a separate frying pan. A good alternative is to use boned chicken breasts, each cut into thirds. The liquid — added very hot or boiling—can be water or chicken broth mixed with fish and shellfish stock. You need approximately twice the volume of liquid to rice, but the liquid from fish and tomatoes counts towards total. Many cooks add a few drops of lemon juice, declaring this keeps the rice from getting sticky. Stir all the ingredients well with a wooden spoon at this point, then never stir the rice again. Shake the pan to redistribute the rice and keep it from sticking.

Remove the rice from the heat before it is quite tender. It should still have a little kernel of hardness in the centre. Let it rest for 10 minutes before serving.

To reheat left-over paella, remove from refrigerator and let it come to room temperature. Place in an oiled oven dish and sprinkle with water. Cover with foil and bake in a medium oven just until heated through, about 15 minutes. Or heat in microwave or in a steamer over simmering water.

SPANISH RICE WITH CHICKEN AND SEAFOOD

Paella

1. Clean the clams or mussels and steam them open. Set aside the clams in half shells, removing and discarding the empty half shells. Strain and reserve the liquid in which they cooked.

2. Peel the prawns, saving several unpeeled for garnish. Cook them in a little water, adding the other shells. Strain and reserve the liquid.

3. Cut the chicken into serving pieces. (The bony pieces can be cooked in water to make a stock for cooking the paella.)

4. In the paella pan heat half the olive oil and in it toast two cloves of garlic and the bay leaf. Remove them and set aside.

5. In the same oil, slowly brown the chicken pieces with the cubes of pork, turning them often. Remove to a dish when nicely browned.

6. Now add the minced onion and chopped peppers to the oil. Let sauté a few minutes, then,

7. Add the rings of squid and sauté.

8. Add the tomatoes and raise the heat to high so that they fry in the oil. Add remaining oil at this point so that mixture doesn't stick.

9. Add the rice and cook briefly, stirring, so that the grains become slightly opaque.

10. Combine the reserved cooking liquids with water or stock and bring to a boil. Add to the rice with the chicken and pork and continue cooking on a high heat.

11. In the mortar or blender crush the fried garlic and bay leaf with the saffron, peppercorns, paprika,

1 dozen clams and/or mussels
1/2 kg prawns
1 small chicken or rabbit
200 g pork loin, cut in cubes
75 ml olive oil
3 cloves garlic
1 bay leaf
1 small onion, minced
2 green peppers, cut in strips
300 g squid, cut in rings
2 large tomatoes, peeled, seeded
   and chopped
500 g rice
1 1/4 litre liquid, very hot or boiling
1/2 teaspoon saffron
10 peppercorns
1/2 teaspoon paprika
2 teaspoon salt
1 small tin red pepper
100 g cooked peas

one clove raw garlic and salt. Dilute in a little of the liquid from the pan or in a little white wine and add to the paella. Stir it in well to mix.

12.   Now turn down the heat and let the paella continue cooking.

13.   Decorate the top with the reserved clams and mussels, cooked prawns, strips of tinned pepper and cooked peas.

14.   Shake the pan to prevent the rice from sticking on the bottom. Do not stir.

15.   Remove from heat and let the paella sit for 10 minutes before serving. Serve with quartered lemons to be squeezed over rice, chicken and shellfish. Makes six servings.

PAELLA, VALENCIA STYLE
Paella valenciana

Rabbit or duck can be substituted for chicken in this recipe or all three can be incorporated in the paella.

If using the dried butter beans, soaked overnight, cook them in boiling water for 20 minutes. Drain and set aside.

Blanch the green beans in boiling water for one minute. Drain, refresh in cold water and set aside. Sprinkle the chicken (or rabbit or duck) with salt. Place a 35cm paella pan on the hob and heat the olive oil over medium heat. Sprinkle one teaspoon salt into the oil, then add the chicken pieces. Brown them slowly, turning occasionally. Add the fresh lima beans or par-boiled butter beans and the blanched green beans. Continue sautéing.

Add the garlic, then the tomato. Fry the mixture another five minutes. In a small bowl combine the saffron and paprika. Add two tablespoons of water and stir to dissolve. Add this mixture to the pan.

Add the stock and turn the heat to high. Add the snails and rosemary. When the liquid is boiling, add the rice, stirring to distribute it evenly. Continue to cook over high heat for six minutes. Remove the rosemary.

Turn the heat to medium-low. Cook 15 minutes more without stirring. When the liquid is mostly absorbed and the rice al dente, remove from heat. This is a total cooking time of about 20 minutes once the rice is added. Allow the paella to set for 10 minutes before serving. Serves four.

100 g fresh lima beans or dried butter beans, soaked overnight
250 g wide, flat green beans
1 kg chicken drumsticks
salt
4 tablespoons olive oil
2 cloves garlic, finely chopped
1 tomato, peeled and chopped
1/2 teaspoon saffron, crushed
1 teaspoon paprika
900 ml chicken stock or water
12 cooked or tinned snails, in their shells
sprig of fresh rosemary
380 g medium-short-grain rice

SAILOR'S RICE
Arroz a la marinera

Put the fish head and trimmings in a pot with prawn shells, onion, one clove garlic, sprig parsley and water. Season with salt and pepper and bring to the boil. Simmer for an hour and strain the stock.

Scrub the clams, steam them open, discard empty shells and strain and reserve their liquid.

In a paella pan or large earthenware casserole heat the olive oil and sauté the sliced eel. Turn to brown the other side and add the slices of angler fish. Add the shelled prawns and the squid, and sauté. Then add the peeled, large prawns or chunks of lobster.

Meanwhile, cook the Dublin bay prawns in a little water and set aside. In the mortar crush the saffron with the other garlic clove, one tablespoon parsley and two teaspoons salt. Dissolve in a little liquid and add to the pan with the rice.

Combine the strained fish stock and clam juice to make about 3/4 litre of liquid. Add it hot to the rice. Cook on a high heat for five minutes, then reduce heat and cook until rice is just tender. Place the cooked Dublin bay prawns and clams on top of the rice during the last few minutes of cooking. Let sit several minutes before serving garnished with parsley and lemon wedges. Serves six.

fish head and trimmings
prawn shells
2 cloves garlic
1 sprig parsley
1 litre water
salt and pepper
1/2 onion
1/4 kg clams
1/4 kg conger eel, sliced
1/4 kg angler fish, sliced
1/4 kg prawns, shelled
1/4 kg Dublin bay prawns or large
    prawns or lobster
400 g squid, cleaned and cut in rings
50 ml olive oil
1/2 teaspoon saffron
400 g rice
parsley
lemon wedges

RICE AND FISH, FISHERMAN'S STYLE
Arroz abanda

Clean the fish and it cut it into slices or fillets. Set them aside. Put all the heads, bones and trimmings into a pot with half an onion, two tomatoes, thyme, bay leaf, parsley, salt and pepper. Cover with the water and 200 ml white wine. Bring to the boil, skim and simmer, covered, for an hour.

Strain the fish stock into another pot and bring it to a simmer. In it poach the prepared fillets or slices of fish, removing them with a skimmer as they are done and placing on a platter. Continue with the prawns and the clams or mussels, placing each on the platter as it is cooked.

In a casserole or paella pan heat the olive oil and in it sauté the remaining onion, minced. Add the other two tomatoes, chopped, two cloves garlic, minced, and pepper cut in strips. On a high heat stir in the rice.

Measure out about one litre of the stock in which the fish was cooked and add to the rice. Crush the saffron and the peppercorns with one teaspoon salt. Dissolve in the remaining wine and add to the rice.

Cook over a high heat for five minutes, then cook slowly or put in a medium oven, uncovered, until done, about 20 minutes.

Meanwhile, crush the remaining two cloves of garlic and mix with the mayonnaise, preferably home-made and flavoured with lemon juice.

Serve the rice in its casserole, accompanied by the platter of cooked fish and shellfish and the garlic mayonnaise. Serves six.

2-3 kg fish, preferably 2 or 3 kinds (such as bass, grouper, meagre, rascasse, redfish, scorpion fish, gurnard, mullet, pompano, bream, angler fish)
fish heads, trimmings
1 onion
4 tomatoes
thyme, bay leaf, parsley
2 litres water
250 ml white wine
1/2 kg large prawns
1 dozen clams or mussels, scrubbed
salt and pepper
50 ml olive oil
4 cloves garlic
1 green pepper
500 g rice
1/2 teaspoon saffron
10 peppercorns
1/2 cup mayonnaise

CATALAN BLACK RICE WITH GARLIC SAUCE
Arros negre amb all i oli

Clean the squid or cuttlefish, saving the ink sacs. If the fish are tiny, leave whole, otherwise cut in pieces.

Heat the olive oil in a pot and sauté chopped onion and peppers. Add the squid and fry for another few minutes. Add the tomatoes, cut into small pieces. Cook for a few minutes, then add 100 ml water or stock and cook until quite reduced, about 20 minutes.

Add the rice and about 3/4 litre of the water. Season with salt and a dash of cayenne. Let the rice simmer.

In a small bowl crush the ink sacs and dissolve them in the sherry. Stir this into the rice and continue cooking until rice is done (can be finished in the oven). Let the rice rest for several minutes before serving. Garnish with the cooked prawns and mussels — a bright contrast to the blackened rice. Spoon a little of the sauce over and serve the rest in a small bowl. Serves six.

To make the sauce, crush the garlic in mortar or blender with the salt. Beat in the oil very slowly.
Variation: omit rice, add squid in ink sauce to cooked spaghetti, cook briefly and serve.

1 kg small squid or cuttlefish
6 tablespoons olive oil
1 onion, chopped
2 peppers, red and green, chopped
1/4 kg drained tinned tomatoes
400 g rice (2 1/2 cups)
1 litre water or stock
1 teaspoon salt
cayenne
50 ml sherry
cooked prawns and mussels

FOR THE SAUCE:
3 cloves garlic
1/2 teaspoon salt
100 ml olive oil

CRUSTY RICE, ALICANTE STYLE
Arros amb crosta

This rice dish, served on special occasions, can be cooked to order, making a rich stock (similar to the following recipe) with chicken, lamb, beef, sausages and salt pork. Or the stock, chickpeas and leftover meats from the previous day's *cocido* can be used.

Heat the olive oil in shallow earthenware casserole. Cut the sausage in slices, fry them and remove. In the same oil fry the prepared tomatoes with the diced pork. (Other uncooked meats can be added.) Stir in the rice, then add the hot stock.

Crush the saffron with the salt and pepper and stir into the rice. Bring to the boil, then reduce the heat and add the fried sausage, the cooked chickpeas and cooked chicken or meats. Simmer until rice is cooked.

Beat the eggs with a few drops of water and a pinch of salt. Pour over the rice and put the casserole in the top part of the oven until the eggs have set and browned slightly on the top. Serves six.

50 ml olive oil
200 g *butifarra* or other sausage
2 tomatoes, peeled, seeded and chopped
100 g pork, diced
500 g rice
1 1/2 litres stock
1/2 teaspoon saffron
salt and pepper
150 g chickpeas, cooked
pieces of cooked chicken, meat, sausage, rabbit, meatballs
6 eggs, well beaten

RICE AND LAMB CASSEROLE, VALENCIAN STYLE
Arroz rosetxat

Put the water in a large pot to heat with the lamb (bones can be added too). When it boils, add the soaked chickpeas, the carrot, turnip and celery, peeled and cut in pieces. Skim the froth and simmer until everything is half-cooked, about one hour. Then add two teaspoons salt, *butifarra* sausages and salt pork.

Meanwhile, make the *pelota* or sausage ball. Crumb bread in food processor, add the minced pork, beaten egg, salt and pepper, cinnamon and chopped parsley. Form it into a ball and add to the pot. Cook until everything is quite tender, about another hour.

Strain out the broth and reserve. Cut the *butifarra* sausages and the meatball into slices and set aside.

Heat the olive oil or lard in an earthenware casserole and sauté the chopped garlic. Stir in the rice and let it fry in the oil briefly. Crush the saffron, dissolve it in a little broth and add to rice with the meat, chickpeas and vegetables from the pot and approximately 3/4 litre of the hot broth. Cook over a hot fire for a few minutes, then place the pieces of *butifarra* and meatball on top of the rice and put in a medium oven to finish cooking, about 20 minutes.

Garnish with chopped parsley, and serve after letting the casserole rest for several minutes. Serves six to eight.

3 litres water
400 g boneless lamb
150 g chickpeas, soaked overnight
1 carrot pinch
1 turnip
1 stalk celery
1 Valencian onion *butifarra* negra
2 white *butifarra*
50 g salt pork
2 slices toasted bread
200 g minced pork
1 egg, beaten
salt and pepper
cinnamon
1 tablespoon chopped parsley
75 ml olive oil or lard
2 cloves garlic, chopped
400 g rice
1 tomato
1/2 teaspoon saffron, crushed
chopped parsley

RICE WITH "PARTRIDGE"
Arroz en perdiu

A Lenten dish in Valencia, this is made similarly to the previous casserole, but adding a whole head of garlic — the "partridge" — to cook with the chickpeas and eliminating all the meats. Add the vegetables and chickpeas to the rice and put the cooked head of garlic in the centre of the casserole.

PASTA

Close behind the paella and other rice dishes on many menus are the listings for *macarrones*, *espaguetis* and *canelones*. Can this be typical Spanish food? Absolutely, especially Catalan. Whether pasta got to Spain via Italy is beside the point — most of the Spanish ways with pasta are unique to this cuisine.

Pasta is, basically, a flour and water paste, either hand-rolled and cut or forced through a die to shape it. Commercial pastas are made from durum wheat semolina, the best for a chewy consistency. They may or may not contain eggs, or may be coloured green with spinach or pink with tomato paste. Making pasta at home is easy and rewarding.

Spanish supermarkets offer more than 25 varieties of pasta, from the tiny ones for soups to chunky shells and tubes to big squares of *lasagne* noodles. However, they're seldom named in Spanish so the shopper has to choose by sight.

Fideos may be the most typically Spanish pasta. These can be as thin as *capelini* or as fat as spaghetti and are often sold packaged wound into nests. The thin varieties are used in soups and every region has its version of *sopa de fideos*. The thicker ones are preferred for casserole-type dishes. Pasta squares for *canelones* and *lasagne* come packaged in small boxes. They are like slabs of cardboard until boiled.

Allow 80 g of pasta per serving for a main course, about 40 g for a starter or side dish, and about 20 g per serving for addition to a soup. So a quarter-kilo of pasta should make six servings as a side dish. (This is not per person, but per serving — some people eat more than one serving.)

To cook pasta: allow three litres of water for each quarter-kilo of pasta. Bring the water to a full, rolling boil and add a tablespoon of salt and a tablespoon of olive oil. Add pasta gradually so water never stops boiling. Boil, uncovered, stirring occasionally with a fork to separate the pieces. Pasta takes from six to 12 minutes, depending on size and type. The only way to know if it's done is to try it: it should be tender but still firm. Drain in a colander and mix immediately with prepared sauce or coat with olive oil. Don't rinse the pasta unless it's to be used in a cold salad.

MACARONI, SPANISH STYLE
Macarrones a la española

Cook the macaroni in salted water until tender and drain well. Meanwhile heat the olive oil in a saucepan and sauté the onions and green peppers until tender. Add the minced garlic and fry a minute. Add the prepared tomatoes. Continue frying and season with salt and pepper.

Add the ham, cut in dice, and the sliced *chorizo*. Cook another 10 minutes until tomatoes are reduced. Season with salt and pepper to taste (not too much salt with ham and sausage). Either toss the sauce with the cooked macaroni and serve immediately with grated cheese or layer the macaroni and sauce in an oiled oven dish, top with the cheese and bake until cheese is melted. Serves four.

1 package (1/4 kg) macaroni (penne)
3 tablespoons olive oil
1 medium onion, chopped
2 green peppers, chopped
1 clove garlic, minced
4 large tomatoes, peeled, seeded
    and chopped
salt and pepper
100 g *serrano* ham
2 soft *chorizo* sausages
100 g grated cheese

SEAFOOD SPAGHETTI CASSEROLE
Cazuela de fideos

This dish is also called *paella de fideos*, a paella made with spaghetti instead of rice, or *fideua*. I also like it cooked in fish stock without the addition of seafood to be served as a side dish with a fillet of any fish.

Heat the olive oil in a casserole or pot and fry the pieces of fish, which can be left in whole slices or cut into smaller, boneless strips. When browned on both sides, remove to a plate.

In the same oil sauté the chopped onion and peppers. Add the chopped garlic, then the prepared tomatoes and fry until reduced to a sauce. Add the shelled peas then the stock. Bring to the boil.

Meanwhile, crush in a mortar the cumin, saffron, paprika, salt and pepper. Dissolve in some of the liquid from the casserole and stir into the casserole. When the liquid is boiling, add the prawns, clams, pieces of fried fish and the *fideos*. Lower heat and cook until the pasta is just tender, about 10 minutes. This dish should be juicy, but not soupy.

Remove from heat, cover the casserole and let it rest for several minutes. Garnish with the sprigs of mint. Serves six.

500 g angler fish slices
50 ml olive oil
1 small onion, chopped
2 green peppers, chopped
2 cloves garlic
2 large tomatoes, peeled, seeded
    and chopped
100 g shelled peas or broad beans
1 1/2 litres fish stock or water
1/4 teaspoon cumin
1/4 teaspoon saffron
1/4 teaspoon paprika
salt and pepper
200 g prawns, peeled
1/4 kg clams, well scrubbed
500 g *fideos* or spaghetti
sprigs of mint

MACARONI CASSEROLE
Greixera de macarrones

Partially cook the macaroni in water. Drain and return to the pan with the milk.

Cook very slowly until macaroni is done. Most of the milk should be absorbed. Then add half the grated cheese and a pinch of cinnamon. Salt to taste and place the macaroni in a buttered oven dish. Cut the eggs in half and embed them in the macaroni. Dot with the butter, sprinkle lightly with cinnamon and remaining cheese and place in oven or under grill to very lightly brown the top. Serves four.

400 g macaroni
1/4 litre milk, warmed
150 g grated cheese (aged Mahón if available, otherwise aged Manchego or Parmesan)
cinnamon
salt
4 hard-boiled eggs
150 g butter

CATALAN STYLE SPAGHETTI
Fideos a la catalana

Heat the olive oil or lard in a casserole or pot and in it fry the pieces of ribs until nicely browned. Then add the chopped onions and sauté until softened. Add the prepared tomatoes and the paprika and cook a few minutes more. Add the link sausage, cut into pieces, and the sliced *butifarra*. Pour in the stock and bring to the boil.

Add the pasta, lower heat and cook. In the mortar or blender crush the nuts with the garlic, saffron, parsley, cinnamon and toasted bread, adding some of the stock to make a paste. Stir this into the casserole and cook until meat is tender, about 20 minutes. Serve in the same casserole, sprinkled with grated cheese. Serves four.

4 tablespoons olive oil or lard
1/4 kg pork spare-ribs, cut in short pieces
100 g spicy pork sausage links
100 g white sausage *(butifarra)*
1 onion, chopped
3 tomatoes, peeled, seeded and chopped
1 slice bread, toasted
1/2 teaspoon paprika
1 1/2 litres meat stock
500 g fideos or spaghetti
40 g hazelnuts and/or almonds and/or pine-nuts
1 clove garlic
1/2 teaspoon saffron
1 tablespoon parsley
1/4 teaspoon cinnamon
100 g grated cheese

"TATTERS AND RAGS"
Andrajos

This dish, typical of Jaén and Granada, would be made with salt cod or wild hare. I like it made with chicken. The "rags" are made from a very simple flour and water paste, cut in squares or circles. The pasta "rags", when home-made, are sometimes pulled apart with a fork, while they cook, giving them a tattered look. Use any favourite pasta dough or substitute packaged *lasagne* or *cannelloni* squares.

Heat the olive oil in a pot or casserole and sauté the chopped onion and garlic. Add the prepared tomatoes and fry for several minutes. Stir in the paprika. (If using salt cod, add it — soaked overnight and shredded — at this time.)

In the mortar crush the saffron, peppercorns, clove and cumin and dissolve in a little of the stock. Add to the casserole with the stock. When it comes to the boil, lower heat and add the shredded chicken or rabbit and the squares of pasta. Cook until they are tender. Serve in the same casserole, garnished with chopped parsley.

50 ml olive oil
1 onion, chopped
1 clove garlic, chopped
2 tomatoes, peeled, seeded and chopped
1 teaspoon paprika
1/4 teaspoon saffron
10 peppercorns
1 clove
1/4 teaspoon cumin
1/2 litre stock
400-800 g cooked, boned and shredded chicken or rabbit, or desalted dried salt cod
100 g pasta squares, cooked
chopped parsley

BREAD

"*Sin pan, no se puede comer* (You can't eat without bread)" says a Spanish proverb. Bread in Spain is not just food. It symbolises all food. Before breaking bread, village folk will make the sign of the Cross on the loaf and kiss it. A loaf dropped on the floor is quickly retrieved and kissed with a blessing. Children are not allowed to snatch bread, but are taught to treat it with respect. Stabbing the bread with a knife causes shudders among the devout — they will remind you that you are stabbing the body of Christ. Bread is, even in these days of abundance, the staff of life.

Every *barrio* has its *panadería* where fragrant, crusty loaves are produced daily. At breakfast time the small *bollos* (rolls) and *barras* (long loaves) are hot from the ovens, just right for drizzling with fruity extra virgin olive oil or spreading with marmalade. By late morning, in time for the midday meal, the large round loaves are ready. Spanish bread, with no fat and no sugar, does not keep well — it's meant to be consumed fresh, the same day it's baked. Day-old bread is never wasted, however, but is cut up to make *sopas*, filler for soups, thickener for sauces or breadcrumbs for breading croquettes and fish. Spanish bakeries also produce excellent sandwich loaves, *pan de molde*.

In days — not really so long ago — when country folk might not go to the village more than once a week, bread was baked at home in clay ovens fuelled with scraps of wood, rosemary and vine prunings to be found on the farm. Nowadays country people drive off to town to buy fresh bread. Old ovens are converted into chicken coops and storage bins. Yet many get misty-eyed as they tell you about that wonderful, home-baked bread they remember from childhood.

COUNTRY BREAD
Pan cateto

One of my friends, who grew up in the country, taught me to make country bread. Here is her recipe. *"Hay que tener suerte,"* she said — with bread-making, you have to be lucky. From a bakery buy *levadura de masa,* about 150 g. This is the "mother dough" which contains the yeast starter. If you don't have access to a Spanish bakery, substitute two cakes of compressed yeast, about 50 g. Heat a big earthenware bowl slightly, just to take the chill off. The bread dough should never touch a cold surface or it will "catch a cold". Use a wooden tabletop, never tile or marble.

Dissolve the yeast dough or pressed yeast in 200 ml of very warm water. Place two kilos of flour in the warmed bowl with two tablespoons of salt. Mix the yeast mixture into it. Then begin adding water, little by little, working it into the flour with the hands. The bread should contain as little water as possible (500 to 750 ml) only enough to hold the dough together. It is customary to place the bowl on the floor while mixing in the water, to get better leverage. Then turn the dough out on to a floured board or table and knead it for 10 or 15 minutes until very smooth and elastic. Cover the dough with a blanket and let it rest for about an hour in a warm place.

To shape the dough, divide it into two parts for the traditional round loaves, or three or four parts for short Vienna loaves. Roll out and shape them, perfectly smooth, seams on the bottom. Oval Vienna loaves are slashed diagonally. Cover the wooden table with the heavy blanket. Place the loaves on top and completely wrap them up or, as they say, "put them to bed". Leave them to rise about two hours. The dough should almost double in size and leave an imprint if pressed lightly with a finger.

Preheat a baking stone. Heat the oven to hot (200 °C/430 °F). Slide the loaves on to the stone. (If baking stone is not available, slide the loaves onto a baking tin. Bake for 10 minutes, then reduce heat to moderate (180 °C/350 °F) and bake until loaves are golden. To keep the crusts crispy, either brush the loaves with water part way through the baking or put a pan of boiling water on an oven rack. Cool the bread completely before storing.

BREAD WITH TOMATO AND HAM
Pan con tomate y jamón

This Catalan speciality, much appreciated for breakfast, is a tasty way to use slightly stale bread. Cut the bread in thick slices. It can be slightly toasted under the grill or in a toaster. Rub the toasted bread with a cut tomato, drizzle with good olive oil and sprinkle with a very little salt. Top the bread slices with thinly sliced *serrano* ham and serve with more sliced tomato.

MANCHEGO "RAREBIT"
Costrada manchega

Toast the bread slices lightly and brush with olive oil. Mix the grated cheese with the white wine to make a thick paste. Season with salt and pepper. Spread the toast with the cheese mixture and place in an oiled oven dish. Mince the garlic and mix it with the chopped parsley and a little salt.

Break one egg on top of each of the toast slices, sprinkle with the garlic-parsley and put in the oven just until the egg-whites are set, about six minutes. Serve from the same oven dish.

6 slices day-old bread
2 tablespoon olive oil
250 g aged Manchego cheese, grated
100 ml white wine
salt and pepper
1 clove garlic
4 tablespoons chopped parsley
6 eggs

FRIED SANDWICHES
Emparedados

Slice a sandwich loaf fairly thinly. Spread one side of slices with butter or olive oil. Layer with thinly sliced *serrano* ham and semi-cured Manchego cheese. Press the bread together tightly. Cut off crusts and cut the sandwiches into four triangles or squares. Dip them into milk, then beaten egg and then into fine breadcrumbs. Fry the breaded sandwiches in olive oil, turning to brown both sides.

"PIZZA", COSTA BLANCA STYLE
Coquetes

If as many people had emigrated from Alicante as from Naples, perhaps all of today's pizza parlours would be serving *coquetes*. Though these are typically made from bread dough, prepared pizza bases or any favourite pizza dough can be used.

Top the rounds of dough — flattened out to about 30 cm rounds — with spoonfuls of *pisto*, stewed summer vegetables *(page 198) or* sautéed spinach or chard. Add chunks of tuna and bits of olives or capers. Bake until bread is slightly toasted, about 25 minutes in a medium hot oven. Add grated cheese before baking if desired.

SAVOURY PASTRIES

Variously called *empanadas, pasteles* and *tortas*, these pies and pastries are a cross between a pot pie and a pizza. The *empanadas* are made with either bread dough or puff pastry *(hojaldre)*. The *pasteles* and *tortas*, not unlike quiches, are more usually made with a shortcrust pastry. Frozen puff pastry, found in most supermarkets, is a great thing to have on hand in the freezer section of the refrigerator. Quickly thawed, it forms the basis of canapés and flaky pastries which can be put together in minutes with left-over cooked ingredients. For shortcrust dough, use your own favourite pie crust, the *empanadilla* wine pastry (Chapter 4 and Chapter 13), or the following flaky pastry.

FLAKY PASTRY
Pasta quebrada

Cream the butter with the olive oil. Beat in the egg yolk, salt and baking powder. The mixture should be smooth and as thick as cream. Then beat in the ice water. Add the flour gradually, adding only enough to make a dough which is not too sticky. Mix only enough to blend the flour into the fat; don't overwork. Chill the dough for 30 minutes.

On a floured board, roll the dough out into a rectangle. Fold the top third down and the bottom third over it and turn the pastry and roll out again. Repeat this three more times. Then place the dough, covered with plastic wrap or a cloth, again in the refrigerator for two hours. It is now ready to be rolled out to line a flan tin or mould for *pastel* or *empanada*.

100 g butter or lard
150 ml olive oil
1 egg yolk
1 teaspoon salt
2 teaspoons baking powder
150 ml ice water
370 g flour (approx)

YEAST PASTRY
Masa para empanada

Place the yeast in a small bowl. Mix the water with the sugar and three tablespoons of flour and add to the yeast. Let it sit in a warm place for about 40 minutes.

Meanwhile, place the flour in a bowl and add to it the salt and lard, mixing the fat into the flour with the fingers. Make a well in the centre and pour in the yeast water and beaten egg. With the hands or a wooden spoon mix the flour and liquid very well.

Turn out on to a floured board and knead the dough until very smooth and elastic, at least five minutes. (Food processors knead dough in short order.) Add more flour as needed to prevent dough from sticking. Now place in a greased bowl, cover with a dampened cloth and set in a warm place to rise until double in bulk — about one hour depending on room temperature.

Punch it down. The dough is now ready to be formed into the *empanada, coquetes* (pizza) or bread loaves. In Galicia a small quantity of cornmeal is often added to the wheat flour. Whole-grain flour may also be used.

40 g pressed yeast
150 ml very warm water
1/2 teaspoon sugar
3 tablespoons flour
500 g flour
1 teaspoon salt
75 g lard (or butter)
1 egg

GALICIAN PORK PIE
Empanada de lomo a la gallega

The Galician *empanada* is also made with cooked and boned chicken, tuna, sardines, eel or minced meat. A "must" for picnics and fiesta days, the *empanada* is often served cold.

Put the slices of pork loin in a dish and sprinkle with paprika, one clove chopped garlic, oregano, salt and pepper and let them sit for 30 minutes.

Heat the olive oil in a pan and fry the pork very quickly, removing the slices as they are browned. In the same oil sauté the chopped peppers, onions and remaining garlic until softened. Add the prepared tomatoes, parsley, salt and pepper and cook until the tomatoes are reduced and sauce is very thick.

Divide the bread dough in half. On a floured board roll out one half to 2cm thickness. (If using bread dough which contains no fat, spread the rolled-out dough with softened butter or lard, fold into thirds; roll out again and spread with butter. Fold and roll it out a final time.)

Line a 30cm oven tin with the dough (an all-metal paella pan makes a good mould). Spread this with half of the prepared sauce. Arrange the slices of pork loin on top. Cut the peppers into strips and make a layer of them on top with the sliced eggs. Spoon on the remaining sauce.

Roll out the remaining dough in the same manner. Cover the pie with it. Crimp the edges together and trim off any excess. Use scraps of dough to roll into long ropes to decorate the top of the pie,

300 g boneless pork loin, thinly sliced
1/2 teaspoon paprika
2 cloves garlic
1/2 teaspoon oregano
50 ml olive oil
1 large green pepper, chopped
3 onions, chopped
3 tomatoes, peeled, seeded and chopped
1 tablespoon chopped parsley
salt and pepper
500 g bread dough, risen once
1 tin red peppers
2 hard-boiled eggs
1 egg, beaten

moistening with just a little water so they stick. Make a hole in the centre for a steam vent. Put in a medium hot oven for 30 minutes. Brush the top with beaten egg and bake another 15 to 20 minutes. The crust should be golden and the pie loosened from the tin when lifted with a fork. Serves six.

PREGNANT BUNS
Bollos preñados

Use bread dough, puff pastry or shortcrust pastry for these. They can be made fairly large or very tiny for canapés, a good use for scraps of leftover dough. Wrap *chorizo* sausage — or pieces of *chorizo* — in very thinly sliced ham. Roll out dough fairly thinly. Cut it into pieces just large enough to completely enclose the *chorizo*. Bake in a medium hot oven until the pastry is lightly browned.

SPINACH AND CHEESE PIE
Empanada de espinacas y queso

Wash the spinach well and cook until wilted. Drain it very well, pressing out excess water. Return it to the pan and chop. Add the beaten eggs, salt, pepper and nutmeg.

Sauté the finely chopped onion in the oil until softened and add to the spinach. Roll out about 3/4 of the pastry dough and line a 20cm flan tin. Spoon in a layer of spinach. Slice the cheese and place a layer of cheese on top of the spinach. Top with the remaining spinach. Use the remaining pastry to roll long cords and make a criss-cross topping for the pie (or cut rounds or stars, etc.) Put in a medium oven until pastry is golden, about 25 minutes. Serves eight as a starter or side dish.

flaky pastry or other shortcrust
1 kg spinach (500 g frozen spinach) or
    chard greens
2 eggs, beaten
salt and pepper
grated nutmeg
1/2 small onion
2 tablespoons olive oil
200 g soft white cheese or dry cottage
    cheese *(requesón)*

PORRIDGE
Gachas

I resist calling *gachas* by the unappetizing name of gruel, which is really what it is. This is sturdy peasant fare, but ever so well flavoured with garlic, spices and ham. It has many variations, some sweet, some savoury and some both. The porridge can be made with chickpea flour, vetch flour (not much found any more), ground broad beans, wheat flour, maize flour or lentil meal. In some places, made with white flour and spiced with anise and cinnamon and served with honey or molasses, it is a pudding. It can be garnished with grapes, cucumbers, olives, sardines, chocolate, sausage...you see, this is a versatile dish.

In the Canary Islands, a similar preparation, *gofio* or *frangollo,* is made with toasted maize flour. Serve it with fried bananas. *Fariñes, farrapes, pantruque* and *boronchu* are other preparations made with maize, well flavoured with salt pork, ham or sausage, which might be cooked in a cabbage leaf — not unlike Mexican *tamales* — or combined with egg and made into a sort of dumpling to include in the *cocido.*

Heat the oil in a deep frying pan and in it slowly fry the diced salt pork and ham. Add the chopped garlic and fry. Meanwhile, soak the maize flour in the 50 ml of water. Stir it into the oil and season with the paprika, plenty of pepper, caraway, cloves and salt.

Add the boiling water and cook the porridge — stirring with a wooden spoon — on a very low heat for about 20 minutes or until very thick and the oil separates on top.

3 tablespoons olive oil
100 g salt pork or bacon, diced
100 g *serrano* ham, diced
2 cloves garlic, chopped
50 ml water
100 g maize flour (corn meal) or chickpea flour
1 teaspoon paprika
freshly ground pepper
few caraway seeds
sprinkle of cloves
1 teaspoon salt
1/2 litre boiling water

Serve in small earthenware bowls garnished with fried croutons of bread (in which case it's *con tropezones*) or sliced pork loin, fried, or fried *chorizo* or other sausage.

FRIED CROUTONS
Migas

This is one of those homely, satisfying dishes that you'll rarely find on restaurant menus. In Spain it might be served for breakfast or lunch. The flavourful croutons are a good base for fried eggs and sausage. They're excellent added to soups or turned into a stuffing for fish or fowl.

Cut two-day-old bread, crusts and all, into very small dice. Sprinkle with salted water — enough to thoroughly dampen but not soak the bread. Wrap the croutons in a dampened tea towel and tie it tightly. Let sit for a few hours or overnight.

In a little olive oil or lard slowly fry salt pork, or bacon, cut in very small dice. Add chopped red pepper, chopped garlic, chopped parsley and a little chopped chili pepper, if desired. Add the bread cubes and sauté them, stirring constantly, until slightly toasted. Sprinkle with a little paprika to colour, but don't allow them to burn. If the *migas* are served with milk, they're *migas canas*. They can also be served with thick, hot chocolate.

FISH AND SHELLFISH

Seafood is absolutely the glory of Spanish cuisine. For an exquisite sea bass, a pristine gilt-head or giant prawns, Spaniards will gladly pay considerably more than they would for pork fillet, beef entrecote or lamb chops. Not that every entrée from the fish market is so pricey — at the other end of the scale, inexpensive mackerel, sardines or grey mullet provide bargain protein plus flavourful eating.

The glory of Spanish seafood is its freshness and its incredible variety. I have tried to provide recipes here which show how best to prepare some of the less familiar fish as well as the old favourites in new ways. Spanish recipes usually call for a specific fish, such as "hake in green sauce", so in these recipes I have named the preferred fish. That doesn't mean you can't substitute other fish if the one called for is not available, e.g. cod or halibut for hake. Lots more information on buying, storing and cooking fish is to be found in Chapter 2 on marketing, along with a complete listing of the fish most commonly found in Spanish markets. Hopefully, this manual will give enough user-friendly instructions to increase your enjoyment of the many exciting Spanish seafood dishes.

Most fishmongers will clean fish for you. But if you are going to do it yourself, here's how. Place the fish on several thicknesses of newspaper on a flat surface. If it needs scaling, use a dull knife or a scaling tool and scrape the scales off from tail to head. This is a good chore to do outside, if convenient, as the scales do tend to fly. Then, with the knife point, slit all along the belly of the fish from the anal fin to just below the head. Pull out the entrails and discard with first layers of newspaper. You may want to save the roe (huevas), if there is any, and the liver of some fish.

Cut out the fins on the belly side, then slit along either side of the dorsal fin on top of the fish. Grasp it firmly and give a quick pull up and towards the head to release the fin and the bones attached to it. Fish vendors usually use scissors to trim fins and tails, but this operation doesn't release the attached bones. You can now remove the head (cut it off or snap it on the edge of the counter) if you wish, and the fish is ready for cutting into steaks or slices.

Because fish in Spain is so good, it's most frequently prepared whole, grilled, fried or baked. But there are other dishes for which you might want fillets of fish. Though not difficult, filleting is a little tedious until you get the knack. Lay the fish flat on the table and, starting either at the tail or just below the head, slice down at an angle until the knife blade reaches the backbone. Then turn the blade almost flat against the bone and slowly work down the length of the fish, freeing the top fillet. Turn the fish and repeat the operation. You now have two fillets. The thin and bony belly flaps can be cut out if desired. To skin the fillet, lay it skin side down, slice through the tail to the skin and with the blade taut against the skin, pull the skin away from the flesh.

Mixed Fish Fry (*Pesca'ito Frito*) with, clockwise from left, fresh anchovies, squid and hake; page 228.

Flat-fish such as sole are skinned by making an incision above the tail, holding the tail down firmly with one hand and with the other hand sharply pulling the skin up and towards the head. The skin peels off in one piece. A fish that is to be skinned needn't be scaled. Bones, head and skin can be saved for making flavourful fish stock, a basis for soups and sauces or a poaching liquid for the fillets.

The "magic touch" Spanish cooks have with fish is knowing not to overcook it. Fish is very quick cooking. To keep it moist and flavourful, don't overcook. Probe the fish with a fork during cooking and remove from heat when the flesh just pulls away from the spine and is opaque and flaky.

MIXED FISH FRY
Pesca'ito frito

The coasts of Cádiz and Málaga are famous for their fried fish. The art is in shaking off excess flour and keeping the oil — preferably olive — at the perfect temperature, so the fish turns golden and crispy, and is scooped out with a skimmer while the flesh is still meltingly moist. A mixed fish fry includes fresh anchovies (boquerones), rings of squid (calamares), a slice of hake (pescadilla or merluza), diminutive red mullet (salmonete), tiny whole sole (lenguado) and a few prawns. When all is cooked to perfection and served piping hot, it is one of the most perfect dishes of Andalusian cooking. So simple. Olive oil is the best for frying fish. Heat it until shimmering, but not smoking (180°C/355°F).

400 g cleaned small fish and squid rings
per person
flour for dredging
olive oil for frying
salt
lemon wedges

Heat oil in a deep frying pan to a depth of at least 4cm.

Working with each kind of fish separately, dredge it in the flour, shake off the excess and fry the fish until golden, three to six minutes.

Remove and drain on kitchen towels. Sprinkle with salt. Serve with lemon wedges.

SOLE, FLAT-FISH & ANGLER FISH

Of all the flat-fish (see Chapter 2 for descriptions), sole is certainly the most popular. Use the following recipes for sole or any of the flat-fish.

BRILL OR JOHN DORY WITH LEMON
Gallo o pez de san pedro al limón

Allow one fish per person. Slice the lemons very thinly and arrange half in a layer in a baking dish. Place the fish on top and cover with the remaining lemon slices. Put the fish in a hot oven for about five minutes. Meanwhile, heat the oil in a pan and toast the garlic, cut in slices. Pour this over the fish and return to the oven until flaky, about 10 minutes. Serves six.

6 flat-fish, skinned
3 lemons
100 ml olive oil
3 cloves garlic

ANGLER FISH IN ALMOND SAUCE
Rape en salsa de almendras

The large head of the angler fish can be used to make the fish stock. Boil it for an hour with onion, carrot, celery, parsley, bay leaf and a glass of white wine. Season with salt and pepper. Strain and reserve.

Dust the fish steaks with flour. Heat the oil in a frying pan and very quickly brown the fish on both sides. Remove them to an oven casserole. In the same oil fry the blanched almonds, the peeled cloves of garlic, the parsley and the slice of bread until garlic is golden and bread crisp. Remove to a mortar or blender and crush with the saffron, adding the white wine to make a paste.

In the same oil, fry the chopped onions until softened. Add the prepared tomato and fry for several minutes. Stir in the mortar mixture and simmer the sauce for several minutes, then add the fish stock or water. Season with salt and pepper and pour over the fish slices. Bake in a medium oven until fish flakes easily, about 15 minutes. Serves four.

3/4 kg sliced angler fish
65 ml olive oil
flour
20 blanched almonds
2 cloves garlic
1 sprig parsley
1 slice bread, crusts removed
1/2 teaspoon saffron
50 ml white wine or fish stock
1 medium onion, chopped
1 medium tomato, peeled, seeded
    and chopped
100 ml fish stock or water
salt and pepper

ANGLER FISH, SAILOR STYLE
Rape a la marinera

Place the fish slices in an oven dish and sprinkle with the salt. Arrange the peeled prawns and well-scrubbed clams around it and sprinkle the chopped pepper on top.

In a frying pan heat the oil and sauté the onions and chopped garlic. Pour this, oil included, over the fish. Chop the hard-boiled egg and sprinkle on to fish. Mix the tomato sauce and fish stock and pour over. Bake in a medium oven until fish flakes easily and clam shells have opened, about 20 minutes. Serves four.

500 g sliced angler fish
1 teaspoon salt
200 g peeled prawns
1 dozen clams
1 red tinned pepper, chopped
3 tablespoons olive oil
3 scallions, thinly sliced
1 clove garlic, chopped
1 hard-boiled egg
50 ml tomato sauce
50 ml fish stock or white wine

FAKE LOBSTER
Rape a la langosta

The angler fish has sweet-tasting, slightly chewy flesh very similar to lobster, for which it can be substituted. Poach the angler fish in a well-seasoned *court bouillon,* or in a *fumet* made with lobster or prawn shells. Let it cool, then pull the flesh into pieces with the fingers or using two forks. Serve on a bed of lettuce, covered with mayonnaise and garnished with quartered hard-boiled eggs, sliced tomato and lemon wedges.

ROCKFISH

GURNARD IN ORANGE SAUCE
Rubio a la naranja

Grouper *(mero)* can be prepared in the same manner.

Clean the fish, but leave whole. Rub them inside and out with salt and place in the cavity of each a few orange slices. Let them sit for 30 minutes, then dust with flour.

Heat 50 ml oil in a heat-proof oven pan big enough to hold the fish. Add the chopped garlic and put the fish in. Turn to brown the reverse side, then put in a medium oven for about 30 minutes.

Meanwhile, remove zest from one of the oranges. Chop the peel and cook it in a little water for five minutes. Reserve the peel.

In a saucepan heat four tablespoons olive oil and sauté the onion until softened. Stir in two tablespoons flour and cook a few minutes without browning. Then add the stock, the orange juice and the reserved, cooked orange peel. Cook, stirring, until the sauce is thickened. Remove the fish from the oven and place on a serving dish. Spoon a little of the sauce over the fish and garnish with additional orange slices. Serve the remaining sauce separately. Serves four to six.

2 gurnards, each about 700 g
2 oranges
salt
120 ml olive oil
3 cloves garlic
1 chopped onion
flour
1/4 litre fish stock
60 ml orange juice

SCORPIONFISH, REDFISH, RED SNAPPER OR RASCASSE IN GREEN SAUCE

Cabracho en salsa verde

Cut the fish into slices or fillets, salt the pieces and set aside. In a heat-proof casserole heat the oil and fry the chopped leeks. Add the garlic, then the parsley and potatoes, peeled and very thinly sliced. Cover with the water, add one tablespoon salt and cook on a medium heat until the potatoes are almost tender, 25 minutes.

Dredge the pieces of fish in flour and place in the casserole. Pour in the wine. Cook the fish five minutes, turn the pieces of fish and cook another 10 minutes. Don't stir the potatoes after adding the fish, but shake the casserole to keep from sticking. Garnish, if desired, with a sprinkling of cooked peas. Serves four.

1 1/2 kg whole fish
salt
6 tablespoons olive oil
3 leeks, finely chopped
2 cloves garlic, chopped
4 tablespoons chopped parsley
600 g potatoes (4 medium)
1/4 litre water
flour
175 ml white wine
cooked peas to garnish

SCORPIONFISH, REDFISH, RED SNAPPER OR RASCASSE WITH GARLIC

Cap roig

Clean the fish but leave it whole. Rub with salt and let sit for 30 minutes. Place the fish in an oiled oven dish and pour over the water and the wine. Put in a medium oven until the fish flakes easily, about 25 minutes.

Meanwhile, heat the oil in a saucepan and sauté the sliced garlic until lightly golden. Add the chopped parsley. Pour this sauce over the fish. Serves four.

1 1/2 kg whole fish
salt
100 ml water or stock
50 ml white wine
6 tablespoons olive oil
3 cloves garlic, sliced
1 tablespoon chopped parsley

MULLET

GRILLED RED MULLET WITH SAUCE
Salmonetes a la plancha con aliño

In my early days in Spain, while I was still getting a kitchen together and learning my way around the market-place, I used to lunch every day in the same bar, where I always ordered the same thing: a salad and grilled red mullet with this simple sauce. I was straight out of midwest America, where fresh seafood was unknown. The memory of that superbly fresh fish flavours all my impressions of Spain.

Red mullet is one of the few fish which can be cooked without gutting, as it has no bitter gall. At its simplest, lay the whole, unscaled fish on a hot grill (griddle), brush with oil, and turn once. Or gut and scale it and cook under the broiler/grill or over charcoal.

For the sauce: mix three cloves chopped garlic with three tablespoons chopped parsley. Add 50 ml extra virgin olive oil and the juice of one lemon. Drizzle this over the grilled fish. Or serve with *romesco* sauce (page 346).

RED MULLET WITH ANCHOVY SAUCE
Salmonetes con salsa de anchoas

Clean the red mullet (one per person) and rub with lemon juice and salt. Let them sit for 15 minutes. Then dip them in oil and in breadcrumbs. Place on an oven tin and bake in a moderate oven until the fish flakes, about 20 minutes. Place on a serving platter and keep warm.

To the juices in the pan add the tomato purée and the butter and let it heat, stirring. Mash the anchovy fillets in the mortar and add to the pan with the water and wine. Season with pepper (salt may not be necessary) and cook for several minutes. Pour the sauce over the baked mullet and garnish with chopped parsley. Serves six.

6 red mullet
lemon juice
salt
olive oil
breadcrumbs
6 tablespoons tomato purée
100 g butter
4 anchovy fillets, well drained
50 ml water or stock
2 tablespoons white wine
pepper
chopped parsley

GREY MULLET IN SAFFRON SAUCE
Lisa en amarillo

Pez espada en amarillo (swordfish in saffron sauce) is prepared in the same manner.

Either fillet the fish or cut them into slices. Rub the pieces with salt and lemon juice and let them sit for an hour at room temperature or longer, covered, in the refrigerator.

Arrange in a *besuguera,* a rectangular, metal fish-cooking pan, or in a casserole. In a frying pan heat the oil and fry the slice of bread until golden and crisp. Remove. Then fry the garlic and chopped onion. Put the contents of the pan into a mortar, food processor or blender with the fried bread, saffron, parsley and water and blend to a smooth paste. Pour this sauce over the fish with the juice of the lemon and place on a moderate heat until it begins to bubble.

Cover the pan with foil and cook until the fish flakes easily, about 10 minutes, adding a little more liquid if needed. Diced potatoes can be incorporated in this dish, adding them before the fish. Serves four.

2 grey mullet, each about 450 g
salt
lemon juice
50 ml olive oil
1 slice bread, crusts removed
2 cloves garlic
1 small onion, chopped
1/2 teaspoon saffron
1 tablespoon chopped parsley
100 ml water or fish stock
1 lemon

BLUEFISH

BAKED MACKEREL
Caballa al horno

Clean the fish but leave them whole. Pour the oil into a baking dish large enough to hold the fish comfortably. Arrange the sliced onions on the bottom and place the fish on top. Sprinkle with salt and top with the sliced lemon. Bake in a medium oven until the fish flakes easily, about 25 minutes. Serve in the same dish. Serves four.

4 mackerel, about 300 g each
60 ml olive oil
4 small onions, sliced
salt
1 lemon, thinly sliced

STUFFED MACKEREL
Caballas rellenas

This excellent preparation can be used for other fish as well. Try it with *lubina* (sea bass), *dorada* (gilt-head), salmon or trout. Use any white fish such as hake, angler or sole, for the stuffing. Left-over cooked fish or shellfish can be substituted.

To bone the fish: slit the fish along the belly from tail to head. Gut the fish and wash them. Starting at the tail, ease the knife along the backbone, freeing the flesh of the top fillet all the way to the head. Turn the fish over and repeat the operation. Now cut the backbone free at the tail and head and remove it, leaving the whole, boned fish. Repeat with the remaining fish.

Finely mince (can be done in a food processor) the boneless white fish. Mix it with the breadcrumbs, egg yolks, salt and pepper, minced onion, brandy, nutmeg and chopped parsley. Stuff the fish with this mixture.

6 medium mackerel
300 g boneless white fish, such as
    hake, angler, sole
50 g fine breadcrumbs
2 egg yolks
salt and pepper
1 chopped onion
1 tablespoon brandy
grated nutmeg
1 tablespoon chopped parsley
2 tablespoons olive oil
50 ml white wine
1 tomato, sliced

Sew up the cavity openings with needle and thread. Pour the oil into an oven dish and place the fish in it. Pour over the wine and top the fish with the slices of tomato. Bake in a medium oven until the fish flakes easily, about 35 minutes. Serves six.

BONITO, BILBAO STYLE
Bonito a la bilbaína

Clean the fish and cut into thick slices. Place in a pan with the water, salt, wine, vinegar, bay, garlic, peppercorns, parsley and slice of onion. Bring to the boil, lower the heat and simmer for five minutes.

Remove the fish from the heat and let it cool in the liquid. Remove it, draining well and discarding all skin and bones. Arrange on a serving dish.

Chop the eggs and mix with chopped onion, chopped parsley, chopped pickle and pickle juice. Spread this mixture over the pieces of bonito and serve garnished with lettuce leaves, sliced tomato, cucumbers and lemon. Drizzle with olive oil.

Accompany with mayonnaise to which a spoonful of tomato sauce has been added. Serves six as an hors-d'oeuvre.

1 bonito, about 1 1/4 kg
1/2 litre water
1 teaspoon salt
100 ml white wine
1 tablespoon vinegar
1 bay leaf
1 clove garlic, slivered
peppercorns
sprigs parsley
slice onion
2 hard-boiled eggs
1/2 onion, finely chopped
1 tablespoon chopped parsley
1 tablespoon chopped pickle or capers
2 tablespoons pickle juice
lettuce
sliced tomato
sliced cucumber
lemon wedges
extra virgin olive oil
75 ml mayonnaise
1 tablespoon tomato sauce

FISH PÂTÉ
Fiambre de bonito

This fish pâté can be made with any fish. It's a delightful starter.

Clean the fish and cut the flesh from the skin and bones. Chop the fish in a processor or meat grinder. Place in a bowl and add the breadcrumbs, sherry, two tablespoons chopped parsley, thyme and 1/2 teaspoon salt. Let the mixture sit for 30 minutes.

Mix in the beaten eggs. On a clean cloth or kitchen towel, dampened, spread a third of the fish paste in a layer. Arrange half of the sliced ham, strips of pepper and chopped olives on it. Spread with another layer of paste and repeat with the ham, peppers and olives. Spread the remaining paste. Wrap it tightly in the cloth, forming a rectangle about 18 x 14 cm, and secure it with string or sew up with thread.

In a deep pan put about two litres of water, one onion, carrot, herbs, garlic, white wine and one teaspoon salt. Bring to the boil and reduce heat to a simmer. Add the pâté and cook very slowly for about an hour.

Drain it well, then place on a board with a weight on top and let it cool completely. Refrigerate. Unroll from the cloth and cut in slices to serve cold or room temperature. Makes 12 hors-d'oeuvre servings.

1 bonito, about 1 1/2 kg
50 g breadcrumbs
50 ml dry sherry or brandy
2 tablespoons chopped parsley
1/2 teaspoon thyme
1 1/2 teaspoons salt
1/4 teaspoon pepper
dash of cayenne
2 eggs
200 g sliced ham or bacon
1 small tin red peppers
50 g pitted olives, sliced
1 onion, quartered
1 carrot
bay, thyme, parsley, celery
1 clove garlic
200 ml white wine

FRESH TUNA BAKED IN TOMATO SAUCE
Atún con tomate

Sprinkle the tuna steak with salt and lemon juice and let it marinate 15 minutes. Then dredge in the flour and brown on both sides in a frying pan. Remove and place in an oven casserole.

In the same oil, fry the tomatoes, peeled and cut up. Add the bay leaf, salt, pepper and sugar and let cook on a high heat for five minutes. Pour over the tuna and sprinkle with the chopped garlic. Put in a medium hot oven until the tuna flakes easily, about 25 minutes. Sprinkle with parsley. Serves six.

1 thick slice tuna (750 g to 1 kg)
1 lemon
4 tablespoons olive oil
3/4 kg tomatoes, peeled and chopped
    (or tinned ones, drained)
1 bay leaf
salt and pepper
1 clove garlic
1 teaspoon sugar
1 tablespoon parsley, chopped

TUNA AND POTATO CASSEROLE
Marmitako

There are dozens of versions of this Basque dish, all of them wonderful. Because it originated as a fisherman's stew, prepared aboard a boat, I have chosen the simplest version and, in my opinion, the tastiest. This dish can be cooked with more liquid, making a soupier stew which is served over a slice of bread. It can also be made with tinned tuna packed in olive oil. Drain it and add the tuna chunks to the casserole at the very end of cooking to heat thoroughly.

Cut the tuna into chunks, discarding the bone. If using bonito, cut it first into slices, then with a knife or fork pull off chunks of the flesh from the bone.

Heat the oil in a heat-proof casserole and in it sauté the chopped onions, garlic and peppers, cleaned of seeds and cut in strips. When soft, add the tomatoes, peeled, seeded and chopped, the paprika, salt and pepper and chili. When tomatoes are somewhat reduced, add the potatoes. Stir for a few minutes, then add the wine and water.

Cover the pot and cook on a high heat until potatoes are nearly tender, about 20 minutes. Add the fish to the casserole, cover and cook another five minutes, or until fish flakes easily but is still juicy. Let the casserole rest, covered, for five to 10 minutes before serving. Serves four to six.

1 kg tuna or bonito
50 ml olive oil
1 onion, chopped
4 cloves garlic, chopped
2 sweet bell peppers, red and/or green
1/2 kg tomatoes (2 large)
2 teaspoons paprika
salt and pepper
1 small chili pepper
1 kg potatoes (7-8 medium), diced
200 ml white wine
100 ml water

CHARCOAL GRILLED AMBERJACK WITH FENNEL
Pez limón al hinojo

This is one of my favourites for charcoal grilling on the patio. Besides the meaty amberjack, sea bass, pompano, trout, mackerel or grey mullet are good choices for barbecuing. A hinged grill makes turning the fish much easier. A few sprigs of fennel can be laid on the fire as well — the aromatic smoke further flavours the fish.

Put the cleaned fish in a shallow dish and pour over them a marinade made with the oil, sherry, lemon juice, garlic, salt and pepper and chopped fennel. Let them marinate for an hour.

Drain the fish and stuff the cavities with a few sprigs of fennel. Have charcoal prepared. Oil the grill and heat it before placing the fish on it. Grill the fish over the hot coals, basting with the marinade until done, about five minutes on each side. Serves four.

2 amberjack (each about 1/2 kg)
50 ml olive oil
50 ml dry sherry
1 lemon
1 clove garlic, crushed
salt and pepper
1 tablespoon chopped fennel
sprigs of fennel

FRIED POMPANO
Palometa frita

Other fish fillets, such as John Dory or frozen fish, can be used in this recipe.

Fillet the fish and skin it. Cut the fillets into regular-sized pieces and place in a shallow dish. Sprinkle with salt, lemon juice and parsley and let them sit for 30 minutes.

Combine the hazelnuts and breadcrumbs on a plate. Dip the fillets first in flour, then beaten egg, then in the hazelnut mixture.

Heat enough oil to cover the bottom of a frying pan. Fry the pieces of fish, turning to brown both sides. Serves four to six.

1 pompano (about 1 kg) or 500 g fillets
salt
1 lemon
1 tablespoon chopped parsley
50 g hazelnuts, finely ground
50 g breadcrumbs
flour
1 egg, beaten
olive oil

SARDINES IN A ROW
Moraga de sardinas

Moraga means sardines grilled on spits *(espetones)* at the beach. This way of cooking them is suitable for the home kitchen.

Clean the fish, scale them, but leave whole. Arrange in a rectangular pan in rows, alternating the direction of heads and tails. Sprinkle them liberally with salt. Pour over the oil. Add the bay leaf, broken into several pieces, and the pine-nuts.

Arrange the well-scrubbed clams around the edges and between rows. Pour in the white wine and sprinkle with the chopped garlic and parsley. Cook on a medium heat (or in a hot oven) until the sardines are cooked and the clam shells have opened, about 15 minutes. Serve in the same pan. Serves six.

1 kg fresh sardines
60 ml olive oil
salt
1 bay leaf
25 g pine-nuts
1 dozen clams, scrubbed
150 ml white wine
4 cloves garlic, chopped
1 tablespoon chopped parsley

STUFFED SARDINES
Sardinas rellenas

For the stuffing, grapes, seeded and chopped, can be used instead of raisins and chopped walnuts can be added in addition to the pine-nuts. This extraordinary stuffing is equally good for mackerel or sea bass. If preferred, the fish can be floured and fried instead of baked.

Clean the sardines, scale them, cut off the heads and open them by slitting up the belly. Carefully remove the spines, leaving the fillets attached at the tail. Wash and pat dry.

Heat the oil in a small pan and in it toast the breadcrumbs. Remove from heat and add the seeded and chopped raisins, the pine-nuts, parsley and the anchovy fillets, well drained and chopped. Mix well and season with salt and pepper.

Stuff the filleted sardines with this mixture, pressing them together and fastening with a toothpick. Place in an oven dish, drizzle with oil and sprinkle with breadcrumbs. Bake in a medium oven until cooked, about 20 minutes. Serves four.

1/2 kg fresh sardines
2 tablespoons olive oil
2 tablespoons fine breadcrumbs
1 tablespoon raisins, seeded and chopped
1 tablespoon pine-nuts
1 tablespoon chopped parsley
2 tinned anchovy fillets
salt and pepper
olive oil

MOORISH-STYLE SARDINES
Sardinas a la moruna

During the Moorish era in Spain, tomatoes would not have been included, but they are an excellent addition. Left-overs make a delicious hors-d'oeuvre, served cold or spread on bread.

Clean the sardines, scale them, remove heads and spines. Wash and pat dry.

Chop the onions, peppers, and the skinned and seeded tomatoes all very finely (the food processor does this quickly). Add the chopped garlic, chopped parsley, minced chili, crushed saffron, cumin, paprika, salt and pepper to the vegetables.

In a casserole spread a layer of the chopped vegetables and on top a layer of the filleted sardines. Repeat the layers, ending with a layer of the vegetables. Drizzle with the oil and put the casserole over a medium heat. Cook fairly slowly until sardines are cooked, about 30 minutes. Serve hot or cold.

3/4 kg sardines
400 g onions (3 small)
400 g peppers
400 g tomatoes (2 large)
2 cloves garlic
2 tablespoons chopped parsley
1 chili pepper (optional)
1/4 teaspoon saffron
1/4 teaspoon cumin
1/4 teaspoon paprika
salt and pepper
2 tablespoons olive oil

FRESH ANCHOVIES IN BATTER
Boquerones rebozados

Clean the fish, cut off the heads. To fillet them, grasp the top of the backbone firmly against the knife blade and pull it down sharply across the belly of the fish. Cut off the bone at the tail, leaving the two fillets attached by the tail. Wash and pat them dry.

Make the batter by beating together the flour, water, egg, parsley, minced garlic, saffron and salt. Let the batter sit for an hour. Heat the oil.

1/2 kg fresh anchovies
130 g flour
100 ml water
1 egg, beaten
1 tablespoon chopped parsley
lemon wedges
4 cloves garlic, minced
1/8 teaspoon saffron
1 teaspoon salt
olive oil for frying

Dip the fish fillets in the batter and fry them in the hot oil until golden and crisp. Drain on absorbent paper and serve hot with lemon wedges. Serves four.

SWORDFISH

SWORDFISH KEBAB
Brocheta de pez espada

Angler fish, tuna and shark may be prepared in the same manner.

Cut the swordfish into cubes of about 4cm and place them in a bowl. Add the oil, parsley, garlic and lemon juice. Let marinate for 30 minutes.

Cut the tomato, onion and green pepper each into eighths. Thread the swordfish on to skewers, alternating with pieces of vegetable. Brush with marinade and grill over hot coals or on a griddle, turning frequently and basting with marinade until the fish is done, about eight minutes.

1/2 kg swordfish
2 tablespoons olive oil
2 tablespoons chopped parsley
5 cloves garlic
1 lemon
1 tomato
1 onion
1 green pepper

SWORDFISH, MÁLAGA STYLE
Pez espada a la malagueña

This recipe is equally good with any large fish steak — tuna, haddock, cod, halibut, shark, etc.

Into an earthenware casserole large enough to hold the fish put the chopped onion, garlic, green pepper and tomatoes. Add the bay leaf, cloves and peppercorns. Place the fish on top, sprinkle with salt and add the oil. Place on a medium heat until it begins to sizzle. Add the wine and just bring it to the boil.

Cover and simmer (or bake in a medium oven) until fish is done and flakes easily, about 25 minutes. If desired, the fish can be removed to a serving dish and the sauce boiled to reduce and thicken it. Serve garnished with parsley. Serves six.

1 medium onion, chopped
4 cloves garlic, chopped
1 large green pepper, chopped
2 tomatoes, peeled, seeded and chopped
50 ml olive oil
1 bay leaf
2 cloves
5 peppercorns
1 kg swordfish steak
1 teaspoon salt
100 ml white wine

HAKE

When, years ago, I acquired the typical traveller's malady after a sojourn in another country, the village doctor prescribed some strong medicine and a diet of white fish and white rice — with only red wine. At the local restaurant I presented my menu prescription. A few minutes later the waiter brought for my inspection a whole hake *(merluza)*, about 50cm long and gleamingly fresh. I nodded my approval. I was served a thick slice of the flaky white fish, perfectly poached, with a serving of white rice, a sprig of parsley and a slice of lemon. So moist and flavourful was the fish that, although I've since enjoyed many stupendous fish dishes, perhaps no other was as good as that one. I like to think I was cured on the spot and certainly recommend this invalid's diet to even the most demanding gourmet.

Hake may be Spain's favourite fish, particularly on the north and the south coasts, where you come across several quite different ways of cooking it. It's a good choice for "fish and chips", simple and straightforwardly fried, but lends itself to many fancier preparations. Where not available, try substituting cod, haddock, whiting or coley in these recipes.

HAKE, BASQUE STYLE
Merluza a la vasca

This dish is also called *koskera* or *salsa verde* and may only include the parsley, with no peas or asparagus.

Cut the fish in fairly thick steaks or in bone-free medallions. Salt them and let sit for 15 minutes. Then dredge them in flour.

In a heat-proof casserole heat the oil. Add the pieces of hake and quickly brown the fish on both sides. Add the chopped garlic and immediately the white wine. Don't stir, but shake the casserole, adding water, stock or liquid from peas, asparagus or clams, drop by drop, until the sauce is the consistency of thick cream.

Add the cooked peas and garnish with the cooked asparagus tips and quartered eggs. Season with salt and pepper and add lots of chopped parsley. Total cooking time for the fish should be less than 15 minutes, the sauce thickening while the fish cooks. Serves four to six.

1 kg hake steaks
flour
50 ml olive oil
6 cloves garlic, chopped
100 ml white wine
75 g cooked peas
2 dozen asparagus tips, cooked or tinned
3 hard-boiled eggs
salt and pepper
3 tablespoons chopped parsley

HAKE, BILBAO STYLE
Merluza a la bilbaína

For presentation, spoon this lovely sauce onto the plate and place a slice of poached fish on top. Serve with boiled potatoes and garnish the plate with chopped parsley.

Sprinkle the fish steaks with salt and let them sit while preparing the sauce. Heat the oil in a frying pan and sauté the chopped onion, chopped garlic and skinned peppers, cut in dice. Season with bay leaf and salt and pepper and cook until very soft, adding a few drops of water if necessary. Purée this mixture in the blender or sieve it.

Oil an oven-proof dish and put the fish steaks in it. Pour over the white wine and put in a medium hot oven until fish is partially cooked, about 10 minutes. Spread the puréed pepper sauce on top and bake another five minutes or until the fish flakes easily.

1/2 kg sliced hake (4 steaks)
50 ml olive oil
1 onion, chopped
2 cloves garlic, chopped
2 large red peppers, roasted and
    skinned, or tinned peppers
1 bay leaf
salt and pepper
50 ml white wine

POACHED HAKE WITH MAYONNAISE
Merluza con mayonesa

The liquid in which the fish is poached makes a wonderful basis for soup.

Put the water in a pot large enough to hold the whole fish. Bring to the boil and add the sliced leeks, salt, sliced carrot, parsley, bay leaf, white wine and lemon zest. Boil this *court bouillon* for 30 minutes.

Place the cleaned fish on a clean cloth or kitchen towel and put it into the poaching liquid. Reduce heat so the liquid just simmers and cook until the

1 whole fish, about 1400 g
1 1/2 litres water
2 leeks
1 tablespoon salt
1 carrot, peeled and sliced
2 sprigs parsley
1 bay leaf
50 ml white wine
1 piece lemon zest
200 ml mayonnaise
parsley and lemon
lettuce

fish flakes easily, about 20 minutes. Remove the fish to a platter and let it cool slightly.

Skin it if desired, and garnish with parsley, lemon and lettuce. Spoon the mayonnaise over it and serve cold. Serves four to six.

HAKE MORSELS IN GREEN SAUCE, SAN SEBASTIÁN STYLE
Kokotxas en salsa verde a la donostiarra

This is, inevitably, the priciest item on any menu where it is available. The tiny morsel of flesh from the fish's throat, so delicate and so perishable, is more commonly gobbled up by the fishermen. In northern markets, cod's cheeks can be used in this dish. Clams can be added to the *kokotxas* to extend the portions.

1 kg *kokotxas* (hake morsels or cod cheeks)
100 ml olive oil
6 cloves garlic, chopped
1 chili pepper (optional)
2 tablespoons chopped onion
100 ml water
freshly ground pepper
2 tablespoons chopped parsley

Heat the oil in an earthenware casserole and sauté the chopped garlic, chopped chili pepper and onion. Add the hake morsels and fry for a minute. Then add the water very slowly, swirling the casserole to combine it. Season with pepper. Cook about five minutes, garnish with parsley and serve. Serves eight as a starter.

SEA BREAM

Spanish markets offer a variety of different sea bream in various hues of pink and grey, from the small and cheap to the big and very expensive. They can all be used in the following recipes fairly interchangeably, though the named fish is the preferred choice. *Besugo* may be the favourite in Spain, a good fish for grilling or baking. A *besuguera* is a rectangular metal pan, or fish-kettle, just right for holding a *besugo,* which goes from gas hob to oven.

BAKED BREAM, MADRID STYLE
Besugo a la madrileña

Clean and scale the fish and rub inside and out with the salt and let sit for 15 minutes. Chop the garlic and mix with the chopped parsley and breadcrumbs.

Heat the oil in a heat-proof oven pan and put the fish into it. Sprinkle the garlic-crumb mixture on top of the fish and add the white wine. When the liquid starts to simmer, put the pan in a medium oven. Bake the fish until it flakes easily, about 20 minutes, basting frequently with the liquid in the pan. Sprinkle with a few chopped olives. Serves three or four.

1 whole fish (about 750 g)
salt
8 cloves garlic
4 tablespoons chopped parsley
3 tablespoons breadcrumbs
50 ml olive oil
1/4 litre white wine
chopped olives

BAKED BREAM
Pescado al horno

A large bream, such as gilt-head or dentex, is excellent for this dish, but any large fish — bass, salmon, grouper — could be used. This is a speciality of the beachside restaurants on the Cádiz and Málaga coasts.

Rub the fish inside and out with salt and let sit 15 minutes.

Pour the oil into the bottom of a heat-proof oven dish and add a layer of half the thinly sliced potatoes. Sprinkle half the chopped garlic, parsley and peppers over them and sprinkle with salt and pepper. Add a layer of the sliced onions and tomatoes. Add the rest of the potatoes, the remaining garlic, parsley and peppers and sprinkle with salt and pepper. Lay the fish on top of the

1 whole fish (about 1 1/4 kg)
100 ml olive oil
1 kg potatoes, thinly sliced
5 cloves garlic, chopped
3 tablespoons chopped parsley
2 small green peppers, chopped
salt and pepper
1 onion, sliced
2 tomatoes, sliced
100 ml white wine
1 bay leaf

potatoes and top with a few remaining slices of tomato. Put pieces of bay leaf around it. Pour the wine over and when it begins to simmer, cover with foil and put the pan into a medium oven until potatoes and fish are done, about 30 minutes.

Remove the foil during the last 15 minutes of baking. If using smaller fish, it will be necessary to put the potatoes in to bake before adding the fish. Serves six.

GRILLED BREAM, SAN SEBASTIÁN STYLE
Besugo asado a la donostiarra

If the fish is split open and boned, it is called *a la espalda*, on its back. Prepare other large bream, sea bass, redfish, grey mullet in the same way

Rub the fish inside and out with the salt and oil and let it sit for an hour. Prepare broiler/grill, charcoal or griddle *(plancha)* for cooking the fish. Preheat the grill, brush it with oil and place the fish on it. (If using a griddle, brush it with heavy brine and heat until the salt turns white.)

Brush the fish with oil as it cooks, turning it to toast both sides. The skin should be quite crisp. When done, place it on a platter and serve with sauce made by frying the chopped garlic in the remaining oil. Add the lemon juice, minced chili pepper and chopped parsley. Serves four.

1-2 whole fish, about 1-2 kg
salt
100 ml olive oil
6 cloves garlic
3 tablespoons lemon juice
1 chili pepper, minced
1 tablespoon parsley, chopped

BREAM IN ONION SAUCE
Pargo encebollado

Clean the fish, rub with salt and let them sit for a while.

Chop or shred the onions (food processor works well — no tears) and mix with the garlic and parsley. Put the oil in the oven dish and put the onion mixture on the bottom. Place the fish on it and squeeze over it the juice of the lemon. Put in a medium oven until fish is done, about 20 minutes, spooning the onion mixture over the fish occasionally while it bakes.

Fry the almonds or pine-nuts in a little oil until toasted. Sprinkle them over the fish before serving.

1 or 2 whole fish
salt
2 onions
4 cloves garlic, chopped
3 tablespoons parsley
75 ml olive oil
1 lemon
25 g almonds or pine-nuts

FISH, ROTA STYLE
Urta a la roteña

Sprinkle the fish lightly with salt and dredge in flour. Heat 60 ml oil in a heat-proof casserole and brown the pieces of fish on both sides. Pour in the brandy, set it alight and gently swirl the casserole until flames subside.

Meanwhile, in another pan, heat the remaining oil and sauté the chopped onions and the peppers, cut in strips. Add the puréed tomato, thyme, bay leaf, salt and pepper and the sherry. Simmer this sauce until somewhat reduced, about 10 minutes. Add it to the fish, combine well, and simmer until the fish is flaky, about 10 minutes more. Serves four.

1 1/2 kg fish fillets
flour
110 ml olive oil
50 ml brandy
1 onion, chopped
4 small green peppers, cut in strips
1 large tomato, peeled and puréed
1/2 teaspoon thyme
1 bay leaf
salt and pepper
50 ml dry sherry

GILT-HEAD BAKED IN SALT
Dorada a la sal

The salt bakes into a crust, sealing in the fish juices. Crack the crust and peel it away with the skin. Spoon the flesh off the bones on to plates and serve accompanied by two or three sauces, such as *alioli* and *aliño*. Use a large bream, especially gilt-head, or sea bass, snapper or redfish for this dish.

If possible, have the fish drawn through the gills. Wash and dry well. Measure it at the thickest part and allow 15 minutes in a hot oven for every 2cm, or about 20 minutes for a fish weighing 3/4 kilo. Mix 1/2 cup of water with 2 kg of coarse salt. Oil an oven pan and put in a layer of the salt. Place the fish on top and cover with the remaining salt. Place in a preheated hot oven and bake as indicated above. A fish of this weight serves two people.

SEA BASS

This is my personal favourite, which I would choose over steak or lamb chops any day. I prefer it very simply grilled. I place it on a pre-heated, oiled grill pan and put under the grill until the top is browned, about eight minutes, then remove and serve it without turning. However, because it is such an expensive fish, it merits fancier preparations.

SEA BASS, ASTURIAS STYLE
Lubina a la asturiana

Cut the fish in crosswise slices, season with salt and pepper and place in an oven dish. Pour over the oil, the chopped onion and sprinkle with the paprika. Add the cider and bake in a medium oven until fish is cooked, about 20 minutes.

While it is baking, steam the clams open and discard the shells. Reserve them in a little of their strained liquid. Place the fish on a serving platter and keep warm. Pour the juices in the pan through a sieve and add the clams. Pour this sauce over the fish and serve with triangles of fried bread and sprigs of parsley. Serves four.

1 kg sea bass
salt and pepper
2 tablespoons olive oil
1 small onion, chopped
1 teaspoon paprika
fried bread to serve
sprigs of parsley for garnish
100 ml cider or white wine
2 dozen clams
parsley

SEA BASS WITH WILD MUSHROOMS
Lubina con gibelurdiñas

Clean the fish, scale it and rub with salt and pepper and let it sit for 30 minutes. Place in an oiled oven dish and put in a moderately hot oven for 10 minutes. Add the cleaned mushrooms to the pan (saving 2 of them) and pour over the oil. Return the fish to the oven to bake until it flakes easily, about 30 minutes in all. Baste frequently with the liquid in the pan.

Put the white wine, parsley and reserved mushrooms in the blender and whirl until puréed. Put in a small saucepan and simmer. Place the fish on a serving dish with the cooked mushrooms and add the liquid in the pan to the saucepan. Heat thoroughly and pour over the fish. Serves six.

1 whole fish (about 1 1/2 kg)
salt and pepper
250 g chanterelles or other wild
    mushrooms, wiped clean
50 ml olive oil
150 ml white wine
1 tablespoon parsley

FISH WITH CANARY ISLAND RED SAUCE
Sancocho canario

This is typically made with *sama,* a Canary Island fish for which either sea bass or a large sea bream can be substituted. The fish could be grilled instead of boiled and served with a *mojo verde,* green sauce, in addition to the *mojo colorado,* red sauce (see recipes in Sauce chapter).

Cut the fish into slices or into bone-free chunks. Peel the potatoes and, if small, quarter them, or cut into regular-sized chunks. Put them to cook in salted water to cover. When half-cooked, about 10 minutes, add the pieces of fish and simmer about eight minutes.

1 kg bass or bream
1/2 kg potatoes
1/2 teaspoon cumin
2 cloves garlic
salt
1 chili pepper
1 teaspoon paprika
2 tablespoons vinegar

Drain the fish and potatoes, reserving the liquid. In the mortar or blender crush the garlic with salt and the chili pepper, cumin, paprika and vinegar. Add two or three pieces of cooked potato and enough of the reserved cooking liquid to make a smooth sauce. Put the cooked fish and potatoes on a serving dish and pour some of the sauce over. Serves four.

MEAGRE IN CAPER SAUCE
Corvina en salsa de alcaparras

A very bland fish, meagre or corb profits from the sharp taste of capers. Spain is the world's largest producer of this piquant condiment. Use this preparation for *mero* (grouper), *cherna* (wreckfish), *brótola* (forkbeard), *merluza* (hake) and any frozen fish.

650 g fish steak
2 tablespoons white wine
4 tablespoons capers (50 g)
1 tablespoon minced scallion or onion
2 tablespoons olive oil
1 head garlic, roasted (for how-to see
    page 142)
20 almonds, blanched and toasted
salt and pepper

Rub the fish steak with salt and let it sit for 30 minutes. Place in an oiled oven dish with the white wine and cover the casserole. Bake in a medium oven until the fish flakes easily, about 25 minutes.

Drain off the cooking liquid and keep the fish warm while making the sauce. In mortar or blender mash the roasted and peeled garlic with the almonds, capers, scallions and oil. Beat in the cooking liquid from the fish and season with salt and pepper. Serve the fish in the same dish, covered with the sauce. Serves four.

GROUPER IN VINAIGRETTE
Mero a la vinagreta

This wonderful fish can be substituted in almost any of the preceding recipes. It's especially good served cold with piquant sauces.

Poach a whole fish or steaks in a flavourful *court bouillon,* to which have been added orange and lemon peel. Remove when flesh flakes easily and let cool. Chop hard-boiled eggs, onions, olives, capers or pickles and parsley. Stir in vinegar, olive oil, salt and pepper to taste. Serve the fish cold, accompanied by the sauce.

DOGFISH

MARINATED DOGFISH
Cazón en adobo

In Spain, instead of man-eating sharks, we have shark-eating men. The dogfish is one of several edible sharks. This tapa bar favourite is also a good way to treat frozen fish, as the marinade adds lots of flavour. If shark isn't on your shopping list, make this recipe with angler or other solid-fleshed fish.

Cut the fish into cubes about 4cm square, discarding any skin and bone. Put it in a glass or ceramic bowl. Mix together the oil, vinegar, water, chopped garlic, paprika, oregano, pepper, cumin and salt. Pour over the fish and toss it well. Marinate for at least six hours or overnight.

Drain the fish well, dredge it in flour and fry in hot oil until golden and crisp. Drain on absorbent paper and serve hot.

3/4 kg dogfish
50 ml olive oil
50 ml vinegar or lemon juice
1 tablespoon water
3 cloves garlic, chopped
1/4 teaspoon paprika
1 teaspoon oregano
1/4 teaspoon ground pepper
pinch of cumin
1/2 teaspoon salt
flour
olive oil for frying

Bottom: Sizzling Cod (*Bacalao al Pil Pil*), page 268, and
Squid in Inky Sauce (*Calamares en Su Tinta*), page 282

SKATE

SKATE IN PAPRIKA SAUCE
Raya en pimentón

Any solid-fleshed fish, such as gar and angler, or shellfish such as prawns, mussels or scallops, can be prepared in this manner.

Cut the fish into pieces. Heat the oil in a pan and fry the garlic and remove when golden. Add the skate to the pan and sauté it on a hot fire.

In the mortar or blender crush the garlic with the parsley, cayenne, paprika, saffron, oregano and vinegar. Add this to the fish with salt and pepper to taste and cook a few more minutes. A little water can be added if desired to dilute the sauce. Serves four.

3/4 kg cleaned skate
70 ml olive oil
6 cloves garlic
1 sprig parsley
dash cayenne
1 teaspoon paprika
1/4 teaspoon saffron
1 teaspoon oregano
2 teaspoons vinegar
salt and pepper

EEL

When I made a trip to the Basque Country, on the Bay of Biscay, I wanted to have a first-hand look at the capture of *angulas*, the tiny, baby eels that are a favourite dish, especially for holidays. I called various companies and begged for an appointment, but met with no cooperation. "Too early in the season," said one. "All secret," said another. My most productive conversation was with José, whose family has been in the business for a couple of generations. He told me he was very bitter about the fishing of baby eels, so traditional in the Urbion river near San Sebastián. "The Chinese are buying the elvers to raise up to be eels to sell to the Japanese. They can pay more than we can. We Basques can't afford to eat angulas any more."

Tiny baby eels are an expensive treat, in the luxury category with caviar and truffles. Elvers, spawned in the Sargasso Sea, find their way across the Atlantic to the mouths of rivers in northern Spain. Some survive to grow into mature eels (see recipe for *anguila*). But many are scooped up in nets, quickly cooked and frozen.

Basques, especially, love to serve elvers on special occasions such as Christmas. At holiday time, supermarkets feature "fake" *angulas*, called *gulas*, made of surimi, a fish paste, complete with the pale gray line down their backs.

In fact, what makes angulas so delicious is their texture and the manner of preparing them, quickly sizzled in oil with garlic and a touch of chili. I found an excellent substitution: enokitake mushrooms. They look the part, are similar in texture, but they don't have eyes. Elvers are usually prepared and served in individual ramekins and eaten with wooden forks. Accompany with bread.

BABY EELS WITH GARLIC
Angulas en cazuela

Thaw elvers or clean mushrooms. In an earthenware casserole or small frying pan heat the oil with the garlic and chili. When it is hot, add the elvers (or mushrooms) all at once and stir them in the oil on a hot fire for one to two minutes. Sprinkle with salt (the imitation *angulas* need no salt).

Serve immediately, while still sizzling. Serves four as a tapa or two as a starter.

1/2 pound elvers, frozen surimi "gulas"
   or enokitake mushrooms
5 tablespoons olive oil
4 cloves garlic, sliced
4 crosswise rings of dry red chili pepper
salt

VALENCIAN EEL STEW
Anguila al all i pebre

Cooked vegetables in season, peas, broad beans or green beans, can be added to the stew.

Clean and skin the eel and cut it into 8cm lengths. Season with salt and pepper.

In an earthenware casserole, heat the oil. When hot, remove the casserole from the heat and stir in the paprika. Add the hot water and return to the heat, letting it cook for several minutes. Then add the pieces of eel and continue simmering, adding more water if necessary so they are just covered.

In the mortar or blender crush the saffron, garlic, parsley, almonds or walnuts and salt and pepper. Dissolve this paste in some of the liquid from the casserole and add it to the stew. Cook several minutes more until eel is done. Garnish with parsley. Serves six.

1 1/2 kg eel
100 ml olive oil
1 tablespoon paprika
1/2 litre hot water
1/4 teaspoon saffron
3 cloves garlic
1 tablespoon parsley
1 dozen blanched and toasted almonds or
    8 toasted walnuts
salt and pepper
parsley to garnish

CONGER EEL, RIOJA STYLE
Congrio a la riojana

Use the head and upper portion of conger, which is full of tiny bones, for making flavourful fish stock. Use the tail part of the fish in this recipe.

Clean the conger and cut it into slices. Rub them with salt and pepper and dredge in flour.

Heat the oil in a casserole and fry the peppers, which have been seeded and cut in wide strips. Remove to a plate when softened. Add the garlic, and when just golden, add the floured slices of conger. Brown them on both sides, then add the puréed tomatoes, fried peppers, wine, salt and pepper and chili pepper, if desired. Cook for 15 minutes until the conger is cooked.

1 1/4 kg tail of conger eel
100 ml olive oil
flour
1/4 kg sweet red peppers
6 cloves garlic, sliced
2 tomatoes, peeled and puréed
500 ml red wine
salt and pepper
1 chili pepper (optional)

SEAFOOD STEWS

Some are more like soups, others like casseroles, but all have two or more kinds of fish and shellfish. Savouring them is like touring all the coastlines of Spain.

MALLORCAN FISH AND AUBERGINE CASSEROLE
Tumbet de pescado mallorquín

This can be made with any combination of fish or with frozen fish fillets.

Put the fish in an oven dish, salt it and squeeze the juice of the lemon over it. Drizzle with one tablespoon oil and pour in the white wine. Bake the fish until partially done, only about 10 minutes, and remove.

Meanwhile, prepare each of the vegetables. Put the sliced potatoes in a frying pan with two tablespoons of oil, fry them for a few minutes, then cover the pan and let them cook, turning occasionally, until almost done.

Peel the aubergines and slice them. Dredge in flour and fry in oil (or, to decrease oil in this dish, brush the slices with oil, put them on a tin and bake until tender).

Roast the peppers, peel and cut them in wide strips.

In a saucepan, heat remaining oil and sauté the chopped onion and garlic until softened. Add the prepared tomatoes, bay leaf, salt and pepper, cinnamon, sugar, and the liquid from the pan in which the fish baked. Cook this sauce for about 15 minutes, then sieve it or purée in a food processor. It should be fairly thick.

3/4 kg fish fillets
1 lemon
100 ml olive oil
50 ml white wine
1/2 kg potatoes, sliced
2 aubergines
flour
2 large sweet red bell peppers
1 onion, chopped
1 clove garlic, chopped
3 large tomatoes, peeled, seeded and
    chopped
bay leaf
salt and pepper
1/2 teaspoon cinnamon
1 teaspoon sugar

Place a layer of half the potatoes, half the fish and half the aubergine and peppers in a *greixonera,* an oval, earthenware casserole, or other oven dish. Repeat the layers and cover with the prepared sauce. Put in a medium-hot oven until bubbly, about 15 minutes. Serves four to six.

ASTURIAN FISH STEW
Caldereta asturiana

Instead of sherry and white wine called for in this recipe, *vino rancio* or cider can be used.

2 to 3 kg solid-fleshed fish (angler, mullet, redfish, scorpionfish, gurnard, bass)
1 kg shellfish (prawns, clams, mussels, razorshells)
1 kg onions, thinly sliced
4 tablespoons chopped parsley
1 small tin peppers
freshly ground pepper
grated nutmeg
cayenne
200 ml olive oil
50 ml sherry
250 ml white wine

Clean the fish. Leave small ones whole and cut large ones into pieces. Scrub the clams; scrape and wash the mussels well; leave prawns unpeeled.

In a large pot or fish-kettle with a tight-fitting lid, put a layer of the sliced onions, then a layer of fish. Put the scrappiest, least good fish in the bottom layers and the best fish at the top. Continue layering onions and fish, sprinkling them with the chopped parsley.

Purée the peppers in the blender with a little water. Drizzle this sauce on to the fish (or substitute paprika). Sprinkle with pepper, nutmeg and cayenne. When the pot is filled, pour over the oil, sherry and wine and just a little water. Cover the pot, bring to the boil, then simmer gently for 15 minutes. Serve the stew in the same pot. Serves eight.

SEAFOOD OPERETTA
Zarzuela

This is an opera in three acts, a lavish but simply staged production if all the ingredients are prepared before starting to cook. The dish is usually served in a shallow earthenware casserole or a paella pan. A separate frying pan is used to sauté all the ingredients first. They are then combined to finish cooking in the casserole. The *suquillo del pescador*, fisherman's stew, is a similar Catalan dish, somewhat soupier and usually without tomatoes.

Four servings each of three or four different kinds of fish, e.g. "meaty" fish (such as angler, conger or lobster), flaky fish (bass, grouper, bream, meagre, gurnard), and lean, delicate fish (hake, sole, turbot) — the servings can be cut into fillets or steaks

Heat some of the oil in the frying pan and fry the floured pieces of squid (the flour keeps the oil from splattering) until golden and transfer them to the casserole. Next add the pieces of angler, conger or lobster, sautéing them very slowly, turning once to brown the other side. The pieces of flaky fish (bass, grouper, etc.) can be added while the first are still cooking, as they take less time. Remove them to the casserole as they are done.

Next fry the pieces of delicate fish that need only quick browning on each side. Add more oil to the pan as needed. Now sauté the prawns and crayfish (prawns can be peeled, leaving tails and heads intact). Place them in the casserole and add the prepared mussels and clams.

Wipe the pan clean and add more oil. Sauté the finely chopped onions just until soft. Add the

1/2 kg squid, cleaned and cut in rings and dredged in flour

1/2 kg mussels, cleaned, steamed open and empty half-shells discarded

1/2 kg clams scrubbed, steamed open and half-shell discarded (strain and save liquid from cooking mussels and clams)

8 large prawns, or 4 prawns and 4 Dublin Bay prawns (sea crayfish) — the large red prawns, *carabineros*, are a good choice

100 ml olive oil

1 onion, finely chopped

3 large tomatoes, peeled, seeded and finely chopped

50 ml sherry or white wine

50 ml brandy, rum or, for those who like the taste, anise brandy

1 bay leaf

1/2 teaspoon saffron

2 cloves garlic

6 blanched and toasted almonds

2 plain biscuits *(galletas María)*

salt and pepper

dash of cayenne

chopped parsley

lemon wedges

triangles of fried bread

pitted black olives or anchovy- stuffed green olives (optional)

prepared tomatoes and fry for a few minutes. Add the sherry or wine and the brandy, rum or anise and the bay leaf. In the mortar or blender crush the saffron, garlic, almonds, biscuits, salt and pepper and cayenne. Dissolve in a little liquid and add to the tomatoes with the strained broth from the mussels and clams. Cook a few minutes, then pour this sauce over the fish and shellfish in the casserole. Shake the casserole to distribute the sauce and continue cooking for about 10 minutes until all the fish are cooked.

Serve the casserole garnished with chopped parsley, lemon wedges, fried bread and a sprinkling of olives, if desired. Serves four.

SALT COD

The small village where I live had no supermarkets when I first settled there. Staples like sugar, flour and chickpeas (*garbanzos*) were purchased in tiny shops, often the front room of someone's house. Sugar was scooped from bins, oil poured from jugs into a bottle that was perpetually recycled and wine was measured into the drinking glass, later to be set at the father's place. If you bought from the tiny selection of canned foods, tuna, sardines, jam, the shopkeeper offered to open the tin, as no one had can-openers at home.

On my first forays into these shops, there were a few things I took pains to avoid. These included ropes of evil-looking sausages, hanging from the beams and sweating and dripping a little in the summer heat, and chunks of salt pork which gave a rancid pungency to the shop. And then there were some strange-smelling objects hanging on a line like grey bats. This was *bacalao*, dry salted cod, and village women bought a lot of it.

I first ate *bacalao* on *Viernes Santo*, Good Friday, as processions were wending their way through village streets; while penitents, many barefoot with candles, followed the images and the sombre, throbbing drums. In a tapa bar — which, as on any Spanish holiday, was doing a brisk business — I was served two fishy tapas, one in sauce, the other a croquette. They were both made of *bacalao*.

Since then I've learned to prepare it in many more ways, all of them quite delicious. Though the

Basques seem to have the most and the best recipes for *bacalao,* some others of interest are *a la manchega,* with anise brandy, *soldaditos de Pavía,* fried in a crisp batter, and *porrusalda,* with leeks.

Salt cod is the "in" dish on stylish menus these days, though it's still dearly loved by simple village people all over Spain, especially during Holy Week. Today you can buy it in supermarkets, cut in pieces and packaged in plastic. Quality and price vary. The larger the fish, the better it is and, though dry, it should never be stiff as a board, but slightly pliable. The best *bacalao* has a thin skin and is white or grey, not yellow. Nowadays it can be purchased in small packets, ready for cooking.

If starting with salt cod, clean *bacalao* in running water. Put it to soak in water to cover for 24 to 36 hours, changing the water twice a day. Drain it, then cut into pieces, removing all skin and bones. Do not salt a dish made with salt cod until tasting it at the end of cooking time.

SALT COD, BISCAY STYLE
Bacalao a la vizcaína

There are those who say this dish should be made only with dried peppers and no tomatoes, and others who say that tomatoes must be included. In either case, the sauce is a deep ruddy red. The dried peppers (*ñoras* or *pimientos choriceros*) are first soaked in boiling water. If not available, use a big spoonful of paprika mixed to a paste with water.

Put the fish, soaked overnight, in a pot with fresh water and heat it almost to boiling. Remove from heat and take out the fish, saving the liquid. Cut it into regular-sized pieces, discarding all bone.

Heat 100 ml oil in a saucepan and sauté the chopped onions. Add the chopped tomatoes and fry for several minutes, then add the soaked peppers, the bread and chili pepper. Add some of the liquid from the fish and let this sauce cook for several minutes on a hot fire. Add more liquid and simmer for 30 minutes adding extra liquid as

1 kg salt cod soaked 24 hours
12 dried peppers (not chili), soaked overnight
150 ml olive oil
2 onions, chopped
1 kg tomatoes, chopped
2 slices toasted bread
chili pepper or cayenne
2 sweet red bell peppers, roasted and skinned
6 cloves garlic

needed. Purée the sauce in a processor then pass it through a fine sieve.

Spread some of the sauce in an earthenware casserole, place the pieces of cod on top and cover with the remaining sauce, adding a little more liquid if sauce seems too thick. Cut the peppers in wide strips and sauté them in oil until very soft. Garnish the top of the casserole with strips of pepper and put in a medium hot oven until bubbly, about 15 minutes.

Meanwhile, fry the garlic, slivered, in the remaining oil. Drizzle the top of the fish with the garlic, and serve. Serves six.

SIZZLING COD
Bacalao al pil pil

Put the soaked cod in a pan with water to cover and heat until it almost boils. Remove from heat and drain, saving the liquid. Remove any bones and scales, but do not skin the fish. Pat it dry on a clean cloth.

Put the oil in a flame-proof casserole and heat it. Add the garlic, cut in crosswise slivers, and the chili pepper, seeds removed and broken into several pieces. Fry until the garlic is toasted lightly and skim out with the chili. Reserve.

Put the pieces of cod into the oil in one layer, skin side down, and cook for a few minutes. Then sprinkle with the flour and, grasping the casserole with pot-holders, swirl it gently from side to side, lifting it off the stove slightly. Add a spoonful of the water in which the fish heated and swirl it in. The gelatinous quality of the skin causes the oil and liquid to amalgamate into a sauce the consistency of cream. Add a few more spoonfuls of liquid and cook the fish about 30 minutes, adding liquid as needed and shaking the casserole. Sprinkle with the reserved garlic and chili, and serve. Serves six.

1 kg salt cod, cut in 12 pieces and soaked 24 to 36 hours
150 ml olive oil
10 cloves garlic
1 chili pepper
1 tablespoon flour

SALT COD, MULETEERS' STYLE
Bacalao al ajo arriero

Before the days of modern transport, the muleteers who carried fresh seafood inland from the coasts were vital to the economy. Like modern-day lorry drivers, they ate very well in the posadas and ventas en route, enjoying excellent and unpretentious dishes like this one. So good is this that the same preparation is used for lobster!

Put the fish in a pot with water, bring it almost to the boil and drain. Remove all skin and bones and, with the fingers, tear the cod into thin strips. Pat dry.

Heat the oil in a casserole and fry the chopped garlic and chili pepper, broken into small pieces. Add the red peppers and fry a few minutes, then the pieces of cod. Continue frying this mixture for several more minutes, then add the paprika and the tomato sauce. Depending on the thickness of the tomato sauce more liquid might be required to give the consistency of a thick soup. Simmer for 20 minutes and serve garnished with chopped parsley. Serves six.

1 kg salt cod, cut in thin strips and soaked
   24-36 hours
100 ml olive oil
8 cloves garlic
1 chili pepper
2 red peppers, cut in strips
1 teaspoon paprika
200 ml tomato sauce
parsley

CODFISH BALLS
Albóndigas de bacalao

Cook the desalted cod in water with the bay leaf for five minutes without letting it boil. Remove and drain, squeezing out all the liquid. Remove all skin and bones and put the cod in the processor or mortar.

Soak the slice of bread in milk until softened. Squeeze it out and add to the processor with the pepper, cinnamon, nutmeg, parsley, one tablespoon of flour and the baking powder. Process until smooth.

Make small balls of the paste, roll them in flour and fry in oil until nicely browned. They may be served as is or added to an almond or hazelnut sauce.

350 g salt cod, soaked 24-36 hours
1 bay leaf
1 thick slice bread
milk
pepper
pinch of cinnamon
grating of nutmeg
1 tablespoon chopped parsley
flour
1/2 teaspoon baking powder
olive oil

SALMON, TROUT and TENCH

SALMON, GALICIAN STYLE
Salmón a la gallega

Boil equal parts of *aguardiente de orujo,* clear brandy distilled from grapes (similar to French *marc* or Italian *grappa),* and salted water with bay leaves, peppercorns, clove and onion. Reduce heat and poach salmon steaks in the liquid. Remove from heat and let them cool in the liquid. Marinate, refrigerated, for several days.

SALMON, ASTURIAS STYLE
Salmón a la ribereña

Salt the salmon steaks, let them sit for 30 minutes, then dredge with flour. Heat the butter and oil in a frying pan and put in the fish, moderating the heat so the fish cooks in the time it takes to brown both sides, about 10 minutes. Remove to a platter and keep warm.

In the same fat sauté the diced ham. Stir in the flour, then add the cider or *cava* and salt and pepper. Simmer, stirring, until the sauce is thickened, adding a small quantity of fish stock, if needed, to thin the sauce. Pour over the salmon (or reheat the fish in the sauce) and serve with sprigs of parsley.

4 salmon steaks
flour
4 tablespoons butter
2 tablespoons olive oil
100 g diced ham
1 tablespoon flour
100 ml cider or *cava* (sparkling wine)
salt and pepper

TROUT, ASTURIAS STYLE
Truchas a la asturiana

Melt lard in a frying pan and fry a little chopped salt pork or bacon. Clean the trout, dredge them in flour and fry in the lard, turning to brown both sides. Garnish with fried salt pork.

TROUT, NAVARRE STYLE
Truchas a la navarra

Slit fairly large trout (350 g) along the belly, removing the backbone, but leaving head and tail intact. Wash and pat dry. Put a thin slice of *serrano* ham inside the cavity. Salt the fish and let it sit for 15 minutes. Then dredge it in flour and sauté gently in oil until nicely browned on both sides. Serve with lemon.

TROUT, ZAMORA STYLE
Truchas a la zamorana

Salt the trout and let them sit for 15 minutes.

In a pan large enough to hold the fish put the oil, slivered garlic, chopped parsley, vinegar, water and peppercorns. Bring to the boil, reduce the heat so the liquid just simmers, and add the trout. Cover the pan and steam the trout just until done, about eight minutes. Remove from heat. Serve hot or let the fish cool in the liquid.

4 trout, cleaned
4 tablespoons olive oil
4 cloves garlic
2 tablespoons chopped parsley
2 tablespoons vinegar
100 ml water
5 peppercorns

MARINATED TENCH
Tencas en escabeche

Clean the fish and fillet it or cut into slices. Put it into a bowl and cover with a marinade. For the marinade, mix these ingredients:

Marinate for two hours. Drain well. Then flour the pieces of fish and fry them in oil.

The fish can also be poached in equal parts of the marinade and water. Other freshwater fish — carp, barbel, shad — can be prepared in the same manner.

100 ml olive oil
50 ml vinegar
1 sliced onion
2 crushed cloves of garlic
1/2 teaspoon paprika
1 sprig parsley
1 sprig fennel
1 bay leaf
10 peppercorns
salt

PRAWNS

These being perhaps my favourite food, I was all set to list lots of recipes for their preparation. However, when I combed through my collection of Spanish recipes, I found relatively few. Prawns are served, if they are beautifully fresh, in their pristine glory: boiled for an instant in sea-water and adorned with nothing more than lemon wedges. The floors of tapa bars are crunchy with the shells. They're also much appreciated for their baroque beauty as garnish — on paella, *zarzuela* or a plate of hors-d'oeuvres. Additionally, here are a few very Spanish ways of cooking prawns.

SIZZLING PRAWNS
Gambas al ajillo

This dish, favourite tapa bar fare, is also called *pil pil* , because the prawns arrive at the table *"pil-pileando"*, a word that sounds like spluttering oil. It is traditionally made in individual earthenware ramekins and topped with a plate of chunks of bread for sopping the savoury juices. One daren't remove the plate nor taste the first morsel until the oil stops sizzling, for fear of singeing the tongue. Here is the classic, tapas bar version for a single serving. If you make it in a frying pan to serve four, the dish won't have quite the sizzle, but will still taste delicious. By the way, the tails of the prawns are peeled too, for easy eating.

Per serving: put three tablespoons olive oil, one chopped clove of garlic, one minced piece of dry red chili pepper and a pinch of paprika, into an earthenware ramekin. Put it on the heat until the oil is quite hot. Add 10 peeled prawns and cook only until they turn pink and curl slightly. A few drops of water will start the oil sizzling. Serve immediately, accompanied by bread.

GRILLED PRAWNS
Gambas a la plancha

Select large prawns for this preparation. Wash them, drain well and pat dry. Brush a grill (griddle) with olive oil then with salted water and heat it until the salt shows white. Lay the unpeeled prawns on the grill and cook them, brushing with oil, until they turn pink. Turn and grill the other side. Serve with an *alioli* sauce or a *romesco* and a tomato sauce (Chapter 12). Everybody peels the prawns. Those in the know remind you to "suck the heads". That's because the tasty coral or roe is in the head segment. Don't forget to follow the prawns with "lemon soup", finger-bowls with slices of lemon floating in them.

SAUTÉED PRAWNS
Langostinos salteados

Freshwater crayfish (cangrejos de río) can be substituted for king prawns (langostinos) in this recipe.

In a pan heat the oil and sauté the chopped onion and garlic. When softened, add the prawns and turn up the heat. Stir-fry briefly, then add the sherry, tomato sauce, thyme and salt and pepper, with a little additional water as needed.

Cook just until the prawns are pink and curled slightly. Serve garnished with chopped parsley.

1 kg large prawns, peeled
50 ml olive oil
2 tablespoons chopped onion
1 clove chopped garlic
50 ml dry sherry
2 tablespoons tomato sauce
1/4 teaspoon thyme
salt and pepper
chopped parsley

CLAMS, SAILOR STYLE
Almejas a la marinera

This dish appears, with little variation, in all the countries bordering the Mediterranean, using a little olive oil, garlic, wine and clams and a sprinkling of parsley. This version — very simple — adds the tang of tomatoes. Cockles or mussels can be substituted for clams.

Heat the oil in a deep frying pan or casserole. Add the minced onion and garlic and fry. Add the prepared tomatoes, bay leaf, pepper and white wine and simmer the sauce until tomatoes are reduced, about 10 minutes.

Add the clams. On a high heat cook the clams just until the shells open, shaking the pan or stirring constantly. Serve in small bowls garnished with chopped parsley.

1 kg clams, well scrubbed
75 ml olive oil
1 small onion, minced
4 cloves garlic, minced
1 kg tomatoes, peeled, seeded and
   finely chopped
1 bay leaf
pepper
chopped parsley
50 ml white wine

CLAMS AND BEANS
Almejas con alubias blancas

Drain the soaked beans and put them to cook in water to cover with the onion, cut in quarters, one clove of garlic, the bay, thyme and parsley. When the beans are half-cooked, about 40 minutes, add the oil and salt.

Meanwhile, scrub the clams very well and put them in a pot with a very little water and steam them open over a high heat, shaking the pan until the clam shells open. Remove immediately from the heat. Strain the liquid and reserve it.

Shuck the clams, discarding the shells. In a mortar, crush the saffron with remaining clove of garlic and breadcrumbs. Dissolve in a little of the liquid from the beans. Now add the shucked clams to the beans with the mortar mixture. Simmer for a minute and let sit for a few minutes before serving. Serves four to six.

250 g cannellini beans, soaked overnight
2 cloves garlic
bay, thyme, parsley
3 tablespoons olive oil
1 teaspoon salt
1 onion
1 kg clams
1/2 teaspoon saffron
1 tablespoon breadcrumbs
salt and pepper

MUSSELS

An extraordinarily inexpensive source of excellent protein and a delicious basis for many dishes. Use mussels in any way suitable for pricier shellfish such as oysters or scallops, add them to pasta sauces, star them in seafood cocktails, use in soups. Mussels sold in Spanish markets are farmed in mussel beds on the Galicia coast and are safe to eat year-round — as long as they are alive and shells tightly closed when tapped (see Chapter 2 for more information on marketing and storing).

Mussels come tangled in a seaweedy-looking growth called the beard. Pull it down to the hinge and cut it off with a knife. Use a dull knife to scrape off the various protuberances and scum on the mussels' shells. Wash them very well in running water or several changes of water.

To steam mussels open, put the cleaned mussels in a deep frying pan or pot. Add very little water (about 50 ml for one kilo of mussels), as they release quite a lot of liquid when they open. Cover the pot and put it on a hot fire. When the liquid begins to boil, shake the pot vigorously back and forth or remove the lid and, with a long-handled skimmer, stir them well. The shells should open within minutes. Remove them as they open or remove the whole pot from the heat.

Mussels served plump and juicy are a delight. Allowed to overcook and they are not very appetising. Discard any mussels that do not open. Mussels can be served at this point. Or they may be shucked, both shells discarded or, if to be served on the half-shell, only the empty shell discarded.

Strain the liquid in the pan through a sieve lined with dampened paper towelling. It can be incorporated in sauces and soups. It is quite salty, so don't add salt to a sauce without tasting first. To store cooked mussels, pour the strained broth over them in a bowl or jar, cover tightly and refrigerate. Use within two days. The whole mussel is edible, but in large specimens the mantle, or dark outer rim, which is quite chewy, can be removed. For those who are lesser aficionados of mussels, try chopping them before adding to sauces and soups.

MUSSELS, SAILOR STYLE
Mejillones a la marinera

Put the oil, chopped garlic, wine and water into a pan big enough to hold the mussels. Bring it to the boil and add the mussels. Cover the pan and shake it until shells open. Sprinkle in the breadcrumbs, pepper and chopped parsley and cook for another minute.

Serve mussels and their broth in soup bowls. For a soupier version, increase wine and water. If broth seems sandy, remove mussels before adding breadcrumbs. Strain the broth, then reheat. Serves four.

1 kg mussels, cleaned
2 tablespoons olive oil
4 cloves garlic, chopped
50 ml white wine
50 ml water
2 tablespoons fine breadcrumbs
freshly ground pepper
2 tablespoons chopped parsley

SCALLOPS

These shells don't close tightly, so they're very easy to open by inserting a knife between the shells and cutting the muscle at the hinge. Or they can be steamed open (as for mussels, above) or opened in a hot oven. They will probably need rinsing to remove grit. Cut away the mantle, which is tough, and the black stomach sac. Both the white muscle and the coral "foot" are edible.

SCALLOPS, GALICIAN STYLE
Vieiras a la gallega

A few drops of Galician *aguardiente de orujo*, a clear brandy made from grape lees, is added to the sauce. The closest equivalents are French *marc* and Italian *grappa*. Or substitute brandy.

Open the scallops as described. Cut off and reserve the coral. Clean four of the shells and oil them. Place three or four of the white scallop muscles in each and set on an oven tin.

In a frying pan heat the oil and sauté the chopped onion and garlic. Chop the corals and add to the pan with the paprika. Then add the wine and *aguardiente*, salt and pepper, cinnamon and cayenne. Cook this sauce until it is reduced. Spoon it over the prepared scallops. Top with breadcrumbs which have been mixed with the parsley and drizzle with a little oil.

Put under the broiler/grill or at the top of a hot oven just until the crumbs are lightly browned. Serve immediately with lemon wedges. Serves four as a starter.

12-16 scallops *(coquilles St. Jacques)*
3 tablespoons olive oil plus additional for
    drizzling over tops
1 onion, finely chopped
1 clove garlic, chopped
1 teaspoon paprika
100 ml white wine
50 ml Galician *aguardiente de orujo*
salt and pepper
1/8 teaspoon cinnamon
pinch of cayenne
3 tablespoons fine breadcrumbs
1 tablespoon chopped parsley
lemon wedges

CRAB

Crabs should be purchased live and cooked immediately.

Bring a large pot of salted water (150 grams salt to four litres of water) or sea-water to the boil. Put in the crabs, bring the water again to the boil, then simmer for 15 minutes. Remove crabs and plunge them in cold water to stop the cooking.

To clean and extract the crab meat, place the cooked crab on its back and twist off the legs and claws. With thumbs under the tail flap, push upwards until the body snaps away from the shell. Remove and discard the mouth, stomach bag and spongy gills. Scrape all soft brown meat from the shell and reserve it. Save the liquid in the shells. Discard hard, finger-like protuberances, and extract remaining meat. Scoop white meat from leg sockets. Crack the claws and legs and remove meat from them. The shells may be trimmed, scrubbed and oiled for use as a casserole.

BASQUE CRAB CASSEROLES
Txangurro

One crab does not provide a lot of meat. Extend the casserole by adding 200 grams boneless, cooked and flaked fish to the crab. *Rape*, angler fish, is a good choice.

In a frying pan sauté the onion in the oil until soft. Add the dark meat from the crab. Pour over the brandy, set it alight and stir gently until flames subside.

Add the wine, tomato sauce, parsley, salt, pepper and cayenne and simmer about 15 minutes, adding a little water or stock if sauce seems too thick. Add the remaining crab meat to the sauce and spoon it into two or four of the prepared shells. Top with breadcrumbs and dot with butter. Put under the grill or in the top of a very hot oven until lightly browned, about five minutes.

4 spider crabs about 1/2 kg each or 100 g per person of tinned crab
4 tablespoons olive oil
1 onion, minced
100 ml brandy
100 ml white wine
5 tablespoons tomato sauce
1 tablespoon chopped parsley
salt and pepper
dash cayenne
4 tablespoons breadcrumbs
butter

LOBSTER

Both *langosta,* clawless, spiny lobster, and *bogavante,* larger lobster with heavy claws, are found in Spanish markets. Buy them live.

To cook, place in a large pot of cold water and bring very slowly to the boil. Simmer for about 20 minutes. Drain.

While still hot (use a cloth to protect hands), place the lobster on its back and with sharp scissors split the underside of the tail shell lengthwise and extract the tail meat. Discard the stomach (a sac near the head), the dark, intestinal vein which runs through the tail meat, and the spongy lungs. Save the eggs or coral, if there are any, and the green liver or tomalley. Crack claws, if there are any, and remove tendrils of meat. Cooked lobster meat may be served cold with mayonnaise.

Lobster which is to be grilled, baked or sautéed needs to be cleaned before cooking. Kill it by inserting the knife between the head and the body and severing the spinal cord. Slit the undershell lengthwise and remove stomach sac and vein. Or cut the whole lobster in half lengthwise and remove viscera.

GRILLED LOBSTER, MALLORCA STYLE
Langosta a la mallorquina

Cut the lobsters in half lengthwise, allowing half a lobster per person.

In a blender whisk the oil, vinegar and pepper together. Brush the lobster halves with this and grill them over charcoal, brushing with more of the basting sauce, until done, about 12 minutes.

Serve with the garlic sauce or mayonnaise and lemon wedges. The liver and roe can be mashed and combined with the sauces if desired.

2 lobsters (each about 750 g)
100 ml olive oil
50 ml vinegar
1/2 teaspoon pepper
ajoaceite or mayonnaise
lemon wedges

LOBSTER, COSTA BRAVA STYLE
Langosta a la costa brava

After severing the spinal cord, open the lobsters and cut the meat from the shell into chunks. Save all the liquid as well as the liver and roe, if there are any.

Heat the oil in a casserole and sauté the finely chopped onion. Add the pieces of lobster and sauté briefly on a high heat with the bay leaf, thyme and orange peel.

Meanwhile in a mortar or blender crush the saffron, garlic, paprika, nuts, parsley, ladyfingers, chocolate and cayenne. Add the juices from the lobster, and the liver and roe. Dissolve in a little white wine or a stock made by boiling the lobster shell. Pour into the casserole and cook the lobster in the sauce for about 15 minutes. Add more liquid as needed. Serves four.

2 lobsters, each about 3/4 kg
100 ml olive oil
1 onion, finely chopped
1 bay leaf
1 teaspoon thyme
1 piece orange peel
1/2 teaspoon saffron
2 cloves garlic
1 teaspoon paprika
1 dozen almonds or hazelnuts, skinned, blanched and toasted
1 tablespoon parsley
3 sponge fingers (bizcochos secos) or use toasted bread
50 g dark chocolate
dash of cayenne
50 ml white wine
water or shellfish stock, as needed

LOBSTER, GALICIAN STYLE
Bogavante a la gallega

Cut the spinal cord of the lobster, open it and cut the meat from the shell into chunks. Crack the claws and extract the meat from them. Save all the liquid and the liver and roe.

Heat the oil in a frying pan or casserole and sauté the chopped onion and garlic. When softened, add the chopped tomato and fry for a few minutes. Add the pieces of lobster. Stir in the wine, bay leaf, paprika and the liquid from the lobster as well as the chopped liver and roe. Cook, covered, about 15 minutes. Serves three to four.

1 large lobster (1 1/2 kg)
salt and pepper
100 ml olive oil
1 onion, finely chopped
2 cloves garlic, chopped
1 tomato, peeled and chopped
100 ml white wine
1 bay leaf
1 teaspoon paprika

SQUID, CUTTLEFISH AND OCTOPUS

The great tentacle adventure needn't be scary. Here are some instructions.

The squid, *calamar,* is the most delicate of this trio. Its body is a slender pouch out of which protrudes a head with short tentacles. Grasp the head and pull gently. It will come away from the body pouch bringing the innards with it. Still inside is the cartilage, which looks like a strip of transparent plastic. Grasp the top of it and pull — it should come out in one piece.

Rinse out the pouch and pull off the purple-coloured membrane covering it. The wing flaps will come off too. Save them and the pouch. Now, cut off the tentacles just above the eyes. Save the tentacles, pulling off their outer membrane. Discard the remaining head and innards — unless you need the ink. The ink is enclosed in a tiny silver sac, like a dot of mercury, along the innards. Cut it free without breaking. (Tiny plastic envelopes of squid's ink can be purchased in many markets, useful for making squid in ink sauce with frozen squid, which contain little ink.) The squid is now ready for cooking. Whether fried, poached or braised, it cooks in little time.

Cuttlefish, *jibia or sepia,* is often found already dressed. If not, the fish vendor will usually do it for you. Otherwise, slit the wide body section open, remove and discard the cuttlebone and innards. The flesh is usually cut into pieces for slow braising.

Octopus, *pulpo*, needs long, slow cooking. To avoid unnecessary queasiness about cooking it, simply dump it whole into a pot of boiling water and cook for 15 minutes. Drain it and put in a fresh pot of water with salt, bay, onions and celery and cook until tender, about three hours. Drain. Then use kitchen scissors to cut the flesh and tentacles into pieces, discarding the stomach, eyes and mouth beak.

FRIED SQUID RINGS
Calamares a la romana

A la romana, Roman style, means floured and fried. Prepare squid as described above. With scissors, cut the body pouch into rings about 1.5cm wide. Dry them well. Dredge in flour, then put in a sieve and shake lightly to remove excess flour. Fry the rings and tentacles in deep, hot oil until golden and crisp. Serve with lemon wedges.

SQUID IN INKY SAUCE
Calamares en su tinta

Serve the tender squid in black sauce accompanied by white rice or pieces of fried bread. For an exotic variation, stuff the cooked squid inside *pimientos de piquillo,* tinned and skinned red peppers, then add sauce. This dish is also made with *chipirones,* tiny cuttlefish.

Clean the squid as described, saving the ink sacs in a cup. Finely chop the wing flaps and tentacles and mix with the breadcrumbs and one clove minced garlic. Stuff the squid with this mixture and close them with toothpicks. Dredge in flour, shake off excess and sauté in the hot oil until lightly browned. Remove to a casserole.

In the oil (or use fresh oil if flour bits have blackened in the pan) sauté the chopped onion and remaining clove garlic until soft. Add the tomato sauce, wine, brandy, bay leaf, salt, pepper and cayenne. Simmer for a few minutes, then pour the sauce over the squid in the casserole.

Cover and cook until very tender, about 25 minutes, adding more stock if necessary.

A few minutes before the squid are done, break the ink sacs with the back of a spoon and dilute the ink in a little white wine. Stir into the casserole and cook another few minutes. Garnish with chopped parsley.

1 kg small squid
4 tablespoons fine breadcrumbs
2 cloves garlic
flour
50 ml olive oil
1 onion, finely chopped
100 ml tomato sauce
100 ml white wine
1 tablespoon brandy
1 bay leaf
salt and pepper
dash of cayenne
chopped parsley

STUFFED SQUID
Calamares rellenos

Clean the squid. Finely chop the tentacles and wing flaps and mix in a bowl with the minced beef, chopped ham, nutmeg, 1/2 teaspoon salt, one clove minced garlic, breadcrumbs, lemon juice and beaten egg. Mix well with hands or a wooden spoon and stuff the squid. Fasten them with toothpicks.

Heat the oil in a pan, flour the squid and fry until golden. Remove them and add the chopped onion and pepper and remaining garlic, chopped. Add the prepared tomatoes, remainder of salt, pepper, cloves and wine. Bring to the boil, reduce to a simmer and return the squid to the pan. Cover and simmer until quite tender, about 45 minutes. Serves six.

1 kg medium squid
200 g minced beef
50 g ham, chopped
grated nutmeg
1 1/2 teaspoons salt
2 cloves garlic
3 tablespoons breadcrumbs
1 teaspoon lemon juice
1 egg, beaten
50 ml olive oil
flour
1 onion, chopped
1 green pepper, chopped
5 tomatoes, peeled, seeded and chopped
   (or large tin tomatoes)
pepper and dash of cloves
100 ml white wine

SQUID WITH BROAD BEANS
Chocos con habas

This is a speciality of the Atlantic coast of Cádiz and Huelva. Clean the squid and cut them into rings or pieces. Heat the oil in a casserole and add the slivered garlic and the pieces of squid. Cook for 10 minutes, then add the shelled beans and about 100 ml of water, the salt and pepper.

Cover and cook until beans are tender and most of the water has evaporated, about 15 minutes. Sprinkle with parsley. Serves six.

1 kg squid
4 cloves garlic, slivered
1/4 kg shelled broad beans
salt
100 ml olive oil
freshly ground pepper
chopped parsley

SAUCED CUTTLEFISH
Jibia en salsa

Clean the cuttlefish and cut into pieces. Heat the oil in a pan and fry the bread, garlic and almonds until toasted. Remove. Add the pieces of cuttlefish to the oil with the chopped green pepper and fry for several minutes. Add the white wine.

In mortar or blender crush the saffron and peppercorns with the toasted bread, garlic and almonds. Dissolve in a cup of water and add to the pan, stirring it in well. Add salt and cook the cuttlefish, covered, about 20 minutes. Add the diced potatoes and continue cooking, adding water as needed, until everything is tender, another 20 minutes. Alternatively, omit potatoes and serve with rice. Garnish with parsley and cooked peas, if desired. Serves four.

3/4 kg cuttlefish
50 ml olive oil
1 slice bread
3 cloves garlic
10 blanched almonds
1 green pepper
100 ml white wine
1/2 teaspoon saffron
10 peppercorns
2 potatoes, cut in dice
salt
parsley
cooked peas (optional)

OCTOPUS, GALICIAN STYLE
Pulpo a la gallega

With scissors cut cooked octopus into pieces about 2cm square. Put them in a wooden bowl with boiled potatoes. Sprinkle with salt, minced garlic, paprika and extra virgin olive oil.

OYSTERS

Fried Oysters
Ostras fritas

Pry open the oyster shells and scoop the oysters out. Drizzle them with lemon juice, then dip in beaten egg, dredge in maize flour and fry in hot olive oil until crisp. Drain briefly on absorbent paper, then stack the fried oysters in a pile and garnish with lemon wedges. Accompany them with a tomato sauce.

OYSTERS, CÁDIZ STYLE
Ostiones a la gaditana

Ostiones are the so-called Portuguese oyster. Open the oysters and put them on an oven tin. Mix breadcrumbs, chopped parsley, minced garlic and ground pepper and spoon over the oysters. Drizzle with olive oil and put in a hot oven just until the edges curl. Serve with lemon.

CRAYFISH

RIVER CRAYFISH, JEREZ STYLE
Cangrejos de río al jerez

Wash the crayfish in several changes of water. To eviscerate them, grasp the middle of the three tail flaps and give it a sharp pull and twist. The vein will pull out with the fin.

Heat the oil in a large pot or casserole and sauté the chopped onion and garlic. On a high heat add the crayfish and turn them in the oil for a few minutes. Sprinkle with the thyme, parsley, salt, pepper and cayenne. Pour in the sherry and cook just until the crayfish turn red and curl. Ladle them into individual bowls and serve with bread, spoons and a side dish for the shells. Follow with finger-bowls. Serves six.

1 kg live crayfish
100 ml olive oil
1 small onion, chopped
6 cloves garlic, chopped
1/2 teaspoon thyme
1 tablespoon chopped parsley
salt and pepper
dash of cayenne
100 ml dry sherry

SNAILS

Snails are quite popular in Spain, a speciality of simple bars and restaurants, rather than a home-cooked delicacy. They're often strongly spiced or else combined in all sorts of interesting ways: with fish or eel in paella ; with rabbit in a country stew, with ham and sausage.

Either fast the snails for two or three days or feed them maize flour or wheat flour. This is so they are purged of any foods they have eaten which could be harmful to those consuming them. Another method is to sprinkle them liberally with salt and let them froth for a while. In either case, wash them in several changes of water, then let them soak in a basin of water for about 30 minutes. This, supposedly, coaxes them to poke their heads out, making the cooked snail much easier to extract from its shell. Plunge them into a pot of boiling water for five minutes and drain.

Prepare a well-flavoured *court bouillon* (onions, parsley, wine, fennel, thyme, etc.) and bring it to the boil. Put the snails into it. Simmer for about two hours then drain.

In Spanish preparations, the snails are not previously removed from the shell — each person extracts the snails with a toothpick. Eating snails is a "hands on" experience, and licking the fingers is part of the pleasure. Allow between two and four dozen per person.

SNAILS, LEVANT STYLE
Caracoles a la levantina

Cook the snails according to the preceding directions. In an earthenware *cazuela* (casserole), heat the oil and sauté the chopped onion, garlic and ham. Add the chopped tomato, paprika, cumin, chili, salt and pepper, cloves, thyme and white wine. Add the snails and cook, covered, for 30 minutes, adding water or stock as needed to keep the sauce just a little thick.

Serve in the same casserole sprinkled with chopped mint, fennel or parsley. Serves four.

12 dozen snails
100 ml olive oil
1 onion, chopped
4 cloves garlic, chopped
150 g diced ham
1 tomato, peeled and chopped
2 teaspoons paprika
1/2 teaspoon cumin
cayenne or chili pepper
salt and pepper
dash of cloves
1/2 teaspoon thyme
200 ml white wine
chopped mint, fennel or parsley

GRILLED SNAILS, CATALAN STYLE
Caracoles a la patarrallada

Prepare the snails for cooking as described above. Cook them on a grill over charcoal, placing with the openings uppermost so each one forms its own cooking pot. Serve with *alioli*.

COOK'S NOTES:

POULTRY AND GAME

Going through my collection of Spanish cookbooks, I made a surprising discovery — there are more classic recipes for rabbit and partridge than for chicken. This is a reflection of less prosperous times, when hens were kept for laying, not the stew-pot, but small game birds, rabbit and hare were free for the taking on scrubby hillsides and in dry ravines.

Today chicken is, with seafood, Spain's most consumed protein food. Since both rabbits and partridge are now farm-raised, they are widely available for you to try some of these tempting ways of preparing them. Please see Chapter 2 on marketing for more information on buying and storing chicken and other poultry, game birds and rabbit.

Serving sizes are very approximate — a small chicken (one and a half kilos) in some households will easily serve four; in others, that's a meal for two or three. With cut-up chickens, a piece — such as the thigh or breast — is considered one serving, but many people will eat two servings.

ROAST CHICKEN
Pollo asado

The village *feria*, in honour of the town's patron saint, marked with religious processions and plenty of merry-making, is heralded by the pop of rockets and the arrival of vendors of roast chickens and *turrón* (nougat). The roast chickens turning on big rotisseries waft a tantalizing aroma throughout the fairgrounds.

To rotisserie-roast chicken, choose small ones, about one and a half kilos. For oven roasting, any size is acceptable. Regulate oven heat so a large chicken does not brown before it is thoroughly cooked.

Rub cleaned chicken inside and out with salt, lemon juice and crushed garlic. Place inside the cavity a few sprigs of thyme, bay, rosemary and celery leaves. Rub the chicken all over with lard or olive oil. Place it in a very hot oven for five minutes. Then lower the heat to moderate and roast the chicken, basting frequently with the drippings. If it browns too quickly, cover with foil or greased paper. Allow about 18 minutes' roasting time per half kilo of chicken (weighed without feet or head).

Allow the chicken to rest 10 minutes before serving. Skim fat from the pan juices, add a little white wine and boil briefly. Serve in a sauce bowl with the chicken. Roast partridge and squab in the same way, barding them with thinly sliced pork fat to prevent the birds from becoming too dry.

Chicken with Garlic (*Pollo al Ajillo*), page 292

CHICKEN WITH GARLIC
Pollo al ajillo

If you like crisp garlic bits, remove them before adding wine, then sprinkle over the chicken at the end. Some cooks prefer to fry whole, unpeeled garlic cloves. The skins prevent the garlic from scorching.

Rub the chicken pieces with salt, pepper and paprika and let them sit for 15 minutes.

Heat the oil in a large frying pan and in it very slowly brown the chicken. Turn the pieces to brown the other side and add the garlic.

When the chicken is browned, remove the pan from the fire and add the brandy or sherry and bay leaf. Cover the pot and simmer until chicken is tender, about 20 minutes more. Serves four to six.

1 chicken, cut in serving pieces
salt, pepper and paprika
75 ml olive oil
10 cloves garlic, coarsely chopped
75 ml brandy, sherry or Montilla
1 bay leaf

CHICKEN WITH PEPPERS
Pollo al chilindrón

Rub the chicken pieces with salt and pepper and set aside.

Roast the peppers under the grill flame, turning them, until blistered and charred. Remove and let them sit, covered, until cool enough to handle. Peel them and cut the flesh into wide strips.

Heat the oil in a pan or earthenware casserole and brown the chicken pieces, a few at a time. Add the garlic, cut in slivers, the ham, cut in thin strips, and the chopped onion. When this has fried

2 chickens, legs and breasts only
salt and pepper
4 red bell peppers
50 ml olive oil
4 cloves garlic
200 g cured or cooked ham
1 onion, finely chopped
5 large tomatoes, peeled, seeded
  and chopped

several minutes, add the strips of pepper and the prepared tomatoes.

Cook the chicken, partially covered, until quite tender. The sauce should be considerably reduced and thick. Serves six to eight.

CHICKEN, GRANADA STYLE
Pollo granadina

A friend who collects recipes with six or fewer ingredients says this is one of her favourite dishes.

Heat the oil in a large frying pan. Add the whole, peeled garlic cloves and fry until golden. Remove. Fry the chicken in the same oil, turning occasionally until nicely browned on all sides, adding the diced ham part way along.

Add the sherry, salt and pepper and the toasted garlic. Cover and simmer until chicken is fork-tender, about 25 minutes more. Serves four to five.

50 ml olive oil
6 cloves garlic
1 chicken, jointed
200 g diced *serrano* ham
100 ml sherry
salt and pepper

CHICKEN WITH VEGETABLES, CATALAN STYLE
Pollo en samfaina a la catalana

Rub the chicken pieces with salt and pepper.

In a frying pan heat half the oil or lard and fry the aubergines. Add the peppers, cut in large pieces and then the diced courgette.

In another pan heat the remaining fat and sauté the chicken pieces with the sliced onions. Add the chopped garlic, then the prepared tomatoes. Fry a few minutes more, then add wine, salt and pepper, bay, thyme and parsley. Cover and cook until chicken is nearly tender, then add the fried aubergines, peppers and courgette and cook another 15 minutes. Serves four to six.

1 chicken, jointed
salt and pepper
2 medium aubergines, peeled and diced
100 ml olive oil or lard
2 green or red peppers
1 courgette, diced
2 onions, thinly sliced
3 cloves garlic, chopped
2 tomatoes, peeled and finely chopped
75 ml white wine
bay, thyme, parsley

CHICKEN WITH TOMATO
Pollo con tomate

So absolutely simple. No, don't add onions, garlic, peppers or fancy herbs. Fresh, ripe Spanish tomatoes are highly flavourful. Use extra virgin olive oil for best taste.

Rub the chicken with salt, pepper and a little paprika. Heat the oil in a pot and brown the chicken pieces slowly on both sides.

While they are browning, dip tomatoes in boiling water, peel, seed and chop them. Add to the pot with the bay leaves and one teaspoon salt. Simmer, uncovered, until tomatoes are reduced to a thick sauce and chicken is tender, about 30 minutes. Serves six.

1 large chicken
salt, pepper and paprika
50 ml olive oil
8 tomatoes (2 kg), peeled seeded and
    chopped coarsely
2 bay leaves

CHICKEN WITH SHERRY
Pollo al jerez

Use either a dry *fino* or medium-dry *amontillado* sherry for cooking the chicken.

Rub the chicken pieces with salt and pepper. Heat the oil in a frying pan and brown the pieces, transferring them to a casserole as they are done. In the same oil sauté the spring onions, sliced, and the diced salt pork. Stir in the flour and cook a minute, then add salt and pepper, the sherry and water.

Cook for a few minutes, stirring up the browned bits from the bottom of the pan, and pour over the chicken pieces. Add the bay leaf, cover and simmer (or bake) until chicken is tender, about 25 minutes longer.

Meanwhile, clean the mushrooms, slice them and sauté in a little oil. Add to the chicken during the last few minutes and garnish with chopped parsley. Serves six.

1 chicken, jointed
salt and pepper
50 ml olive oil
3 spring onions or 1 onion
50 g salt pork, diced
1 tablespoon flour
200 ml sherry
100 ml water
1 bay leaf
100 g mushrooms
chopped parsley

CHICKEN WITH LOBSTER
Mar i terra

This Catalan dish reminds me of an American one, "surf'n'turf", which is steak with lobster. Somehow I think the chicken is a better companion for the lobster than beef — at least you don't have to argue about whether to drink white or red wine.

Heat the oil and lard in a large earthenware casserole. Season the chicken pieces with salt, pepper and cinnamon and brown them in the fat with the chicken liver. Remove the liver when browned. When chicken is nicely golden, add the chopped onion. Sauté a few minutes, then add the bouquet garni, chopped tomatoes, wine and anise brandy. Cover and let the liquid reduce by half.

Add the flour or breadcrumbs mixed in a little water. Add water or stock to just barely cover the pieces of chicken. Simmer, covered.

Cut the lobster into eight pieces (see Chapter 9 for how-to). Heat a little oil in a separate frying pan and sauté the pieces of lobster and the green lobster liver briefly. Transfer the lobster meat to the casserole with the chicken.

In a mortar or blender crush the saffron, garlic, toasted almonds and hazelnuts, grated chocolate and the chicken and lobster livers. Add reserved lobster juices to make a smooth paste. Add this mixture to the casserole and cook a few minutes more to blend the flavours. The sauce shouldn't be too soupy. Garnish with triangles of fried bread and sprinkle with chopped parsley. Serves four to six.

50 ml olive oil
30 g lard
1 chicken, cut in serving pieces
salt and pepper
cinnamon
1 chicken liver
200 ml white wine
50 ml anise brandy or brandy
2 teaspoons flour or fine breadcrumbs
water or stock
1 lobster of about 1 kg
1 onion, chopped
bouquet garni of bay, thyme, oregano,
    leek, parsley and orange peel
4 tomatoes, peeled, seeded and chopped
1/2 teaspoon saffron
2 cloves garlic
30 g almonds and hazelnuts,
    blanched and toasted
25 g grated chocolate or cocoa powder
fried bread to serve
chopped parsley to garnish

CHICKEN BREAST, SEVILLE STYLE
Pechuga de pollo a la sevillana

Flatten the chicken breasts slightly. Heat the oil in a frying pan and put in the chicken. Let them just firm in the oil, without browning, turning once. Remove them to a plate.

In the same oil sauté the chopped onion and pepper until softened. Add the chopped garlic, then the prepared tomato. Fry for a few minutes, then add the sherry and water, salt and pepper. Cook on a medium heat about 10 minutes.

Return the chicken breasts to the pan and cook very slowly until done, about 10 minutes. Transfer to a heated serving dish and garnish with the sliced olives. Makes two servings.

1 boned chicken breast (about 250 g), split into halves
50 ml dry sherry
2 tablespoons olive oil
1/2 onion, chopped
1 red pepper, chopped
1 clove garlic, minced
1 large tomato, peeled
50 ml water
salt and pepper
10 anchovy-stuffed olives

ROAST TURKEY, CATALAN STYLE
Pavo asado a la catalana

This has become my favourite holiday recipe. Clean the turkey and rub it inside and out with salt and a little of the wine or sherry, or with lemon juice.

Heat the lard in a large pan and sauté the turkey liver until browned on all sides. Remove, and chop it. To the fat add the chopped ham and the sausages, chopped. When browned, add the chopped liver, the chopped prunes and apricots, raisins, apples, celery, onion, pine-nuts, chopped chestnuts, cinnamon, salt and pepper. Stir in the wine or sherry and cook for a few minutes until the mixture is "dry". Add breadcrumbs.

Stuff the turkey with this mixture. Sew up the openings and truss the bird with string, tying the legs and wings close to the body and covering the breast with thin slices of pork fat. Put the turkey in a roasting pan with the bouquet garni of herbs.

Put in a very hot oven for 10 minutes, then reduce heat to moderate and roast the bird, basting frequently. After an hour's roasting, add a glassful of wine and continue adding wine as it is cooked away. Remove fat from breast towards end of cooking time so skin browns.

Allow approximately 18 minutes per half kilo of turkey (weighed unstuffed, without head and feet). Remove turkey to a serving platter. Remove excess fat from the pan drippings and serve the sauce with the turkey. Makes about 12 servings.

1 turkey, 4-5 kg
50 g lard
1/4 kg ham, chopped
6 pork sausages
50 g prunes, soaked, pitted and chopped
50 g dried apricots, or peaches, soaked, pitted and chopped
25 g Málaga raisins, seeded
2 apples, peeled, cored and diced
1 stalk celery, chopped
1/2 onion, chopped
25 g pine-nuts
10 chestnuts, roasted, peeled and chopped
1/2 teaspoon cinnamon
salt and pepper
100 g breadcrumbs
100 ml *vino rancio* or *amontillado* sherry
pork fat
thyme, oregano, bay, rosemary

DUCK, SEVILLE STYLE
Pato a la sevillana

Try duck with figs — fresh or dried — or with *membrillo,* quince jelly. The classic duck *a l'orange* is, of course, made with Seville bitter oranges. This dish, however, is made with olives.

Cut the duck into quarters. Heat the oil in a large casserole and brown the pieces of duck in it with the sliced onion. Remove duck when browned and pour off excess fat.

Stir the flour into the drippings. Let it begin to brown, then add the wine. Return the duck to the casserole with the quartered orange, parsley, bay leaf, carrots, salt, pepper and enough water or stock to nearly cover the duck. Cover the casserole and cook until the duck is fork tender, about one and a half hours.

Strain the sauce and return to pot with the chopped olives. Serve the duck from the same casserole or cool it, chill overnight, and remove the congealed fat from the sauce. Reheat before serving. Serves six.

2 ducklings, each about 2 kg
80 ml olive oil
1 onion, sliced
1 tablespoon flour
1/2 litre white wine
1 bitter orange or 1 orange plus 1
    tablespoon vinegar
1 sprig parsley
1 bay leaf
2 carrots, peeled and quartered
salt and pepper
water or stock
150 g olives, drained, rinsed and chopped

DUCK BREAST WITH FIGS
Magret de pato con higos

Put the duck breasts in a deep dish. Combine the crushed garlic, sliced onion, vinegar, anise brandy, thyme, salt and pepper and pour over the duck. Cover tightly and marinate, refrigerated, overnight, turning the duck occasionally.

In a saucepan combine the red wine, stock, honey, orange and lemon zest, clove, pepper and half a teaspoon of salt. Add the figs, bring to the boil and simmer until figs are very soft, about 40 minutes. Remove duck breasts from marinade and place in an oven casserole and bake, uncovered in a hot oven, basting with the marinade, for 20-25 minutes, or until the meat is medium rare.

Remove a few of the figs from the sauce, purée them and return to the sauce. Strain the marinade and add to the fig sauce. Cook until thickened. Serve the duck surrounded by the figs and with some of the sauce spooned over.

4 duck breasts
2 cloves garlic, crushed
1 small onion, sliced
75 ml sherry vinegar
1 tablespoon anise brandy
1/2 teaspoon thyme
salt and pepper
150 ml red wine
150 ml duck or chicken stock
3 tablespoons honey
1 strip of orange zest
1 strip of lemon zest
1 clove
1/2 teaspoon coarsely cracked pepper
250 g dried figs

PARTRIDGE, HOME STYLE
Perdices a la casera

Allow one partridge per person for a main course dish. Heat the oil in a pot large enough to hold the birds. Brown them very slowly. Add the chopped onions and peeled garlic cloves. When golden, add the peeled and quartered tomatoes. Fry for a few minutes, then add the remaining ingredients.

Cover and simmer until the partridges are tender, about an hour. Place on a serving dish, pass the sauce through a sieve and spoon some of it over the partridges. Accompany with slices of fried bread. Serves two.

2 partridges (or squab,
    Cornish game hens), cleaned
50 ml olive oil
2 medium onions, chopped
5 cloves garlic
3 tomatoes, peeled
100 ml Málaga wine
100 ml brandy
50 ml water
2 bay leaves
5 cloves
5 peppercorns
2 teaspoons salt

MARINATED PARTRIDGE, TOLEDO STYLE

Perdices en escabeche a la Toledana

Clean the partridges and rub them inside and out with salt and pepper. Truss them with string so they keep their shape. Heat the oil in a frying pan and slowly brown them, one or two at a time. When golden, transfer the birds to a casserole.

Peel the very small onions and cut a slit in their stem end (helps to keep them from opening out) and add them to the oil with the crushed garlic and the carrots, peeled and halved lengthwise. Then add the bay, thyme, oregano, paprika, peppercorns, cloves, salt and white wine. Pour this over the partridges in the casserole and add the vinegar and water. Bring to the boil, then cover and cook very slowly until the birds are very tender, about one hour, adding more water as needed so there is always plenty of liquid in the casserole.

When the birds are done, remove the pan from the heat and let cool thoroughly. Then remove the partridges and discard the string. Place in a glass or crockery bowl. Strain the cooking liquid and pour it over the partridges, which should be covered by the liquid. Slice the carrots and add them and the onions to the bowl. Cover tightly and chill for at least two days.

Serve at room temperature or reheat very gently. Garnish with sliced lemon and parsley. Serves four or eight, depending on whether the birds are split.

4 partridges (or other bird)
75 ml olive oil
8 small onions
3 cloves garlic, crushed
2 carrots
2 bay leaves
1 teaspoon thyme
1 teaspoon oregano
1 teaspoon paprika
10 peppercorns
3 cloves
salt
100 ml white wine
100 ml vinegar
200 ml water
lemon
parsley

PARTRIDGE WITH CABBAGE, CATALAN STYLE

Perdices con coles a la Catalana

Rub the cleaned and split partridges with salt and pepper, cinnamon and nutmeg. In a pot heat the oil or lard and very slowly brown the partridges, adding the bacon, cut in strips, the chopped onion and chopped carrot.

When the birds are nicely browned, add the herbs and the wine and stock. Cover and simmer until partridges are quite tender, about an hour, depending on their size.

Meanwhile, cut the core out of the cabbage and blanch the cabbage in boiling water for five minutes. Drain and very carefully separate the leaves from the head of cabbage. Spread out four or five leaves overlapping on a flat surface. Place a half partridge on the leaves and fold over to enclose the partridge in a packet. Do this with the remaining partridge halves.

Dip them in beaten egg and roll in flour. Fry the rolls in a frying pan until lightly browned. Place them in an oven casserole. Pour over the sauce from the pan in which the birds cooked, adding more liquid if necessary. Add sliced *butifarra*. Cover the casserole and bake in a medium oven for 25 minutes. Serves eight.

4 partridges, split in half
salt and pepper
cinnamon
ground nutmeg
2 tablespoons olive oil or lard
100 g unsmoked bacon
2 onions, chopped
1 carrot, chopped
bay, thyme, oregano
100 ml Málaga wine or medium sherry
100 ml veal stock
1 cabbage
1 egg, beaten
flour
100 g *butifarra* (white) sausage

PARTRIDGE, NAVARRE STYLE
Perdices a la navarra

Rabbit is good prepared in the same manner as partridge, in a chocolate-embellished sauce.

Clean the partridges and rub them inside and out with salt, pepper and brandy. Let them sit for 30 minutes, then dredge in flour and brown them slowly in the hot oil or lard.

When browned, add the chopped onion and garlic. Fry a few minutes more, then add the parsley, bay, thyme, cinnamon, whole peeled tomato, and water or stock. Add one teaspoon salt and the vinegar. Cover and simmer until the birds are tender.

Remove them to a serving dish. Pass the sauce through a sieve and return to the pan. Add the grated chocolate and cook very slowly until it is completely dissolved, adding more stock as needed to make a smooth sauce. Pour over the partridges. Serves four.

4 partridges
salt and pepper
brandy
flour
4 tablespoons olive oil or lard
1 onion, chopped
4 cloves garlic, chopped
2 tablespoons chopped parsley
1 bay leaf
1 teaspoon thyme
1/4 teaspoon cinnamon
1 tomato, peeled
1/4 litre water or stock
1 tablespoon vinegar
50 g dark chocolate, grated

QUAIL IN GRAPE LEAVES
Codornices en hojas de parra

Clean the quail, and wrap each in a slice of ham or bacon.

Place a quail on two overlapped grape leaves, fold the leaves around the bird and tie with twine. Put the wrapped quail in an oven pan with the stock and roast in a hot oven for about 20 minutes. (Traditionally, the leaf-wrapped quail were grilled over a wood fire.)

Remove the grape leaves and place each quail on a slice of fried bread on a serving platter. Keep them warm.

Add the sherry to the pan juices and reduce by half on a hot fire. Pour some of the sauce over the birds and serve the rest separately. Garnish with lemon slices and watercress. Serves four.

8 quail
8 thin slices ham or bacon
16 grape leaves, blanched
50 ml veal stock, boiling
100 ml sherry
8 slices fried bread
lemon and watercress for garnish

DRUNKEN QUAIL
Codornices emborrachadas

Clean the quail, rub them with salt and brown in the lard with the diced salt pork.

Add the white wine and brandy to the pan, cover and cook them gently until tender, about 25 minutes.

Remove the quail to a plate. Beat the egg with the sugar and milk. Whisk a little of the hot liquid from the pot into the egg, then whisk the egg into the liquid in the pot. Stir until sauce is thickened. Return the quail to the pot to reheat, and serve. Serves four.

8 quail
1 tablespoon lard
100 g salt pork, diced
1/2 litre white wine
100 ml brandy
1 egg
1 teaspoon sugar
50 ml milk

SQUAB, DOVE OR TURTLEDOVE
Pichón, paloma o tórtolo

Finely mince the liver, heart and cleaned gizzard of the birds. Sauté briefly in a little olive oil. Add fine breadcrumbs and enough brandy to moisten. Stuff the birds with the mixture and truss them. Brown well in oil with a little minced garlic. Add sherry or white wine, cover, and simmer until tender.

RABBIT, HUNTER STYLE
Conejo a la cazadora

Rub the rabbit pieces with salt and pepper and set aside.

Heat the oil in a frying pan and sauté the diced ham, salt pork, chopped onion and garlic. With a skimmer, transfer them to a casserole.

In the same fat brown the pieces of rabbit, placing them as they are browned in the casserole. Add the brandy, wine and water to the pan and bring to the boil, scraping the pan to deglaze it. Add the liquid to the casserole with the tomato paste, thyme, salt and pepper. Cover and simmer slowly until rabbit is tender, about 30 minutes for young, domestically raised rabbits.

Slice and sauté the mushrooms and add them to the casserole during the last 15 minutes. Sprinkle with chopped parsley. Serves four.

1 rabbit, cut in pieces
3 tablespoons olive oil
100 g diced *serrano* ham
50 g diced salt pork
1 onion, chopped
2 cloves garlic, chopped
50 ml brandy
200 ml white wine
100 ml water
3 tablespoons tomato paste
1 1/2 teaspoons thyme
salt and pepper
200 g mushrooms
chopped parsley

RABBIT IN ALMOND SAUCE
Conejo en salsa de almendras

Rub the pieces of rabbit with salt and pepper and set aside. Heat the oil in a pan and fry the onions, four cloves garlic and almonds with the rabbit liver, if available, just until toasted. Remove them to mortar or blender and crush with the cinnamon, parsley, raw garlic, peppercorns, cloves, saffron and salt. Dissolve in the water.

Meanwhile, in the oil in the pan slowly brown the rabbit pieces. Add the mortar mixture to the rabbit with the white wine and bay leaves. Cover and simmer until rabbit is very tender, 30 minutes to an hour, depending on size of rabbit, adding water or light stock if more liquid is needed. Serves four.

1 rabbit, cut in pieces
50 ml olive oil
1 onion, chopped
5 cloves garlic
20 almonds, blanched and skinned
1/4 teaspoon cinnamon
1 tablespoon chopped parsley
10 peppercorns
2 cloves
1/2 teaspoon saffron
1 teaspoon salt
50 ml water
1/4 litre white wine
2 bay leaves

RABBIT, TARRAGONA STYLE
Conejo tarraconense

Heat the oil in a casserole or pot and slowly brown the rabbit pieces and the liver. Remove the liver and reserve it.

When rabbit is partially browned, add the chopped onion. Continue frying, then add the prepared tomatoes, then the red wine, herbs, salt and pepper, nutmeg and fennel seed. Cover the pan and let the rabbit cook very slowly.

Meanwhile scrub the small new potatoes very well and parboil them for five minutes. Drain, then cut in half. (If using regular-sized potatoes, cook them until nearly tender, then cut in quarters.)

In a mortar or blender crush the saffron, fried

1 rabbit (about 2 kg), cut in pieces
100 ml olive oil
1 onion, chopped
4 tomatoes, peeled, seeded and chopped
150 ml red wine
bay, thyme, parsley and rosemary
salt and pepper
grated nutmeg
1/2 teaspoon fennel seeds
3/4 kg new potatoes
1/2 teaspoon saffron
1 dry chili pepper (or more)
2 cloves garlic
20 g chocolate
1 tablespoon toasted flour
chopped parsley

rabbit liver, seeded chili pepper, garlic, chocolate and toasted flour. (To toast flour, put it in a frying pan with no fat and no liquid and stir it over a low flame just until slightly coloured. Do not let it scorch or it will be bitter.)

Dissolve this mixture in about 100 ml of boiling water and stir it into the casserole with the parboiled potatoes. Cover and cook another 20 minutes, or until rabbit and potatoes are very tender, about one and three-quarter hours total. Garnish with chopped parsley. Serves four or five, depending on the size of the rabbit.

STEWED HARE, CASTILIAN STYLE
Liebre estofado a la castellana

Season the pieces of hare with salt and pepper and a little of the wine.

Put the soaked beans to cook in fresh water with a few slices of the onion and a bay leaf. Simmer until tender, about one and a half hours, adding salt to taste when partially cooked.

Meanwhile, put the hare, sliced onions, garlic, green peppers, bouquet garni, wine, vinegar, water, oil, salt, pepper and chili pepper cut into small pieces into a pot. Bring to the boil, then reduce heat and simmer until the hare is quite tender, adding a little of the liquid from the beans as needed.

Add the drained beans to the hare and cook another 15 minutes to combine the flavours.

1 hare, cut up
1/4 kg white beans, soaked overnight
2 onions, sliced
3 cloves garlic, slivered
2 green peppers, cut in strips
bouquet garni of bay, parsley, thyme and
    cinnamon stick
150 ml white wine
2 tablespoons vinegar
50 ml water
75 ml olive oil
salt and pepper
1 dry red chili pepper

SHEPHERD'S STEW, LA MANCHA STYLE
Gazpachos manchegos

This dish, concocted by shepherds and hunters, is also called *galianos*. The plural, *gazpachos*, distinguishes it from Andalusian cold gazpacho. Though typically containing several partridges and rabbits, a home version can be made with chicken and squab or domesticated rabbit. Dark-meat turkey is a good substitute.

Torta, a flat, unleavened bread baked on the hearth stone, is added to the soup to thicken it and another is used as a dinner plate. Hebrew *matzoh* or even water biscuits can be substituted for the *torta*. They turn into a thick pasta in the stew. Traditionally *gazpachos* would be made in a wide and deep two-handled frying pan. Everyone eats from the pot in which it is cooked.

3 partridges or squab
2 rabbits
100 ml olive oil
1 slice bread or torta
3 cloves garlic
1 onion, sliced
1 tomato, peeled and cut up
2 green peppers, cut in half
bay, thyme, rosemary
salt and pepper
3/4 litre white wine
1 litre water
1/2 teaspoon cinnamon
1/2 teaspoon saffron
tortas or matzoh or water biscuits

Cut the partridges in half and the rabbits in quarters and rub the pieces with salt. Heat the oil in a large frying pan and first fry the rabbit livers, the slice of bread and the garlic and remove when browned.

Add the birds and rabbit to the oil and fry slowly, adding the sliced onion. When the meat is browned, add the cut up tomato, peppers, herbs, salt and pepper, wine and water. Bring to the boil, cover the pan and simmer.

In the mortar or blender crush the fried livers, bread and garlic with the cinnamon and saffron. Dissolve in a little liquid and add to the pan.

When the meats are tender, cut two or three *tortas* into small pieces and add to the pot. Cook another five minutes and remove from heat. Let sit, covered, for 10 minutes before serving. Serve additional *tortas* for dunking. Serves eight to 10.

COOK'S NOTES:

MEAT

There are feast days that appear on the calendar, like Christmas and Easter. There are feast days that mark special events: a wedding, a baptism, a first communion. And then there is the *matanza*, the greatest of the secular holidays and an excuse for serious feasting.

The *matanza* is a hog slaughtering and still takes place in small communities during cool winter months (though nowadays the butchering must be done by authorised personnel). Several families gather, usually at a country cottage far from electric lights and mains water. Once the pig is "sacrificed" (that is the verb in Spanish), great cauldrons of fresh pork are put to cook in flavourful sauces.

The liver is fried up and the ribs barbecued to be served to the assembled people, from small children to old *abuelas*. And the work begins. The hams are rubbed down with salt, the first step in curing. The belly fat also is salted. The blood is added to spices, rice and pine-nuts for black puddings. Lean and fat are ground together and macerated with garlic and paprika for making *chorizo* and other sausages, depending on the region. Sausage casings are prepared. Late at night, while the women take turns stirring the pots and everyone has eaten and drunk his fill, someone starts strumming a guitar and the dancing starts. The work goes on till dawn and sometimes the dancing does too.

Meat in Spain has never been plentiful. Perhaps that is why its "sacrifice" is cause for celebration. I used to marvel at the village butcher shop when Spanish housewives would walk away with a big package of meats to feed a family of six for considerably less money than I paid for two not-very-tender *filetes de ternera*, thin veal cutlets. Their package would include a chunk of boiling beef, a quarter of stewing hen, a piece of salt pork, a ham bone, a few pork ribs, black pudding and red sausage. It all went into the *cocido* (see Chapter 5) with chickpeas and vegetables and provided a nutritious and filling meal for a whole family.

Pork and its by-products are the favourite meats in most parts of Spain. Lamb and baby kid, though very expensive in most markets, are still traditional in the grazing regions of central and western Spain. Beef and veal are very good quality now, but were once confined to the few regions with good grazing, in particular Galicia, Asturias, Salamanca and Ávila. This is why there are so few traditional recipes for their preparation.

Bring meat to room temperature before cooking. In general, the most tender cuts of meat can be cooked on the hottest heat for the shortest length of time (served rare) and the least tender pieces need very gentle and long cooking. Pork doesn't need to be cooked as long as previously thought necessary — it just gets dry. Pale meats such as baby lamb, kid and veal are usually served well cooked, but spring lamb is best enjoyed medium-rare, still pink..

Much more information about kinds of meat and meat cuts can be found in Chapter 2.

Baby Kid in Casserole (*Cazuela de Chivo*), page 327.

BEEF AND VEAL

In Spain *ternera,* veal, generally means young beef. In the following recipes either beef or veal can be used.

VEAL CUTLETS, HOME STYLE
Filete a la casera

Pound the cutlets thin with a wooden mallet or pestle. Rub them with salt and pepper.

Heat the oil in a frying pan and put in one cutlet at a time with some of the chopped garlic. Fry the meat very quickly on both sides. Remove and reheat the oil. Fry the remaining cutlets in the same manner. Serve with lemon wedges and chopped parsley. Makes four servings.

4 thin veal cutlets
salt and pepper
50 ml olive oil
5 cloves garlic, chopped
lemon wedges
chopped parsley

VEAL CUTLETS, GRANADA STYLE
Granadina de ternera

Pound the cutlets thin with a mallet or pestle and trim them to an even shape. Cut the thinly sliced ham into four strips.

Cut three slits in each cutlet and thread the slice of ham through it. Rub with salt and dust with flour.

Heat the oil and fry the cutlets one at a time. Remove and keep them warm. In the same oil sauté the sliced mushrooms, diced ham and chopped garlic for a few minutes. Add the sherry and cook for five minutes. Pour over the cutlets and serve with a garnish of parsley or watercress. Serves four.

4 thin veal cutlets
100 g *serrano* ham or bacon
salt and pepper
50 ml olive oil
flour
150 g mushrooms, sliced
50 g diced ham
1 clove garlic
50 ml dry sherry

VEAL POT-ROAST
Ternera mechada

Mechada refers to larding or threading with strips of pork fat which helps keep the meat juicy during cooking. Classically it's done with a larding needle. The village cooks I watched simply use a sharp knife, cutting deep gashes into the meat which are plugged with thin strips of salt pork. The *redondo* or round, a long, tubular piece of meat, is most favoured for this dish, but any "roast beef", such as rump, would be suitable.

Serve the sliced meat with potato purée or potatoes that have been browned in lard with a little garlic. Cooked vegetables such as carrots and peas are often added to the meat. Pork roast is prepared in the same manner.

Wipe the meat with a cloth. In the mortar grind together the peppercorns, clove, nutmeg, parsley, garlic cloves, egg and two teaspoons oil to make a paste. Cut the salt pork into very thin strips.

With a sharp knife cut deep gashes into the piece of meat and with the knife blade insert some of the paste and a piece of salt pork. Continue, spacing the gashes regularly on the meat's surface. Tie the meat with twine, giving it a good shape (thin slices of pork fat can be used to bard it, if desired).

Heat the oil or lard in a deep pan big enough to hold the piece of meat and brown the meat, very slowly, on all sides. Add the quartered onion, carrot, tomatoes, and roasted garlic cloves. Put in the bay leaf, sherry and stock and cook the meat very slowly until fork-tender, about two hours, adding more stock as needed.

Remove the meat to a serving dish, discard the string, and slice. Sieve the sauce and spoon it over the meat. Serves six.

1 1/2 kg veal or beef in one piece
5 peppercorns
1 clove
1/4 teaspoon grated nutmeg
2 tablespoons chopped parsley
2 cloves garlic
1 hard-boiled egg
2 teaspoons olive oil
50 g salt pork, cut in thin strips
4 tablespoons olive oil or lard
1 onion, quartered
3 carrots, cut in half
2 tomatoes, quartered
1 head roasted garlic
   (for how-to see page 142)
1 bay leaf
100 ml sherry or Málaga wine
150 ml stock or water

POT-ROAST, SEVILLE STYLE
Carne asada a la sevillana

If desired, the meat can be larded as in the previous recipe, using slivers of almonds and garlic and salt pork.

Dredge the meat in flour, then brown it slowly in the oil or lard. In the mortar or blender crush the garlic, parsley and lemon juice. When meat is browned add to pan with the Montilla wine, salt and pepper and a piece of cinnamon stick.

Cover and simmer, adding water and stock as needed, until the meat is quite tender, about 2 hours. Remove the meat to a serving platter.

Rinse the olives in water, drain well and add to the sauce in the pan. Pour over the meat and garnish with strips of red pepper. Serves six.

1 1/2 kg beef pot-roast
flour
4 tablespoons olive oil or lard
3 cloves garlic
2 tablespoons parsley
1 lemon
100 ml Montilla or sherry
salt and pepper
cinnamon stick
100 g pitted olives
1 small tin red pimiento

"OLD CLOTHES"
(BEEF WITH AUBERGINES)
Ropa vieja

A good dish for leftover roast beef or boiled beef. It is typically made with meat from the *cocido*.

Cut the meat into slices or strips. Peel the aubergines and slice them. Fry them slowly in the oil until slightly browned and soft. Remove and set aside.

In the same oil sauté the chopped onion and garlic until softened. Stir in the flour and let it cook briefly. Add the tomato sauce and stock, the salt and pepper, the red pepper cut in pieces, the cut up meat and the fried aubergines. Stir and let cook for 10 minutes. Serves four.

3/4 kg cooked beef
2 medium aubergines
75 ml olive oil
1 onion, chopped
1 clove garlic, chopped
2 teaspoons flour
100 ml tomato sauce
100 ml beef stock
salt and pepper
1 red pepper, roasted or tinned

STUFFED FLANK
Falda rellena

Have the butcher trim the piece of meat so it is an even rectangle. Grind the trimmings.

Mix the minced meat with the chopped ham. Squeeze out the soaked bread and add to the meat with the chopped olives, chopped onion, one clove garlic, minced, chopped parsley, chopped eggs, chopped pimiento, salt and pepper and beaten egg. Spread this mixture on top of the meat.

Starting at a long side, roll up the meat as tightly as possible. Either sew it closed or fasten with skewers. Wrap securely in string.

Heat the oil in a pot large enough to hold the roll and very slowly brown it on all sides. Add the quartered onion, two cloves slivered garlic, the tomato sauce and white wine.

Cover and simmer until meat is very tender, about two hours, adding more liquid as needed. Remove it to a serving platter. Sieve the sauce. Let the meat rest for 10 minutes, then remove strings and cut it in slices. Serve with the sauce. Serves six to eight.

1 1/2 kg beef or veal flank, skirt or
    boned breast
100 g cooked ham, finely chopped
1 slice bread, soaked in milk
1 dozen pitted olives, chopped
1 tablespoon finely chopped onion
3 cloves garlic
2 tablespoons parsley, chopped
3 hard-boiled eggs
1 tinned red pepper
salt and pepper
1 egg, beaten
75 ml olive oil
1 onion, quartered
100 ml tomato sauce
200 ml white wine

ANDALUSIAN VEAL STEW
Estofado a la andaluza

Other vegetables — peas, pumpkin, artichoke hearts, broad beans, etc. — can be added to this stew and it's perfectly acceptable to add quartered pears or apples as well.

Cut the meat into cubes of about 3cm. Place in a stew-pot with the green pepper, cut in strips, the tomato cut in quarters, the onions and carrots.

In the mortar crush the saffron, peppercorns, cloves, roasted garlic, cinnamon, and dissolve in the water. Add this to the pot with the oil, bay leaves, parsley, salt and white wine.

Cover and cook about one hour, adding more water or stock as needed to keep the meat just covered with liquid. Then add the potatoes and cook another 30 minutes. Serves four to six.

1 kg stewing beef or veal
1 large green pepper
1 large tomato, peeled
2 onions, sliced
2 carrots, halved lengthwise
1/2 teaspoon saffron
8 peppercorns
2 cloves
1 head garlic, roasted
  (for how-to see page 142)
1/4 teaspoon cinnamon
100 ml water
50 ml olive oil
2 bay leaves
1 sprig parsley
2 teaspoons salt
1/4 litre white wine
4 potatoes, peeled and cut up

CHOPPED BEEF, ALMERÍA STYLE
Picadillos almerienses

Cut the meat and salt pork into dice of the same size.

Heat the oil in a casserole and brown the meat and pork or bacon. When browned, add the onions and fry for a few minutes. Add the prepared tomatoes, pine-nuts, cinnamon, nutmeg, saffron, pepper, salt, wine and water. Cover and cook until meat is tender, about 45 minutes, adding more water to keep the mixture just juicy.

Serve in the same casserole garnished with sliced eggs, chopped parsley and triangles of fried bread. Serves four.

1/2 kg beef, cut into dice
150 g salt pork or bacon, diced
50 ml olive oil
1 onion, finely chopped
2 tomatoes, peeled, seeded and chopped
40 g pine-nuts
1/2 teaspoon cinnamon
1/4 teaspoon grated nutmeg
1/4 teaspoon crushed saffron
1/2 teaspoon ground pepper
1 teaspoon salt
100 ml white wine
100 ml water
hard-boiled eggs
chopped parsley
fried bread

GRILLED MEATS

The most tender cuts of beef — fillet, entrecote, chateaubriand, tournedos — are best enjoyed simply grilled or pan fried and served medium to rare. Use tongs or spatula to turn the meat, so as not to pierce with a fork. As grilled meats are pretty much the same in any language, no recipe is given for their preparation. However, in serving them, try some of the Spanish sauces (see Chapter 12) as an accompaniment. Especially good are *romesco* (pepper sauce), olive sauce, Cabrales blue cheese, and *mojo* (a paprika sauce).

BEEF CHOPS, BASQUE STYLE
Chuletón a la vasca

Trim the steaks of fat and place them on a platter. Pour over the oil and the juice of the lemon. Let macerate for 2 or 3 hours.

Drain the steaks, sprinkle with pepper and grill on a hot griddle or under broiler or over charcoal. Sprinkle the steaks with the chopped garlic and parsley while they are grilling. Serve accompanied by the fried peppers. Serves four big eaters.

4 rib steaks, thickly cut
100 ml olive oil
1 lemon
pepper
5 cloves garlic, chopped finely
3 tablespoons chopped parsley
1 dozen fried green peppers

PORK

Boneless cutlets (*filetes*) and chops can be interchanged, adjusting the cooking time. Other boneless pork roasts can be substituted for the loin (*lomo*). A particularly good cut for roasting or braising is *babilla*.

GRILLED PORK CUTLETS
Filetes a la plancha

When the cutlets are cut into small pieces (about 6 x 4 cm), they become the *planchitas* served in tapa bars.

Put the cutlets in a shallow bowl. Sprinkle with the chopped garlic, parsley and juice of the lemon. Let them marinate for two hours.

Heat a griddle or a heavy frying pan and brush it very lightly with oil. Place the cutlets on the griddle and cook, turning once, until browned on both sides. Sprinkle with salt and pepper.

Serve with lemon wedges. Makes four servings.

4 pork cutlets (or thin pork chops)
olive oil
3 cloves garlic, coarsely chopped
2 tablespoons chopped parsley
1 lemon
salt and pepper

BREADED PORK CUTLETS
Empanados de cerdo

Flatten the cutlets slightly, then place them in a shallow bowl and sprinkle with the chopped garlic, parsley, thyme, salt and pepper. Squeeze over the juice of the lemon and let them marinate for one hour.

Dip the cutlets into beaten egg, then breadcrumbs. Fry slowly in oil until browned on both sides. Serves four.

Prepare veal cutlets in the same manner.

4 pork cutlets (or chops, thinly cut)
4 cloves garlic, chopped
1 tablespoon chopped parsley
1/2 teaspoon crushed thyme
salt and pepper
1 lemon
1 egg, beaten
50 g fine breadcrumbs
60 ml olive oil

MARINATED PORK LOIN
Lomo en adobo

This is a classic way of brining pork. In this recipe, the loin is roasted. But, instead of roasting, the pork loin can be thinly sliced and the pieces fried in olive oil.

Put the pork loin in a deep bowl. In the mortar crush the garlic, oregano, saffron and peppercorns with the salt and paprika. Dissolve the paste in a little of the vinegar. Pour over the meat with the rest of the vinegar. Cover and marinate, refrigerated, for about 48 hours, turning the meat two or three times a day.

Drain the piece of meat and pat it dry. Place in an oiled oven tin and rub with the oil. Place in a very hot oven for five minutes, then reduce heat to moderate and roast the pork until done, about 40 minutes. (In roasting pork, allow 20 minutes for each 500 grams of meat.) Baste with pan drippings. Makes four servings.

3/4 kg boned pork loin
4 cloves garlic
1 teaspoon oregano
1/4 teaspoon saffron
10 peppercorns
1/2 teaspoon salt
1 teaspoon paprika
100 ml vinegar
2 tablespoons olive oil

PORK LOIN WITH MÁLAGA WINE
Lomo a la malagueña

Heat the oil in a large pot and very slowly brown the piece of meat on all sides. Place in a roasting pan and pour over the wine. Put the piece of cinnamon in the pan and put the pan in a very hot oven for five minutes, then reduce the heat and bake until meat is done, about 50 minutes.

Meanwhile, seed the raisins and plump them by soaking in a little hot water. Sliver the blanched almonds and toast them lightly in the oven or in a frying pan.

When meat is done, place on a serving dish and slice. Pour over a little of the pan juices and sprinkle with the raisins and almonds. Serve the remaining juice in a sauce bowl. Serves six.

50 ml olive oil
1 kg boned pork loin
200 ml Málaga muscatel wine
1 piece cinnamon stick
25 g Málaga raisins
25 g almonds, blanched

PORK LOIN WITH MILK
Lomo con leche

This is a Galician dish. Good served with potato purée and fried peppers.

Trim the piece of meat of excess fat and melt the fat in a large pot, adding lard or oil to make enough in which to brown the meat.

Rub the meat with the garlic and slowly brown it on all sides. Then add the milk, pepper, salt and cinnamon. Bring to the boil, then simmer very slowly until meat is really tender, about one hour.

Remove the loin to a serving platter and slice it. Reduce the sauce by boiling it. Pour over the meat and serve. Serves six.

1 kg boned pork loin
lard or olive oil
1 clove garlic
1/2 litre milk
1/2 teaspoon coarsely ground pepper
1 teaspoon salt
1/4 teaspoon cinnamon

STUFFED PORK LOIN, CÁDIZ STYLE
Lomo de cerdo relleno a la gaditana

Cut the piece of meat open lengthwise, opening it up like a book. Arrange a layer of half the ham slices on one half. Mix the chopped eggs, chopped almonds, two cloves, chopped garlic and beaten egg and spread on top. Place on top the remaining sliced ham. Close the meat and sew up with thread and tie with string to make an even-sized roll.

Rub it with lard or oil and sprinkle with thyme. Place in an oven tin with head of garlic, peppers and salt. Put in a hot oven for five minutes, then reduce the heat to medium. Pour over the sherry and roast the meat until done, about one and a quarter hours, adding water so there is always liquid in the bottom of the pan. (The meat can also be cooked, covered, on top of the cooker.)

When tender, remove to a serving platter. Let the meat sit for five or 10 minutes, then remove string and thread. Slice the meat. Sieve the sauce in the pan and spoon it over the sliced meat. Serves eight.

1 1/2 kg boned pork loin
200 g cooked ham, thinly sliced
2 hard-boiled eggs, chopped
75 g almonds, blanched, and/or
    walnuts, chopped finely
1/2 teaspoon salt
2 cloves garlic
1 egg, beaten
2 tablespoons lard or olive oil
1 teaspoon thyme
1 head garlic
10 peppercorns
100 ml dry sherry
water

PORK FILLET WITH SHERRY
Solomillo de cerdo al jerez

Lard the fillets with strips of ham or lay strips of ham over the "tail" end of the fillets, double them over the ham and secure with string.

Rub them with lard and put in a baking dish. Put in a preheated hot oven for five minutes, then add the garlic and onions which have been peeled and parboiled in boiling water for two minutes, and the sherry and rosemary. Lower the heat to moderate and roast about 45 minutes, basting occasionally.

Remove to a serving dish and slice the fillets. Serve covered with the pan juices and surrounded by the onions. Serves four.

2 pork fillets (about 750 g)
50 g *serrano* ham
2 tablespoons lard
1 head garlic
1-2 dozen small onions
100 ml sherry
sprig of rosemary

ROAST PORK, CATALAN STYLE
Asado de cerdo a la catalana

Any piece of pork can be prepared in this manner — a whole fresh ham, cuts from the leg or shoulder, or the unboned loin.

In the mortar crush the cloves of garlic to a paste and rub the piece of pork all over with it. Let sit for an hour.

Melt the lard in a casserole or flame-proof oven dish and brown the meat on all sides. Add the cinnamon, thyme, oregano, onion, bay, parsley, celery, pepper and cloves. Put in a very hot oven for five minutes, then reduce the heat and add the brandy or anise and the sherry or Málaga wine (or a *vino generoso*).

1 1/2 kg pork roast
4 cloves garlic
2 tablespoons lard
1 piece cinnamon stick
1 teaspoon thyme
1 teaspoon oregano
1 onion, sliced
1 bay leaf
1 sprig parsley
1 stalk celery
1 teaspoon coarsely ground pepper
pinch of cloves
50 ml brandy or anise
100 ml medium dry sherry or dry
    Málaga wine

Roast the meat until done, about one and three-quarter hours, adding small quantities of water as needed so there is always some liquid in the roasting pan.

Remove to a serving platter and let sit for 10 minutes before carving. Strain the pan juices and serve in a sauce bowl. Garnish the meat with cooked vegetables and potatoes. Serves six.

ROAST SUCKLING PIG
Cochinillo asado

Buy an oven-ready suckling pig and have the butcher split it in half lengthwise (it can also be roasted whole).

Crush the garlic cloves and mix them with the lard. Spread the pig with about half the lard and place, skin side down, on a bed of bay leaves and thyme in a large roasting pan or earthenware platter.

Put in a preheated medium oven for about one hour, basting frequently (if browning too fast, partially cover with foil).

Turn the pig skin-side up. Raise the oven temperature to hot. Prick the skin with a fork and brush with lard. Mix the salt, vinegar and water and brush over the skin. Return the pig to the oven and roast it another 45 minutes, brushing frequently with the water to crisp the skin. The meat should be tender enough to be "carved" with the edge of a plate. Serves eight.

1 whole pig, 3 to 4 weeks,
   weighing 3 1/2-4 kg.
100 g lard
4 cloves garlic
bay leaves
thyme
1 tablespoon salt
1 tablespoon vinegar or lemon juice
1/4 litre water

PORK WITH TOMATO
Magro con tomate

A tapa bar speciality, this is simple and flavourful. Made with fresh, ripe tomatoes, it really needs no extra spices or herbs. Choose a juicy cut such as butt, from the shoulder. This makes a good sandwich when served on bread rolls.

Fry the pork cubes in oil until browned. Add the chopped tomatoes, salt and bay leaf. Fry on a high heat for a few minutes, then simmer until pork is cooked and tomatoes reduced to a sauce, about 20 minutes. Serves four.

1/2 kg pork, cut in cubes
50 ml olive oil
1 kg tomatoes, peeled, seeded
  and chopped
2 teaspoons salt
1 bay leaf

BARBECUED SPARE-RIBS
Costillas a la parrilla

Mix together the water, salt, parsley, oregano, thyme, bay leaf, pepper and quartered lemon. Cut the ribs into three-rib segments and place in a shallow pan. Pour over the marinade and let sit for four hours.

Grill the ribs very slowly over charcoal or on a griddle, brushing with the marinade, until thoroughly cooked, about 15 minutes on each side. Serve with *alioli* and *picante* sauces (see Chapter 12). Serves four.

100 ml water
1 teaspoon salt
3 tablespoons chopped parsley
1 teaspoon oregano
1 teaspoon thyme
1 bay leaf
freshly ground pepper
1 lemon
1 3/4 kg spare-ribs

BAKED SPARE-RIBS
Costillas al horno

Make up the stuffing as in the recipe for Stuffed Turkey, Catalan Style (page 298).

Put the stuffing in a roasting pan and put the rack of spare-ribs on top of it. Cover with foil and bake in a medium oven until the meat is tender, about one and a half hours.

Remove the foil during the last 15 minutes and let the ribs brown slightly. Serves four.

1 rack spare ribs, about 1 3/4 kg

KEBABS, MOROCCAN STYLE
Pinchitos

Cooked over charcoal braziers at fiestas and in tapa bars, these kebabs are relatives of the ones made in Tangier just across the Straits of Gibraltar. The difference is that in Morocco, a Muslim country, they are made with lamb or beef and in Spain they are usually made with pork. The *especias para pinchitos*, a mixture of spices, can be purchased in many markets. Where not available, use a curry powder to which is added extra cumin. (Use one tablespoon curry powder and one tablespoon ground cumin.) These are usually served as snacks, accompanied by bread.

Cut the meat into fairly small cubes (about 2cm square).

In a deep bowl, glass or crockery, put a single layer of meat. Sprinkle with chopped parsley, minced garlic, a pinch of salt, a teaspoon of spice and a tiny pinch of cayenne. Squeeze the juice of a half-lemon over it. Add another layer of meat and other ingredients. Continue until all the meat is used. Cover and marinate in the refrigerator six to 12 hours, turning the mixture two or three times.

Thread four or five pieces of the meat on thin, metal skewers and grill over charcoal, on a griddle or under broiler/grill until browned on all sides. Makes about 20 kebabs.

1 kg pork, lamb or veal
4 tablespoons chopped parsley
10 cloves garlic, minced
2 lemons
1 tablespoon Morrocan spices
  (*especias para pinchitos*)
1/2 teaspoon cayenne or red pepper flakes
1 teaspoon salt

LAMB AND KID

Milk-fed baby lamb and kid are much appreciated in Spain and can be used in the following recipes fairly interchangeably. Except when roasted whole, the meat is usually hacked into even-sized pieces, which, unfortunately, makes for bone splinters. You can have the meat jointed instead, but then allow longer cooking time. In markets outside Spain where the suckling animals are not available, use small lamb chops, well-trimmed, or slices from a leg of lamb for these dishes. In general, Spaniards like their meat well-cooked, so spring lamb is usually braised rather than roasted and is never served still pink.

BABY KID IN CASSEROLE
Cazuela de chivo

I first had this dish at a wedding feast in the country, where two baby goats were cooked in a huge cauldron, almost a metre in diameter, which then went into a domed bread oven to cook for many hours. I've made the casserole on a much smaller scale in my gas oven, using lamb chops instead of the kid. It's an easy dish and wonderfully spiced.

Have the butcher cut the lamb or kid into even-sized pieces. Pour the oil into the bottom of a large roasting pan or deep casserole. Put a layer of sliced potatoes on the bottom and alternate with layers of sliced tomatoes and onions.

Place the meat on top of the potatoes. Cover with strips of green pepper, chopped parsley, cloves of roasted garlic, bay leaves and another layer of sliced potatoes, tomatoes and onion.

In the mortar crush the salt, two cloves of garlic, peppercorns, cloves, cinnamon and saffron. Dissolve in a little white wine and add to the pot with the rest of the wine.

Put the casserole in a hot oven for 10 minutes, then reduce the heat to moderate and cook until meat and potatoes are very tender, about two and a half hours, removing cover for last 20 minutes. Serves six to eight.

1 1/2-2 kg baby lamb or kid, or use
    lamb chops
150 ml olive oil
8 medium potatoes, peeled and sliced
6 medium tomatoes, sliced
2 large onions, sliced
3 small green peppers, cut in strips
2 tablespoons parsley, chopped
1 head garlic, roasted
    (for how-to see page 142)
4 bay leaves
2 teaspoons salt
2 cloves garlic
10 peppercorns
4 cloves
1 teaspoon cinnamon
1 teaspoon saffron
1/2 litre white wine

LAMB SAUTÉ, NAVARRE STYLE
Cochifrito a la navarra

Cut the lamb into small cubes. Heat the lard in a heavy frying pan and on a high heat sauté the meat. When it is partially browned, add the chopped onion and garlic. Keep stirring the lamb while it browns. Then add the paprika and pepper and immediately add the water.

Continue cooking on a hot fire until the liquid is evaporated and the meat begins to fry again, then add the juice of the lemon and the parsley. Cover the pan and cook slowly another 15 minutes. Serves four.

1 kg boned lamb
3 tablespoons lard or olive oil
1 onion, chopped
2 cloves garlic, chopped
2 teaspoons paprika
1/4 teaspoon pepper
300 ml water
1/2 teaspoon salt
1 lemon
parsley

BABY KID WITH GARLIC, GRANADA STYLE
Choto ajillo a la granadina

Cut the lamb or kid into even-sized pieces. Cut the liver in several pieces.

Heat the oil in a frying pan and sauté the liver until lightly browned and remove it. In the same oil fry five cloves of garlic and the bread until toasted, and remove. Continue browning the meat in the same oil.

Meanwhile, in mortar or blender crush the peppercorns, oregano, cayenne, paprika, salt and two cloves raw garlic with the fried garlic, bread and liver. Add the vinegar and a little wine to make a smooth paste.

Place the meat in a deep pot or casserole. Add the remaining wine to the frying pan and scrape up

1 1/2 kg baby lamb or kid, or use lamb
    chops
the animal's liver or 150 g chicken livers
75 ml olive oil
7 cloves garlic
1 slice bread
10 peppercorns
1 teaspoon oregano
pinch of cayenne
1 teaspoon paprika
1/2 teaspoon salt
1 tablespoon vinegar
2 bay leaves
1/2 litre white wine

all the browned bits. Dissolve the paste from the mortar in the wine and pour over the meat with the bay leaves. Cover and simmer until meat is tender, about one and a half hours. Serves six.

Caldereta extremeña, a lamb stew from Extremadura, is prepared similarly.

LAMB WITH PEPPERS
Cordero al chilindrón

A speciality of Aragón, this dish is prepared as for Chicken with Peppers *(Pollo al Chilindrón)* in Chapter 10. Though baby lamb should be used, it's a very good dish made with lamb chops intead.

LAMB, SHEPHERD STYLE
Cordero a la pastora

Cut the lamb into regular-sized pieces. In the mortar crush the peppercorns, clove, garlic and half a teaspoon of salt. Mix with the vinegar and wine and rub the pieces of meat with this mixture. Marinate overnight.

Put the oil in a deep pan or casserole and warm it. Turn the meat in the oil just to seal it, without letting it brown. Stir in the flour and blend well, then add the bouquet of herbs and the water. Peel the potatoes, but if small leave them whole.

Add to the casserole, cover and simmer until liquid is reduced, about one hour. Add the milk, salt and pepper to taste, and cook until the sauce is smooth, about 15 minutes more. Serve in the same casserole sprinkled with chopped parsley.
Serves six.

1 1/4 kg baby lamb
5 peppercorns
1 clove
2 cloves garlic
2 tablespoons vinegar
50 ml white wine
75 ml olive oil
1 tablespoon flour
thyme, rosemary, bay leaf, mint and parsley
1/2 litre water
3/4 kg small potatoes
1/4 litre milk
salt and pepper
chopped parsley

LAMB STEW
Caldereta de cordero

Cut the lamb into cubes and put in a pot. Add enough water to just cover the meat. Bring to the boil, skim the froth and reduce to a simmer. Add the onion, tomatoes, peppers, roasted garlic, bouquet of herbs, salt and oil. Cover and simmer until the meat is tender, about 45 minutes.

In the mortar or blender crush the peppercorns, clove, paprika, cumin and soaked bread. Dissolve in a little water and add to the lamb. Cook another few minutes and serve. Serves four to six.

1 kg boned lamb
1 onion, quartered
2 tomatoes, quartered
4 small peppers, cut in half
1 head garlic, roasted
   (for how-to see page 142)
bay leaf, parsley, thyme
1/2 teaspoon salt
50 ml olive oil
6 peppercorns
1 clove
1 teaspoon paprika
1/2 teaspoon cumin
1 slice bread, soaked in water

BRAISED LEG OF LAMB WITH WHITE BEANS
Pierna de cordero guisada con judías blancas

Have the butcher bone the leg of lamb, roll and tie it. Rub it with salt and pepper.

In a large pot, heat the oil and very slowly brown the meat on all sides. Add the garlic cut in slivers, the whole, peeled onions, and the carrots, peeled and cut in chunks. Let them brown in the fat for a few minutes, then add the meat stock. Cover and simmer the meat until very tender, about one and a half hours.

While the meat is cooking, put the soaked beans in another pot with the onion and bay leaf and plenty of water to cover. Bring to the boil, then simmer until tender, about one hour. Add salt when the beans are partially cooked.

1 leg of lamb or mutton, about 1 1/2 kg
4 tablespoons olive oil or lard
4 cloves garlic
1 dozen tiny onions
4 carrots
1/2 litre meat stock
salt and pepper
1 /4 kg white beans, soaked overnight
1 slice onion
1 bay leaf

Drain them and add to the pot in which the lamb is cooking. Cook another 20 minutes and serve the lamb, sliced, on a platter surrounded by the beans, onions and carrots. Serves six.

ROAST BABY LAMB, CASTILIAN STYLE
Lechazo asado al castellano

Choose a lamb of about four weeks. Split in half lengthwise. Rub inside and out with salt and pepper.

In a bowl mix finely chopped thyme, parsley, garlic and onion with a little paprika. Rub the meat with this mixture and let it sit for two hours.

Rub the meat with lard and place in a roasting pan. Put in a very hot oven, skin side up, until browned, basting with the fat in the pan. Reduce the heat and pour over a little white wine. Roast the lamb until tender, about 45 minutes, adding extra wine as needed. Remove to a serving platter and cut into serving pieces. Add a little extra wine to the pan and boil it briefly. Serve the sauce with the lamb. Serves about eight.

LAMB CHOPS WITH SHERRY
Chuletas de cordero al jerez

Sprinkle the lamb chops with salt and pepper.

Heat the oil in a large frying pan and brown the chops on both sides. Remove them to a plate. In the same oil sauté the chopped onions and diced carrots until softened. Return the chops to the pan and add the bay leaves, ground cloves, pepper, 1/2 teaspoon salt and sherry. Cover and simmer, adding a little water if necessary, until chops are tender and sauce reduced, about 40 minutes. Serves four.

8 lamb chops
salt and pepper
50 ml olive oil
2 medium onions, chopped
4 carrots, diced
2 bay leaves
pinch of ground cloves
1/2 teaspoon ground pepper
1/4 litre sherry

LAMB CHOPS, PAMPLONA STYLE
Chuletas de cordero a la pamplona

Heat the oil and lard in a frying pan and fry the lamb chops. As they are browned, transfer them to an oven casserole.

In the same fat fry the diced ham and chopped onion. Add the tomatoes, sugar, salt and pepper. Let cook for several minutes, then pour the sauce over the lamb chops. Put in a medium oven until the meat is tender, about 20 minutes.

Cover the casserole with a layer of sliced *chorizo* and return to the oven to cook for several minutes. Serve in the same casserole. Serves four.

12-16 baby lamb chops
2 tablespoons olive oil
2 tablespoons lard
100 g diced ham
1 onion, chopped
3 tomatoes, peeled and chopped
1 teaspoon sugar
salt and pepper
1/4 kg Pamplona *chorizo* sausage

HAM

Two kinds of ham are used in Spanish cookery: the salt-cured *jamón serrano*, usually served raw, and *jamón cocido*, or cooked ham, which might be baked English style or fried and sauced with sherry. The raw ham is used in small quantities to flavour beans and potages. Soften it before cooking by soaking in water.

CURED PORK SHOULDER
WITH TURNIP TOPS
Lacón con grelos

The *"grelos"* in this Galician speciality are the flowering stems of the turnip. If not available, use turnip leaves, cabbage or other greens. *Lacón* is salt-cured pork hand or shoulder. (Ham can be used instead.) Other salted meats — the feet, ears and cheeks — are usually added to this tasty stew.

Put the soaked *lacón*, pig's ear, cheek and foot to cook in plenty of water to cover. Bring to the boil, skim, then simmer until the *lacón* is tender, about one and a half hours.

Remove to another pan with a little of the liquid to cover. Wash the *grelos*, chop them into pieces, blanch in boiling water and drain. Add them to the same broth in which the *lacón* cooked. Add the *chorizo* and let cook 10 minutes, then add the potatoes, peeled and left whole. Add salt, if necessary, and pepper. Cook until potatoes and greens are tender, about 20 minutes.

With a skimmer, remove the *grelos* to a serving platter. Cut the meat into pieces and put on top and arrange the *chorizo* and potatoes around the side of the platter. Serves six.

1 kg *lacón*, soaked, or cooked ham
200 g ear, cheek, etc.
1 pig's foot, split
1 1/2 kg grelos
1/2 kg *chorizo* (red sausage,
    preferably Galician)
12 small potatoes
salt and pepper

MINCED MEAT, PÂTÉS AND SAUSAGE

Minced (ground) pork or a combination of pork and veal is more widely used in Spanish dishes than minced beef. Sometimes chopped ham or pork fat is added to the mixture both to flavour it and to keep it juicy.

MEATBALLS
Albóndigas

Spanish-style meatballs are usually first browned in olive oil, then added to a sauce to simmer for another 20 minutes. Use either almond sauce or tomato sauce (see Chapter 12). This same mixture is used to stuff peppers, tomatoes, courgettes, aubergines, onions, etc.

Place the minced meat in a bowl. Soak the sliced bread in water or milk to cover until softened. Squeeze out and add to the meat with the minced garlic, chopped onion, chopped parsley, salt, pepper, nutmeg and beaten egg. Knead well to make a smooth mixture. Form into small balls. Roll them in flour and fry slowly in hot oil until browned on all sides. Remove.

Make the almond sauce. Fry the blanched almonds, bread and garlic in the oil until toasted. Remove. In a mortar or blender, crush the peppercorns, saffron, clove and salt with the toasted almonds, bread and garlic. Add the wine to make a smooth paste.

Add to the oil remaining in the pan, then add the stock or water. Cook for a few minutes, then add the fried meatballs. Simmer the meatballs for 25 minutes, adding more liquid if needed. Immediately before serving, add a squeeze of lemon juice and a sprinkling of parsley.

1/2 kg minced pork and/or veal
2 slices bread (50 g)
1 clove garlic, minced
2 tablespoons finely chopped onion
2 tablespoons chopped parsley
1/2 teaspoon salt
1/4 teaspoon ground pepper
freshly grated nutmeg
1 egg, beaten
flour
olive oil

ALMOND SAUCE:
25 almonds, blanched and skinned
1 slice bread (25 g)
2 cloves garlic
3 tablespoons olive oil
10 peppercorns
1/2 teaspoon saffron
1 clove
1/2 teaspoon salt
100 ml white wine
1/4 litre meat stock or water

CASTILIAN BAKED LAMB ROLL
Hornazo a lo castellano

Put the minced lamb in a bowl with the chopped ham and chopped salt pork. Put the bread to soak in 50 ml wine until softened. Squeeze it out, reserving the wine, and add the bread to the meat. Season with salt and pepper, nutmeg and cinnamon.

Blanch cabbage, chard, spinach or grape leaves in boiling water until wilted, drain and cut out the stem. Make an overlapping layer of leaves on a flat table.

Form the meat into a roll and place it on top of the leaves. Roll the leaves around the meat and tie with string.

Dip the roll in beaten egg, then dredge in flour. Fry it in oil, turning to brown on all sides. Add the chopped onion, the oregano, thyme, reserved white wine and enough additional wine to partially cover the roll. Season with salt and pepper.

Bake in a medium oven until done, about one hour. Serves six.

3/4 kg minced lamb or veal
50 g chopped ham
50 g chopped salt pork
2 slices bread
300 ml white wine
grated nutmeg
1/4 teaspoon cinnamon
cabbage, chard, spinach or grape leaves
1 egg, beaten
flour
75 ml olive oil
1 onion, chopped
1/2 teaspoon oregano
1/2 teaspoon thyme
salt and pepper

OFFAL (VARIETY MEATS)

Though pork and lamb liver are most frequently used, calf or beef liver can be used in these dishes if preferred. Lamb and veal kidneys are considered the most delicate in flavour but, again, any can be used. Pork tongues are the most usual; if substituting beef tongue, which is much larger, increase cooking time.

LIVER IN ALMOND SAUCE
Hígado con salsa de almendras

Cut the liver into 3cm cubes. Heat the oil in a frying pan and in it fry the garlic, almonds and bread until toasted. Remove and set aside.

In the same oil sauté the pieces of liver until browned.

Meanwhile, in the mortar crush the saffron, peppercorns, clove and salt with the garlic, almonds and bread. Dissolve this paste in a little water and add to the pan with the wine and bay leaf. Return the liver to the sauce and cook gently for 20 minutes.

Garnish with chopped parsley. Serves four. Serve accompanied by potatoes cut in dice and fried until browned.

1/2 kg liver
50 ml olive oil
1 clove garlic
1 dozen almonds, blanched and skinned
1 slice bread
1/4 teaspoon saffron
8 peppercorns
1 clove
1/2 teaspoon salt
100 ml white wine
1 bay leaf
2 tablespoons chopped parsley

LIVER IN SOUR SAUCE
Hígado en adobo

Cut the liver into strips. Heat the oil in a pan and sauté it.

In a mortar or blender crush the garlic, chili pepper, vinegar, water, salt, paprika, pepper and oregano. Pour this over the liver and cook until liquid is reduced by half. Serves six.

1 kg liver
50 ml olive oil
4 cloves garlic
piece of chili pepper
50 ml vinegar
100 ml water
1/2 teaspoon salt
1 teaspoon paprika
1/2 teaspoon pepper
1 teaspoon oregano

SAUTÉED CHICKEN LIVERS
Higadillos salteados

Heat the oil in a frying pan and sauté the pieces of chicken liver with the diced salt pork. Add the onion and garlic, then the sherry, salt, pepper and thyme. Cook 10 minutes.

Sprinkle with parsley and garnish with strips of red pepper. Makes two servings. Good served in a rice ring.

3 tablespoons olive oil
1/4 kg chicken livers, cut up
150 g salt pork or bacon, diced
1/2 onion, finely chopped
1 clove garlic, minced
100 ml dry sherry
salt and pepper
1/2 teaspoon thyme
chopped parsley
strips of red pepper

SAUTÉED KIDNEYS WITH SHERRY
Riñones al jerez

Very fresh lamb or veal kidneys should not need soaking or blanching. Pork or beef kidneys can be blanched for 15 minutes in simmering water to which has been added lemon juice or vinegar. Peel off the thin membrane that encases the kidney and cut out the core of fat. Small lamb kidneys may be sliced crosswise; the larger veal kidney should be cut in quarters and sliced. If desired, add sliced mushrooms to the kidneys.

Heat the oil or lard in a frying pan and sauté the kidneys very gently — high heat and overcooking cause kidneys to harden. When lightly browned, remove them and reserve.

Add the chopped onion and garlic to the fat and sauté until softened. Stir in the flour and cook for a minute, then add the bay leaf, sherry and stock. Season with salt and pepper and simmer the sauce for 10 minutes.

Return kidneys to the pan and heat gently for a few minutes. Serve sprinkled with chopped parsley. Makes six first-course portions.

1/2 kg kidneys, prepared for cooking
4 tablespoons olive oil or lard
1/2 onion, finely chopped
1 clove garlic, chopped
1 tablespoon flour
1 bay leaf
100 ml dry sherry
100 ml meat stock
salt and pepper
chopped parsley

FRIES
Criadillas

I first encountered this dish in a Seville restaurant where it was translated into English as "the moo cow's delight". *Criadillas* is kitchen terminology for the testicles of bulls or sheep, in English called "fries", "mountain oysters" or "animelles". The texture is between that of kidneys and brains.

Blanch the fries in simmering, salted water for five minutes. Remove and let them cool.

Peel off the outer layer of membrane. Slice them thickly and put in a bowl. Add enough water to cover, and the vinegar. Soak for two hours.

Drain well and pat the slices dry. Place the beaten egg and salt in a bowl and the crumbs on a plate. Dip the slices first into egg, then into breadcrumbs and sauté in oil until golden on both sides. Serve garnished with lemon slices. Serves six as a starter.

4 calves' or lambs' fries
2 teaspoons vinegar
1 egg, beaten
1/2 teaspoon salt
50 g fine breadcrumbs
75 ml olive oil
lemon slices

SWEETBREADS WITH SHERRY
Mollejas al oloroso

Soak the sweetbreads in water for one hour. Blanch them in simmering salted water for 10 minutes. Drain. Then cut them in slices.

Melt the butter in a pan and sauté the diced ham and onion. Add the sweetbreads and sauté gently for several minutes. Add the sherry, stock, lemon juice, salt and pepper, and simmer, covered, for 20 minutes, adding more stock if necessary.

1/2 kg sweetbreads
50 g butter
50 g ham, diced
1 tablespoon chopped onion
50 ml *oloroso* sherry
50 ml chicken broth
1 tablespoon lemon juice
salt and pepper
50 ml cream

Remove the sweetbreads, stir in the cream and heat thoroughly. Pour over the sweetbreads and serve. Makes four servings.

BRAISED TONGUE
Estofado de lengua

Scrub the tongues under running water then put them to soak in a basin of salted water for two hours. Rinse again.

Put them in a lidded pot with water to cover, adding the quartered onion, carrot, a bay leaf, salt and pepper. Bring to the boil, skim off the froth, and simmer the tongues for 40 minutes. Remove from the water, reserving the broth. As soon as they are cool enough to handle, but while still warm, slit the skins and peel off.

Cut the tongues crosswise into thick slices, discarding any bone and fatty parts from the thick ends.

Heat the oil in a pot and fry the almonds, garlic and bread until toasted and crisp. Remove. In the mortar or blender crush the saffron, peppercorns and cloves with the fried almonds, garlic and bread. Dissolve in the sherry.

Add the sliced tongue to the oil and sauté it, turning with a fork, for a few minutes. Add the almond mixture, half a teaspoon of salt, potatoes peeled and cut in small pieces, the two bay leaves and enough of the reserved broth to just cover the meat and potatoes. Cover and simmer until tongue is very tender, about one hour. Serves six.

1 kg pork tongues
1 onion, quartered
1 carrot, cut in half
3 bay leaves
salt and pepper
75 ml olive oil
1 dozen almonds, blanched and peeled
6 cloves garlic
1 slice bread
1/2 teaspoon saffron
10 peppercorns
2 cloves
100 ml dry sherry
8 medium potatoes

STEWED TRIPE, MADRID STYLE
Callos a la Madrileña

I had never eaten tripe in my life — nor ever expected to — until one chill night in one of Madrid's *tascas*, when friends ordered plates of a hot and fragrant potage, full of rich, deep flavours. So satisfying was the experience, that I have loved tripe ever since. Though time-consuming, this is not a difficult dish to prepare at home.

To clean and prepare the tripe: first wash it well under running water, scraping it with a knife to clean off bits of fat clinging to the surface. Then spread the tripe out and sprinkle it with coarse salt. Use a half-lemon to "scrub" the tripe well on both sides, adding more salt and another lemon as needed. Rinse well.

With scissors, cut the tripe into 4cm squares. Put in a bowl, sprinkle with salt and pour over a glass of vinegar. Let it sit for an hour, turning occasionally. Rinse again.

Put in a pot and cover with water. Bring to the boil, skimming off the froth, and boil five minutes. Drain.

Put the pieces of tripe in fresh water with bay leaf, chili pepper, peppercorns, an onion stuck with cloves and several cloves of garlic. Bring to the boil, skim, then simmer until tripe is tender, about three hours for veal tripe, five hours if it is cow's tripe.

A calf's foot is often cooked with tripe. It should be skinned, split, well scrubbed and blanched with the tripe.

After cooking, remove bones and cut the meat into pieces similar to the tripe. The tripe can be prepared up to this point and refrigerated, with the broth, until the following day.

Drain the tripe, saving the broth. Put the tripe and cut-up calf's foot into a casserole.

In a pan heat the oil and sauté the chopped onion, carrot, diced ham and garlic. Stir in the flour and the paprika, then the tomato sauce and about one-quarter litre of the reserved broth. Season with pepper, cayenne, cumin and salt. Pour over the tripe and add the *chorizo*. Cook slowly for an hour, adding more broth as needed. The sauce should be thick.

Before serving, cut the *chorizo* into slices and arrange on top of the tripe. Serves six.

1 kg veal tripe, cooked
1 calf's foot, cooked
75 ml olive oil
1 onion, chopped
1 carrot, chopped
100 g ham, diced
1 tablespoon flour
4 cloves garlic
1 tablespoon paprika
100 ml tomato sauce
1 teaspoon freshly ground pepper
cayenne or chili to taste
1/2 teaspoon cumin
200 g *chorizo* or *longaniza*
salt to taste

ANDALUSIAN-STYLE TRIPE
Callos a la andaluza

In Seville this is prepared similarly to Madrid tripe, with the addition of chickpeas and chopped mint. In the village where I live it is usually made with pig tripe instead of veal, and includes the trotter, ears and tail. Because it contains all the parts of the pig, it is a favourite dish for the festival of San Anton, St. Anthony Abbot, patron of farm animals.

Clean and blanch the tripe, trotters, ears and tail as in the previous recipe. Drain and put all of them to cook in water to cover for one hour. Drain again.

Cut the tripe into pieces, remove bones from the trotter and dice the meat, cut the ears and tail into pieces. Place in a pot with the piece of pork, the salt pork, the soaked chickpeas, roasted garlic, bay leaves and parsley. Cover with water, bring to the boil and simmer, partially covered.

In the mortar or blender crush the saffron, peppercorns, cloves, chili pepper, raw garlic, paprika and salt. Dissolve in a little liquid from the pot and add to the tripe.

Heat the oil in a frying pan and sauté the chopped onion. Add the chopped tomato and continue frying for 10 minutes until reduced to a sauce. Add this to the tripe with the black pudding and red sausage. Continue simmering until tripe is done, about three hours. Cut the sausages, pork and salt pork into pieces. Serves eight.

1 kg pig tripe
2 pig trotters, split
2 pig ears
1 pig tail
1/4 kg pork
100 g salt pork
300 g chickpeas, soaked overnight
1 head garlic, roasted
    (for how-to see page 142)
3 bay leaves
2 sprigs parsley
1/2 teaspoon saffron
15 peppercorns
4 cloves
1 chili pepper
2 cloves garlic
2 teaspoons paprika
2 teaspoons salt
3 tablespoons olive oil
1 onion, chopped
1 tomato, peeled and chopped
100 g *morcilla* (black pudding)
150 g *chorizo* (red sausage)

SEVILLE BRAISED OXTAILS
Rabo de toro a la sevillana

After a bullfight, this is, indeed, made with bulls' tails. Otherwise, the butcher's oxtails will do nicely.

Have the butcher cut the tails into segments of about 7cm. Blanch them in boiling water and drain.

In a pot heat the oil and add the chopped onion, leek, carrots, garlic and ham. Sauté until softened, then add the blanched pieces of oxtail and sauté on a high heat.

Add the brandy, set it alight, and stir with a long-handled spoon until flames subside. Add the red wine or sherry, the herbs and spices, chili pepper and chopped tomato. Simmer until meat is very tender, about two hours, adding stock or water as needed. When cooked, the sauce should be fairly thick from reduction. If not, thicken with a little flour mixed with water. Serves four.

1 oxtail, about 1 1/4 kg
50 ml olive oil
1 onion, chopped
1 leek, chopped
3 carrots, chopped
2 cloves garlic, chopped
50 g ham, diced
75 ml brandy
100 ml red wine or sherry
bay leaf, parsley, thyme
salt, pepper, cloves
1 piece chili pepper or cayenne
1 tomato, peeled and chopped

SAUCES AND SALAD DRESSINGS

Few Spanish cookbooks include a chapter on "sauces". In Spanish cookery, a sauce is an integral part of a dish rather than a separate preparation. There are, of course, some notable exceptions — mayonnaise and *romesco* are two — plus some others too good to be relegated exclusively to the dishes in which they are cooked. Olive oil is the basic ingredient for all of these Spanish sauces.

FRIED TOMATO
Sofrito

This is the starting point of many Spanish dishes. *Sofrito* is not exactly a sauce, it's a procedure — the ingredients are fried in olive oil, then added to meat, fish, vegetables or eggs to finish cooking together. After frying, the sauce can be sieved or puréed in a blender if a smooth consistency is desired. More often it is left as is to reduce slowly during cooking.

Heat the oil in a frying pan and sauté the chopped onion, garlic and pepper until softened. Add the diced ham, if using, then the prepared tomatoes. "Fry" the tomatoes on a high heat for several minutes. Season with salt, spices and herbs and continue cooking briskly until the tomatoes "sweat" out their liquid and it has evaporated.

Mash the tomatoes with the back of a fork as they fry. The tomatoes need to cook only about 15 minutes. At this point they can be sieved or the *sofrito* added to food to continue cooking. Makes about 300 ml of sauce.

50 ml olive oil
1 small onion, chopped
1 clove garlic, chopped
1 green pepper, chopped (optional)
50 g ham, diced (optional)
1 kg tomatoes (4 large), peeled, seeded
  and chopped
1/2 teaspoon salt
pinch of paprika, cumin and pepper
bay leaf, parsley

Clockwise from left: Almond Sauce (*Salsa de Almendras*), page 350; Garlic Mayonnaise (*Alioli*), page 352, and Tarragona Pepper Sauce (*Romesco*), page 346.

ALMOND SAUCE
Salsa de almendras

Use this sauce with sliced, hard-boiled eggs, meatballs, cooked chicken, sautéed liver, etc. Finish the sauce with a squeeze of lemon juice and a sprinkling of parsley.

Fry the almonds, bread and garlic in the oil until toasted, and remove.

In mortar or blender crush the peppercorns, saffron, clove and salt. Add the toasted almonds, bread and garlic and mash to a smooth paste. Dilute with the wine and stir into the oil in the pan. Fry for a minute, then add the stock or water. Cook for 10 minutes.

15 almonds, blanched and skinned
1 slice bread
2 cloves garlic
50 ml extra virgin olive oil
5 peppercorns
1/2 teaspoon saffron
1 clove
1/2 teaspoon salt
100 ml white wine
1/4 litre stock or water

PINE-NUT SAUCE
Salsa de piñones

In blender or processor purée the pine-nuts and garlic. Beat in the oil, lemon juice and water. Season with salt and pepper and stir in the chopped parsley. Serve with fish, vegetables, pasta.

200 g pine-nuts
1 clove garlic
100 ml extra virgin olive oil
1 lemon
50 ml water
salt and pepper
2 tablespoons chopped parsley

MAYONNAISE
Salsa mayonesa

I lived for several years in a beautiful mill house in the country, where the sound of running water was a constant backdrop, but where there was no electricity, thus no modern appliances like blenders. Making mayonnaise by hand became one of my favourite rituals: a big stone mortar, olive oil measured into the eggshell, and a particular patience in stirring that indicated one really had nothing more important to do than confect a perfect mayonnaise. When I built a new house and put in electricity, I bought a blender the day I moved in. I still make mayonnaise regularly, but now it takes minutes.

The most flavourful mayonnaise is made with olive oil. However, if you want the mayonnaise as a sandwich spread or a bland salad dressing, other vegetable oils can be used instead of, or in addition to, olive oil. Likewise, vinegar or lemon juice or both can be used, adjusting the quantity to taste. Some people like a very tart mayonnaise.

Have the eggs and oil at room temperature. In the winter, it is helpful to rinse out the bowl in very hot water and dry it well and very slightly warm the oil near the stove.

Place the yolks in the bowl or in a large mortar. Beat them until mixed, then add a few drops of vinegar or lemon juice and a few grains of salt. Have the oil in a small pitcher.

Stirring the yolks with a wooden spoon or the pestle, begin adding the oil, a drop at a time. Stir in the same direction until the oil is completely absorbed before adding another drop of oil.

When about half the oil has been incorporated, beat the rest of it in in a slow stream. By this point the mayonnaise should be thickened. Add the remaining vinegar and salt to taste. If necessary, thin with a little milk or water. If the mayonnaise should "break", it can be reconstituted by placing a fresh yolk in another bowl and adding the first sauce to it, drop by drop, until emulsified.

Makes about 300 ml mayonnaise. Store refrigerated.

2 egg yolks
1/4 litre olive oil
3 tablespoons vinegar and/or lemon juice
1/2 teaspoon salt

BLENDER MAYONNAISE

Put the whole egg in the container of blender or food processor with a spoonful of oil and the mustard and cayenne. Whirl until the egg is mixed.

With the motor running add the oil in a very slow stream until the mayonnaise is thick. Add the vinegar or lemon juice and salt and whirl again. Store refrigerated.

1 whole egg
175 ml olive oil
pinch of mustard and cayenne
2 tablespoons vinegar or lemon juice
1/2 teaspoon salt

ANDALUSIAN MAYONNAISE
Mayonesa a la andaluza

Add one tablespoon tomato purée or two tablespoons tomato sauce to 150 ml of mayonnaise with 25 grams finely chopped tinned pimiento, one clove of garlic, minced, and two tablespoons chopped parsley. Season with pepper and additional lemon juice. Serve with seafood cocktail, cold vegetables, cold cuts and as a sandwich spread.

GARLIC MAYONNAISE
Alioli

Alioli just means "garlic oil", and is variously called *ajiaceite, ajoaceite* and *all-i-oli*. At its simplest — the original formula — the sauce is crushed garlic to which oil is added, drop by drop. Today, it is usually made with egg yolk as well. Serve it with grilled lamb chops, grilled fish, snails, rabbit, chicken, squab, prawns, lobster.

Crush three cloves garlic in mortar, then proceed as for handmade mayonnaise, using good olive oil. For blender *alioli,* whirl three cloves garlic with the egg, then proceed as for blender mayonnaise.

VINAIGRETTE
Salsa vinagreta

Spanish green salads are usually served accompanied by cruets of olive oil and vinegar. A vinaigrette sauce would more likely be used on vegetable salads, such as potatoes or beans, or drizzled over fish or served with many cold foods.

In a mortar or bowl crush the egg yolks with the garlic and salt. Add the pepper, then beat in the vinegar until creamy.

Add the oil, drop by drop, beating well, until it is all incorporated. Makes 200 ml. Can also be made in the blender.

2 hard-boiled egg yolks (optional)
1 clove garlic
1/4 teaspoon salt
freshly ground pepper
50 ml wine vinegar
150 ml extra virgin olive oil

GALICIAN SAUCE
Salsa gallega

This is served with boiled potatoes, grilled octopus, prawns, fish, meat and also makes a good salad dressing.

In a bowl mix the crushed garlic, paprika, cayenne, salt, pepper and vinegar. Beat in the oil until blended.

1 clove garlic, crushed
1 teaspoon paprika
pinch of cayenne
1/2 teaspoon coarse salt
pinch of white pepper
3 tablespoons vinegar
100 ml extra virgin olive oil

BLUE CHEESE SAUCE
Salsa de Cabrales

Serve this sauce with crisp bread as a dessert course, as an hors-d'oeuvre with crudités for dipping, as a salad dressing, or as a steak sauce. Crushed garlic, minced onion, mustard, herbs or butter can be incorporated in the sauce as desired.

Beat Cabrales blue cheese with a wooden spoon or in the blender, adding just enough cider, white wine or cream to make it of spreading consistency. For a thinner, pouring sauce, add more liquid until the cheese is about the consistency of cream.

PASTRIES, PUDDINGS AND DESSERTS

In Spain as in Arabic countries sweets of all kinds are a gesture of hospitality. Platters of small cakes and pastries are proffered to guests, usually accompanied by decanters of anise, brandy and sweet wine. They're also essential ingredients of every holiday, often with special puddings or sweet bread made in honour of a local patron saint. A feature of village fairs are vendors with push-carts laden with candies and other confections: *turrón*, nougat; sugared almonds and pine-nuts; candied fruits moulded to look like real fruits; *yemas*, egg yolk candies; marzipan confections; and much more.

Many of the finest sweets are available only from Spanish convents from recipes used for centuries. Others are packaged and sold in *pastelerías* and are favourite souvenirs for travellers. Be sure to sample them on your tours through Spain.

Though tarts, tortes, cakes, pastries, biscuits and confections are consumed at all hours of the day, perhaps with coffee or sweet wine, they are seldom served as dessert. Fruit, preferably fresh, is the preferred dessert everywhere in Spain, though a pudding, such as *flan*, caramel custard, is quite acceptable.

Holiday sweets: left, Lard Cakes (*Mantecados*), page 358, and Wine Doughnuts (*Roscos de Vino*), page 357.

PASTRIES, CAKES AND BISCUITS

GALICIAN WALNUT ROLLS
Casadielles

Shortcrust pastry or *empanadilla* dough can be used instead of puff pastry. The *casadielles* can be fried instead of baked.

Grind the walnuts or chop them finely in food processor.

Put the sugar, sherry, water, cinnamon and lemon peel in a saucepan and bring to the boil. Cook five minutes. Remove the lemon peel and stir in the walnuts.

Roll out the pastry and cut squares of about 10cm. Spread a spoonful of the walnut mixture on each square. Fold the top edge to the centre and the bottom edge to meet it and pinch together. Crimp the ends with the tines of a fork and put the packets, seam side down, on a lightly buttered oven tin. Brush with beaten egg and bake in a hot oven until golden.

Makes about 15.

200 g walnuts
100 g sugar
50 ml sherry or anise brandy
100 ml water
1 teaspoon cinnamon
1 piece lemon peel
500 g puff pastry
1 egg, beaten

ALMOND MERINGUE PUFFS, GRANADA STYLE
Soplillos granadinos

These can be baked on tins or in small, fluted paper cups. If using tins, coat with non-stick spray or line them with baking parchment. The meringue puffs will flatten somewhat as they bake, so leave space between them.

Toast the skinned almonds in a frying pan or in a low oven until lightly golden, stirring frequently so they do not scorch. Cool.

In a mixing bowl, beat the egg whites until stiff. Beat in the sugar a little at a time and fold in the lemon juice and grated lemon zest. Fold in the ground almonds.

Spoon small mounds of the meringue on to prepared oven tins or into paper cups set on an oven tray. Bake in a low oven (150°C/300°F) until the puffs are very slightly coloured, about 30 minutes. Makes about 40 meringues.

250 g almonds, blanched, skinned
and slivered
4 egg whites
juice and grated zest of 1 lemon
400 g sugar

WINE DOUGHNUTS
Roscos de vino

Sift together the flour, baking powder, and cinnamon. Combine the oil, wine and sugar in a mixing bowl and whisk to blend. Add the zest, sesame seed, and salt. Stir in the dry ingredients to make a soft dough. Turn the dough out on a lightly floured board and knead until it is shiny, about four minutes.

Divide the dough into 24 walnut-sized balls. Roll each ball into a cord, about 15cm long and 1cm thick. Pinch the ends together forming a ring. Place the rings on baking sheets lined with parchment.

Bake in the middle of preheated medium oven, changing position of sheets once, until rings are lightly golden, 40 to 45 minutes. Cool the rings on a rack. Sift icing sugar over them. Makes 24.

450 grams flour plus more for board
3 teaspoons baking powder
1/2 teaspoon cinnamon
235 ml olive oil
120 ml white wine
50 grams sugar
1 teaspoon grated lemon zest
1 teaspoon sesame seed, toasted
Pinch of salt
Icing sugar for dusting

CINNAMON LARD BISCUITS
Mantecados

Mantecados along with *polvorones* and *roscos* are beloved Christmas pastries. These are called *mantecados* because they are made with *manteca*, lard, a by-product of winter's hog slaughtering. Butter can be substituted, but they are not as authentic. If desired, the biscuits can be wrapped individually in a square of tissue paper, twisting the ends to enclose them.

270 g plain flour
30 g ground almonds
170 g lard
130 g icing sugar
1 egg yolk
2 tablespoons ground cinnamon
pinch of salt
1 tablespoon sesame seeds
icing sugar, for dusting

Spread the flour in an oven tin and toast it in a hot oven until lightly coloured, stirring so it browns evenly. When the flour is cooled, mix with the ground almonds. Beat the lard until very creamy.

Beat in the sugar, egg yolk and cinnamon with salt and two teaspoons of water.

Add the flour-almond mixture a little at a time with the sesame seeds. Turn the dough out on a board or marble work surface. Combine the dough by kneading it with a few squeezes. Gather into a ball and let it rest at room temperature for one hour.

Roll or pat the dough to a thickness of 2cm. Cut into rounds about 5cm in diameter and place on an oven tin.

Bake in a moderate oven (180°C/350°F) about 10 minutes. Transfer to wire racks to cool. Dust with icing sugar. Makes about 20 biscuits.

SPONGE CAKE
Bizcocho

In a large mixing bowl beat the eggs with half the sugar until well combined, then beat for 15 minutes.

Mix in remaining sugar. Sift together the flour and baking powder. Add to the sponge batter a little at a time. Stir in the grated lemon zest.

Butter a sponge cake mould (18cm) and line with a round of paper, well-buttered. Pour in the batter and bake in a preheated, medium oven (180°C/ 350°F). The cake is done when a knife inserted in the centre comes out clean, about 40 minutes.

Let it sit a few minutes, then unmould to cool on a rack. Serves 10. Once cool, the cake can be sprinkled with icing sugar or split horizontally into two or three layers and filled with fruit or cream filling.

6 eggs
375 g sugar
185 g plain flour, sifted
2 teaspoons baking powder
1 teaspoon grated lemon zest

DRUNKEN CAKES
Borrachos

Use leftover sponge cake for this recipe. Or prepare the cake batter in the preceding recipe and bake it in a flat, rectangular pan instead of a round mould.

Cut the cooled cake into squares.

Put the sugar, water and orange zest in a saucepan and boil five minutes. Remove from heat and discard the strip of orange zest. When partially cooled add the sherry or Málaga wine.

Drizzle the wine syrup over the squares of cake. Place each one in a paper cup and dust the tops with cinnamon.

1 sponge cake, cut in squares
100 g sugar
100 ml water
strip of orange zest
100 ml medium sherry or Málaga wine
cinnamon

"GYPSY'S ARM" CAKE ROLL
Brazo gitano

Combine the flour and baking powder and set aside. Beat the egg whites until stiff.

In another bowl, combine the yolks, granulated sugar and lemon zest. Beat until thick and pale.

Whisk in a quarter of the egg whites, then fold in the remaining whites. Stir in the flour until combined.

Spread in a 30x40cm Swiss roll tin that has been lined with buttered baking parchment. Bake the cake in a preheated medium-low oven (160°C/325°F) until the top springs back when pressed in the centre, about 15 minutes.

150 g plain flour, sifted
1/2 teaspoon baking powder
4 eggs, separated
150 g granulated sugar
grated zest of 1 lemon
2 tablespoons icing sugar
cream filling (recipe follows)

While still hot, unmould the cake on to a sheet of greaseproof paper or parchment sprinkled with one tablespoon of icing sugar. Trim off any crisp edges of the cake and remove the parchment from the surface.

Spread the cake with the cream filling. With the help of the paper beneath, roll up the cake, enclosing the filling. Place it on a platter, seam side down. Sprinkle with remaining icing sugar. Serves 10.

CUSTARD CREAM
Cremadina

Used as a filling for cakes as in the previous recipe, the custard cream can also be served as a pudding or spooned over fruit. To make a chocolate cream filling, melt 60 grams of dark chocolate with the milk. A tablespoon of instant coffee gives a mocha flavour.

450 ml milk
5 tablespoons cornflour
150 g sugar
3 egg yolks
1 teaspoon vanilla extract

In a bowl, combine a quarter of the milk with the cornflour. Stir until it is smooth. Add the sugar and egg yolks to the cornflour mixture and beat until smooth.

Scald the remaining milk and pour it through a sieve into a heatproof jug. Whisk the hot milk into the egg mixture.

Pour the custard mixture into a saucepan and cook, beating constantly, until it thickens. Cook on a very low heat for five minutes.

Remove from heat and stir in the vanilla. Beat the custard well. Cool it before spreading on a cake.

CÓRDOBA PASTRY
Pastel cordobés

The filling for this pie, *cabello de ángel* ("angel's hair"), is confected from a type of squash called *cidra*, which cooks up into golden strands. Buy it in tins. Or make the jam with pumpkin instead of *cidra*. Cook the pumpkin, drain well, purée and weigh the pulp. Put in a heavy saucepan with the same weight of sugar plus slivers of lemon peel. Cook very slowly until as thick as a jam. Cool. Or substitute peach jam or orange marmalade. Frozen puff pastry could be used instead of the pastry dough given here.

Mix the flour and salt. Cut in the lard, rubbing the mixture through the fingers to combine. Add the iced water and vinegar and combine in a few strokes. Roll into a ball, knead very briefly, and refrigerate the dough, covered, for 30 minutes.

Knead the butter until softened. Divide it in half. Place half between sheets of cling film and with a rolling pin spread it to a circle. Roll out second piece of butter in the same manner and refrigerate both, still enclosed in plastic wrap, until chilled.

Divide the dough in half. Roll out one half on a floured board. Cover it with a slab of butter. Fold it in thirds, turn and roll out again. Repeat the folding and rolling twice more, then gather into a ball and chill. Repeat with the second piece of dough, layering it with the remaining butter. Chill.

Roll out one piece of the dough to line a round or rectangular oven tin. Spread it with the "angel's hair" or other preserve. Sprinkle with grated lemon peel.

1/2 kg plain flour
2 teaspoons salt
100 g lard
200 ml iced water
1 tablespoon vinegar
250 g butter
1 egg, beaten
450 g "angel's hair" or other fruit preserve
grated lemon peel
cinnamon
sugar

Roll out the remaining dough and fit it over the filling. Roll the edges together to seal. Chill the pastry for 20 minutes.

Preheat the oven to very hot (200°C/400°F) Brush the pastry with beaten egg and bake until golden, about 25 minutes. Remove and brush again with egg. Sprinkle with sugar and cinnamon and return to oven for a few minutes to dry. Serves 10.

ALMOND TORTE SANTIAGO
Torta de Santiago

You can use a template to form the design of the Santiago pilgrims' cross on the top of the torte, if desired. This cake is delicious served with tart fruit purée.

450 g almonds, blanched and skinned
150 g butter
1/2 kg sugar
7 eggs
150 g plain flour
grated zest and juice of 1 lemon
icing sugar

Toast the skinned almonds in the oven to bring out their flavour, then grind them finely.

Cream the butter with the sugar until fluffy, then beat in the eggs, one at a time. Stir in the flour and the ground almonds. Add the grated lemon zest. Put in a buttered, springform mould and bake in a moderate oven until a knife inserted in the centre comes out clean, about one hour.

Cool for five minutes, then sprinkle the juice of the lemon over the top. Remove from the mould and cool on a rack. Sprinkle the top with icing sugar Serves 10.

FROZEN TORTE
Tarta helada

In a saucepan place the chocolate, broken into pieces, 50 grams sugar and 75 ml milk. Cook on a low fire, stirring constantly, until chocolate is melted. Cool completely.

In a bowl, cream the butter until soft and fluffy. Gradually beat in 100 grams sugar, then 50 ml brandy, a few drops at a time, beating well after each addition. Beat in the egg yolk, then add 50 ml of the melted chocolate, reserving the rest.

Into a shallow bowl put the remaining milk, brandy, cinnamon and sugar. Dip the biscuits quickly, one at a time, into the milk mixture. Arrange a layer of them in the botton of a buttered loaf pan. Spread the biscuits with a layer of the butter cream, then add another layer of biscuits dipped in the milk mixture. Continue until all the biscuits and all the cream filling have been used, ending with a layer of the biscuits.

Put the mould in the freezer for at least five hours. Run a knife around the edges and dip the mould briefly into hot water. Unmould the torte on to a serving platter. Cover it with a frosting of the sweetened whipped cream (it can be decorated with rosettes piped with a pastry gun). Use the reserved melted chocolate to drizzle a decorative pattern on the cream. Return to the freezer, covered in plastic wrap, until firm. Let sit at room temperature a few minutes before slicing.
Variation: After 2 layers of the biscuits and cream filling, spread a layer of softened ice cream, 3-4 cm thick, and follow with two more layers of biscuits and filling. Freeze, unmould and frost the torte as described above.

150 g dark chocolate
175 g sugar
125 ml milk
65 g butter
100 ml brandy
1 egg yolk
1/2 teaspoon cinnamon
200 g plain biscuits (*galleta María* or similar)
sweetened whipped cream

Addition: Blanch and skin 75 grams almonds. Chop them coarsely. In a frying pan toast them with one tablespoon butter and two teaspoons sugar, stirring constantly to prevent their scorching. Sprinkle a layer of the toasted almonds between layers of the biscuits.

CRISPY PINE-NUT BISCUITS
Mostachones

Beat the eggs in a saucepan with the sugar until thick. Heat, whisking constantly until sugar is dissolved. Remove from heat and beat well. Beat in the flour, cinnamon and toasted pine-nuts.

Drop tiny spoonfuls on to a buttered oven tin. Sprinkle with icing sugar and bake in a moderate oven about 15 minutes. Makes about six dozen small biscuits.

3 eggs
1/4 kg sugar
1/4 kg plain flour, sifted
pinch of salt
1/4 teaspoon cinnamon
100 g pine-nuts, toasted
icing sugar

GALICIAN DESSERT CRÊPES
Filloas

These crêpes are lovely served with strawberry puré or apples sautéed in butter and sprinkled with cinnamon.

Beat together the eggs, milk, water, flour, salt and melted butter. The batter should be the consistency of thick cream.

Rub a frying pan with a little pork fat or butter and pour in a little of the batter to make a thin film. Fry on both sides, as for crêpes. The edges will crisp slightly. Remove and stack on a plate.

Beat the soft cheese or cottage cheese until soft. Whip the cream and fold in the sugar, lemon peel and vanilla and fold it into the softened cheese.

Spoon this mixture on to the crêpes and roll or fold them. Serves six.

3 eggs
100 ml milk
100 ml water
6 tablespoons plain flour
pinch of salt
1 tablespoon butter, melted and cooled
200 g *queso fresco* or *requesón*
   (soft cheese or cottage cheese)
200 ml cream
50 g sugar
1 teaspoon grated lemon zest
1 teaspoon vanilla extract

FRIED PASTRIES

This is a very special category in Spanish cookery, especially in regions such as Andalusia where few homes had ovens but where olive oil was plentiful. There are several types of pastry doughs, each with its particular texture and flavouring. Many of these pastries are especially beloved at Christmas time — *roscos, empanadillas* and *pestiños,* in particular — but any of them make a nice tea-time snack. I especially enjoy them as an accompaniment to fruit compotes. Many can be baked instead of fried, though they are emphatically not the same. Please read the section about *fritos* in Chapter 4.

FRUIT PASTIES
Empanadillas

These little fried pies are usually filled with *cabello de ángel* ("angel's hair"), a candied squash, or *dulce de batatas*, candied sweet potatoes. *Cabello de ángel* can be purchased in tins. The sweet potato jam is made by cooking sweet potatoes with an equal weight of sugar, cinnamon and lemon zest until it forms a thick paste. Or substitute any fruit jam for the filling.

Melt the lard and butter in a saucepan. Add the wine, then beat in enough of the flour with the salt and aniseed to make a smooth dough. Knead very briefly and let it rest, refrigerated, for at least two hours.

Meanwhile, put the fruit jam, if using, in a saucepan and boil until very thick.

Roll out the pastry dough quite thinly. Cut in very small circles (about 6cm). Place a half-teaspoon of the fruit paste on each circle, fold over, and seal the edges by pressing with a fork.

Fry the tiny pies in deep, hot oil until golden. Remove and drain on absorbent paper.

Boil the honey, water and brandy until thickened, about 15 minutes. Dip the fried pies in the honey syrup and place them on a serving platter. Sprinkle with sugar. Makes about 50 tiny *empanadillas*.

25 g lard
25 g butter
100 ml white wine
200 g plain flour
1/4 teaspoon salt
1/2 teaspoon aniseed
sugar
100 ml *cabello de ángel, dulce de batata* or any fruit jam
olive oil for frying
100 ml honey
50 ml water
50 ml brandy

SWEET FRITTERS
Pestiños

These are frequently made with the scraps of dough left from making the above *empanadillas*. Roll out the dough and cut into 5cm squares. Fold two opposite corners to the middle and pinch them together. Slip a fork under the fold and drop into hot oil and fry until golden. They will puff up like pillows.

Drain on absorbent paper and dip into honey syrup, as above recipe. Sprinkle with sugar.

EGG DOUGHNUTS
Roscos de huevo

This recipe makes enough doughnuts to last all 12 days of Christmas. To increase or decrease the quantity: for each egg use eight tablespoons of olive oil, milk and sugar and one teaspoon of baking soda, with *"la harina que admite"*, enough flour to make a smooth dough that doesn't stick to the fingers.

Put the 300 ml oil in a saucepan and heat until hot, but not smoking. Add the aniseed and cook for a few minutes just until the spice is fragrant. Remove and cool the oil.

In a large bowl mix the lemon zest, 275 grams sugar, milk and juice, cinnamon, cooled oil and aniseed. Add two cups of the flour, then beat in the egg yolks and baking soda.

In another bowl beat the whites until stiff and fold them into the batter. Add flour using the hands to work it in. At first the dough will be very sticky. Continue adding flour until the dough is just stiff enough to roll without sticking to the hands.

300 ml olive oil
30 g aniseed
grated zest of 1 lemon
675 g sugar
300 ml milk (or 1/2 milk
    and 1/2 orange juice)
2 tablespoons cinnamon
3 eggs, separated
3 teaspoons baking soda
1 1/2 kg plain flour
olive oil for frying

Take a small ball of the dough and roll it into a thick cord about 12cm long. Pinch the ends together to form a circle. Continue forming the *roscos*.

Heat deep oil until hot, but not smoking, and add the *roscos*, a few at a time. Fry until golden brown. Remove with a skimmer, drain briefly and, while still hot, dredge them in sugar on both sides. Makes about 10 dozen.

PUFFS OF WIND
Buñuelos de viento

The puffs can be split in half with a knife and filled with a cream filling or spoonful of jam, then pressed together again and dusted with icing sugar.

Place the milk, butter, anise, sugar and salt in a saucepan and heat just until it boils. Lower the heat and add the flour all at once, beating it hard with a wooden spoon until it forms a smooth ball of dough.

Remove from heat and beat in the eggs one at a time.

Dip spoons into oil and use them to drop balls of dough into deep, hot oil. Fry until golden and puffed. If the oil is too hot, the *buñuelos* will not puff.

225 ml milk
70 g butter
1 tablespoon anise brandy (optional)
2 tablespoons sugar
1/4 teaspoon salt
125 g plain flour
4 eggs
olive or vegetable oil for frying
icing sugar

BREAKFAST FRITTERS
Churros

Churros, typically, either start the day or finish it. At the end of a village *feria,* after the last fireworks and rockets have died down and the band is packing away the instruments, the last stall still open is the *churrería,* where these crisp strips of fried dough are served with thick, hot chocolate. And so to bed.

Then, very early in the morning at cafés near big market-places, great cauldrons of oil are put to heat to serve *churros* to the wholesalers bringing fresh produce, meat and fish to the markets. Later, shoppers can stop for a breakfast of *churros* with *café con leche* while doing the day's marketing. On Sundays when no one has to hurry off to work or school, *papá* gets up first and takes the smallest child with him to buy *churros* for the family — the earlier the better, to avoid a long queue. They may be fried in rings and these strung, a dozen or more, on a loop of reed for carrying home. By the time he gets back, *mamá* has the chocolate ready. *Churros,* by the way, were invented for the sole purpose of dunking. They must be eaten fresh and hot.

Put the water in a saucepan with the 75 ml oil, the lemon zest and salt. Bring to the boil. Skim out zest. Add the flour all at once and beat hard with a wooden spoon, working it on a low fire for a minute or two until it forms a ball. The batter will be quite stiff.

Put it in a pastry bag and pipe long strips or rings of the batter into deep, hot oil. It takes a bit of muscle to push it through. Fry until golden brown, remove and drain. With scissors, cut long strands into short lengths. Sprinkle generously with sugar. Makes about 30 strips.

250 ml water
75 ml olive oil
1 piece lemon zest
1/2 teaspoon salt
200 g plain flour
olive oil for frying
sugar

PUDDINGS

SPANISH CARAMEL CUSTARD
Flan

In a heavy saucepan melt 100 grams sugar until a golden caramel colour. Remove from heat and pour into a single mould or four individual custard cups, tilting to coat the mould.

Scald the milk with the cinnamon and lemon peel or vanilla. Beat the egg yolks and whole eggs until mixed and beat in remaining sugar. Whisk in the hot milk, then pour the custard through a sieve into the mould or moulds.

Set them in a pan and add hot water to half their depth. Put in a medium oven until the custard is set, about 40 minutes. Cool the custards, then unmould on to serving plates. Serves four.

175 g sugar
1/2 litre milk
cinnamon and lemon zest or vanilla bean
2 egg yolks
2 whole eggs

CREAMY CUSTARD WITH MERINGUE
Natillas

Place the half litre of milk, cinnamon, lemon zest and vanilla in a saucepan, bring the milk to the boil and remove. Let it sit until slightly cooled and strain it.

Beat the egg yolks and 100 grams sugar in the top of a bain-marie (double boiler) until thick. Whisking the yolks, pour in the hot milk.

Dissolve the cornflour in the three tablespoons milk and whisk it into the yolks.

Set the pan over boiling water and cook, stirring, until custard is thickened, about 10 minutes. It should be thick enough to coat a spoon. Remove and let it cool.

Place sponge fingers or other biscuits in individual pudding bowls and divide the custard among them. Chill. The custard will be the consistency of very thick cream.

Meanwhile whip two egg whites until stiff. Beat in four tablespoons of sugar, salt and lemon juice. Line an oven tin with baking parchment. Spoon the meringue into four heaps. Sprinkle the tops with cinnamon.

Place in a medium oven until meringues are lightly coloured, about 10 minutes. Turn off the oven and let them dry in the oven until nearly cooled.

Serve each custard topped with a meringue. Serves four.

1/2 litre plus 3 tablespoons milk
cinnamon stick
lemon zest
vanilla bean
4 egg yolks
150 g sugar
1 tablespoon cornflour
sponge fingers (*bizcocho soletilla*) or biscuits
2 egg-whites
pinch of salt
1/2 teaspoon lemon juice
1 teaspoon cinnamon

CATALAN CUSTARD WITH BURNT SUGAR TOPPING
Crema catalana

Beat the egg yolks with 150 grams of the sugar. Combine 750 ml of the milk in a pan with the zest and cinnamon. Bring to the boil and remove from the heat. Strain the milk and whisk it into the beaten yolks.

Stir the remaining milk and cornflour together in a small bowl. Add it to the custard mixture.

Pour the custard into a clean saucepan and cook over low heat, stirring constantly, until it just begins to bubble. Remove from the heat and divide between six shallow pudding dishes or ramekins. Allow the custard to cool.

Shortly before serving, sprinkle the tops of the custards with the remaining 50 grams of sugar. Caramelise the tops with a heated iron (salamander) or a kitchen blowtorch.

6 egg yolks
200 g sugar
900 ml milk
zest of 1 lemon
cinnamon stick
3 tablespoons cornflour

FRIED MILK
Leche frita

Place 400 ml of the milk in a heavy saucepan with the lemon zest and cinnamon stick. Bring to the boil. Remove from heat and let infuse for a few minutes. Strain the milk into a heatproof jug.

Combine the remaining 100 ml milk, two eggs, flour, cornflour and sugar in a blender and blend until completely smooth. With the blender running pour in the hot milk.

Return the custard mixture to the saucepan and place over boiling water. Cook, stirring constantly, until the custard just begins to thicken. Remove it from the heat and beat it hard to prevent lumps from forming. Place the pan over boiling water again and cook, stirring constantly, for five minutes. Remove from the heat and beat the custard until very smooth.

Spread the custard to an even thickness in a 20cm square mould or cake tin that has been generously oiled. Cover with plastic wrap and refrigerate at least six hours.

Cut the custard into squares or triangles. Beat the remaining egg with two teaspoons water in a shallow bowl. Spread half the bread crumbs in a shallow tray.

Dip each custard piece into beaten egg, then lift it out and place it in the bread crumbs. Sprinkle the remaining bread crumbs over the custard pieces. Shake the tray gently to coat the edges. Place the breaded custard pieces on a tin and refrigerate for at least 30 minutes.

500 ml milk
strip of lemon zest
cinnamon stick
3 eggs
50 g plain flour
30 g cornflour
70 g sugar, plus additional for sprinkling
100 g fine dry bread crumbs
olive or vegetable oil for frying
ground cinnamon for sprinkling

Heat the oil in a large frying pan. Fry the custard pieces in two batches, until browned on both sides, one to two minutes per side. Transfer them to a tray lined with paper towels to drain.

Sprinkle with sugar and cinnamon. Serve warm or cold. Serves six. Nice accompanied with fruit jam or fruit purée.

ALMOND PUDDING
Menjar blanc

Grind or finely chop the almonds. Reserve three tablespoons of almonds and place the rest in a heatproof bowl. Pour over the boiling water and let them sit for 10 minutes.

Place a sieve lined with cheesecloth over another bowl and pour through the liquid, squeezing the cloth to extract all of it.

Place this almond milk in a saucepan with the cinnamon, lemon zest, 200 grams sugar and salt. Bring to the boil and simmer for a few minutes. Remove cinnamon and zest.

Dissolve the cornflour in a little cold water and whisk it into the almond milk. Cook, stirring constantly, until the pudding is thickened.

Pour into six or eight individual pudding bowls or into a mould oiled with almond oil. Chill well.

Toast the reserved chopped almonds in the oil or butter until golden. Add the remaining 50 grams sugar and stir until it is dissolved. Cool and sprinkle the almond-sugar mixture over the puddings. Serve with whipped cream, if desired. Serves six to eight.

400 g almonds, blanched and skinned
1 litre boiling water
1 cinnamon stick, 4 cm
1 strip lemon zest
250 g sugar
1/4 teaspoon salt
6 tablespoons cornflour
2 tablespoons olive oil or butter
whipped cream (optional)

CREAMY RICE PUDDING
Arroz con leche

Combine the rice, water, salt, cinnamon stick and lemon zest in a saucepan. Bring to the boil, then cover and cook slowly until the water is absorbed, about five minutes. Remove from heat and let stand five minutes.

Rinse the rice under running water, reserving the zest and cinnamon. Rinse out the pan. Return the cinnamon stick and zest to the pan with milk and 100 grams of sugar. Bring to the boil and add the rice. Return to the boil.

Reduce the heat to a simmer and cook the rice until it is very soft, about 12 minutes. The rice will still be very soupy.

Pour the pudding into a pudding bowl or ladle into individual pudding dishes. Sprinkle the tops with remaining one tablespoon of sugar and ground cinnamon. Chill the pudding. It will thicken as it cools. Serves six.

225 g medium-short-grain rice
450 ml water
pinch of salt
5cm cinnamon stick
strip of lemon zest
1 1/4 litres milk
100 g plus 1 tablespoon sugar
1 tablespoon ground cinnamon

SWEET TOASTS
Torrijas

In America this is called "French toast" and is served for breakfast. In Spain it's a dessert, especially enjoyed for Holy Week preceding Easter.

Cut stale bread into thick slices, remove crusts and trim into evenly-sized rectangles or circles. Dip them into white wine or sherry or Málaga wine, or milk for a few minutes. Remove and dip into beaten egg, then fry the slices in olive oil until browned on both sides.

Sprinkle liberally with sugar and cinnamon or drizzle with honey. Serve hot or cold.

CHEESE CUSTARD TART
Tarta cuajada

A layer of sliced apples or pears can be placed over the crust before adding the cheese custard.

Line a pie tin or spring-form mould with the *mantecado* dough or crumb crust.

Beat the cheese until soft. Set aside two tablespoons of sugar. Beat remaining sugar into the cheese. Add the eggs, one by one. Beat in the milk, biscuit crumbs, lemon zest and cinnamon.

Pour into the pie tin and bake in a medium-hot oven until set, about 45 minutes.

Sprinkle the top with reserved sugar and cinnamon. Serves eight to 10.

1/2 recipe for *mantecados* (page 358)
    or any crumb crust
400 g *requesón* (dry cottage cheese)
250 g sugar
4 eggs
200 ml milk
50 g plain biscuit crumbs
grated lemon zest
1/4 teaspoon cinnamon

"HEAVENLY BACON" (RICH CUSTARD SQUARES)

Tocino de cielo

In a heavy saucepan, boil the sugar and water until the mixture turns golden. Cook it a little longer to caramel and immediately pour the liquid caramel into a square mould, approximately 16x16cm. Tip the mould to coat it evenly with the caramel.

In a heavy saucepan, heat the remaining 250 grams of sugar, water and vanilla bean. Cover for a few minutes, then uncover and boil the syrup to the thread stage, 10-15 minutes. A drop of syrup, cooled, will spin a thread off the tip of a spoon. Remove the vanilla bean.

Stir the yolks together and pass them through a sieve. Whisk the hot syrup into the yolks, stirring constantly. Pour the mixture into the prepared mould. Cover with foil and stand the mould in an oven dish. Partially fill with boiling water and place in preheated slow oven (150°C/300°F) until the custard is set, about 25 minutes or when a thin skewer comes out clean.

Let it cool for 15 minutes, then turn the custard out onto a serving dish. Cut into eight squares.

FOR THE CARAMEL
200 g sugar
150 ml water

FOR THE CUSTARD
250 g sugar
400 ml water
1 vanilla bean
12 egg yolks

RENNET PUDDING
Leche cuajada

A country pudding in the Basque region, where it is made with sheep's milk.

Add one teaspoon rennet powder (*cuajo*) to one litre full cream milk heated to 36°C. Stir, then divide between small bowls and leave to set two hours until thickened. Chill. Serve with honey or fruit jam.

WALNUT CREAM
Intxaursalsa

A Basque Christmas Eve speciality. In Toledo a similar cream pudding is made with almonds.

Finely chop the walnuts. Grind the toast or crumb it in a food processor.

Cook the milk, sugar, nuts and breadcrumbs together for 30 minutes. Serve cold in small bowls or cups. Serves eight.

150 g walnuts
4 slices bread, toasted
2 litres milk
300 g sugar

FRUIT DESSERTS

A slice of chilled melon in August, a bowl of glowing oranges in December, a dish of sweet strawberries in the spring — fresh fruit in season is the favourite dessert in Spain. There are quite a few compotes, conserves and other fruit dessserts as well. See Chapter 2 on marketing for lots more information about fruits. Also consult the Spanish/English glossary at the back of the book to find out the names for those unusual fruits.

SPRING FRUIT CUP
Macedonia de frutas de primavera

Slice the bananas into a bowl with the hulled and sliced strawberries. Chop the oranges and apricots and add with the cherries.

Mix the water and sugar in a saucepan and cook for five minutes and let cool. Add the syrup to the fruit with the brandy or liqueur. Chill the fruit. Serves eight.

4 bananas
300 g strawberries
3 oranges
5 apricots
200 g cherries, pitted
100 ml water
200 g sugar
50 ml brandy or liqueur

SUMMER FRUIT SALAD
Frutas de verano

Melons are delectable. The best variety is *piel de sapo* ("toad skin"), which has a ridged green rind and pale yellow flesh.

Cut the melon and peaches into bite-size pieces or use a melon ball cutter to remove melon from its shell. Put in a bowl with the grapes. Add the sherry and the grated zest of the lemon with a little of its juice. Chill well. Serves six.

1 ripe melon, such as *piel de sapo*
3 peaches
400 g muscatel grapes, seeded
100 ml *oloroso* sherry
1/2 lemon

FRUIT MOUSSE
Espuma de fruta

Spain produces some exotic fruits: custard apple, loquat, prickly pear, persimmon, to name a few. Any of these fruits work especially well in a smooth mousse. The recipe can be used for the more usual strawberries, apricots and peaches. If frozen, the mousse can be unmoulded. Otherwise it is spooned into pudding dishes.

400 ml fruit pulp
2 tablespoons orange juice
150 g sugar
60 ml water
2 teaspoons powdered gelatine
2 tablespoons water
400 ml cream
1 teaspoon vanilla extract

Combine the fruit pulp with the orange juice. Place the sugar and water in a saucepan and bring to the boil. Cook a few minutes.

Meanwhile, sprinkle the gelatine into the two tablespoons of water until softened, then stir into the hot sugar syrup until completely dissolved. Mix with the fruit pulp and let the mixture cool. Whip the cream with the vanilla. Fold it into the fruit mixture.

Either chill the mousse for six hours (it will not be solid) or else place in a decorative mould, cover with foil and freeze.

To unmould the frozen mousse, dip into hot water and turn out onto a serving dish. Serves eight.

APPLES BAKED IN WINE
Manzanas asadas al vino

Remove cores from the apples and put them in a baking dish. Put a tablespoon of sugar or honey in each, sprinkle with cinnamon and top with a teaspoon of butter. Pour over the wine and put in a hot oven until the apples are cooked, about

6 apples
6 tablespoons sugar or honey
cinnamon
6 teaspoons butter
1/2 bottle white or red wine

35 minutes, spooning some of the liquid over the apples from time to time. Serve hot or cold.

Serves six.
Note: quince can be baked as for apples, allowing more than an hour. In Aragón, peaches are cooked in wine.

STUFFED APPLES
Manzanas rellenas

Remove cores from the apples. Chop the walnuts and the dates, figs or seeded raisins and stuff the centres of the apples.

Place them in a baking dish, pour over the sherry and water and sprinkle with the sugar. Bake until done, about 35 minutes. Serve hot or cold. Serves six.

6 apples
40 g walnuts
150 g dates, figs or raisins
50 ml sweet sherry
1/4 litre water
75 g sugar

BAKED PEARS
Peras al horno

These luscious pears can be served with sweetened meringue, whipped cream or sabayon sauce. Pumpkin, (calabaza) peeled and cut in chunks, can be prepared in the same manner as the pears.

Peel the pears, halve them and remove cores. Sprinkle with the juice and place in a oiled oven dish. Sprinkle with the sugar and raisins.

Pour over the wine and bake in a medium oven until pears are quite soft, about 30 minutes.

Meanwhile, toast the slivered almonds in the oil. Sprinkle the pears with the almonds. Serve hot or cold. Serves six.

1 kilo firm pears (8-10)
3 tablespoons orange juice
100 g sugar
2 cloves
50 g raisins, seeded
200 ml Málaga wine or oloroso seco sherry
50 g almonds, slivered
1 tablespoon olive oil

BANANA PANCAKES
Tortitas de plátano

A speciality of the Canary Islands, Spain´s southernmost territory, where bananas thrive.

Peel and mash the bananas. Whisk in the eggs, milk, salt, cinnamon, lemon zest and beat well.

Sift the baking powder, soda and flour and stir into the banana mixture. Stir in the brandy. Let the batter stand for 30 minutes.

Heat enough oil to cover the bottom of a frying pan. Drop spoonfuls of the batter into the hot oil, flattening them slightly. Fry until browned on bottom, then turn to brown the other side.

Drain on absorbent paper. Sprinkle with sugar or drizzle with honey that has been boiled with a little water.

1/2 kilo bananas
6 eggs
100 ml milk
pinch of salt
1 teaspoon cinnamon
grated zest of 1 lemon
1 teaspoon baking powder
pinch of bicarbonate of soda (baking soda)
130 g plain flour
2 tablespoons brandy
olive or vegetable oil for frying

FRESH FIGS, MÁLAGA STYLE
Higos a la malagueña

Peel the figs and cut them in half. Place in a fruit bowl and add the lemon juice, sugar and Málaga wine.

Chill for several hours before servings. Makes eight servings. Good served with whipped cream or dollops of yoghurt.

2 dozen ripe figs
1 tablespoon lemon juice
50 g sugar
100 ml Málaga moscatel wine

Spanish Caramel Custard (*Flan*), page 371, bottom, and "Fried Milk" (*Leche Frita*), page 374.

FIG FRITTERS
Buñuelos de higos

Wash and dry the figs. If they are large, halve or quarter them.

In a bowl beat the egg yolks with the milk, oil, salt and lemon zest. Stir in the flour and sugar and combine well. Refrigerate the batter for two hours.

Beat the egg whites until stiff and fold into the batter.

Dip the figs into the batter and fry them in deep, hot oil until golden. Drain briefly and sprinkle with sugar.

2 dozen firm ripe figs (about 1 kilo)
2 eggs, separated
150 ml milk
1 tablespoon olive oil
pinch of salt
grated lemon zest
125 g flour
1 tablespoon sugar plus
    additional for sprinkling
olive or vegetable oil for frying

SPICED FIG ROLL
Pan de higos

Pan de higos translates as "fig bread". It's not really a bread, but a dense fig pâté, especially appreciated at Christmas time. Incidentally, the traditional fig roll does not contain chocolate. This is an addition I adapted from a neighbour of mine. It's such a good idea that I'm pleased to see my recipe appear in other cookery books. Fig roll keeps very well. Slice it and place on a sweets tray or serve with cheese as an hors d'ouvre.

Sprinkle the figs with two tablespoons of the icing sugar and put them through a mincer or chop them in batches in a food processor. Place the pulp in a bowl.

Reserve 16 almonds. Chop the rest of them and add to the figs.

1 kilo dried figs, stems removed
4 tablespoons icing sugar
200 g blanched and skinned almonds
1 teaspoon ground cinnamon
1/4 teaspoon ground aniseed
1/4 teaspoon ground black pepper
1/4 teaspoon ground ginger
grated lemon zest
pinch of ground cloves
75 g dark chocolate, melted (optional)
4 tablespoons anisette or brandy
3 tablespoons sesame seeds, toasted lightly

Mix the remaining two tablespoons icing sugar with the cinnamon, aniseed, pepper, ginger, zest and cloves. Sprinkle it over the fig mixture and mix it in.

Add the chocolate, if using, and the anisette or brandy. Knead the mixture with the hands to blend it well.

Divide the fig mixture into four equal portions. Roll each into a log, about 15cm long and 4cm thick.

Spread the sesame seeds on a sheet of greaseproof paper or baking parchment. Roll the fig logs in the sesame, patting to flatten the logs slightly. Press four reserved almonds into the top of each of the fig rolls.

Let the rolls dry for 12 hours, then wrap them tightly in clingfilm.

To serve, cut the rolls crosswise into 12mm thick slices and place on a serving dish. Makes four 15cm rolls.

CONFECTIONS AND CANDIES

As many of these take some expertise to prepare, it's better to buy them ready-made from those who specialise in their confection. However, for those far from Spain and yearning for some of these sweets, here are a few to try at home.

SUGAR-COATED ALMONDS
Garrapiñadas

These are sold by street vendors, who stir the almonds and sugar in a copper pan until the sugar makes a crunchy, caramelised coating around the almond. The aroma is delicious and so are the almonds, so it's hard to say how many servings. Can you eat just a few? Or all? A round-bottomed wok is a good pan for making these, as there are no corners where the caramel can get stuck.

Combine a third of the sugar, the vanilla extract and the water in a heavy pan, preferably round-bottomed. Bring to a boil over high heat, stirring to dissolve the sugar.

Add the almonds. Cook, stirring constantly, until the syrup thickens and begins to adhere to the almonds, four to five minutes.

Sprinkle with another third of the sugar. Stir the almonds constantly until the sugar begins to liquefy and adhere to the almonds.

Sprinkle with the remaining sugar. Continue stirring, just until the sugar melts and coats the almonds. Remove from heat and turn the almonds out onto a tin. The process takes about 10 to 12 minutes.

When they are cool enough to handle, separate any almonds that are stuck together.

200 g sugar
1/2 teaspoon vanilla extract
120 ml water
200 g almonds (not skinned)

CANDIED EGG YOLKS
Yemas

This famous sweet is made by nuns in convents and varies somewhat from one region to another. The candies can be individually wrapped in tissue paper or placed in bon-bon papers. Keep refrigerated.

In a saucepan bring to the boil the sugar, water and orange zest. Cover the pan and cook for three minutes. Uncover and cook, without stirring, until the syrup forms a soft ball (112°C/234°F) when dropped into cold water, about 10 minutes.

Using a wooden spoon, stir in the egg yolks, little by little. Continue beating the syrup on a low heat until it thickens and leaves the sides of the pan.

Remove from heat and continue beating as the syrup cools.

Sprinkle some of the icing sugar on a marble slab or on a tray covered with baking parchment and spread out the yolk candy. Leave to cool.

Dust the hands with additional icing sugar and form small balls of the paste (about 15 g) into little cones or cylinders. Roll them in icing sugar. Makes about 18 sweets.

225 g sugar
200 ml water
1 teaspoon grated orange zest
12 egg yolks, stirred together and strained
50 g icing sugar

ICE CREAMS AND ICES

Ice cream used to be a purely seasonal phenomenon. Corpus Christi day in early June marked the first day for eating ice cream and bathing in the sea. Now ice cream is available year-round, and I have never seen it consumed with more gusto than in midwinter at the Sierra Nevada ski station. Which is, of course, where it all started. Centuries ago Moorish kings, and later their Christian counterparts, sent runners to the snow-covered mountains to carry back snow, which was sweetened with syrups and fruits. What a marvel that icy sweetness must have seemed in the languid heat of the city!

Ice creams are easily made at home, with or without an ice cream-maker. The trick is to freeze the mixture, then break it up and beat it by hand or in a food processor until it is slushy, then refreeze it, repeating the process if desired. This breaks down the ice crystals so the cream or sorbet freezes smooth — exactly what the paddle in an ice cream-maker does. Another kind of ice made in Spain is the *granizado* — see the following chapter for how to make it.

FRUIT SORBET
Sorbete de fruta

Use any kind of fruit pulp for this sorbet, fresh, frozen or in conserve, preferably unsweetened. If you have such exotica as *chumbos* (prickly pears), *chirimoyas* (custard apples) or *nísperos* (loquats) in your garden, try this refreshing ice with any of these fruits. Fresh fruit should be moistened with lemon juice to prevent its darkening. Peel the fruit, remove seeds and mash or purée it with the orange or lemon juice. To make the sorbet with juice instead of pulp, such as orange, lemon, grapefruit, pomegranate, tomato, substitute about 350 ml juice for the fruit pulp.

450 ml fruit pulp
2 tablespoons orange or lemon juice
200 g sugar
250 ml water

Put the sugar and water in a saucepan and boil five minutes. Cool the syrup, then mix it with the fruit purée. Chill.

Pour into a metal pan, cover and freeze until almost firm. Then break the ice into chunks and beat it in a mixer or food processor until slushy.

Return to pan, cover and freeze until firm. Or freeze in electric ice cream maker according to directions. Makes one litre of sorbet.

MOULDED FRUIT ICES
Helados de frutas

Put the sugar in a saucepan with the lemon zest and water. Boil until it makes a syrup that spins a fine thread.

Meanwhile, beat the egg whites until stiff. With the mixer running, add the hot syrup to the meringue in a slow stream. Allow to cool, then fold in the whipped cream, the fruit purée and the vanilla extract.

Spoon into small moulds such as hollowed orange shells or custard cups and put them into freezer until solid.

To unmould, dip them briefly into hot water and turn out onto dessert plates. Serves six.

125 g sugar
1 strip lemon zest
100 ml water
3 egg whites
200 ml cream, whipped
150 ml fruit purée
1 teaspoon vanilla extract or liqueur

SHERRY ICE CREAM
Helado oloroso

Put the sherry and 250 g sugar in a saucepan and cook for 15 minutes.

Meanwhile, beat the yolks with a pinch of salt and the remaining sugar until thick. Put in a bain-marie (double boiler) over boiling water and cook, stirring, until they thicken.

Whisk in the wine syrup and continue cooking until thick enough to coat a spoon. Remove from heat and whisk until the mixture is creamy and cooled.

Beat in the cream and chill the mixture. Mix again before freezing, preferably in an ice cream maker. Otherwise, freeze, then beat the mixture, and refreeze. Beat again before letting the cream freeze finally. Makes about one litre.

250 ml *oloroso seco,* medium sherry
300 g sugar
8 egg yolks
pinch of salt
500 ml cream

NOUGAT ICE CREAM
Helado de turrón

Turrón, nougat candy, is famous in Spain. Buy it from vendors at village fairs and in any supermarket at Christmas time. The best nougat is made from almonds. Very good, and less expensive, types are made from peanuts and hazelnuts. *Turrón*, which comes in bars covered with an edible wafer paper, is of two main types: the hard, white Alicante, studded with whole almonds, and a soft, brown one, like a nut fudge, from Jijona. Use the soft *turrón* in this ice cream. Crush some of the hard *turrón* in a mortar to sprinkle over the top.

Scald the milk and/or cream with the sugar. Whisk the egg yolks with the salt until frothy, then slowly whisk in the hot cream. Cook this custard until thickened.

Remove from heat and add the vanilla. Cool the mixture, then chill it before freezing.

Put in an ice cream maker and when cream is partially frozen add the nougat diced small.

850 ml milk or part milk and part cream
175 g sugar
6 egg yolks
pinch of salt
150 g soft nougat candy (turrón de Jijona)
1 teaspoon vanilla extract

ICE CREAM WITH MUSCATEL RAISINS
Helado moscatel

Scoop vanilla ice cream into coupes or tall glasses, sprinkle over each a spoonful of muscatel raisins and pour over a shot of Málaga wine.

SWEET BREADS AND BUNS

These are always good, for breakfast, tea-time or dessert. Knead yeast doughs until smooth and elastic, adding only enough flour to keep them from being sticky.

MALLORCAN SPIRAL BUNS
Ensaimadas mallorquinas

These are traditionally made with lard. Instead of buns, the dough can be divided to form two very large spirals. After baking, pipe sweetened whipped cream in the spirals and top with pieces of glacé fruit.

Dissolve the yeast in four tablespoons warm water with one teaspoon of the sugar and 100 grams of the flour. Put in a bowl and cover with a damp cloth and leave to rise in a warm place.

In a large bowl mix 400 grams flour, salt, eggs, hot water and remaining sugar. Add the yeast sponge to it. Turn out on to a floured board and knead until very smooth, adding the oil a little at a time and enough additional flour to make a soft, smooth dough.

Place the dough in an oiled bowl, turn it to coat evenly and cover with a dampened cloth. Put in a warm place until doubled in bulk, one to two hours.

Cream the lard or butter until soft.

Punch down the dough and knead it again briefly. Divide it into pieces each of about 40 grams. Roll each one out quite thinly, brush it with the lard, fold in quarters and roll and brush again with lard.

10 g pressed yeast
80 g sugar
4 tablespoons very warm water
500 g plain flour plus additional for kneading
1 teaspoon salt
2 eggs
100 ml hot water
2 tablespoons olive oil
50 g lard or butter
icing sugar

Roll the piece of dough into a cord about 25cm long. Twist the cord into a spiral, pinching the end underneath so it does not unwind. Place on a lightly greased oven tin. Continue with the remaining pieces of dough, spacing them apart on the tin. Cover with a damp cloth and put in a warm place until they have risen, about 30 minutes.

Sprinkle the rolls with cold water and put in a preheated hot oven (200°C/400°F) until golden, 10 to 12 minutes. Remove and cool on a rack. Sprinkle with icing sugar when cool. Makes 20 buns.

CATALAN ALMOND ROLL
Tortells

Use the preceding recipe for *ensaimada* dough, substituting butter for the lard. Prepare the dough up to the point of rolling out.

1 recipe for spiral buns (above)
1 small potato
125 g sugar
125 g almonds, ground
1 teaspoon grated lemon zest
50 g butter
1 egg
sugar for sprinkling

For the filling, cook the potato, grind it into a purée and whip it with the sugar. Add the ground almonds and lemon zest. Divide the filling into six portions.

Divide the dough into pieces of about 150 grams. Roll each out on a lightly floured board into a rectangle and spread it with softened butter. Place a strip of filling across one end and roll the dough up. Bring the ends together, forming a circle, and pinch them together. Place on a buttered baking sheet. Proceed to fill and roll the remaining dough.

Cover with a damp cloth and put in a warm place to rise until nearly doubled in bulk (about one hour depending on temperature).

Brush the rolls with beaten egg and sprinkle with sugar. Bake in a medium-hot oven (190°C/375°F) until golden, about 20 minutes. Makes six rolls.

KINGS' DAY CAKE
Roscón de reyes

In Spain it isn't jolly old St. Nicholas who brings toys and sweeties to good girls and boys, but the Three Kings, *los Reyes Magos*, who arrive by camel (or helicopter) from Bethlehem. And they don't come on Christmas Eve, but on the Twelfth Day of Christmas, January 6. This cake, which can be purchased in pastry shops during the holiday, always contains a tiny trinket — the one who finds it can be sure of a year's good fortune. This makes a lovely tea-cake any time of the year.

Sugar makes the dough very sticky. Use a large wooden spoon to stir in as much flour as possible. Then use one hand to knead in the remaining flour, keeping one hand clean. Before turning the dough out, lightly rub the board and hands with butter or oil.

Dissolve the yeast in the hot milk with one tablespoon of the sugar. Add 50 grams of the flour and mix it to make a soft dough. Cover with a damp cloth and set in a warm place until doubled in bulk.

Put the remaining flour in a large bowl. Make a well in the centre. Beat the whole eggs together with the egg yolk and pour into the flour with the salt, rum, orange-flower water and the remaining sugar. Add the orange and lemon zest.

Work the flour into the liquids in the centre with the hands or a wooden spoon. Add the yeast dough and mix very well. Divide the butter into four parts and sprinkle it with flour.

15 g pressed yeast
4 tablespoons hot milk
200 g sugar
500 g plain flour
3 whole eggs
1 egg, separated
1 teaspoon salt
1 tablespoon dark rum or brandy
1 tablespoon orange-flower water
  (agua de azahar)
1 teaspoon grated orange zest
1 teaspoon grated lemon zest
100 g butter, softened
50 g almonds, blanched, skinned
  and slivered
candied fruits for decorating

Divide the dough into four parts. On a lightly floured board work a piece of butter into each of the pieces of dough, then knead them together again. Knead the dough until smooth and elastic.

Lightly butter a bowl, put the ball of dough into it, turn it, cover with a dampened cloth and set in a warm place for one hour.

Punch the dough down, turn out on to the board and knead again. Insert a coin or non-toxic, heat-resistant trinket in the dough. Shape the dough into one or two rings by making a flattened ball, then inserting a finger into the centre and gently easing the dough outwards to create a hole in the centre. Either stuff the hole with crumpled foil and place on a buttered oven tin, or set the ring in a lightly buttered ring mould.

Cover and set in a warm place to rise again. The dough will not double in bulk, but will rise substantially during baking.

Lightly beat the reserved egg white. Brush the cake with the egg. Sprinkle on the slivered almonds and decorate with candied fruits. Sprinkle lightly with sugar and bake in a medium-hot oven (190°C/375°F) until nicely browned, about 35 minutes. Makes one large cake or two medium ones.

CONSERVES AND PRESERVES

Ten different kinds of fruit trees grew in the small garden of the old village house where I once lived. I was delighted to see an orange tree, my first, heavily laden with fruit. When the oranges looked sufficiently ripe and juicy, I picked one, peeled it and popped a sliver in my mouth. It was unbelievably bitter. I had a tree that had never been grafted. What to do with bitter oranges? I started making marmalade. Wonderful marmalade it was, too. I made so much that I put a sign on the front door and sold it to passers-by.

Very small quantities of marmalades, jams and preserves can be stored refrigerated. To preserve in quantity, they must be packed in sterile jars. Canning jars can be purchased or ordinary jars recycled, as long as the lids are not damaged.

To sterilise jars, first wash them well in soapy water then rinse. Set them in a large pan and partially fill with water. Set their lids on top. Fill the pan with water to about three-quarters the height of the jars. Bring the water to the boil and boil for 15 minutes. Remove carefully, pour out water and drain the jars on a clean cloth. Fill them while still hot.

ORANGE MARMALADE
Mermelada de naranja

The Seville orange is the bitter marmalade orange. Actually, the juice is sour and the skin is bitter. For each kilo of fruit, allow one litre of water and one kilo of sugar. If you like a very bitter marmalade, use equal quantities of bitter oranges and sweet oranges, plus a couple of lemons. If you prefer it sweeter, use more sweet oranges, fewer bitter ones and only one lemon. Soaking the orange seeds provides pectin that helps the marmalade to jell.

This is a three-day procedure.
Day 1: Wash the oranges, weigh them and soak them in fresh water for several hours. Then shred, chop or finely slice them, catching all the juice and reserving the seeds in a separate bowl. Add enough water to cover the seeds. Add one litre of water for every kilo of fruit. Cover the shredded oranges with the water and allow them to stand for 24 hours.

Day 2: Cook the oranges very slowly until tender, about one hour. Cover and let them stand overnight.

Day 3: Add one kilo of sugar for every kilo of oranges and let the oranges stand for six hours. Put the seeds and their liquid (it will be quite gelatinous from the pectin) into a strainer and strain the liquid into the oranges.

Bring the oranges to the boil and regulate the heat so they just bubble gently. Cook until thickened. The marmalade is done when a small quantity dropped on a cold surface does not run. Stir occasionally to prevent scorching. Time depends on quantity of oranges, but the jelling can easily take an hour.

Pack the marmalade while hot into sterile jars and seal.

FRUIT JAM
Mermelada de fruta

Recipes for fruit jams generally call for equal weight of sugar and fruit. I find this excessively sweet and usually use about three-quarter kilo sugar for each kilo of fruit. Lemon juice helps to give a tart flavour and a pinch of salt enhances flavour. Don't add water to soft fruits such as peaches, apricots, strawberries, figs, etc. Mix the sugar gently with the cut-up fruit and allow it to stand for several hours. The sugar draws out the fruit's juice and it is ready to cook. Low-pectin fruits, such as strawberries and figs, take a long time to set and benefit from the addition of high-pectin fruits such as apple and quince.

QUINCE JELLY
Carne de membrillo

Quince jelly, also called quince paste, is sold in Spanish shops and is increasingly available in stores abroad (look for it with the cheeses). Unlike other fruit preserves, this one is solid enough that it can be sliced. Serve it for breakfast with toast, for dessert with a few walnuts and fresh white cheese or as an hors d'oeuvre paired with Manchego cheese. Quince fruit looks like a knobbly, leathery apple. It comes into the market in autumn.

Wash the quinces, put them in a pot with water to cover and cook until quite tender, about 25 minutes. Drain, reserving a little of the water.

Peel and core the fruit and put it through a sieve or purée in a food processor, adding some of the reserved liquid as needed. Weigh the fruit pulp and add the same weight of sugar. Cook the fruit and sugar until very thick, stirring constantly so it does not scorch. When ready, the fruit pulls away in a solid mass from the bottom of the pan and a spoonful dropped on a cold plate turns solid immediately.

Pour the jelly into shallow rectangular moulds and let it cool. It solidifies as it cools. Wrap tightly and store in a cool place.

BEVERAGES

Spain is a wine-drinking country and no meal is complete without it. On special occasions this means fine, aged *reservas*. But day-to-day, drinking wine is accompanied by no ceremony or ritual: the bottle is opened, the wine poured — in simple restaurants into ordinary water glasses — and drunk. Simple red wine, *vino común*, sometimes is diluted with *gaseosa*, bubbly lemonade, which makes it possible to return to work after a midday meal of three courses with wine. You'll find lots more about Spanish wines in Chapter 2 on marketing.

Tapa bars serve wines by the glass, often from several different wine regions. However, a *bar de copas*, is a cocktail bar, serving cocktails and mixed drinks, rarely with food. These bars tend to be late-night clubs, sometimes with music.

Cocktails and mixed drinks based on wine — such as the concoction so adored by tourists, *sangría* — can be ordered in most bars. My own favourites are those based on sherry, which seems to have a special affinity for orange juice. A "screwdriver" of sherry and orange juice over ice, is a lovely, sunny brunch drink, and a sherry sour — sherry, lemon juice and sugar — is richer but less potent than its whisky counterpart. In addition, there are wonderful festive drinks like *coctel de champán*, "champagne" cocktail made with Spanish *cava*.

Brandy de Jerez is made by sherry bodegas. Aguardiente is a strong clear brandy flavoured with anise. Pacharán, usually served as a digestive, is subtly flavoured with anise and sloe berries.

Refrescos (refreshers) is the word for cool, non-alcoholic drinks, which include lemonade, orangeade and other fruit drinks, as well as bottled drinks. Many bottled waters are sold in Spain. Those who don't drink wine with meals usually order a bottle of water, either *sin gas*, still, or *con gas*, fizzy. (Nobody in Spain would dream of drinking coffee, or tea, with a meal.)

A *batido* is a milk shake or flavoured milk, which you can buy bottled in cafés but is much better freshly made. *Horchata* is an exotic summer drink which makes me think of Arabic *souks* and cushioned harem rooms. This is the orgeat of the Moors, originally sweetened almond milk. Today it is made with the *chufa*, tiger nut. The sweet, milky drink has a faint flavour of coconut. It's available bottled, but can be made at home with either *chufas* or almonds.

As much a part of Spanish life as wine is coffee. Indeed, how would any business get done or social engagements arranged if it were not for the café, a veritable institution in Spain? Coffee begins the day: boiled in a *puchero* pot or made with a filter, served half-and-half with hot milk. And coffee ends the day: a strong, espresso brew drunk black in tiny cups with plenty of sugar. In between are

Spanish Hot Chocolate (*Chocolate a la Española*), page 405,
and Coffee with Milk (*Café con Leche*), page 406,
with Breakfast Fritters (*Churros*), page 370.

numerous espresso coffees with varying degrees of milk: a *sombra* has lots of milk, a *cortado* has a tiny bit of milk, and so forth. In cafés, coffee is very often served in small glasses, a very satisfying hand-warmer in the winter. In the summer, I order my *café con leche* with a glass full of ice cubes on the side and, after sweetening the brew, pour it over ice. Some cafés specialise in hot chocolate, thick and rich, for dunking *churros*. At home chocolate would be scented with cinnamon and liberally infused with sugar.

RED WINE PUNCH
Sangría

There are many versions of this favourite — rather too sweet to be served with a meal, though it makes a nice afternoon or evening refresher. Some prefer the fruit macerated in brandy for several hours and others like crisp, fresh fruit added at the last minute. Some aficionados insist on only brandy with the wine, others mix a syrup of sugar and fruit liqueurs. Some say no soda water, others — wishing to be able to walk home afterwards — dilute the punch.

In a pitcher mix a litre of chilled red wine with 1/4 litre brandy or orange liqueur. Stir in 100 grams sugar until dissolved. Add a variety of sliced fruit; oranges, lemons, bananas, apples, strawberries are typical. Chill the punch. Before serving add 1/2 litre soda water or *gaseosa*.

MANCHEGO WHITE WINE COOLER
Zurra

Boil the sugar and water for five minutes. Remove from heat and add the mint, celery, cinnamon, lemon and orange slices. Let steep until the syrup is cool.

Strain into a pitcher and add the chilled wine and a few slices of lemon, orange and peach. Dilute to taste with soda water and garnish with fresh mint sprigs.

1 litre white wine, chilled
200 ml water
50 g sugar
several sprigs of mint
1 stalk celery
1 piece cinnamon, 4 cm
1 sliced lemon
1 sliced orange
1 sliced peach

BASQUE LEMONADE
Ardaurgozatza

Soak the lemon peel in the water for 24 hours. Add the sugar and red and white wines to the water with sliced lemons. Serve chilled.

3 lemons, peeled
1/2 litre water
75 g sugar
1/2 litre red wine
1/2 litre white wine

MULLED WINE, MENORCAN STYLE
Sangri Menorquí

Put the wine, water and sugar in a pot and add the cinnamon stick and zest of a lemon and an orange. Heat until the mixture begins to bubble, but do not boil. Remove from heat and sprinkle with grated nutmeg. Squares of toasted bread can be added, to be consumed when nicely sodden.

2 litres red wine
1 litre water
100 g sugar
cinnamon stick
lemon and orange zest
nutmeg
toast

SPANISH HOT TODDY
Ponche

Put a shot of brandy in a small glass with a lump of sugar. Fill the glass with hot water and add a slice of lemon. The drink may also be made with a bottled liqueur called Ponche, omitting the sugar.

GALICIAN FIRE DRINK
Queimada

This is made with Galician *aguardiente de orujo,* a strong, clear brandy distilled from the pressed grapes left after the wine-making. This firewater is powerful stuff and would probably make suitable aviation fuel. If you can't get *aguardiente,* use French *marc,* Italian *grappa,* brandy or rum.

In the bottom of a warmed earthenware bowl mix 50 ml *aguardiente* and one tablespoon sugar per person. Stir to blend. Turn off the lights. Dip up a spoonful, light it and add to the bowl. Continue stirring until the alcohol is more or less burned off. While still burning, you may add a few shots of brandy, Cointreau and Crema de Café. Serve as it is, while telling ghost stories, or extinguish the flames by adding a small pot of freshly made coffee.

CHERRIES IN ANISETTE
Guindas en anís

Fill clean jars with cherries, which have been well washed and stems removed. Put in a cinnamon stick, and 1/4 kilo sugar for each kilo of fruit. Fill the jars with *aguardiente* (anisette) Cap tightly. The fruit will keep for years as long as it is covered with anise. Serve the anise as a cordial and the fruit as a punchy addition to cakes, punches, ice cream and puddings. If you don't like the flavour of anise, try this with brandy or rum.

CHRISTMAS CUP
Copa de navidad

Mix 1/2 kilo raisins, which have been well washed and dried, with one litre of *aguardiente dulce*, sweet anisette. Let sit two or three months. Serve in brandy snifters at Christmas — or any time.

HONEYED LEMONADE
Limonada de miel

Mix the juice of one large lemon with two tablespoons of honey. Dissolve in a little hot water, then add cold water to taste, about 400 ml. Chill.

ORANGEADE
Naranjada

Cut the rind from 12 oranges, without taking any of the white part. Squeeze the oranges, strain the juice and set aside. Cut the peel into strips and put in a bowl. Pour a litre of boiling water over them, add 100 grams of sugar (or to taste), cover and let stand several hours. Strain and mix with the orange juice. Chill well. Lemonade can be made in the same way.

ORGEAT
Horchata

Wash 1/4 kilo *chufas*, tiger-nuts, and put them to soak in water for 24 hours (or use blanched and skinned almonds). Wash them again, drain and dry well in a towel, rubbing to whiten them.

Put the *chufas* through a grinder or finely chop in processor. Add one litre hot water or milk to the pulp. Let it soak for several hours, then press the liquid through a sieve. Add 1/4 kilo of sugar and chill well. Sprinkle with cinnamon.

LEMON ICE
Granizado de limón

Make one litre of lemonade, adding sugar and water to taste. Put it in metal pans and freeze. Before serving whirl the ice in blender or processor until it is slush. Serve in tall glasses with straws.

COFFEE ICE
Granizado de café

Make coffee, adding sugar and water to taste. Put in metal pans and freeze. Proceed as in the previous recipe. A tablespoon of brandy can be added to the coffee.

WINE ICE
Granizado de vino

Mix one bottle of Málaga wine or medium sherry with 50 grams sugar and 50 ml orange juice. Put in metal trays and freeze. Proceed as above.

SPANISH HOT CHOCOLATE
Chocolate a la española

A bewildering array of chocolate bars is on sale in supermarkets. Besides eating chocolate you'll find *chocolate a la taza,* chocolate meant for making this hot drink. It contains starch which will thicken the chocolate as it cooks. If you can't get Spanish chocolate, mix two tablespoons cornflour for each litre liquid and use any dark chocolate, grated.

Allow 50 grams of chocolate for each cup. Chop or grate it and put in a pan with one 1 cup of water or milk per person. Heat the mixture and whisk it continually to keep it very smooth. Remove the chocolate from the heat the instant it begins to boil and beat it hard for a few minutes. Pour into cups, adding sugar to taste and thinning as desired with cold water. Sprinkle with a little cinnamon.

COFFEE
Café

For Spanish-style coffee brewed at home choose a dark roast, what in Spain is called *natural,* and have it ground very fine. Espresso coffee served in cafés is usually made with coffee beans which have been very darkly roasted with sugar, giving a slight caramel taste. This is called *torrefacto* and you can buy it in Spanish supermarkets. It also must be finely ground.

Whether making morning *café con leche* or after-dinner *café solo,* use one measure of coffee (a heaped tablespoon, about eight grams) per cup, but change the quantity of water from 200-250 ml for the big cup to 100 ml for demitasse. Use either a filter pot or an espresso pot, which forces the water up through the coffee into the top section of the pot.

For *café con leche,* heat milk just to boiling point, remove and strain it. Serve hot.

SPANISH/ENGLISH GLOSSARY

aceite: oil
aceituna: olive
acelga: chard, Swiss chard, spinach beet
achicoria: chicory
adobo: marinade
agrio: sour
agua: water
aguacate: avocado
aguardiente: distilled liquor
aguardiente de anís, anise brandy
aguardiente de orujo, clear grape brandy
aguja: (fish) needlefish, gar
ahumado: smoked
ajo: garlic
ajoaceite, ajiaceite: garlic sauce
ajonjolí: sesame seed
albahaca: basil
albaricoque: apricot
albóndiga: meatball
alcachofa: artichoke
alcaparra: caper
alcaravea: caraway seed
alfalfa: alfalfa
aliño: dressing, sauce, marinade
alioli: garlic mayonnaise
alitán: type of edible shark
almeja: clam
almendra: almond
almíbar: syrup
almirez: mortar and pestle
almuerzo: lunch, midday meal
alondra: lark
altramuz: lupin
alubia: bean
amargo: bitter
anacardo: cashew nut
anca de rana: frog's leg
anchoa: anchovy
angelote: angel shark
anguila: eel

angula: baby eel
anís: aniseed
añojo: year-old, yearling
apio: celery
araña: (fish) weever
arándano: blueberry
arbitán: (fish) ling
arenque: herring
arete: (fish) red gurnard
armado: fish similar to gurnard
arroz: rice
asado: roast, roasted, from verb *asar*
atún: tunny, tuna
ave: fowl, poultry
avena: oats
avellana: hazelnut
azafrán: saffron
azahar: orange blossom
azúcar: sugar
azúcar tamizado, icing sugar
azúcar moreno, brown sugar

B

bacaladilla: (fish) blue whiting
bacalao: cod
baila: (fish) type of bass
barbo: (fish) barbel
batata: sweet potato
becada: woodcock
bejel: (fish) tub gurnard
berberecho: cockle
berenjena: aubergine, eggplant
berro: watercress
berza: cabbage
besugo: red bream
bicarbonato sódico: sodium bicarbonate, baking soda
bizcocho: sponge cake
bocadillo: sandwich
bocarte: young sardine

bodio: (fish) type of wrasse

boga: (fish) a small bream

bogavante: lobster

boleto: boletus mushroom

bollo: bun, bread roll

boniato: sweet potato

borracho: drunken, as in *tarta borracha,* cake soused in wine or liqueur; also (fish) grey gurnard

boquerón: fresh anchovy

brasa: ember; *a la brasa,* charcoal grilled

breca: (fish) a small bream

brécol: broccoli

breva: early fig

bróculi: broccoli

brote: sprout, i.e. beansprout

brótola: (fish) forkbeard

brut: dry sparkling wine

buey: ox; also, beef from older animal; also (shellfish) a type of crab

buñuelo: fritter

búsano: whelk

butifarra: type of catalan sausage

C

caballa: mackerel

cabeza: head

cabeza de ajo: head of garlic

cabra: goat; also (fish) type of rascasse

cabracho: scorpion-fish

cabrillo: (fish) comber

cabrito: kid, baby goat

cacahuete: peanut

cacerola: cooking pot, saucepan

cachorreña: bitter orange

cailón: type of edible shark

calabacín: courgette, small marrow; zucchini

calabaza: pumpkin, squash

calamar: squid

caldereta: stew

caldo: broth, stock, consommé

callos: tripe

camarón: small prawn, shrimp

canela: cinnamon

canelones: cannelloni

cangrejo: crab

cangrejo de río, river crayfish

capitón: (fish) type of grey mullet

caqui: persimmon

carabinero: large prawn

caracol: snail

caracola: sea-snail

carbonera: type of wild mushroom

carbonero: (fish) coley, saithe, coalfish

cardamomo: cardamom

cardo: cardoon

carne: meat

carne picada, minced meat, ground meat

carnero: mutton

carpa: carp

cártamo: safflower

castaña: chestnut

cayena: chili pepper, cayenne

caza: hunt, game

cazón: dogfish

cazuela: casserole

cebada: barley

cebado: fattened

cebolla: onion

cebollino: chive

cecina: dried beef jerky

cena: evening meal, supper

centeno: rye

centollo: spider crab

cereal: cereal, grain

cereza: cherry

cerdo: pig, pork

cerveza: beer

chacina: cured meat

chalota: shallot

champiñón: mushroom, sp. cultivated

chanquete: (fish) type of goby

charcutería: meat curing; shop where cured meats are sold

cherna: wreckfish, stone bass

chicharro: (fish) horse mackerel, scad

chipirón: small squid

chirimoya: cherimoya, custard-apple

chirivía: parsnip

choco: small cuttlefish

chivo: kid, baby goat
chopa: (fish) red bream
chopito: small cuttlefish
chorizo: red sausage
choto: baby kid
chufa: tiger-nut
chuleta: chop, cutlet
chuletón: large beef chop
chumbo: prickly pear
churro: breakfast fritter
cidra: a type of gourd
ciervo: deer
cigala: Dublin Bay prawn, sea crayfish
cilantro: coriander
ciruela: plum
clavo: clove
clementina: a type of mandarin orange
cochinillo: suckling pig
cocido: cooked, from verb *cocer* (also a type of meal-in-a-pot)
cocina: kitchen; cuisine
coco: coconut
codorniz: quail
cogollo: heart, core, as in *cogollo de palmito,* palm heart
col: cabbage
col de Bruselas: Brussels sprout
coliflor: cauliflower
colza: rape seed
comida: food; meal
comino: cumin
concha: (seafood) shell
concha fina: venus-shell clam
conejo: rabbit
confitura: jam, preserve
congelado: frozen, from the verb *congelar*
congrio: conger eel
coquina: wedge-shell clam
corazón: heart
corcón: (fish) a type of grey mullet
cordero: lamb
corvina: (fish) meagre
corzo: roe deer
cosecha: harvest, vintage
costilla: rib

crema: cream; cream soup, as in *crema de espárragos,* cream of asparagus soup
criadilla: testicle
criadilla de tierra, truffle
cuajada: curd, rennet pudding, junket
cuajo: rennet
cúrcuma: turmeric

D

dátil: palm date
dentón: (fish) dentex
desayuno: breakfast
diente: tooth; clove, as in *diente de ajo,* clove of garlic
doncella: (fish) type of wrasse
dorada: (fish) gilt-head
dulce: sweet
dulce de membrillo, quince jelly

E

eglefino: (fish) haddock
embutido: sausage
empanada: pie
empanadilla: little pie, pastie
empanado: breaded
emperador: swordfish
encurtido: pickle
endibia: endive, chicory
endrina: sloe berry
enebro: juniper berry
eneldo: dill
ensalada: salad
entremeses: hors-d'oeuvre
erizo de mar: sea urchin
escabeche: marinade; *en escabeche,* pickled
escalonia: shallot
escarola: escarole, endive
escolano: (fish) ling
escorpión: (fish) weever
espagueti: spaghetti
espárrago: asparagus
especia: spice
espinaca: spinach
estofado: stew, stewed

estornino: mackerel
estragón: tarragon

F

faba: type of dried bean
faisán: pheasant
falda: (meat) flank
fesol: type of dried bean
fiambre: pressed meat, pâté
fideo: vermicelli noodle
filete: (meat) slice of steak; (fish) fillet
fino: fine; also (wine) type of dry sherry
frambuesa: raspberry
frejol: type of dried bean
fresa: strawberry
fresón: strawberry
frigüelo: black-eyed pea
frijol: type of dried bean
frisuelo: type of dried bean
frito: fried, from verb *freír*
fruta: fruit
fuerte: strong

G

galleta: biscuit; cookie
gallina: hen
gallineta: redfish, bluemouth, Norway
 haddock
gallo: (poultry) cock, rooster; (fish) whiff,
 megrim
galludo: dogfish
galupe: (fish) type of grey mullet
gamba: prawn; shrimp
ganso: gander
garbanzo: chickpea
garneo: (fish) piper
gayano: (fish) type of wrasse
germen de trigo, wheatgerm
girasol: sunflower
granada: pomegranate
granadina: grenadine
granel, al: in bulk
gratinado: au gratin
grelo: flowering turnip green

grosella: currant
guayaba: guava
guinda: cherry
guindilla: hot chili pepper
guisante: pea

H

haba: broad bean, fava
habichuela: green bean or dried bean
harina: flour
helado: iced; ice cream
hierbabuena: mint
hierba luisa: lemon verbena
hígado: liver
higo: fig
hinojo: fennel
hojaldre: puff pastry
hongo: fungus; also, certain types of wild
 mushrooms
horno: oven
hueso: bone
huevas: fish roe
huevo: egg

I

infusión: herbal tea

J

jabalí: boar
jamón: ham
jarabe: syrup
jengibre: ginger
jerez: *(wine)* sherry
jibia: cuttlefish
judía: bean
judía verde, green bean
judía seca, dried bean
jurel: horse mackerel

L

lacón: cured pork shoulder
langosta: spiny lobster, rock lobster
langostino: large prawn
laurel: bay leaf

lecha: fish roe, esp. milt
lechal: milk-fed
leche: milk
lechuga: lettuce
legumbre: vegetable, especially legume, pulse
lengua: tongue
lenguado: sole
lenteja: lentil
levadura: leavening
levadura en polvo, dry yeast, baking powder
levadura prensada, cake yeast
liebre: hare
lima: lime
limanda: lemon sole
limón: lemon
lingote: a type of dried bean
lisa: (fish) grey mullet
llisera: flat-fish similar to whiff or megrim
lombarda: red cabbage
lomo: loin, especially pork
lota: (fish) ling
lubina: sea bass
lucio: (fish) pike

M

macarrones: macaroni
macis: mace
magro: pork, lean
maíz: corn
malva: hibiscus flower
mandarina: mandarin, tangerine
manojo: handful, bunch
manteca: lard
mantequilla: butter
manzana: apple
manzanilla: chamomile (also a type of sherry and of olive)
maragota: (fish) a type of wrasse
margarina: margarine
marisco: shellfish
maruca: (fish) ling
masa: pastry or bread dough
matadero: slaughterhouse
matalahuva: aniseed

mayonesa: mayonnaise
mazapán: marzipan
mejillón: mussel
mejorana: marjoram
melaza: molasses
melocotón: peach
melón: melon
membrillo: quince
menta: mint
merlan: (fish) whiting
merlo: (fish) a type of wrasse
merluza: hake
mermelada: jam, marmalade
mero: grouper
miel: honey
miel de caña, molasses
mielga: type of edible shark
migas: breadcrumbs, a dish of fried croutons
mijo: millet
mojama: cured tuna
molleja: sweetbread
monjete: type of dried bean
morcilla: blood sausage, black pudding
morena: (fish) moray eel
mostaza: mustard
mujol: type of grey mullet
musola: type of edible shark

N

nabo: turnip
ñame: yam
naranja: orange
nata: cream
navaja: (shellfish) razor-clam
nécora: small crab
níscalo: type of wild mushroom
níspero: loquat
ñora: sweet dried red pepper
nuez: nut, walnut
nuez moscada: nutmeg

O

oblada: fish similar to dentex
oca: goose

olla: pot
oloroso: (wine) type of sherry
orégano: oregano
orejón: dried apricot
ostión: portuguese oyster
ostra: oyster

P

pajarito: small bird
paletilla: shoulder of an animal
palmito: palmetto, palm heart
paloma: squab, pigeon, dove
palometa: (fish) pompano
palometa negra: (fish) pomfret, ray's bream
palometón: (fish) pompano
pan: bread
pan rallado, breadcrumbs
panceta: streaked pork fat, fresh bacon
pardete: type of grey mullet
pargo: fish similar to dentex
parrilla: grill
pasa: dried fruit, as in *uva pasa,* dried raisin,
    ciruela pasa, dried plum, prune
pastel: pie, pastry
pata: leg of an animal
pata negra: cured ham from ibérico pig
patata: potato
pato: duck
pavo: turkey
pechuga: (poultry) breast
peluda: scaldfish
pepinillo: cucumber pickle
pepino: cucumber
pera: pear
perca: (fish) perch
percebe: barnacle
perdiz: partridge
peregrina: (shellfish) scallop
perejil: parsley
perifollo: chervil
perlon: (fish) gurnard
pescadilla: small hake
pescado: fish
pez: fish
pez ángel, angel-fish

pez espada, swordfish
pez limón, amberjack
picante: hot, spicy, piquant
pichón: squab, pigeon, dove
picota: cherry
pierna: leg
pijota: (fish) hake
pimentón: paprika
pimienta: (spice) pepper
pimiento: (vegetable) pepper
piña: pineapple
piñón: pine-nut
pintada: guinea fowl
pintarroja: dogfish
plancha: grill, griddle
plátano: banana
platija: (fish) flounder
pocha: type of dried bean
pollo: chicken
pomelo: grapefruit
potaje: pottage
puchero: stock-pot, boiled dinner
puerro: leek
pulpo: octopus

Q

queso: cheese
quisquilla: small prawn

R

rábano: radish
rábano picante, horseradish
rabo: tail
rape: anglerfish, monkfish
rascacio: rascasse
rata: (fish) stargazer
raya: (fish) skate, ray
rebeco: chamois
rebozado: batter-dipped and fried, from verb
    rebozar
redondo: (beef) round
remojo: soaking
remol: (fish) brill
remolacha: beet

reo: sea-trout
repollo: cabbage
requesón: cottage cheese
reserva: (wine) aged wine
riñón: kidney
rodaballo: (fish) turbot
romero: rosemary
rombo: (fish) brill
rosada: (fish) cusk-eel, marketed frozen
rosco: doughnut
rubio: (fish) gurnard

S

sábalo: (fish) shad
sal: salt
salado: salted, salty
salchicha: fresh pork sausage
salchichón: cured sausage
salema: (fish) bream
salmón: salmon
salmonete: red mullet
salsa: sauce
salteado: sautéed (from verb *saltear*)
salvia: sage
salvado: bran
sandía: watermelon
sangre: blood
San Pedro: (fish) John Dory
sardina: sardine
sargo: (fish) bream
sartén: frying pan
sebo: suet
seco: dry, dried
sepia: cuttlefish
serandell: scaldfish
serrano: mountain style, as in *jamón
    serrano,* mountain-cured ham
sesos: brains
seta: wild mushroom
sidra: cider
soja: soy
solla: (fish) plaice
solomillo: (meat) fillet, tenderloin
sopa: soup
sortija: French sand sole

suela: fish similar to sole

T

tambor: fish similar to sole
tarta: cake
tenca: (fish) tench
ternera: veal, young beef
tienda: shop
tigre: fish similar to sole
tila: linden flower
tocino: pork fat, salt pork
tomate: tomato
tomillo: thyme
tordo: type of wrasse
torta: round, flat bun or cake
tortilla: omelette
tórtola: turtle dove
tostado: toast, toasted, from the verb *tostar*
trigo: wheat
trucha: trout
trufa: truffle
tuétano: bone marrow
turrón: nougat

U V Y Z

uva: grape
urta: fish similar to dentex
urogallo: wood-grouse
vacuno, carne de: beef
venado: venison
verdura: green vegetable
vieira: (shellfish) scallop
vino: wine
vino rancio, mellowed wine

yema: egg yolk; also, a sweet made of yolks

zanahoria: carrot
zapata: fish similar to dentex
zarzamora: blackberry
zorzal: thrush

INDEX

Useful references

www.oliveoilfromspain.com
www.winesfromspain.com
www.spaingourmetour.com
www.foodsfromspainnews.com
Guide to the Seafood of Spain and Portugal,
by Alan Davidson (Santana Books, 2002).

QUICK CONVERSIONS

In the recipes in this book, quantities are given in metric measurements. The charts on this page show approximate equivalents of Imperial, American and metric measures.

FLUID MEASURES
Metric/British Standard

10 MILLILITRES	1/3 OUNCE
50 MILLILITRES	1 3/4 OUNCES
100 MILLILITRES	3 1/2 OUNCES
250 MILLILITRES	8 1/2 OUNCES
500 MILLILITRES	17 1/2 OUNCES
1 LITRE	1 3/4 PINTS
1 TEASPOON	5 MILLILITRES
1 TABLESPOON	18 MILLILITRES
1 OUNCE	28 MILLILITRES
1 PINT	570 MILLILITRES
1 QUART	1.14 LITRES
1 GALLON	4 1/2 LITRES

FLUID MEASURES
Metric/U.S. Standard

10 MILLILITRES	2 TEASPOONS
50 MILLILITRES	3 TABLESPOONS
100 MILLILITRE	3 1/2 OUNCES
250 MILLILITRES	1 CUP + 1 TABLESPOON
500 MILLILITRES	1 PINT + 2 TABLESPOONS
1 LITRE	1 QUART + 3 TABLESPOONS
1 TEASPOON	5 MILLILITRES
1 TABLESPOON	15 MILLILITRES
1 OUNCE	30 MILLILITRES
1 CUP	235 MILLILITRES
1 PINT	475 MILLILITRES
1 QUART	950 MILLILITRES
1 GALLON	3 3/4 LITRES

WEIGHT
Metric/Ounces & Pounds

10 GRAMS	1/3 OUNCE
50 GRAMS	1 3/4 OUNCES
100 GRAMS	3 1/2 OUNCES
250 GRAMS	8 3/4 OUNCES
500 GRAMS	1 POUND + 1 1/2 OUNCES
1 KILO	2 POUNDS + 3 1/2 OUNCES
1/2 OUNCE	14 GRAMS
1 OUNCE	28 GRAMS
1/4 POUND	110 GRAMS
1/2 POUND	230 GRAMS
1 POUND	450 GRAMS

OVEN TEMPERATURE

TEMPERATURE	DIAL NUMBER
VERY SLOW = 250F/120C	= 1/4
SLOW = 300F/150C = 1	
MODERATE = 350F/180C	= 4
HOT = 400F/200C = 6	
VERY HOT = 450F/230C	= 8

TEMPERATURE

F.	C.
500	
	250
475	
	240
450	230
425	220
	210
400	
	200
375	190
350	180
	170
325	
	160
300	150
275	140
	130
	120
225	110
	100 (Water boils)
200	
	90
175	
	80
150	70
	60
125	
	50
100	
	40
	30
75	
	20
50	10
	0 (Water freezes)
25	
	-10
0	- 20
	- 30
	- 25
	- 40
	- 50
	- 50
F.	C.